*The publisher and the University of California Press
Foundation gratefully acknowledge the generous support
of the Ahmanson Foundation Endowment
Fund in Humanities.*

Thinking Black

BERKELEY SERIES IN BRITISH STUDIES

Edited by James Vernon

Thinking Black

BRITAIN, 1964–1985

Rob Waters

UNIVERSITY OF CALIFORNIA PRESS

University of California Press, one of the most distinguished university presses in the United States, enriches lives around the world by advancing scholarship in the humanities, social sciences, and natural sciences. Its activities are supported by the UC Press Foundation and by philanthropic contributions from individuals and institutions. For more information, visit www.ucpress.edu.

University of California Press
Oakland, California

Library of Congress Cataloging-in-Publication Data

Names: Waters, Rob, author.
Title: Thinking black : Britain, 1964–1985 / Rob Waters.
Description: Oakland, California : University of California Press, [2018] | Series: Berkeley series in British studies ; 14 | Includes bibliographical references and index. |
Identifiers: LCCN 2018020264 (print) | LCCN 2018024304 (ebook) | ISBN 9780520967205 | ISBN 9780520293847 (cloth : alk. paper) | ISBN 9780520293854 (pbk. : alk. paper)
Subjects: LCSH: Blacks—Great Britain—History—20th century. | Great Britain—Race relations—History—20th century. | Radicalism—Great Britain—History—20th century. | Blacks—Great Britain—Politics and government—20th century.
Classification: LCC DA125.N4 (ebook) | LCC DA125.N4 W38 2018 (print) | DDC 305.896/04109045—dc23
LC record available at https://lccn.loc.gov/2018020264

Manufactured in the United States of America

26 25 24 23 22 21 20 19
10 9 8 7 6 5 4 3 2 1

For Fay

CONTENTS

ILLUSTRATIONS

ACKNOWLEDGMENTS

Many years ago, when I was an undergraduate at the University of Edinburgh, Enda Delaney encouraged me to think about postgraduate study. I am very grateful to him. University was not a tradition in my family, and certainly I had not considered further study. Such paths simply were not part of my social horizon at the time. Under Enda's tuition at Edinburgh, and later under the brilliant supervision of Bill Schwarz and Rachael Gilmour at Queen Mary, I began to find my feet in academia. The writing of this book owes a lot to their encouragement, enthusiasm, and of course their intellects. Upon finishing my postgraduate study, I was caught in the scourge of modern university life in this neoliberal age: underpaid, short-term, part-time contracts, long intervals between jobs. I worked at many institutions in this period, as well as in jobs outside the university. I would like to thank my colleagues at these institutions, who have showed sympathy and solidarity, alongside national campaigns such as Fighting Against Casualisation in Education, who fight tirelessly for better academic lives. I also thank those immediate managers who, under difficult circumstances, did what they could to provide better working conditions and security for us. These people kept me afloat.

I have been lucky to also enjoy the support, encouragement and friendship of other brilliant scholars. As I worked through the job of proposing and then writing this book, James Vernon has been a constant source of support and excellent, incisive advice. I want to thank him, and to thank Niels Hooper, Bradley Depew, and the team at the University of California Press for their patience and kindness, and Peter Dreyer for his attentive and informed copyediting. I finished writing the book in my first year as a Leverhulme Early Career Fellow at the University of Sussex, and my thanks also go to the Leverhulme Trust for supporting this work, and to Clive Webb and Tim Hitchcock for mentoring me. Others at Sussex have also been brilliant: Anne-Marie Angelo, Hester Barron, Tom Adam Davies, Martin Evans, Jill Kirby, Claire Langhamer, Melissa Milewski, Nathan Richards, and Lucy Robinson have all been enthusiastic interlocutors as I worked through the ideas here. And beyond Sussex: Justin Bengry, Matt Cook, David Feldman, Tank Green, Hilary Ingram, Hannah Ishmael, Peter Jones, Diarmaid Kelliher, Feriel Kissoon, Jon Lawrence, Anna Maguire, Saima Nasar, Naomi Oppenheim, Kate Quinn, Gavin Schaffer, Robbie Shilliam, Clair Wills, David Winks, the Raphael Samuel History Centre, and my wonderful students on the Black Writing in Britain module. Thank you, all. Particular mention must be saved for my co-conspirators in rethinking the history of race in Britain: Kennetta Hammond Perry, Marc Matera, Radhika Natarajan, Nicole Jackson, and especially Camilla Schofield, a wonderful scholar and friend.

The story that *Thinking Black* tells would not have been possible were it not for the help and advice of four brilliant archives: the George Padmore Institute, the Institute of Race Relations, the Black Cultural Archives, and the Huntley Collection at the London Metropolitan Archives. The archivists and outreach workers here have been fantastic, not only in their intimate knowledge of their collections and dedication to the politics that their archives were built on, but in their willingness to help me as I sought to speak to those people whose stories this book tells. My thanks go to the staff at all these archives, but particularly to Sarah Garrod, who has helped me innumerable times over the years. Many people have also taken the time to speak with me about the stories I attempt to tell in this book, and to share their memories. To my great sadness, some of them are no longer here to see the finished product, but I would like to thank them all here: Jenny Bourne and A. Sivanandan, Leila and Darcus Howe, Jessica and Eric Huntley, Sarah White, Ansel Wong, Michael McMillan, Neil Kenlock, Paul Gilroy, and Peter Davis. I'd also like to thank Una Howe, Shakka, Horace and Indra Ové, Peter Davis, and Neil and Emelia Kenlock, for helping me to locate some of the images I include in this book, and for allowing me to include them.

Final thanks go to my family, and to Fay. This book is for you, Fay.

ACRONYMS AND INITIALISMS
OF BLACK BRITAIN

ACER	Afro-Caribbean Education Resources Project
AYM	Asian Youth Movement
BBWG	Brixton Black Women's Group
BLF	Black Liberation Front
BPIC	Black People's Information Centre (Notting Hill, London)
BPM	Black Panther Movement
BUFP	Black Unity and Freedom Party
CAM	Caribbean Artists Movement
CCCS	Centre for Contemporary Cultural Studies (University of Birmingham)
CECWA	Caribbean Education and Community Workers' Association
CARD	Campaign Against Racial Discrimination
CORE	Congress of Racial Equality (United States)
CRC	Community Relations Commission
CRE	Commission for Racial Equality
ESN	educationally subnormal (children)
GPSS	George Padmore Supplementary School (Finsbury Park, London)
ILEA	Inner London Education Authority
IMG	International Marxist Group
IRR	Institute of Race Relations
LEA	local education authority

NAACP	National Association for the Advancement of Colored People (United States)
NCCI	National Committee for Commonwealth Immigrants
NLWIA	North London West Indian Association
NUFF	National Union of Freedom Fighters (Trinidad and Tobago)
OWAAD	Organisation of Women of Asian and African Descent
PPP	People's Progressive Party (British Guiana)
RAAS	Racial Adjustment Action Society
RTC	Race Today Collective
SNCC	Student Non-Violent Coordinating Committee (United States)
TAR	Teachers against Racism
UCPA	Universal Coloured People's Association
WISC	West Indian Students Centre

Introduction

HISTORY MOVING FAST

> History moves very fast these days and can quickly leave the
> dull behind.
>
> C. L. R. JAMES
> *at London's West Indian Students' Centre, August 1967*[1]

> We need bodies, and we need cats that think black.
>
> DICK GREGORY
> *at London's West Indian Students' Centre, February 1968*[2]

ON A CHILLY SATURDAY EVENING on February 3, 1968, the African
American novelist James Baldwin addressed an audience at the West Indian
Students' Centre in London's Earl's Court neighborhood. He spoke on the
question of freedom, and the meaning of black experience in the pursuit of
freedom. An acclaimed writer, a celebrity of the American civil rights movement, and a famously good speaker, Baldwin drew quite a crowd, and he was
joined by the African American comedian and civil rights activist Dick
Gregory, who had addressed a large crowd in the same room a few days previous.[3] Their audience was mostly black but with a scattering of white faces; a
mix of women and men, though men predominated. Everybody listened
intently, and everybody smoked. Many, seduced by Baldwin's warm humor,
laughed. But most were also angry. One man shouted a denunciation of
Baldwin for his continued use of the term "negro," now "black" was the order
of the day; another accused him of a "contemptuous" regard for Africa.

On everyone's mind was the rapidly changing pace of the politics of global
black and anticolonial liberation. Baldwin was speaking just days after the

Viet Cong and the North Vietnamese People's Liberation Army had launched the Tet Offensive against U.S. and South Vietnamese armies, and after a year of tumultuous change in the American civil rights movement, as many African Americans began to reframe the question of racial justice now in the language of Black Power, and as successive American neighborhoods went up in flames. This was a situation that required some urgent decisions.

"How do you envisage the black man's fate, say within fifty years?" one woman asked him.

"Which is better, integration or Black Power?" asked another.

A middle-aged white man, pained by the denunciations of whiteness frequent that night, appealed to Baldwin: "Do you think that there is any place for the white liberal in the Black Power movement? [. . .] Because I've attended a lot of meetings on this subject of Black Power at which, in particular, English people feel very hurt because you get the line from the Black Power, 'we don't want you.'"

Both the speakers and audience at the West Indian Students' Centre that night were clear that they were discussing important questions. Though the address was by an African American, and to an audience mostly of West Indian migrants, they were clear also that the discussion did not refer only to America or the Caribbean. Responding to the self-confessed "white liberal" anxious about his own role in this new global moment, Baldwin reminded his audience of what was at stake in the freedom they were discussing that evening. "It is not a matter of my liberation," he insisted, "it is also a matter of yours." This was an argument that would be heard often. Dick Gregory, wading into the discussion, advised the man on how this liberation was to be achieved. "We need bodies," said Gregory, "and we need cats that think black."

THINKING BLACK

Dick Gregory's call was a common one in the two decades following the rise of Black Power as a transnational political formation in the mid-1960s. It was a call that was heard by many in Britain, the Caribbean, and the United States of America, and it mobilized an extraordinarily rich political culture. In Britain, a network of institutions and organizations, as well as a wide variety of new cultural practices, were held together by Gregory's two ambitions: to get bodies, and to get those bodies "thinking black." This book traces the formation of that political culture and the new purchase that ideas and experiences of blackness had in Britain between the mid-1960s and the mid-1980s. It follows the development of new cultural practices that came to be signified as black by an expansive network of activists and intellectuals who used them to shape a distinctly "black" politics, and "black" ways of thinking. These men and women—teachers, writers, publishers, booksellers, campaigners, picketers, marchers, and revolutionaries—were part of transnational anticolonial and civil rights networks. Many were socialists, some were feminists. Most regarded themselves as radicals. In Britain, they sought to identify, confront, and overturn the racism that they saw, not only structuring British society and politics from top to bottom, but upholding all manner of other inequalities. To transform, they insisted, British society needed to start "thinking black," recognizing how histories of racialized oppression continued to structure social and political life. Their primary focus was often on Britons of African, Caribbean, and South Asian descent, who, they felt, could better fight the oppressions they faced by thinking of and recognizing themselves as "black" people. But they rarely assumed that thinking in this way was of benefit only to those who understood themselves as "black." "Thinking black," indeed, was seen to be the necessary preoccupation of all who sought to build a fairer, more equal and democratic society out of Britain's imperial past.

The legacy of this way of thinking about social and political life in Britain can be seen today perhaps most forcefully in the work of critics like Paul Gilroy and Stuart Hall. They have insisted on the centrality of race in the making of modern Britain, and on the insights offered for understanding this dynamic of British modernity by adopting the vantage point of those whom Satnam Virdee has termed Britain's "racialized outsiders."[4] This book situates such arguments within their wider contexts, locating them as part of a diverse formation of blackness in Britain between the mid-1960s and the mid-1980s, which drew on, dialogued with, and brought to Britain a global black liberation politics forged in the fight for a decolonized world. This was Britain's moment of "thinking black." Hall and Gilroy's work has been remarkably productive in remaking how politics in Britain has been thought about—problematizing the categories by which we explain social life, the divisions that sustain discussions of the political and the cultural, the intellectual and the popular, the epistemological and the ontological. My purpose is to show how the force of this revolution in thought came from the energies of the wider formation of which Hall and Gilroy were a part, and how it animated a political culture.

Today, the word "black," when applied to particular social phenomena—"black politics," "black culture"—appears to hold a self-evident meaning. It refers, or so it seems, to the political or cultural activities or traditions of a particular group of people ("black people"), usually, though not always, people of African descent. But this apparently settled and self-evident meaning of blackness is a relatively new historical development. The ascendency of "black" as the description of an ethnic or racial category, to replace older descriptors such as "negro" and "colored," is in one sense simply a story of changing vocabulary. But it is also a political story. The purchase of "black" as a category of ethnic or racial identity from the mid-1960s on was knitted together with its purchase as a political category, marking an embrace of bodies and cultural practices understood as "black," and a commitment to political changes—usually radical in their ambitions—understood as the consequence of a "black" historical experience.

There are two points here. First, in attempting to define what characterized blackness, activists and intellectuals set out how it referred to a particular kind of critical perspective informed by the experience of racialization, and the politics that this entailed. Second, and related to this, blackness did not coincide neatly with any biological fact or supposed ethnic group. It involved a positioning in relation to the forces that attributed weight to these very categories, and therefore signaled a critical relation more than an already-existing fact. In this, many could come to inhabit or think with blackness. "Black" in these years could refer to African heritage, and many Britons of African descent chose to describe themselves as black in this way, particularly with the rise of the "black is beautiful" movement and the new, transnational music cultures of soul and reggae. But many who were not of African descent also came to think with blackness, or identify as black. Blackness, as Dick Hebdige noted in the mid-1970s, held a powerful cultural capital and promise, particularly for disaffected white youth turning "from a whiteness which wasn't worth much anyway, to a blackness which just might mean something more."[5] In greater numbers, many British Asians also came to articulate their politics through blackness, and to locate themselves within a broad conception of black culture that borrowed often from African American, Caribbean, and Afro-British forms, but deployed these alongside South Asian cultural practices with little sense of contradiction. Blackness, in other words, was unstable, multiple, and multidirectional, which proved to be both its strength and its fragility.[6]

The politics of blackness uniquely promised to address a particular experience of racialized oppression at a time when British social and political life appeared to be consolidating around a revived politics of whiteness. In the two decades between 1962 and 1981, successive British governments passed legislation that effectively attempted to define the rights of British citizenship in racial terms. They did so first through a series of immigration acts restricting the rights of nonwhite Commonwealth citizens to enter Britain freely, and later, with the 1981 Nationality Act, in a redefinition of British citizenship itself.[7] This top-down race politics was joined by a racism from below, soon to be coordinated by the Conservative (and later Ulster Unionist) MP Enoch Powell. Although it had racialized citizenship, the Labour government's simultaneous pursuit of a "race relations" agenda outlawing (some) forms of racial discrimination left it open to a white populist charge that it had abandoned the people and failed to uphold racial order.[8] Powell seized this charge to dramatic effect on April 20, 1968, when he delivered his infamous "rivers of blood" address in Birmingham, denouncing race relations legislation and laying the groundwork for his later calls for "repatriation" of nonwhite Britons. Triggering a groundswell of public support, Powell definitively shifted the terrain of British politics.[9] After his intervention, as Stuart Hall noted at the time, race became "the prism through which the British people [were] called upon to live through, then to understand, and then to deal with the growing crisis."[10]

As the politics of race in Britain tightened, the global politics of Black Power and decolonization came closer to home. The rise of a radical politics of blackness as the defining feature of many anti-racist, anticolonial, and black liberation projects from the second half of the 1960s to the early 1980s marked a new turn in the history of decolonization and black liberation. Certainly, there were continuities with older political projects, and certainly black nationalism had long featured in the political movements of the black Atlantic, from Martin Delany to Marcus Garvey.[11] But the language of blackness assumed a distinctly new weight in the mid-1960s. This was, as William Van Deburg has proposed of the U.S. context, a moment in which black culture became "a tool of liberation," and it is for this reason that Eddie S. Glaude has proposed we read Black Power as a "politics of transvaluation [. . .] best understood as a reassessment of 'blackness' in terms of its value for black lives and struggle."[12] From the mid-1960s on, new political projects couched in a revived language of blackness took root on a global scale. Black Power, black arts, black consciousness, and Rastafarian movements sprang up across the black Atlantic, from the United States and Canada to Europe, Africa, and the Caribbean, as well as in Israel, Australia, New Zealand, and

India.[13] The world appeared to be on the brink of transformation, and many locating themselves through cultures and politics of blackness in Britain were ready to be a part of its transformation. The sense of impending change was palpable. "It soon come," as Linton Kwesi Johnson wrote in a poem of 1975. "It soon come / look out! look out! look out!"[14]

The expansion of "black" feeling, cultures of blackness, and "black" activism marks this era as a key conjuncture in modern British history. To understand how this conjunctural shift moved, this book examines how "black" was made into a category of experience and politics at this time. For the English novelist Colin MacInnes, writing about the rise of blackness in Britain in the early 1970s, depths of feeling were waiting to be mobilized by black activists. "Black Power propaganda, in effect, consists far more in saying simply to fellow blacks, 'Get up off your arse, man' than of telling anyone anything that they didn't already know either through personal experience, or else from a thousand hereditary tales," MacInnes wrote. "Consequently, though Black Power militant groups in England may be few in number, I'd say there are equally few, among the 300,000 West Indians in our country, who disagree with the basic Black Power premises."[15] MacInnes was right to point to potentialities nascent among those of whom he spoke. For many of them, life in Britain had made the indignities of the colonial past come to seem peculiarly close—as one woman explained to the Indian journalist Dilip Hiro in 1969, it was in "coming to this country" that "you get to realise that we're part of slavery."[16] But if MacInnes was correct to note the proximity of such feelings, it was a proximity made speakable through the new cultures of blackness. If "black" arose as a political language in this era, it was one rooted in a culture that generated an outpouring of new energies in music and literature, fashion and hairstyles, modes and mediums of communication. This was the era of soul and reggae, dance halls and deejays, Afros and badges, prison memoirs and *Roots*.[17] These new transnational mediums for communicating blackness had substantial traction in Britain. A Bristol man explaining the causes of friction with his employer to the Jamaican sociologist Ken Pryce in the early 1970s, for example, suggested that it came "from reading too much history of slavery."[18] For a woman from London, following BBC broadcasts of the U.S. television series *Roots* "none of the black workers spoke to the white workers and if any white person had said anything that day there would have been riots."[19] For those activists and intellectuals whom I discuss in this book, "thinking black" was the challenge of coordinating these rapidly expanding cultures into a political formation.

Cultures of blackness provided expressive mediums by which past or new memories and experiences could be created, or find meaning. Black activists sought to build an affective economy of blackness on the back of these new cultural practices, working to bind a new political community together in the name of blackness.[20]

The development of a politics of blackness involved the coordination of a dissimilar, fractious terrain. MacInnes was probably wrong that few would have disagreed with the premises of Black Power. Even given how famously flexible definitions of Black Power could be, there would be those that would reject it outright.[21] When Stokely Carmichael visited London in 1967, for example, local West Indians called a mass meeting to publicly repudiate Black Power, and contacted the local press to express their displeasure that Black Power politics might take root in Britain.[22] Those who did identify themselves through a politics of blackness might find themselves misrecognized by others because of their ethnicity or gender. It was not only among West Indians that memories of the atrocities of slavery in the Caribbean were resonating, for example, as BBC journalists discovered when they interviewed South Asian students about Black Power in 1968 and found such topics being readily recalled, alongside denunciations of British violence in colonial India.[23] But while many articulated their politics through Black Power, this articulation was easier for some than for others. Ansel Wong, a Trinidadian of African and Chinese descent who became a leading figure in the early black arts movement in Britain, lived with all kinds of "inner turmoils and tensions." As he coordinated political, education, and arts programs across London, he was haunted by hints and references to his ethnicity that placed him outside the category of black, and he found himself having to "stick to the ideology and the dogma, as opposed to people's perceptions of identity and colour of skin."[24]

If many came to understand themselves as black, then, they did so by bending the category into many different meanings, making more claims upon it than it seemed it could possibly hold. These are what Brent Hayes Edwards has called the "necessary hauntings" of articulated formations, the points of "misunderstanding, bad faith, unhappy translation."[25] The political culture of blackness was held together by uneasy articulations, described by Edwards as processes of "linking or connecting across gaps."[26] Black projects brought together many different people—women and men, South Asian, Caribbean, African, black and white British. They also brought together many different practices—protests against police brutality, critiques of the authoritarian turn of the state, reformulations of education and modes of self-expression, and critiques of the structure of capital and its social relations. Each of these articulations of blackness involved translations between dissimilar experiences, affects, structures, and histories. This made for an unstable, often contradictory, coalition. But there was nonetheless a certain unity to the political and cultural projects working through a language of blackness in this era, even while this unity did not mean a perfect symmetry of all parts. This was the work that "thinking black" did. Remarkably, blackness held together. Rallies happened. Schools were established and supported. Conferences were organized. Deeply significant cultural and intellectual work was done. The apparent ability of blackness to make sense of so many different phenomena, and to interpellate so many different subjects, makes it a formation worth examining. Despite the volatility and contradictions between its various articulations, the politics of blackness was coordinated to considerable political effect, to the extent that it became a primary means of decolonizing British society in the late twentieth century.

DECOLONIZING BRITAIN

In December 1982, the Indian-born novelist Salman Rushdie published his "The New Empire within Britain" in *New Society*. This essay was a study in what Rushdie termed "a gulf in reality": "White and black perceptions of everyday life have moved so far apart as to be incompatible."[27] His own position in this antagonism was slippery. He spoke with authority on "black perceptions" and clearly identified himself with the "new empire within Britain." But Rushdie defined this new empire variously as "black people" and "black and Asian," while his pronouns occasionally raised him above either designation to talk in equally detached terms of the "them" of white Britain and the "them" of black. Such was the complexity of interpellation into blackness in this moment, and such slippages were common. Rushdie's classic exploration of race and immigration in Britain in *The Satanic Verses* (1987) later made much comedy of the misrecognitions of blackness in its playful depiction of Black Power rallies.[28] His essay, though, focused on a key claim made across the many articulations of blackness common in these years: that to understand contemporary British politics, one had to return to the era of empire, and to move forward, one had to decolonize Britain.

Decolonization was the promise of the politics of blackness. As one West Indian interviewed about involvement in black British politics by the

Trinidadian labor activist Trevor Carter in the mid-1980s explained, "the Black Power movement [. . .] struck a chord with us in the sixties in Britain." It "created the political space for us to redefine our own blackness," and it taught him and others that "we had to decolonise ourselves."[29] Photocopying Rushdie's essay for her personal files, Stella Dadzie, an anticolonial activist of Ghanaian and English heritage, founding member of the Brixton Black Women's Group and the Organisation of Women of African and Asian Descent, underlined the key phrases:

> Racism is not a side-issue in contemporary Britain; it is not a peripheral minority affair. Britain is undergoing the critical phase of its post-colonial period. This crisis is not simply economic or political. It is a crisis of the whole culture. [. . .]
> British thought and British society have never been cleansed of the Augean filth of imperialism. It is still there, breeding lice and vermin, waiting for unscrupulous people to exploit it for their own ends. The British may be the only people on earth who feel nostalgia for pillage and conquest and war.[30]

In such thinking, the empire may have largely come to an end, but in Britain its afterlives continued.

The argument that the empire had a significant impact on metropolitan Britain, and that after empire this impact still reverberated, has only gained consensus among British historians relatively recently, and is not without detractors. For those historical actors who form the subjects of this book, however—those whose politics were premised on "thinking black"—these assumptions underpinned much of their thought and actions. Decolonization, in this mode, meant primarily breaking the hold of a racialized order seen still to structure British society at the end of empire, and seen to be the legacy of empire. In 1987, Paul Gilroy published his famous critique of the racialization of national identity in Britain between the mid-1960s and the mid-1980s, in which he identified the manner in which nonwhite Britons were excluded from imagined communities of Britishness, and demonstrated how such exclusion structured their relationship to the state, and how the politics of race structured the various social, cultural, and political crises of the period.[31] Both Gilroy's critique of the politics of race in Britain and the solutions he tentatively posed to these owed their origins in large part to the wider political projects of "thinking black" developed since the 1960s, and, as I argue in chapter 5, it is within such projects that we can locate his work. But while these projects were subterranean and marginalized for much of this period, following Gilroy's work the positions adopted in such projects have gained greater ascendancy, decisive in shifting historiographical debate on Britain's transition to a post-imperial power, as historians have attended to the ways in which racial imaginaries of the colonial peripheries moved now to the former metropolitan center, and to center of national life.

As questions of race, immigration and decolonization have increasingly come to the forefront in studies of modern British history, this has necessarily led to the need to rethink the process of decolonization. The effects of colonialism lasted beyond the formal acquisition of constitutional sovereignty in the former colonies, and reverberated deep in the culture and politics of the metropole.[32] In the task of understanding both how and when British culture and politics might be described as "decolonized," the role of Britain's postcolonial migrants holds an important place.[33] Decoding British culture, Bill Schwarz has proposed, "came to be the necessary pastime of all who journeyed across the seas" from the colonies and former colonies.[34] These migrants—particularly, Schwarz argues, West Indians—found themselves "having to interrogate the lived culture of the colonizers, in order to comprehend their own discrepant experiences," and in the process offered the potential to dismantle some of the practices and assumptions by which imperial hierarchies were maintained within Britain.[35] While migrants and migration have held a privileged position in this recent turn in the historiography, however, in this book, focusing on a later period than that which has usually preoccupied historians of decolonizing Britain, I look as much to the children of those migrants, to long-settled black and Asian communities in Britain, and to white Britons who took up the task of "thinking black" in an effort to confront the vestiges of empire as it organized late-twentieth-century British culture and politics. Uniting them was less their status as migrant, settler, or native Britons than their shared dedication to and production of a transnational practice of "thinking black" ascendant in this period and reorganizing the meanings of and means for decolonization.

Claims for the wider possibilities of decolonization realized through blackness were common. "We blacks in Britain have been the leavening for a new perspective in Britain," the Trinidadian poet and publisher John La Rose insisted in 1976, writing for the black political magazine *Race Today*. "And it is what Aimé Césaire, the poet, calls our total vision from below that has enabled us to behave here in Britain, in the US, Canada and Africa like we have so far."[36] Bringing their experiences of racialized subordination in the colonies to the former center of imperial power, La Rose and his contemporaries would claim, those able to look upon it with better-trained eyes might better understand, and better contest, the hold of social inequality in Britain. Reading Britain's social order as a colonial order might, finally, allow Britain to be decolonized, too. "We bring to contemporary political life in Britain the unresolved tensions of five hundred years," one contributor to the West Indian Students' Centre's magazine wrote in 1970.

> Surely we must share with the British people the prospect of creating a humane society for all. [...] the popular basic [black] identity has survived oppression, has evolved impulses and insights of resistance, has no muddled ideas of where we're at, and contains the content of the revolutionary impact that a regenerated and whole black community can have in Britain and the world.[37]

In such pronouncements, we can see the promise that advocates of thinking black saw it to hold. The experience of five hundred years of oppression, as this writer put it, constituted a unique basis for a more universal contribution. Impulses and insights evolved in the tensions of colonialism, he proposed, could be shared to the benefit of all seeking to build a humane society out of the ruins of empire.

The politics of thinking black did not reject Britain and Britishness. Rather, it sought to reframe it, challenge it, and make it anew: "It is not a matter of my liberation, it is also a matter of yours." Historians increasingly recognize the extent to which the anticolonial nationalisms of the first half of the twentieth century were not framed in simple opposition to empire. Until the 1950s, as Marc Matera has demonstrated, black intellectuals and activists in Britain sought less a new world of independent, postcolonial nation-states than a reordering of sovereignty within the transnational political formations produced by imperialism.[38] Similarly, Kennetta Hammond Perry's study of postwar black British politics shows that in the era of decolonization, making claims on the political structures of imperial Britain defined anti-racism.[39] Despite this growing recognition of the intertwined nature of imperialism and anticolonialism, however, it remains the case that the story of the development of multiculturalism in Britain is told most frequently as a transition from blackness to black Britishness, as if the two formations only came into contact in the final decades of the twentieth century. Certainly, the difficulties of naming Britishness or Englishness as black identities were many. As Keith Piper remembers of his adolescence in 1970s Birmingham, though he and his friends had never even been to the West

Indies, from where their parents came, "race [. . .] existed as an indisputable and absolute fact in our lives. Our parents were West Indian, and so we would always be West Indian. [. . .] Englishness was never even considered as an option."[40] The negotiation of Britishness by black Britons was fraught, particularly at a moment that Britishness was increasingly defined, culturally, politically, and in the legal structures of the state as a white identity, hooked around a provincial white Englishness. "When Enoch Powell spoke for England," as Hanif Kureishi wrote of his time growing up in the 1960s and 1970s, "I turned away in final disgust."[41] Many looked beyond Britain's shores to understand themselves culturally, and for models of the new political futures they aspired to. Kureishi, for example, turned to the Black Panthers, Jimi Hendrix, James Baldwin, and Muhammed Ali. Others would look to Angela Davis or Bob Marley. But it was precisely by drawing attention to the shared histories of Britain and the colonies that many black activists and intellectuals made their most successful critiques of the British state and insisted that blacks and whites were both victims of an imperial formation still intact after the fall of the colonial empire. As a character in Horace Ové's 1975 film *Pressure* claims, realizing the insights of blackness while in conversation with his political allies, "white people in this country has been colonialized and enslaved in this country—just like we. The only difference between them and us is that we can see the bars and the chains, but they can't."[42] The era of blackness that this book explores is a history of Britain and Britishness; it is a history of projects for Britain's decolonization.

Blackness held this promise for many Britons in the two decades between the mid-1960s and the mid-1980s that this book explores. When James Baldwin and Dick Gregory visited the West Indian Students' Centre in 1968, they were but two of a raft of African American intellectuals, civil rights activists, and entertainers visiting Britain in these years. Since the visits of Martin Luther King Jr. and Malcolm X in 1964, black Atlantic exchange was central to reorienting the politics of race in Britain. These men and women intervened forcefully in British politics at a moment when Britain's fragile and short-lived race relations settlement was first being established, and as it faltered and fell, Black Power and decolonization politics from across the black Atlantic world offered new conceptions of what liberation might mean for the many facing growing institutional and interpersonal racism in Britain. It was the apparent pace of change inaugurated by this new political movement—*history moving fast*, as C. L. R. James would describe it to another audience at the West Indian Students' Centre in 1967—that brought many into its fold in these years, despite the difficulties that negotiating blackness sometimes involved. But this was not only for nonwhite Britons. A broad radical politics within Britain was reinvigorated through its encounter with the politics of thinking black, and in that loose formation we call the New Left, blackness often played a pivotal role in how the political crises of the current moment were conceptualised, and solutions to them proposed. These engagements were hooked around the liberation promise of blackness that Black Power and decolonization offered in this era, a promise sustained throughout the tumultuous 1960s and 1970s. They declined only by the mid-1980s, with the failure of black liberation movements in the Caribbean, the shifting politics of radical anticolonialism brought about by the 1979 Iranian Revolution, and the growing differential incorporation of Britain's ethnic minorities into the structures of the state. The politics of race and decolonization shifted once again, and the era of radical blackness that this book traces closed.

ONE

Becoming Black in the Era of Civil Rights and Black Power

IN JULY 1967, Stokely Carmichael came to London. A civil rights activist in the Student Non-Violent Coordinating Committee (SNCC), Carmichael had gained international fame—or infamy—for his call for "Black Power" at a rally in Greenwood, Mississippi, in June 1966, popularizing the slogan that came to define the global politics of radical blackness for over a decade.[1] He visited London at the height of his fame, at the start of a five-month world tour that his biographer describes as "the culmination of his personal desire and political need to forge relationships with global revolutionaries."[2] For black Britons, as the Barbadian poet Edward Brathwaite later recalled, Carmichael's visit "magnetized a whole set of splintered feelings that had for a long time been seeking a node."[3] Interviewing London's Black Power groups for her undergraduate sociology degree at the University of Edinburgh in 1969, the Trinidadian student Susan Craig found his visit remembered as "the single crystallizing experience which carried them over the threshold into '*becoming Black*.' Two years later, the fervour with which Carmichael and his message were received was spontaneously described by many militants as a 'conversion.'"[4] Carmichael was a confrontational black man in London, and, significantly, a Trinidadian by birth. "Here, for the first time, was 'one of us' telling the whites 'where to get off,'" Craig wrote.[5]

Craig's interviewees were not alone in their "conversion" to blackness through Black Power. "The era of blackness in the USA," the Guyanese-born journalist Mike Phillips remembered, "seemed to show us a direction."[6] Indeed, when Phillips interviewed black Britons of Caribbean descent in the late 1990s, he found them time and again identifying televised images of American Black Power with "the time in which they became black."[7] This chapter asks why Carmichael's presence, and the politics he represented, resonated in Britain, and looks at how British activists took up Black Power, and what the consequences were for the reformulation of the politics of blackness, anti-racism, and anticolonialism. It also, though, refuses a reading of Black Power simply as America's "global export."[8] Black Power was forged globally. Those African Americans whose visits to Britain in the mid-1960s accelerated the building of a new black politics were themselves formed by personal histories and political movements that traversed the black Atlantic—in his youth in a Trinidad in the wake of major labor rebellions, Stokely Carmichael grew up with the electrical charge of anticolonialism "in the air"; Malcolm X, who visited Britain before Carmichael, also to great acclaim, had grown up schooled in the Garveyite politics of black internationalism and West Indian anticolonialism.[9] They came to a Britain in which black internationalism had a long history.[10] And black Britain of the mid-1960s had important links with challenges to neocolonialism and racialized sociopolitical orders in other global locations. The Caribbean politics of decolonization, indeed, played a formative part in reconfiguring blackness in Britain.[11] This chapter shows how becoming black in Britain in the global moment of Black Power was transformative, albeit reworking rather than replacing a longer history of transnational black anticolonial and anti-racist politics. That transformation marked the beginning of the "thinking black" that this book examines.

Becoming black in the era of civil rights and Black Power involved a balancing act. Martin Luther King Jr., Malcolm X, and Stokely Carmichael, with whose visits this chapter begins, were influential in Britain precisely because of how they were changing the profile of black politics in the United States, but their pull also threatened to marginalize or erase from view long traditions of activism within Britain, and the long, transnational coordinates of black internationalism. When, on the eve of Carmichael's departure, C. L. R. James sought to capture and explain the energy unleashed by his visit, he underlined Carmichael's presence as integral to how "the slogan Black Power reverberate[s] in the way that it is doing in political Britain; and even outside of that, in Britain in general."[12] This, James insisted, was "a testimony not merely to him but to the speed with which the modern world is moving politically." It marked a conjunctural shift—a point from which, as Hall describes the conjuncture, there was "no 'going back.' [...] The terrain changes."[13] But for James, this did not mean a clean break, or the substitution of one politics for another; rather, it involved a reorganization and repositioning of the resources of black resistance. "I have to add that much that

I shall now say to you I knew before," James explained, "but I could never have said it in the way that you will hear, unless I had been able to listen and to talk to the new Stokely, the Stokely that we have been hearing."[14]

The first half of this chapter looks to why Black Power reverberated in Britain when U.S. activists visited in the mid-to-late 1960s. These visits were disruptive and transformative, sharpening the existing tensions within British race politics and promising new futures. The second half the chapter, though, turns to James's other concern—the question of how those things "known before" were now to stand in relation to Black Power. The dominance of events in the United States and the visibility of U.S. activists on the world stage were both enabling and restricting. For many of its adherents, Black Power's draw was that it seemed to offer solutions, whereas older politics appeared compromised or ineffective. But this "diasporic resource"—to borrow Jacqueline Nassy Brown's terminology—was utilized through the unequal power relations of diaspora. Using it also meant carving out a space for oneself in the face of marginalization.[15] American activists came to Britain as familiar figures, but their very familiarity as a result of the British media's ready coverage of U.S. race politics, and the different modes of their political engagement compared to those dominating anti-racist politics in Britain, often served to hide the continuities that existed between black British politics pre– and post–Black Power. It made this longer history of black activism either invisible or harder to recognize as "black." Negotiating this was the balancing act that black Britons had to perform.

AMERICAN CIVIL RIGHTS AND BLACK POWER IN BRITAIN

Carmichael's London visit was part of a much longer tradition. In the lead-up to the American Civil War, many African Americans traveled to Britain, raising funds and building support in the movement for abolition.[16] After abolition, many continued to make the journey, seeking to escape American racism for what they often believed to be the less prejudiced shores of Europe. But Britain also remained an important campaigning location in the development of African American civil rights, and for the involvement of African Americans in anticolonial politics, particularly in the 1930s and 1940s. In the late 1950s and early 1960s, the new titans of the U.S. civil rights movement also came to Britain. First, in 1957, Martin Luther King Jr. and Coretta Scott

King visited London on their return from Ghanaian independence celebrations. King returned several times over the following decade, accompanied often by other leading figures in the American civil rights movement. In 1964, Malcolm X came to Britain, again on the first of several tours, the last just days before his assassination.

Coming to Britain, these Americans entered a charged political field. Periodic anti-black riots in Liverpool in 1948, Deptford in south-east London in 1949, and London's Camden Town area in 1954 preceded large-scale rioting in Notting Hill in west London and the city of Nottingham in England's Midlands region in 1958 involving crowds of whites in the thousands.[17] The significance of the events of 1958 is hard to overstate. Average return migration among West Indian migrants in the year following the riots increased from 150 per annum to 4,500.[18] For the Barbadian writer George Lamming, after Notting Hill, "racial antagonism" was "an atmosphere and a background against which my life and yours are being lived."[19] The following year, an Antiguan carpenter, Kelso Cochrane, was murdered in Notting Hill in a racially motivated attack. Cochrane's murder, and apparent police indifference to catching his killers, saw thousands gather for his funeral, including political representatives from the West Indies Federation, the South African anti-apartheid movement, and leaders from the Movement for Colonial Freedom and the London section of the Communist Party of Great Britain.[20]

The 1958 riots hastened political changes that had been in gestation since the early 1950s. On the one hand, they served to draw support for race relations legislation. Since 1950, Labour members of Parliament had proposed legislation against racial discrimination, Fenner Brockway MP leading the campaign with a series of private members' bills in the House of Commons throughout the decade.[21] In late September 1958, just three weeks after the Nottingham and Notting Hill disturbances, the Labour Party's National Executive Committee finally backed this campaign and pledged to introduce race relations legislation if returned to office.[22] On the other hand, the riots provided added stimulus for anti-immigration politicians and lobbyists to argue for the introduction of restrictions on immigration. Though the riots were widely condemned in the British press, and stringent sentences were meted out to perpetrators, many were quick to connect a need to curb immigration to the events of Notting Hill and Nottingham.[23] Many Conservative Party ministers were privately angry about the effects of the riots in *setting back* the introduction of immigration controls—since such controls might be read as concession to racist violence—but calls for restriction quickly passed from the newspapers to the floor of the Commons.[24] In 1961, Prime Minister Harold Macmillan's Conservative government proposed legislating new immigration restrictions. Home Secretary Rab Butler, who presided over the passing of the 1962 Immigration Act found its "great merit" to be that, though ostensibly color-blind, "its restrictive effect is intended to, and would in fact, operate on coloured people almost exclusively."[25] The ruse was easily called out. The Dominican journalist Edward Scobie, whose *Flamingo* magazine had long reported on what he termed the "lunatic fringe" of Britain's Far Right, concluded that the fascist Union Movement and the Conservative Party "could well join forces; it seems after all that there is not very much to choose between them."[26]

After 1958, a consensus on race relations politics grew, developing, by the mid-1960s, into an informal race relations settlement. This race relations policy, summed up in the Labour MP Roy Hattersley's famous aphorism that "without integration, limitation is inexcusable; without limitation, integration is impossible," aimed to remove issues of race and immigration from party political debate and electoral politics, to be managed by a coalition of governmental and research bodies, community relations "experts," and local and national voluntary associations.[27] After Harold Wilson succeeded Hugh Gaitskell as leader of the Labour Party in 1963, Labour abandoned its previous opposition to immigration controls, supporting the continuation of the legislation introduced under Macmillan. Balancing this commitment to immigration controls, Wilson passed the 1965 Race Relations Act and an accompanying program of race relations management. The Conservative front bench in Parliament broadly supported both the measures introduced, and the principle on which these were based. But while the mid-1960s are often remembered as the "liberal hour" of British race relations, before Powellism, the Kenyan Asian "crisis," the 1968 Immigration Act, and the rise of the populist Right both brought "race" firmly back into political life and placed anti-immigration at the center of this politics for both parties, many black Britons were less ready to find cause for celebration in the terms of a race relations settlement that balanced limited protection from racism with support for a racially coded immigration system. In opposition to a race relations politics that traded anti-discrimination legislation for immigration restrictions, Kennetta Hammond Perry notes that "Black British constituencies [. . .] made it clear that their citizenship status was just as much about rights of mobility as it was about the freedom to establish roots and claim Britain as a permanent home."[28]

The 1964 general election saw Labour return to power on a commitment to continuing immigration restrictions, and saw considerable gains for anti-immigration politics in several key seats. The Conservative town councilor Peter Griffiths won the seat of Smethwick in the West Midlands on an explicitly racist platform, defeating Labour's Shadow Foreign Secretary Patrick Gordon Walker. The Tory campaign was accompanied by stickers and posters produced by local activists carrying the slogan "If you want a nigger neighbour, vote Labour!" Griffiths denied responsibility for the slogan, but also refused to condemn it, claiming it to be a legitimate expression of public feeling.[29] He won the seat with a swing of 7.5 percent, despite a national swing to Labour of 3.2 percent. In the same election, Fenner Brockway lost his seat in Eton and Slough, while anti-immigration candidates gained significant votes in Southall and Birmingham Perry Bar.[30] Patrick Gordon Walker stood again three months later in a by-election in Leyton, but again was defeated. Despite the efforts of the leadership of all parties, the Leyton by-election was fought primarily on the issue of immigration.

The events of the 1964 election hung heavy in the minds of Britain's black communities. The *West Indian Gazette*, a vocal supporter of Brockway's campaigns, worried whether manifesto promises on anti-discrimination legislation would be honored.[31] Others felt wholly excluded from politicians' concerns. One Leyton constituent, a 28-year-old Jamaican man who remembered reading about Patrick Gordon Walker as a youth in the West Indies, told the new black British newspaper *Magnet* that the by-election campaign there was "a choice between Caesar and Caesar." As secretary of state for Commonwealth Relations in 1951, Gordon Walker had played a key role in exiling Seretse Khama, the chief of the Bamangwato tribe in the British Protectorate of Bechuanaland, after pressure from the South African government over Khama's marriage to a white woman, Ruth Williams. Unconvinced that Gordon Walker had "changed all that much since then," and noting that "the other candidates [...] were talking in such a soft voice about people like me that I never heard them," this voter wondered whom he had left to vote for.[32] With a memory of colonial racism extending back to his time as an adolescent in colonial Jamaica, he felt unrepresented in British parliamentary politics, from the local platforms of right-wing backbenchers to the international diplomacy of the Labour cabinet. This was the context in which American civil rights leaders visited Britain.

Martin Luther King Jr. visited London in December 1964, two months after the general election and just as Gordon Walker began his by-election campaign. On arriving, King met with the Lord Chancellor and a group of MPs "to discuss racial matters."[33] The appointment spoke to the politics of the emerging race relations settlement, in which matters of racism and anti-discrimination reform were to be managed beyond the play of party or popular politics.[34] King's traveling companion, the civil rights campaigner Bayard Rustin, was similarly appealed to by parliamentarians, and on his return to Britain in the summer of 1965, Rustin advised a group of MPs on civil rights reform in Britain.[35] Alongside these appointments, though, King and Rustin also spoke with local West Indian, African, and South Asian campaigners. Rustin worked with the Trinidadian anti-racist activist Marion Glean, organizing a meeting between King and a party of thirty civil rights campaigners to discuss the foundations of what would become the Campaign Against Racial Discrimination, a national organization aimed at coordinating Britain's various anti-racist campaigns.[36] Alongside further engagements at the Africa Unity House and with Fenner Brockway's Movement for Colonial Freedom, King also delivered a widely reported sermon at St. Paul's Cathedral, in which he condemned Britain's immigration laws, and warned against racial discrimination in housing.[37] He also reacquainted himself with Claudia Jones, C. L. R. James, and the Grenadian Labour politician David Pitt, whom he had met on his earlier visit to the capital in 1957.[38] The Jamaican novelist Andrew Salkey, who interviewed King for BBC radio three times in his short 1964 stay, remembers him galvanizing many black Britons "as persons in a political struggle," and also recalls Rustin being particularly influential.[39]

The Campaign Against Racial Discrimination (CARD) was the most tangible legacy of King's visit, but it also reflected the tensions within anti-racist political strategy at this time. CARD was formed by West Indians, South Asians, Africans, and white sympathizers skeptical about the Wilson government's intentions regarding anti-discrimination legislation. It comprised leading figures in British anti-racist and anticolonial politics, and played an active role in debating with government officials the nature of the anti-discrimination legislation proposed in Labour's manifesto promise, and highlighting its shortcomings, as well as appealing to the national and local press.[40] The closeness of CARD to the political apparatus of government, however, and its failure to build a grassroots movement, soon led to disquiet among some members. In July 1965, only six months after CARD's founding, Marion Glean withdrew her support.[41] "It would be a pity," Glean commented, drawing comparisons with the splits emerging in the American civil rights movement, "if CARD became the NAACP equivalent in Britain." The NAACP (National Association for the Advancement of Colored People), she suggested, represented an "old, coloured, legalistic bourgeoisie"—old in a world where SNCC and the Congress of Racial Equality (CORE) seemed to be radicalizing the civil rights agenda, and building a more confrontational grassroots movement.[42] "Coloured," presumably, in a world that was now becoming black. Legalistic in a world where the law was no guarantee of rights.

Malcolm X, also visiting Britain just then, represented the more confrontational politics of American civil rights that Glean seemed to be wishing for. Malcolm made several trips to Britain, also drawing substantial attention and support. In his initial visits, he stuck closely to discussions of American civil rights, African politics, and Islam, and kept to appointments with students and governing elites.[43] Though he made few pronouncements on British racism in these initial visits, Malcolm's presence alone often had the ability to reframe local race politics. Speaking at the University of Sheffield on the invitation of the Federation of Students' Islamic Societies in December 1964, he arrived at a time when a student magazine had just published an article in support of Smethwick voters, leading to accusations that his visit would stir racial hostility.[44] At the Oxford Union that same month, his visit gave a fillip to the University's Joint Action Committee against Racial Intolerance, which under the leadership of the Jamaican leader of the Oxford Union, Eric Abrahams, had become increasingly active in its protests against both local racism and international race politics.[45] But it was in visiting Smethwick in February 1965 that he intervened in British politics most forcefully. Standing before eager photographers on Marshall Street, where earlier that year the local council had proposed to buy up property for white residents only, Malcolm announced, "I have heard that the blacks in Smethwick are being treated in the same way as the Negroes were treated in Alabama—like Hitler treated the Jews." If he were himself a black in Smethwick, he continued, he "would not wait until the fascists had built the gas ovens."[46] Referring to the black communities as a minority population denied its rights, Malcolm X brought African American experiences close.[47]

Malcolm's demands for grassroots resistance resonated with those who saw the race relations settlement to be disenfranchising and abandoning the interests of black Britons. Certainly, Malcolm did not limit himself to grassroots engagements, and his platform at elite British universities, which he used to condemn British racism, was important in establishing his legitimacy with some of his American audiences. But his notorious call to achieve black liberation by "any means necessary"—uttered, for example, on the steps of the London School of Economics as he railed against the segregation he had witnessed in Smethwick—revealed Malcolm's refusal to allow those in power to dictate the terms of political participation. His presence alone offered a different mode for politics, away from the "respectable" codes of imperial Britishness that structured the culture of the race relations settlement. As Marion Glean later noted over her decision to quit CARD, the failure of the organization, for her, was that it had "alienated potential immigrant members," a problem evolving out of the conviction on the part of some CARD leaders that a recruitment drive among working-class immigrants "would break the 'respectability' of the group."[48] In contrast Malcolm X, as the future black radical leader Darcus Howe, who shook Malcolm's hand as he toured Notting Hill in February 1965, remembered, "legitimised that part of me which 'respectable' Trinidadian and English society feared and despised."[49] This aspect of Malcolm's presence in Britain was equally emphasized by the Guyanese novelist Jan Carew, who met Malcolm at London's Commonwealth Institute in 1965, at the launch of Carew's new newspaper *Magnet*, and through Malcolm saw the incongruity of this event, trapped within this "relic from a dwindling British Empire."[50]

This turn from "respectability" was significant. Caribbean politics—for that is what this was—had never been confined only to "respectable" forms. Garveyism, Rastafarianism, the cultural and political energies unleashed by the labor rebellions of the 1930s: there was always, as Stuart Hall remembers of his native Jamaica, another Caribbean, "darker and less subservient to the sensibilities of colonial order."[51] This, indeed, was a Caribbean with which Malcolm X was intimately familiar. His mother was a Grenadian immigrant who brought to America an enthusiasm for the Grenadian T. Albert Marryshow's radical *West Indian* newspaper, and combined it with commitments to a Garveyism that Lara Putnam has explained as a "community of faith," sure of the coming hour of Africa's redemption. Malcolm grew up embedded in the beliefs and activities of a transplanted Caribbean black radical culture.[52] But, particularly in the Caribbean, these vernacular political cultures existed largely on the margin—or, more properly speaking, they were marginalized from the centers of power. For those seeking to engage and transform colonial power from within its own institutions of governance, the respectable codes of imperial Britishness had long dominated how anticolonial and anti-racist politics were done both in the colonies and at heart of the metropole. Indeed, this imperial Britishness was a cultural formation that, even in the decline of empire, was "difficult to escape."[53] In part this reflected a lack of much real choice: not only was Britishness "largely the only game in town," but in the terms dictated by this hegemony of imperial Britishness, to become a modern subject was to become British.[54] Deploying imperial Britishness could work as a mode of resistance—a means of laying claim to rights of citizenship, in opposition to various forms of racialized exclusion. Such deployments, as Perry notes, might have been strategic articulations of Britishness, and need not signal a wholesale rejection of that deemed beyond its pale, particularly forms of black popular culture.[55] In these ways, accommodations with respectability politics could be important for anti-racism. What Glean, Howe, and Carew identify in the attraction of Malcolm X, however, signals that the readiness to embrace his black politics was a moment of splitting with such codes of respectability and laying hold of the "less subservient" black cultures that had been marginalized by the leaderships of many anticolonial and anti-racist movements, and within the race relations settlement. Certainly, when *Flamingo* asked Malcolm X for his thoughts on "West Indians in England who imitate the English," he rejected them outright: "Any Black man who wants to identify himself with the whites I call an 'Uncle Tom.'"[56]

After Malcolm X left Britain for the last time on February 13, 1965, Carew wrote him a letter. "Your visit was all too short, but folks speak about you as though you'd never left. [. . .] Your visits were short, but your words will echo and re-echo in the minds of generations of Black folk in this country."[57] In the event, he never sent the letter; Malcolm X was assassinated while delivering an address at Harlem's Audubon Ballroom just eight days later. The most immediate and visible impact of his visit in Britain was the formation of the Racial Adjustment Action Society (RAAS). RAAS was established by three men: Carew, a Guyanese Indian named Roy Sawh, who had previously acted as a street vendor for the *West Indian Gazette*,[58] and the Trinidadian Michael de Freitas, who had first made his name in his efforts to organize resistance to white attacks during the Notting Hill riots, but who was better known to many as a "strong arm" and rent collector for the property racketeer Peter Rachman.[59] De Freitas and Sawh would both go on to play important roles in the emerging Black Power organizations of the late 1960s (Carew, on the other hand, was to leave for Ghana soon after the establishment of RAAS). But Malcolm X's legacy was wider than this. As Carew predicted, Malcolm X would provide a constant touchstone for black politics and culture in Britain over the coming years, occupying a space in collective memory and black culture equaling that found among African Americans in the United States. His autobiography remained a best seller at the black bookshops that sprang up in Britain in the late 1960s, and tributes in his memory at the anniversary of his assassination became commonplace among radical black political groups.[60] In large part, for those who celebrated him in Britain, he represented this break from respectability, turn to "grassroots" organizing, and embrace of forms of black modernity divorced from the imperial formation.

NEW ROUTES TO BLACK MODERNITY: STOKELY CARMICHAEL IN LONDON

On July 12, 1967, civil unrest broke out in Newark, New Jersey, instigating a wave of urban uprisings that would sweep across the United States in the following days, from Detroit to Pontiac, Toledo, New York, and Cambridge, Maryland. Jan Carew, staying in Detroit at the time, wrote to Andrew Salkey in London. "Detroit was like a blinding flash, showing the invincible power of the black man's rage ... it's a vindication of Fanon [...], man, those fires were setting us free, Andrew, all of us!"[61] Penguin Books had published Frantz Fanon's *The Wretched of the Earth* (1961) in English translation earlier that summer, and the book was in these months consolidating its reputation as the master text of revolutionary anticolonialism. As yet another wave of violence swept across America's cities, again pointing to the limit of civil rights reforms for addressing African American oppression, Fanon's warnings about the necessarily violent ends to colonialism and racism appealed to Carew. For Fanon, the violence of decolonization was not only unavoidable, it was cleansing, therapeutic.[62] It was in this sense that, for Carew, the fires of Detroit were "setting us free." But this was also about creating new subjects of history. "Decolonization never takes place unnoticed," as Fanon wrote, "for it influences individuals and modifies them fundamentally. It transforms spectators crushed with their inessentiality into privileged actors, with the grandiose glare of history's floodlights upon them."[63] Through Fanon, and through the fires of Detroit, men like Carew felt themselves now at the forefront of history. History's floodlights, for Carew, had shifted from the "relics" of British imperialism, and shone now on blacker, less "respectable" spaces. His sense of excitement captured a significant sense of the reordering of the relationships of blackness, history, and modernity that sharpened in the rise of global Black Power.

Stokely Carmichael arrived in London just days after the Newark uprising began, and he was indelibly marked by those events for all who met him. Visiting for a brief eleven days between July 15 and 25, he had a busy schedule. Many of his engagement retraced the footsteps of the Pan-Africanists who had long visited the capital to organize their politics—he addressed the London West Indian Students' Centre in Earl's Court and an audience at Africa House, he spoke at the soapboxes of Hyde Park's Speakers' Corner, and he met with other Trinidadians invested in anticolonialism, including C. L. R. James and the political organizer and publisher John La Rose. Other engagements saw him in the new centers of black settlement in London, meeting West Indian community activists in Dalston and in Brixton, and getting to know these new "black enclaves." He also, though, held court in big, public-facing events. He spoke three times to an international audience at the Dialectics of Liberation Congress at Camden's Roundhouse, spoke with reporters from all the major newspapers, and was interviewed by Andrew Salkey for the BBC.[64] The print and broadcast media were quick to read Carmichael as representative of the violence sweeping American cities. Speaking of the Detroit "rioters" as mobilized by "a new and dangerous philosophy [. . .] that any rioting, any destruction, any killing of white-skinned people is a battle won in the cause of Negro emancipation," *The Times* warned that "The figure of Mr. Stokely Carmichael, though he was not there in person, dominated the scene with his maxim 'an eye for an eye.'" The paper also recorded that Carmichael—the absent presence of the Detroit uprising—had spent his time in Britain visiting "Brixton, Notting Hill and other areas with large coloured populations, advocating Black Power."[65] An ITV program covering Carmichael's British visit intercut footage of his London addresses with footage of the Detroit uprising.[66] Such accounts usually served the purpose of condemning Carmichael, and insisting on him as an alien presence, unsuited and un-relatable to British race politics.[67] But this connection between Carmichael and the American uprisings was equally made by those eager to see him, and to further his politics in Britain. As the Guyanese activist Jessica Huntley recalled of Carmichael's London visit, a major attraction of going to see him was the feeling that "America was on fire. [. . .] And here was this fire coming. And we go to meet the fire."[68]

Highly publicized, coinciding with the radical turn in black liberation politics in the United States, Carmichael's visit had a seismic impact. Addressing London's West Indian Students' Centre in the weeks following Carmichael's departure from Britain, C. L. R. James reflected that in the slogan "Black Power," Carmichael had provided "a banner for people [...] around which they can rally, a banner which I believe millions already today see and in the not too distant future will see, as the symbol of a tremendous change in life and society as they have known it."[69] A year down the line, John La Rose described Carmichael's visit as "a catalyst in a way that nothing before had been," signaling a new emphasis on the politics of the United States among young West Indians, who now "look [...] to the United States [when] at one time he was concerned with the political leaders and so on who were [...] in the West Indies." "The American experience," Stuart Hall agreed with La Rose, "is the one which is so close to him now; he can see a great deal of connections between himself and [America]."[70] Certainly, there were those who regretted Carmichael's interventions. Carmichael had visited Brixton on the same day that Duncan Sandys, Conservative MP for the nearby constituency of Streatham, called for further immigration controls and a ban on mixed-race marriages. The Brixton publican George Berry, a Jamaican active in Lambeth interracial movement politics, was quick to label both Carmichael and Sandys "fools," both equally damaging to community relations. Courtney Laws, the Jamaican leader of Lambeth's St. John's Inter Racial Club and vice-chairman of the local Council for Community Relations, insisted to the *Brixton Advertiser* that "Stokely Carmichael has had very little effect upon the immigrants living in the borough of Lambeth. These people do not suffer the same oppression as the American negroes although they are sympathetic to the cause."[71] But among the capital's growing band of black radicals, there were few who were not excited at the opportunity to hear Carmichael speak.

Carmichael arrived at a moment of deepening crisis among black activists over the future of anti-racist activism in Britain. From long before his visit, CARD—the leading anti-racist organization in British politics—had been grappling with its significant internal tensions. An anti-racist body only ever partially incorporated into race relations settlement, CARD was pulled in contrary directions. In August 1965, when the government produced its white paper on "Immigration from the Commonwealth" combining anti-discrimination measures with a program to tighten immigration controls still further, two leading CARD members, David Pitt and Hamza Alavi, accepted invitations to join the government-sponsored National Committee for Commonwealth Immigrants, a body receiving funding under the anti-discrimination proposals of the same document.[72] But while Pitt and Alavi sought to work with the government, others saw such an approach, particularly after the fiasco of Rhodesia's Unilateral Independence Declaration, as untenable.[73] Leaders of the West Indian Standing Conference, CARD's largest affiliated body, grew increasingly "impressed with the experience of Negroes in America and Africa," as Benjamin Heinemann noted in his study of CARD conducted in the late 1960s. When Malcolm X visited London, the Standing Conference "warmly welcomed" him and, as Heinemann noted, embraced "negritude" and increasingly distrusted "multiracialism" in anti-racist political organizing. The legacies of Malcolm X's visit continued to pull CARD apart over the following years, and by June 1967, a month before Carmichael's arrival, CARD was already effectively "dead."[74]

At exactly this moment, other organizations also gained ground, making CARD's consensual, inter-racial, state-sponsored politics out of step with the changing face of black politics. Michael de Freitas's RAAS had continued with limited membership and publicity since its founding following Malcolm X's visit in 1965, but when Carmichael came to London, de Freitas assumed the role of his guide to black London, leading him and Angela Davis—also in London for the Dialectics of Liberation conference—around the city's black neighborhoods.[75] Carmichael's visit reinvigorated de Freitas's political career, and following Carmichael's departure, de Freitas shot to fame again as he was arrested under the Race Relations Act for a speech he made in Reading, Berkshire, in Carmichael's place. Alongside de Freitas, Obi B. Egbuna, a Nigerian playwright, also swiftly gained notoriety after he formed Britain's first avowedly Black Power organization, the Universal Coloured People's Association (UCPA), issued a Black Power manifesto that was widely reported in the media, and began regular meetings at Hyde Park's Speakers' Corner, recruiting Carmichael to their platform when he came to London.[76] Four months later, the UCPA would play a key role in finally killing off CARD as a national umbrella organization. It led protests at CARD's third annual convention, where it voted for CARD to declare its support for international anti-imperialism, and to form a new executive committee comprised only of nonwhite representatives. Delegates hung posters of the exiled black internationalist African American leader Robert Williams, and Kenya's anticolonial leader and independence president Jomo Kenyatta, alongside banners proclaiming "Black Power means liberation, not integration as third-class citizens." Mark Bonham-Carter, the chairman of the recently created Race Relations Board, was greeted with shouts of "white liberal" and "resign," while Pitt was heckled as an "Uncle Tom" and "house nigger."[77] The politics that tore CARD apart was the politics that, for many, Carmichael represented: an ascendant confrontational anti-imperialist politics, couched in a language of blackness that regarded black internationalism, black leadership, and a commitment to grassroots involvement as founding principles.

Carmichael's politics built on traditions of internationalism and anticolonialism that had long defined black Atlantic radical politics, but it is surprising how often he was nonetheless greeted as a new phenomenon, breaking through a stale, useless British anti-racism. This was certainly in large part a consequence of the scale of publicity that Carmichael enjoyed, and his skill at exploiting it—something we can hear when we listen to his audiences. "There is not a damn thing the Negro is doing for himself in any way whatsoever as a collective group at all," one man told Carmichael at the Dialectics of Liberation Congress. "I'm sick to death of turning on the television, for instance, and seeing the same old Uncle Tom situations with the downtrodden black man, [saying] 'I'm not downtrodden, nobody's treading me down,' you know?" "For the black people in England, I must say they are sick," another ventured. "Taking into account the successful achievement of the black people in the United States. I personally detest the stand that the black people take in this country. [. . .] I believe it's time for us to wake up."[78] Clearly, on one level, these men were mistaken. There was a history of black resistance in Britain stretching back far, and in recent memory at least until the 1930s, in the League of Coloured People's activities, and in more radical Pan-African projects. In the postwar years, Claudia Jones and the *West Indian Gazette*, and David Pitt, Marion Glean, and CARD, had exerted significant political power, holding the government to account, and intervening in the policy-making process of race relations politics. And yet, it is striking how easily much of this could be forgotten or dismissed as "Uncle Tom" politics, too close to the "white liberal" establishment for any properly *black* political project.

Carmichael offered his politics as new and, like Malcolm X before him, he tapped into the rising identification with grassroots "blackness" as a rejection of the respectability of the race relations settlement. He actively condemned the settlement, proposing instead a realignment, away from

Westminster and toward global black liberation struggles. Asked about Mark Bonham-Carter, the chairman of the Race Relations Board, he was scathingly dismissive.[79] Refusing the decorum of race relations politics, he offered anger, a more populist, less deferential politics; and refusing "to imitate white western society because we wanted to be civilized," he offered a black society, a new model of civilization and modernity.[80] Such an orientation was most evident in Carmichael's addresses to the Dialectics of Liberation Congress— the most public and widely remembered of his London engagements. The speech was electric, prompting the entire Roundhouse to stand on their chairs applauding, as one audience member remembered.[81] Jessica Huntley, present for both of Carmichael's addresses, recalled how he had requested only black people to be in front of him. "That was a bomb. There was all us blacks, you know, 'Move! Move!'"[82] "Man, it was like Carnival!" one of Susan Craig's interviewees remembered, recalling the event two years on.[83] For the Trinidadian journalist Courtney Tulloch, Carmichael "had star quality." "Despite its build-up, the Liberation Conference was pretty routine until Stokely Carmichael set it on fire."[84]

Carmichael's skills in communicating himself as the apex of black modernity were key to this sense of newness that he engendered. The blurred boundaries between Carmichael the political activist and Carmichael the "star" are significant here. "We're not even noticed till we're 'moving in next door,' or going down the street with a pretty chick or something like that," another West Indian man at the Dialectics of Liberation conference told Carmichael. "Then people'll look at you, and say 'look at that black man.' Otherwise, they don't even know we're here. You know, I mean we realize your situation in America, man, but we got an even bigger problem here cos we ain't even noticed. You are."[85] This man found himself erased from national life, his blackness disqualifying him, and making him visible only when he threatened those racialized sites where Englishness was most heavily symbolically invested: the white neighborhood ("moving in next door") and the body of the white woman ("going down the street with a pretty chick").[86] He wanted to control his conditions of visibility, to define himself—something he credited Carmichael with having done. Carmichael's mere visibility, his public profile, was an attraction. Revealingly, the man continued his appeal to Carmichael by arguing about the need for more "Negro" actors on television, "doing a part as a lawyer, or a doctor, or something like that, something I respect, you know."[87] The comment might remind us that previous scarce television appearances for black Britons were far more likely to be framed in terms of "moving

FIGURE 1. Stokely Carmichael at the Dialectics of Liberation conference, July 1967. The bottom-right still is from Carmichael's second address. On stage are (left to right) Michael de Freitas (Michael X), Carmichael, unidentified man, Roy Sawh, Obi Egbuna (standing). From *Stokely Carmichael at the Dialectics of Liberation, London 1967*, directed by Peter Davies (Villon Films, 2013). © Peter Davis / Villon Films (www.villonfilms.ca).

in next door," or mixed-race relationships.[88] In his appeals we might then recognize, beyond its radical political energies, that the attraction of U.S. Black Power was also simply in the everyday concerns with being of consequence, of being *noticed*—and certainly Carmichael could guarantee time on the airwaves. But Carmichael also offered a dynamic, impossible-to-miss presence. When he addressed his audiences resplendent in a gold silk shirt and dark glasses, punctuating his speech with his fist in the air, he embodied a confrontational, modern, stylish black masculine political culture that appealed to men like this beyond just its formal politics. To pick up on the dramaturgical metaphor in Frantz Fanon's *Wretched of the Earth*, it offered scope for the performance of blackness in the "glare of history's floodlights."[89]

Black Power, as historians have recognized, offered new expressions of blackness. Its visual repertoires "recast the relationship between urban culture, modernity, and African American identity."[90] This is most commonly remembered through the Black Panther Party (BPP), gun-toting in their black berets and sunglasses, Afro haircuts and leather jackets. For Earl Anthony, the BPP's deputy minister for education, seeing the Panthers "in black leather jackets, and black pants with black berets pulled down on their heads at a slant," "my heart skipped a few beats." For Eldridge Cleaver, BPP minister for information, it was "love at first sight [. . .] the most beautiful sight I have ever seen."[91] Carmichael, too, offered this: a stylish black modernity that was emphatically political. At the Dialectics of Liberation Conference, his gestures and clothing themselves spoke to his signification—beyond the man and his rhetoric—of a new, radical black modernity. Style here worked as politics, and politics was decidedly stylish. Carmichael's were sartorial and performative expressions "that revealed black visibility."[92]

Recognizing *blackness*, its weight, its potentialities, was key to Carmichael's politics. In his writing and public addresses the experience of racialization was foregrounded. "White America will not face the problem of color, the reality of it," he wrote in 1966. "The well-intended say: 'We're all human, everybody is really decent, we must forget color.' But color cannot be 'forgotten' until its weight is recognized and dealt with."[93] As he later elaborated, "race is an overwhelming fact of life in this historical period. There is no black man in this country who can live 'simply as a man.' His blackness is an ever-present fact of this racist society, whether he recognizes it or not."[94] To discuss race only in abstract terms, evacuated from the intersubjective terrain of the day-to-day, Carmichael proposed, erased the very basis of racism—the racialized body—from which oppression begins. Rather than proposing that one should ignore blackness and become equal, Carmichael demanded equality through blackness. In his public addresses and in his sartorial choices Carmichael, like so many other of the prominent voices of radical black politics, made blackness the starting point for thinking through a new politics and new ways of being.

Becoming black, for Carmichael, meant not only embracing the black body, but assuming a particular politics, rooted in black socialist internationalism. Speaking at his second Dialectics address on Sunday July 23, 1967, advertised on the paper glued to the front of the Roundhouse as a speech for "Black Eyes, Black Voices, Black Power,"[95] Carmichael demanded of his audience that it was time to "come on home." Introduced by Obi Egbuna of the UCPA, flanked by Roy Sawh and Michael de Freitas of RAAS, and with images of Malcolm X hung behind him, Carmichael dominated the stage. In his speech he slipped occasionally into the speech patterns of his native Trinidad, made reference to Winston Churchill, Claude McKay, and British television, and delivered his lines using his characteristic rhetorical devices of anaphora and epistrophe in a delivery that stood somewhere between a Harlem storefront preacher and new black soul-style. This was a speech that was diasporic in its form and content; "coming home," in this sense, meant owning *this* black culture. However, in the speech Carmichael also named a political home for blackness, in an alignment with "Third World" liberation politics. "Black" skin or "black" culture were not all that was at stake:

> We have come to explain to you that, no matter what the shades of your color are, that if you are non-white then you are in the same boat that the rest of us are. Therefore, you had better come on home. You had better come on home.
>
> We have come to tell you that the revolutionary consciousness that is spreading in the Third World today will not only be based on skin color but on ideology. [The former Congolese Premier Moïse] Tshombe[96] is a white man; he will be destroyed. You had better come on home. Had better come on home.
>
> We have come to tell you that if you see your lot and your culture being thrown with that of England then we see you as part of England who suppresses and oppresses us. You will be with England when the lines are drawn. You had better come on home. Home.[97]

Becoming black meant a commitment to a culture of blackness that Carmichael positioned as an opposition to Englishness, as revolutionary and anticolonial, and as resolutely confrontational, constituted in acts of violent resistance. As he told the audience, reflecting on of his Trinidadian childhood when he spent his Saturdays at the cinema watching Tarzan movies: "We should'a burned the movie house down to the ground!"[98] Routing blackness through the most-cited revolutionaries of the day, Carmichael demanded: "Who does the white man think is listening to him any longer? We're listening to the Malcolm Xs, we're listening to the Che Guevaras, we're listening to the Mao Zedongs. That's who we're listening to."[99]

After Carmichael, Black Power was firmly lodged in the British political landscape. Carmichael himself was banned from returning, and the

Department of Public Prosecutions investigated cassette recordings of his London speeches.[100] Michael de Freitas received a year's jail term for his speech in place of Carmichael at Reading, while Obi B. Egbuna claimed that since Carmichael had shared their Speakers' Corner platform in July, members of the organization had been subject to increasing police harassment and arrests.[101] Egbuna was later imprisoned, too. Like Carmichael, Egbuna and de Freitas quickly became television stars, go-to sources for inflammatory rhetoric, or shouting-match debates. Though both were important figures, de Freitas and Egbuna were each amplified far beyond their significance for political organizing by their ability to conform to a media image of angry black men.[102] But the emphasis on black visibility, the insistence on new modes of political engagement distinct from those "respectable" modes that had dominated the politics of race relations, and the alignment away from representatives of the state and toward grassroots communities, beyond the frame of the national and toward the fate of global black liberation politics, increasingly defined the anti-racism of many who now reframed their politics in the language of blackness. And while this was a language often dominated by a particularly chauvinistic model of black masculinity, women remained at the heart of this organizing drive, though they received far less press attention.[103] In the final section of this chapter, we turn to some of the various new or reformulated sites of political and cultural activity cohering around a language of blackness in the late 1960s and early 1970s, as Britain's Black Power took firmer root. Carew, Carmichael, and the Dialectics of Liberation audience members whom we have heard from in this section repeatedly framed the promise of Black Power as the promise of black men coming into history, and coming into visibility. In the next section, we shall see how many others, including many black women, also carved out new political projects in the name of blackness.

THE GROWTH OF BRITISH BLACK POWER AS A TRANSNATIONAL POLITICS: THE WEST INDIAN STUDENTS' CENTRE

Britain's Black Power movement grew substantially following Carmichael's visit. The sheer scale of mobilization and new political organization at this time is staggering. It was protean, varied, and stretched across Britain. In London, a dozen new organisations formed—the Racial Adjustment Action

Society, the Universal Coloured Peoples Association, the Universal Coloured People and Arab Association, the Black Power Party, the Black Panther Movement, the Black Unity and Freedom Party, the Black Regional Action Movement, the Black Eagles, the Black Liberation Front, the Black Active Militants, the South East London Parent's Organisation, and the Fasimbas. Organizations beyond London were fewer, but reports from the early 1970s nonetheless record a network of organizations across England and Wales, many active since the late 1960s. These included Cardiff's Black Alliance; the Black Community Workers in Birmingham's Handsworth; the Black People's Freedom Movement and the Black Workers' Action Committee, both in Nottingham; Leicester's Black People's Liberation Party; Huddersfield's Black People's Liberation Society; Liverpool 8 Black Action; Sheffield's United Black People's Organisation; Leed's West Indian Afro Brotherhood; Coventry's Afro-Asian People's Liberation Movement; and the West Indian Co-ordinating Committee and the Afro-Caribbean Liberation Movement, both in Manchester, where the Black Unity and Freedom Party also set up a satellite branch. Wolverhampton was home to an umbrella organization, the Black People's Alliance.[104] Many of these groups stayed in close contact, moving up and down the country, joining each other for various campaigns and demonstrations, and holding conferences and workshops in cities across Britain.[105]

The sphere and scope of politics was undergoing a radical overhaul in the 1960s. Many in Britain were discontented with existing political structures, and this, as Lawrence Black notes, generated a "more pluralist political culture, mostly located outside of party."[106] On the right, this was most evident in the rise of moral conservative campaigning, particularly under the formidable figure of Mary Whitehouse, and in the rise of racist populism, with its figurehead in Enoch Powell.[107] On the left, it played out in the rapid expansion of the "new social movements" in feminism, gay liberation, environmentalism, student politics, disability politics, and anti-racism.[108] These rising movements were often transnational, prompted by the ramping up of global battles for civil rights and decolonization, and growing discontent over the European postwar settlements entrenched by the Cold War.[109] Of course, little of this was new for black political formations, which had long been transnational, located outside party, and at odds with the political settlements of nation-states. But the shifting global and local conditions were nonetheless important. In this shrinking global world, and in the domestic context of Powellism, black radicalism was on fertile ground in Britain.

As the politics of blackness took hold in Britain in these years, it was of a part with the struggles for secondary decolonization gripping much of the Caribbean, Africa, and other former colonial territories. Richard Drayton coined the term "secondary decolonization" to describe the political and cultural upheavals around blackness in the Caribbean that attempted to end "the persistence of a colonial order after the acquisition of constitutional sovereignty," that condition so memorably described by Frantz Fanon, Achille Mbembe, or Kwame Nkrumah.[110] Rather than "magic thresholds separating slavery radically from freedom," independence celebrations, for most, marked little real change in their relation to freedom.[111] The promises of independence in much of the formerly colonized world were delayed, the colonial economic, political, social, and cultural order not overturned, but entrenched in new ways. Disparate and varied as it was, global Black Power, as Drayton notes, marked a moment when this demand for secondary decolonization crystalized into a transnational movement. "Becoming black" as a transition into a radical politics of blackness in Britain in the 1960s, as we have seen so far in this chapter, was often sparked by or framed through events in the United States, or the visits of African Americans—even while these held their own transnational histories. But it was taken forward by British-based activists deeply tied up in these struggles for secondary decolonization. This is the other key context in the moment of "becoming black" that frames this book. These activists did not suddenly come into activism after American activists visited British shores; they were not just outgrowths of an American movement. Certainly, African Americans visiting Britain carried a particular charge. But black radicalism in Britain drew on long-standing traditions of anticolonial politics, and was built in constant dialogue with anticolonial liberation struggles and the politics of secondary decolonization raging across much of the formerly colonized world. These connections often lacked the flashpoint status of visits of American civil rights and Black Power celebrities, but they are just as crucial to understanding how a particular form of black politics evolved via countless transactions and movements between Britain, the Caribbean, Africa, and North America, and via networks often invisible to the mainstream broadcast media.

The scale of these networks, and the variety of the political and cultural projects produced through them, is too great to give a comprehensive survey. But we can catch some of their energy and preoccupations by using London's West Indian Students Centre as a case study, before taking up some of these strands in later chapters. From the mid-1960s to the mid-1970s, the West

FIGURE 2. James Baldwin speaking at the West Indian Students' Centre, February 3, 1968. From left to right are Andrew Salkey, Locksley Comrie, James Baldwin (standing), Dick Gregory, and Frankie Dymon. From *Baldwin's Nigger*, directed by Horace Ové (1969; London: British Film Institute, 2005). © Horace Ové CBE.

Indian Students Centre (WISC) was a hub of black radicalism. It opened in Earl's Court in 1955, initially as a base for those West Indian students seeking to play their part in preparation for West Indian independence and training up for the governmental posts they hoped to acquire on their return.[112] But in an era in which, as the Guyanese publisher Eric Huntley recalls, it was very difficult to get meeting halls, the building soon became a key meeting place also for other West Indians in the capital, and a center of political activity.[113] By the time James Baldwin spoke there in early 1968, as Horace Ové, filming the meeting, remembers, it had become "One of the great meeting places" in London, "quite radical."[114] It pulled in a wide variety of activists, intellectuals, and local working-class people, including many involved in the new Black Power groups taking root in the city. Such an audience was present at Baldwin's talk, and the success of the event in bringing them together was celebrated by the WISC's newsletter—the "night at the Centre had justified its existence."[115] We know Baldwin's story well, as we know Carmichael's, as we know King's, and Malcolm X's. But if we return to Ové's film of Baldwin's talk, we can begin to unpack the diversity of this crowd of London's black radicals, and see how the event could be judged such a success from those it pulled in. Ové's camera lingers longest, of course, on Baldwin, usually swinging round only to gauge his audience's reaction. But if we freeze the frame for longer on those faces in the crowd, we can see some of the diversity of black politics in the capital pulled together by these events, and its connections to the transnational politics of black liberation and secondary decolonization. In the audience that night at Baldwin's talk were many of the luminaries of black political and cultural activity in Britain, and many ordinary Londoners, too.

Those students who led the WISC's transformation into a radical hub were present the night Baldwin spoke. Sat close to Baldwin was Locksley Comrie, a Jamaican engineering student at Brixton technical college. As the WISC's Discussions and Cultural Officer, Comrie had called for the building to be "open to the bus conductor, the bus driver."[116] He had read Malcolm X to the audience that night as they waited for Baldwin to arrive.[117] Comrie played a key role in transforming the WISC into a site for the discussion of black radical politics, inviting local Black Power leaders and African American and Caribbean activists to speak. Indeed, he had invited Stokely Carmichael during his brief London tour, Carmichael appearing beside RAAS's Roy Sawh in an event that also attracted a large audience.[118] Under Comrie's leadership, together with Jamaican law student and former CARD activist Richard Small and a cadre of young students who would soon take the reins when Comrie and Small returned to the Caribbean, the WISC ran regular discussion events on Black Power politics, built a library of the Black Power literature emerging from the United States and the Caribbean, screened films and played cassette recordings of speeches and documentaries on the American civil rights movement and Black Power, and invited a host of radical speakers from America, the Caribbean, and from the liberation struggles in Rhodesia and South Africa. The WISC's newsletter then also reproduced these speeches, offering a live forum at WISC meetings for ongoing discussion of the politics of blackness.[119] In August 1968, the student executive committee extended this discussion process into a three-day "Seminar on the Realities of Black Power," dedicated to discussing the political and cultural changes taking place around them, complete with a message from Amy Ashwood Garvey, an address by Obi Egbuna, poetry readings, and a performance of Ed Bullins's *The Electronic Nigger*.[120] In 1969, WISC students estab-

FIGURE 3. Althea Jones-Lecointe at the West Indian Students' Centre, February 3, 1968. From *Baldwin's Nigger*, directed by Horace Ové (1969; London: British Film Institute, 2005). © Horace Ové CBE.

lished a supplementary school—the C. L. R. James Supplementary School— teaching black studies to local students. In the same year, Ansel Wong, a member of the WISC's executive committee, established the Black Arts Workshop, focusing on poetry and theatre, and attracting the participation of young black Londoners with whom Wong had made contact as a teacher and youth worker.[121]

This was a wide-ranging program, encompassing arts, education, political campaigning and academic debate. Through this program, the WISC's events brought together the many faces of black radical politics then emergent in Britain. This included revolutionaries working for the overthrow of neo-colonialism in the former colonies and leading campaigns against racist policing, the justice system, and anti-immigration legislation in Britain. It included publishers, booksellers, and educationalists seeking to make the literature of "black experience" better available, and to provide means by which others could read and learn their way into blackness. It included writers and artists seeking to reformulate black aesthetics, and to change the social relations of cultural production, reimagining them through the lessons they sought to draw from the experiences of racialized oppression.

First, there were revolutionaries. Close to the front at Baldwin's talk sat Althea Jones-Lecointe, a Trinidadian biochemistry student and later leader of the Black Panther Movement (BPM). Described by Jessica Huntley as "one of the most powerful black women [. . .] in the country [. . .] in that period," and known nationally among revolutionary groups, Jones-Lecointe is nonetheless, as the historian of British Black Power Rosie Wild notes, largely absent from the historical archive. She "went out of her way to remain anonymous."[122] Her effort to preserve her anonymity is evident in Ové's film. When the camera tracked in her direction, she often held a folder in front of her face—the one covered face in a room of people apparently otherwise too enthralled by Baldwin's talk to notice the camera's presence.[123] Jones-Lecointe's secrecy was of a piece with the BPM's wider strategies. This was, as Wild writes, an "extremely publicity-shy" movement.[124] They kept few written records, were suspicious of outsiders, and were rigorous in screening new members, and testing their dedication. Members were expected to uphold a strict moral code, and underwent demanding ideological training. The Panthers boycotted electoral politics, and they were rumored to have a "military wing" that instructed their members in street fighting.[125] Though they were never engaged in armed resistance to the police like their namesakes in the United States, the BPM were a revolutionary movement, believing in the necessity of anti-capitalist revolution to guarantee black liberation and consistently supporting the anticolonial liberation movements of Africa, the Caribbean, and South-East Asia. They led numerous campaigns against police brutality, racist immigration legislation, and oppression and exploitation in the neocolonial world. The scale of their mobilization is staggering. As Anne-Marie Angelo has noted, over the period that Jones-Lecointe led the Panthers, they catalogued 148 incidents of police harassment and violence in their newsletters and visited at least 60 victims in prisons or hospitals. They staged 147 demonstrations against police brutality and institutional racism, and 77 cultural events. On average they were holding one event every five days, and their activity extended from Birmingham to Bradford, Bristol, Derby, Leeds, London, Manchester, and Nottingham.[126]

This was the revolutionary face of Black Power in Britain. Althea Jones-Lecointe was part of a revolutionary family deeply tied up in the upheavals of secondary decolonization struggles, and for this reason too, she had good reason to seek anonymity where she could. Her mother, Viola Jones, was a member of the Women's League of Trinidad's independence party, the People's National Movement. Since the 1940s, she had wedded the politics of national independence to programs to build public health and child welfare projects, and protest for women's equality. From a young age, her daughters, Althea, Beverley, and Jennifer, accompanied her on marches, knocking on doors, and campaigning.[127] Althea, who excelled at chemistry in school in Trinidad, moved to London in 1965, aged twenty, to pursue doctoral study at University College London. There she immediately faced the racism of her tutors who struggled to understand that she might be the same Althea Jones they had listed on their register. She soon became involved in student anti-racist politics, too, staging a sit-in protest at the union when she found the university's lodgings bureau offering separate accommodation lists for those landladies who would and would not take black lodgers. The BPM came to support the sit-in, and on this introduction she joined the organization.[128] When Egbuna was arrested and imprisoned a few months later for publishing a pamphlet titled *What to Do if Cops Lay Their Hands on a Black Man at Speakers' Corner*, Althea Jones-Lecointe took over leadership. She took to the role with ease. As her fellow Panthers Linton Kwesi Johnson and Tony Sinclair remember, she "could rival any man with her rigid discipline and revolutionary fervour."[129]

In Trinidad, Althea's sisters Beverley and Jennifer became ever more closely embroiled in revolutionary politics. When their mother moved to New York for work in 1968, they moved in with their grandmother, from whose house they would sneak out at night to attend late-night meetings of the National Joint Action Committee.[130] This was the group that would soon spearhead the Black Power revolution in Trinidad and Tobago.[131] In the aftermath of the failed Black Power uprising of February 1970, a new group, the National Union of Freedom Fighters (NUFF) continued the revolutionary movement, inaugurating a four-year armed guerrilla struggle against government forces that took its inspiration from the Cuban revolution.[132] Beverley and Jennifer Jones, both still only in their late teens, joined NUFF, fighting this guerrilla war in the hills around Port of Spain. These, as Trinidad's radical magazine *Tapia* commented, were "women who have chosen to handle bullets, not cyclostyled bulletins written by their men."[133] In this context, it is unsurprising that Althea Jones-Lecointe remembers her world at that time as one of "never ending war."[134]

The worlds of racism and revolution in Britain and the neocolonial Caribbean were closely drawn together for women like Althea Jones-

Lecointe. As she led campaigns in Britain, her comrades in the Panthers traveled to centers of anticolonial struggle, involving themselves in the battles there.[135] Obi Egbuna in July 1968 traveled to Conakry, Guinea, to meet the exiled former president of Ghana Kwame Nkrumah, and published their conversations as a Black Panther pamphlet. He would soon also turn to writing on the civil war in his native Nigeria.[136] Darcus Howe, the Trinidadian great-nephew of C. L. R. James, who had become closely involved with the burgeoning Black Power groups in London in the late 1960s and later worked closely with Jones-Lecointe, traveled to Trinidad in 1969. He joined labor protests there, quickly falling foul of the state in the tense months before the Black Power uprising. Later, he played a strategic part in the uprising itself, before fleeing back to London to evade arrest.[137] As post-independence governments in the Caribbean relied on increasingly heavy-handed tactics to quell political dissent, black activists in Britain, reminding their audiences of what they considered to be a dual struggle against both the British state and the forces of neocolonialism in the former colonies, used their experience of police oppression in Britain and the Caribbean to call out attempts by these governments to win their support. One London Black Power group published an open letter to Michael Manley in 1971, condemning the hypocrisy of his support for anti-police brutality protests in Britain, when "It seems that while one Black Jamaican is being beaten here, there is a fair chance that his family is also being systematically brutalised at home."[138] For Althea Jones-Lecointe, this became a palpable reality when on September 13, 1973, her sister Beverley, only seventeen years old, and three months pregnant, was killed by the police in Trinidad. Her other sister, Jennifer, was captured on the same day.[139] The Panthers in London, now operating under the name Black Workers' Movement, reported that contrary to police reports, Beverly Jones had been tortured and shot at close range.[140]

Althea Jones-Lecointe was not the only member of the audience at James Baldwin's talk who would have first-hand experience of the violent politics of secondary decolonization. A few rows behind her sat Jessica Huntley. A generation older than Jones-Lecointe, Huntley was born Jessica Carroll in 1927 in Bagotstown, British Guiana. In her late teens, she worked in a clothing factory in Georgetown, where she began her lifelong career as an activist, pushing her co-workers to come out on strike over their working conditions. Soon after her entry into trade union politics, she met her future husband, Eric Huntley, an activist in the Post Office Workers' Trade Union and member of the People's

FIGURE 4. Jessica Huntley at the West Indian Students' Centre, February 3, 1968. From *Baldwin's Nigger*, directed by Horace Ové (1969; London: British Film Institute, 2005). © Horace Ové CBE.

Progressive Party (PPP). Jessica soon also joined the party, founding its Women's Progressive Organisation.[141] Both Jessica and Eric backed the social- ist independence platform of the party's leader, Cheddi Jagan.[142] When the British government instigated a coup to overthrow the popularly elected PPP government in 1953, shipping in troops and suspending the constitution, Eric was jailed. Both he and Jessica subsequently found it impossible to get jobs in British Guiana because of their PPP affiliations.[143] Moving to London by necessity in 1956, Eric quickly became involved in anticolonial communist politics there, attending endless meetings at Africa House, just around the corner from the West Indian Students' Centre, where communist anticoloni- alism thrived in the late 1950s.[144] Jessica initially remained in British Guiana, unsuccessfully standing for the PPP in the 1957 election. She joined Eric in 1958.[145] Together, they campaigned for the Communist Party at their new home in London's Haringey, and for an independent socialist Guyana, includ- ing by organizing symposia at the WISC in the mid-1960s.[146]

Like Jones-Lecointe, the Huntleys were actively engaged in battles against the state, in 1975 forming the Black Parents Movement to challenge police harassment of young black people and their failure by the education system, and later playing a key role in the New Cross Massacre Action Committee, challenging the state's indifference to the deaths of thirteen young black people in a suspected arson attack in 1981.[147] At the time of Baldwin's talk, however, Jessica and Eric Huntley were engaged in a different form of activism, on the cusp of launching a career in publishing and bookselling that would define them for the following half century. Their route into publishing, as Jessica remembers, "grew out of political struggles."[148] During their London campaigns for Guyanese independence, they had become acquainted with Walter Rodney, a Guyanese student completing his PhD in African history at the School of African and Oriental Studies, whose father they also knew through the PPP. Rodney's purpose in his academic life at this time, as he later reflected, was to combat a received "old absurd history," and to recover a sense of what slavery, and life in Africa before and during colonization, had been like.[149] He was involved in anti-racist and anticolonial politics in London, and on completing his PhD, after two years teaching in Tanzania, he returned to the Caribbean to lecture at the University of the West Indies's Mona campus in Jamaica. There he made contact with the working class of Kingston's most deprived quarters, joining forces with Rastafarians and holding open meetings ("groundings") discussing the oppressions they faced. When returning to the island after a conference on black liberation in Montreal in October 1968, however, Rodney was banned from reentering, the government fearing that he might stir an uprising. The banning actually prompted a riot, since students protesting the ban were joined by urban poor in Kingston, burning buses and buildings, and fighting police.[150] Jessica Huntley, determined "to give some further voice of protest," resolved to publish Rodney's essays written during his time grounding in Jamaica.[151] Her publication of Rodney's *Grounding with My Brothers* (1969) was concerned with making available this revolutionary set of writings at a time that Rodney was being gagged, and the book soon became the foundational text of Caribbean Black Power. Setting up the Bogle-L'Ouverture publishing house, Jessica, together with Eric, soon also began publishing works emerging from the black cultural renaissance happening in the Caribbean in the early 1970s, which tied together the political demands of Caribbean Black Power with emphases on cultural decolonization that were revolutionizing Caribbean aesthetics.[152] Soon, too, they would begin publishing children's literature, attempting to carve out a space for children facing the onslaught of racism in British schools, and to establish new modes of black self-fashioning.[153]

In these endeavors, the Huntleys worked closely with another key figure at Baldwin's talk that evening: Andrew Salkey, who sat beside Baldwin, chairing the talk. A Panamanian-born Jamaican, he had moved to Britain in the early 1950s, part of that generation of West Indian writers who traveled to the metropole to make their names and their livings.[154] A key figure in the BBC literary program *Caribbean Voices*, Salkey was also politically active from early on, joining the tail end of the League of Coloured People and the Movement for Colonial Freedom in the 1950s, and briefly joining CARD in the mid-1960s.[155] As well as being a novelist of some renown, he was famously a networker and organizer—George Lamming described him as "our bureau." He was in touch with most of black political London and had contacts throughout Britain and stretching across the Caribbean, North America, Europe, and Africa.[156] Restlessly busy in the 1960s, Salkey was a leading voice calling for West Indians to learn from the revolutionary transformations taking place in Cuba, and he followed the Black Power uprisings across the Caribbean with close scrutiny and real hope.[157] He was particularly convinced of the necessity of cultural decolonization—a change in the entire culture, particularly around race—to effect lasting and significant political change. In Britain, he worked to bring together his political and artistic contacts into common projects, and from early 1967 on, together with John La Rose and the Barbadian poet and historian Edward Brathwaite, he had held regular meetings at the WISC of their newly formed Caribbean Artists Movement (CAM).

Distinct from the revolutionary politics of Althea Jones-Lecointe and Jessica and Eric Huntley, or the education and academic activism pursued, in part, by Bogle-L'Ouverture, CAM marks another important dimension of black life in London drawn together in this new politics of blackness that the WISC worked toward, and that aimed at secondary decolonization. Salkey, La Rose, and Brathwaite used CAM to continue conversations active since the 1950s on the role of art in decolonization, and the ways in which artistic practice could be decolonized.[158] These were conversations that had long been sustained, often uncomfortably, within the traditional institutions of the British arts establishment—the BBC, the literary press, the Arts Council. With CAM, though, these conversations were increasingly restaged now as communal practices bringing in those working-class black communities often excluded from such institutions, and aiming to undertake this realignment as part of a wider democratization of political organization, ceding power to those usually excluded from it, and allowing their experiences, interests and modes of organization to dictate the future direction of political and cultural projects.[159] CAM, as Brathwaite would argue, held to "an anti-authoritarianism, a distrust of people who hold power and who like to use power." It advocated new democratic relationships—"You've got to be able to break [power] down, to hand it over, to share it, and this is connected with a sense of community."[160] Blackness was key here. CAM called for artists and intellectuals to connect with the "black sufferers" of Britain and the Caribbean, and to remake a radical project in their name and image. By this, as Gary Burton, president of the WISC, suggested at a CAM conference, they meant an overhaul of black organization in order to learn lessons in social equality, bodily integrity, and economic justice from those whose racialized oppression put all these promises at risk: "We're about to shed the illusion of a middle class sort of white identity and go straight back, straight back to our brothers and sisters, those who catch hell in this community."[161] As this project was taken up by the WISC, one writer explained, "We want to see the structure, rhetoric and programmes of our organisations reflect the unsullied, uncompromising insights of the mass of black sweated female labour in factories and in the cleaners departments of hospitals." This meant "organisations that reflect the feelings of blacks who every morning wake up knowing that their existence in this country leaves them little experience of security or freedom."[162]

Here at the West Indian Students Centre were some of the people and activities that would be at the heart of black radical politics in Britain for next two decades, and in forming that politics they were part of a global politics of black liberation that took many forms. This was a multilayered effort, and the stakes were high. Blackness, as we have seen in so many ways in this chapter, assumed an urgency in this moment. Reorientating political and cultural projects through blackness, for all those present at the WISC, was the basis for moving past an impasse in the politics of race. "Black awareness," as Salkey declared at a CAM–WISC event in 1969, "is the beginning of our search and definition of revolution."[163] For Salkey, black awareness did not begin with U.S. Black Power. "London made me Black, long before Malcolm [X]," Salkey would write in 1972, "long before the Black Revolution in America."[164] Becoming black was a process, and people might be remade or remake themselves as black again and again.[165] In the mid-to-late 1960s, however, the shifting politics of race relations in Britain, the dramatic realignments of British political life, the shifting tone and internationalization of the U.S. civil rights movement and Black Power, and the growth of secondary decolonization politics networked across the black Atlantic, marked a conjunctural shift in the politics of race through which many new ways of becoming black were offered, and, for many, blackness took on a renewed intensity.

It was through American politics that many of these activists first began to frame their understanding of Black Power, but this increasingly shifted to accommodate Caribbean and African secondary decolonization, reworking blackness and black politics again. Gus John, a member of London's BPM in the late 1960s, came into this politics through the American civil rights movement, for example. He was a Grenadian immigrant who came to Oxford in 1964 in order to study philosophy and theology, with ambitions to become a Dominican priest, and the Christian ethics of the U.S. Southern Christian Leadership Conference and SNCC attracted him. Initially a member of CARD, on moving to London in 1967, John joined the fringes of the nascent BPM, of which his brother, Clement, was a member. His reading, at this time, was heavily focused on the United States—Ralph Ellison, James Baldwin, Stokely Carmichael, Richard Wright. And yet, as he recalled some years later, after the Walter Rodney affair in Jamaica this American focus was increasingly challenged by political developments in the Caribbean, and by efforts by many black intellectuals at the center of black radical activity in London to define appeals to blackness through a reconsideration of the Caribbean past: "you were [...] able to [...] make the link between our own colonial experience there and what was happening in Britain in order to place the America thing in its proper perspective."[166]

In this shifting ground of blackness, there was plenty of scope for misrecognition, many "points of misunderstanding, bad faith, unhappy translation," as Edwards has described the "necessary hauntings" of diasporic articulation.[167] Despite long serving as a hub in the struggle for political independence in the Caribbean, the WISC could not be recognized by all as a black space. "The atmosphere was too RAF, too much of colonial administrators, too smelt [sic] of cricket pads and of tea for my taste, and I did not return," one Black Panther told Susan Craig.[168] This atmosphere, however much it was evaded by many at the WISC attempting to focus, instead, on the other parts of their history, is the imprint that reminds us that this turn to blackness could not simply wholesale replace what had gone before; it is a reminder that Carmichael's call to "come on home" would always leave some displacement and dysfunction. But others would instead criticize the readiness of men like Craig's Panther to erase the often-uncomfortable connections between blackness and Britishness that Caribbean migrants brought to Britain. If part of placing "the America thing in its proper perspective" was reading Black Power through its Caribbean coordinates, another part of it was working with and through the particular inheritance of colonialism and Caribbean cultures that structured the response of many in Britain to the new politics of Black Power.

In his 1976 novel *Come Home, Malcolm Heartland*, begun in the early 1970s, when Black Power politics in Britain was at its height, and drawing extensively from his experiences in the WISC, Andrew Salkey was equivocal in his treatment of the British Black Power movement. The Jamaican migrant Malcolm Heartland, the novel's eponymous hero, is suspicious of "the uncritical adoption of the imported Black American revolutionary tenets, theory and practice" among black groups in London. He condemns the Black Power rhetoric of one activist as "emblematic, spuriously symbolic, a kind of London political carnival escapism."[169] Talking about his motivations for traveling to Britain to his young lover, Claudette, he finds she cannot understand the tortuous work he must undertake to square his ambivalent attachment to the culture of the metropole, and to a version of imperial Britishness. In the Indo-Trinidadian novelist Sam Selvon's *Moses Ascending* (1975), which like Salkey's novel sets several of its pivotal scenes in a fictionalized version of the WISC, the adoption of a U.S.-style Black Power politics serves as a form of erasure, covering over a longer history of West Indian life in Britain, which nonetheless keeps peeking through. Selvon reintroduces Sir Galahad, a character from his successful *Lonely Londoners* (1956), now as a man clad in "Black Power glad rags." But these are ultimately ill-fitting. As Galahad seeks to convert his old friend Moses Aloetta, Moses repeatedly misrecognizes the situation, at one point mistaking Galahad's raised fist for an attempt "to bust a cuff in my arse." Insofar as either of the men are won over to a politics of Black Power in the novel, it is one remarkably similar to the irony-rich, comic-tragic hustling traditions that characterized their lives in their previous incarnation as lonely Londoners.[170] A new language, in other words, could not erase all that came before it. Other pasts, and other experiences, haunted its articulation.

Defining the historical moment that this chapter has traced was a passion of and for blackness, and a conception of blackness as a total, radical social, cultural, and political project, often understood in distinction to politics and cultures of Britishness irredeemably steeped in "whiteness." "Black" did not just describe the public of this politics; it described the politics itself. In Britain, the ascendancy of this politics was spurred by the failure of the race relations settlement both to protect the interests and rights of nonwhite citizens and to offer them democratic inclusion in the political processes most concerning them. Black Power politics, with its driving force first in the United States, but soon expanding across the black Atlantic, offered a means to make sense of and challenge this predicament. At the same time, though, the moments of translation between these points of the black Atlantic were fraught, and led to considerable discomfort for some locating themselves ambivalently within the Black Power movement.

The headline actors of Black Power in Britain in the mid-to-late 1960s were usually men, but in Britain, this was a politics driven as often by women. From titans of the civil rights movement like Martin Luther King, Bayard Rustin, James Baldwin, and Malcolm X to new representatives of Black Power like Stokely Carmichael, African American politics in this era was internationalized often through the actions of men, and in the image of a particular type of revolutionary masculinity. But these African American male travelers, as we shall see in the next chapter, were soon replaced by a raft of women, from Penny Jackson to Fania Jordan, Inez Williams, and Angela Davis. Within Britain, women like Althea Jones-Lecointe and Jessica Huntley often took a lead in on-the-ground activism, and rose to prominent places within black radical politics and cultural movements. Black women's groups, as we shall also see in the following chapter, challenged the masculine chauvinism of Black Power, and forwarded their own analyses of black experiences, and agendas of black politics, alongside or even in contrast to those agendas put forward by their male comrades. Althea Jones-Lecointe went on to lead the fight against police brutality in the early 1970s, as we shall see in chapter 3. Women were at the forefront of supplementary school activism, as we shall see in chapter 4.

Those activists and intellectuals we have encountered in this chapter—Jones-Lecointe, Huntley, Salkey, Carew—are representative of many who fill the pages of this book. They were dedicated to creating a black politics, and convinced that to do this meant getting people "thinking black," rereading their social and political worlds through a politics of race forged in the experiences and histories of racialized oppression. The next chapter looks to how some of these activists attempted to get people "thinking black" through building new reading cultures. It also addresses the variety of black political subjectivities generated by black British activism, and how thinking black as an intellectual-critical culture was sustained within the wider transformation of black expressive culture happening in the 1960s and 1970s and 1980s.

TWO

Political Blackness

BROTHERS AND SISTERS

Then, there is blackness. It seems hard for whites to grasp it, but this, to blacks, is an essentially political weapon in their struggle.

COLIN MACINNES,
"Calypso Lament" (1972)[1]

"Brothers and sisters" was the form of address used by almost all the speakers, and it was uttered with a kind of unselfconscious conviction so different from the ritual invocation to comradeship and fraternity of the Trade Union Congress or the Labour Party conference.

ALAN BRIEN,
"Soledad Brothers and Sisters" (1971)[2]

"AS A BLACK WOMAN, I have lately begun to question my own motives and goals concerning my personal life and the life of my people," wrote an anonymous contributor to the Black Liberation Front's *Grassroots* newsletter, in a 1972 article titled "What Is the Role of the Black Woman?" Resolving these "motives and goals," this writer argued, meant being "aware of what your own self is about," and for a black woman "this means additionally, deciding how 'black' she wants to be."

> When I refer to blackness, I do not mean the physical manifestations of the new black culture (Afro-hairdos, Dashikis, Swahili, etc). I am speaking of a mental condition, an awareness of ourselves and our people, a realization of the place we occupy in this society and what we must do for our continued existence. Your degree of "blackness" will determine how well you relate to other people—black or white.[3]

We can take this woman's comments, appearing in one of the many new journals of black liberation emerging in the late 1960s and 1970s, as a manifesto for "thinking black." She began by pointing toward the everyday material cultures of "blackness" gaining popularity in Britain in these years as black Britons adopted new cultural forms and practices. In Afros and dashikis, in Malcolm X posters and Angela Davis badges, and in the recreation of the guerrilla-chic berets, dark sunglasses, and leather jackets popularized by the Black Panther Party, this visual culture drew significant attention from admirers and detractors alike. In this woman's view, however, these "physical manifestations of the new black culture" remained only a pretense at, or early stage of, "blackness." Blackness as a matter of choice, and as a matter of *dedication*, meant not just black culture, but black politics and self-fashioning. It meant, for her, that the "black woman must be a revolutionary. She must revolutionise herself; then her family and eventually all black people."[4] Black radicals were never agreed about what "revolutionary" politics meant. For many of the black women's groups emerging also in the early 1970s and gaining pace throughout the decade, the prescription of this anonymous writer in *Grassroots*—emphasizing a black woman's maternal and matrimonial responsibilities, and particularly her role in helping "her black man [. . .] to realise his potential"—would come in for censure. Agreed upon, however, was the significance of what this writer called "mental condition": the need to cultivate, alongside and out of the new material cultures of blackness gaining pace in this period, practices of "thinking black." This was the task that black radical writers, activists, and community organizers in Britain in these years took upon themselves: to recognize within or carve out from this emergent and assertive culture the tools for political critique, a workable politics of blackness, and a black political movement.

The distinction made by this *Grassroots* writer, however, was a precarious one. Her charge was that blackness as an ontological experience, constituted in the coming-together of "physical manifestations" that made one feel black, must be translated into blackness as an epistemological practice, a "mental condition": *thinking black*. Hers was a Cartesian duality that separated body from mind, and that prioritized the content ("mental condition") over the form ("physical manifestations") of communication. Such distinctions were common, and black radicals would often level the charge against their opponents that their blackness was only skin deep, and required more critical thought. But feeling and thinking, and ideology and its materiality, are never so separate. As recent work on affect and material culture has suggested, to trace the force and hold of an ideological formation, we need to be as attentive to its embodied work as we are to the subject positions it offers. This chapter pursues the question of interpellation into a politics of blackness from these two simultaneous registers at once, looking first to how different groups articulated blackness as they sought to speak in its name, and second to the materiality of black political cultures, how these operated as part of a wider expressive culture, and how they were affectively charged. Black activists frequently championed reading practices as essential to the development of new "mental conditions," the key to thinking black. But this chapter argues that these reading cultures, designed to move beyond the perceived limits of popular expressive cultures, were in fact not so separate from them. Reading and intellectual work, and dressing, dancing, styling, and corporeal work, were in many ways two sides of the same coin. Their mutual imbrication was essential to how black politics took hold for many in Britain in this period, and to the efficacy of that politics. The reading cultures of thinking black were embodied, material cultures. The expressive cultures on which they built were intellectual and political cultures, as easily concerned with explaining, dramatizing, and contesting racism and asserting black integrity as the formal intellectual cultures of black radicalism that activists often prioritized.

Advocates of thinking black hoped to build a black political alliance by uniting a community of readers and thinkers who, with a common focus on what racialized experience could tell them about a globalized post-imperial world, would commonly fight, for and with each other, for an end to racism and imperialism. Blackness here, as Colin MacInnes wrote in a *New Society* article seeking to understand the new articulations of blackness gaining ground in Britain in the early 1970s, was a "political weapon."[5] "Political blackness," though, has come in for a bad press, and certainly does not have the ring that it did in the 1970s. Back then, it was frequently used to speak of an alliance of nonwhite people seeking to end racism and transform British society; today, it is more often invoked to draw attention to the inevitable failures of such alliances. For the political scientist Tariq Modood, one of its chief critics in the 1980s and 1990s, the problem with political blackness was that for all that it sought to speak for a multi-ethnic Britain, its conceptions of blackness were hooked around African diasporic, and particularly African American, particularities. In many respects, he was right in this observation. The content of political blackness was often African diasporic—and African American texts and narratives predominated in its discourse. Indeed, when MacInnes wrote of blackness as a "political weapon," he was concerned with its transformative potential, but West Indians alone were in his sights. If we look, though, not to the starting points in how this black political formation was made, but to its processes, and if we take account of political blackness, not only by the tools it used, but by how it used them, Modood's critique holds less water. Modood was convinced that political blackness could only ever be a thin politics, anchored too much in foreign waters for many who might be encouraged to identify with it. But as the *New Statesman* journalist Alan Brien noted reporting on a rally for the Soledad Brothers at Westminster's Central Hall in 1971—a rally in which both the speakers and the audience were mixed: white English and American, African diasporic and South Asian diasporic, men and women—far from a thin language of alliance, this was a politics that resonated with the thick relations of siblingship. These were "brothers and sisters," and they felt their connection, Brien was sure, deep in the "gut."[6] We must account for such resonances.

This chapter is loosely based around that Soledad Brothers rally, and a case study of the British lives of the African American prison writer George Jackson's *Soledad Brother* (1971), as a way into considering the multiple processes at play as Britons defined themselves through blackness, and found within this definition a political project. It explores the role of texts like Jackson's in the political pedagogy of radical blackness in Britain, and the ways that Britons negotiated the often starkly masculine and African American coordinates of such texts. By focusing on the reception and use of these texts, it draws attention to the processes and problems involved in building up a political blackness premised on alliance across differences of ethnicity and gender. Where both its supporters and its critics have often read political blackness as a strategic, pragmatic call, and an umbrella that reached over, but did not subsume or replace, deeper, more particular and different ethnic or gendered subjectivities, this chapter argues for political blackness as a political culture of substantial depth and variety, even with the contradictions and displacements that locating oneself within it might sometimes produce. It was immersive and intimate, and black political work could be just as much an experience of the gut as the new expressive cultures of black style, entertainment, and leisure that many black activists nonetheless often bemoaned for their supposedly unintellectual focus. Though it sometimes did risk obliterating or marginalizing difference through the centrality of African diasporic or masculinist texts and narratives, political blackness was also embraced as a politics of complementarity and multidirectionality.

I read all the books. Stokely, Cleaver, Jackson.

ANON. IN TREVOR CARTER,
Shattering Illusions: West Indians in
British Politics *(1986)*[7]

Gail Lewis was nineteen years old when Penguin Books published the British edition of George Jackson's *Soledad Brother* in March 1971. She was born in Walthamstow, on the eastern outskirts of London, to a white English mother and an Afro-Guyanese father. The family moved later to the north London district of Kilburn, north of Notting Hill, where their house was firebombed during the white riots of 1958.[8] Her childhood was in many respects a classic 1950s London working-class childhood—multiple-occupancy housing, pie-and-mash shops, pinballing between points in a matrifocal extended family.[9] Her Caribbean heritage, though, also brought both fantasies of other places—particularly the Blue Mountains of Jamaica, which her stepfather fondly described when she was a child—and racial tensions within the family, not least when her uncle demanded that she and her mother move out of her grandmother's home to save him embarrassment when his friends came to visit.[10] As a teenager, she experienced the growing tensions between her mother and stepfather, struggling on a low income; and their conflicts were exacerbated by the pressures of living in a racist society, which seeped into the dynamics of every family argument, always "riddled with race/sex tensions," Lewis remembers.[11] Her route out of these tensions, or her means for turning them into politics, was through books, and particularly through the "accounts of black political prisoners in the USA who 'discovered' their 'brains'" through education.[12] Of all these books, Jackson's *Soledad Brother* was the "formative" one.[13]

Lewis was far from alone in her enthusiasm for *Soledad Brother*. Jackson's title, as Natalie Thomlinson notes of her study of oral histories of the black women's movement in Britain, was the remembered reading that came up most frequently among activists.[14] His book certainly vied with others for space on black radical bookshelves. Bogle-L'Ouverture's best-sellers also included Eldridge Cleaver's prison autobiography *Soul on Ice* (1968), and *The Autobiography of Malcolm X* (1965), also a prison-conversion memoir. Angela Davis's writing was also hugely popular.[15] *Soledad Brother*, however, usually came out on top. For Lewis, the turn to books began as a private indulgence. With "fantasies of going to college," she became an avid reader in her late teens.[16] Her turn to the literature of American civil rights and Black Power was echoed by others of her generation. As this wave of Black Power literature swept the market in the United States, commercial publishers in Britain, recognizing its appeal, quickly gained distribution and publishing rights. Beginning with Hutchinson and then Penguin's publications of *The Autobiography of Malcolm X* (1966 and 1968 respectively), Penguin then also published Stokely Carmichael and Charles V. Hamilton's *Black Power* in 1969, while Jonathan Cape published Cleaver's *Soul on Ice* to rave reviews in the British press. Hutchinson published Black Panther Bobby Seale's memoir *Seize the Time* in 1970, and *Soledad Brother* was published by both Penguin and Jonathan Cape in 1971. Like Lewis, Pauline Black, growing up a mixed-race child adopted into a white household, recounts devouring these texts in the late 1960s and early 1970s, reading Malcolm X, Cleaver, and Carmichael and Hamilton in Romford Library.[17] Hanif Kureishi, also mixed race with a father from Bombay, remembers reading "all the time" as he planned his escape from suburban boredom in south London, working his way through the writings of James Baldwin and Richard Wright.[18]

Lewis's engagement with George Jackson was also, though, a part of her entry into black political activism, where such texts played a central role in political education. From a young age, her mother and grandmother had involved her in local Labour Party politics, and as a teenager she joined the Young Communist League. By her late teens, Lewis decided to find out more about anti-racist politics, and made trips to Notting Hill, picking up the leaflets and newsletters of local Black Power groups. Through this, she found her way to the West Indian Students Centre (WISC), and here met Gerlin Bean, a leading organizer in the Black Liberation Front (BLF). She joined the BLF's reading group, which met at their Finsbury Park headquarters on Wightman Road.[19]

Reading was at the heart of the BLF's project for making new black political subjects. An early edition of their *Grassroots* newsletter distilled the transformative promise of reading into an image of a man of African descent literally split in two, between his "almost white" and his "black" selves (fig. 5). The transition into blackness is marked on the man's body, in his clothes (from a suit to a dashiki), stance (from a stiff detachment to a relaxed, easy relationship with his environment), and hair (from close-cropped to long "natural," and from clean-shaven to bearded). The transition is equally marked, though, by his surroundings. He is flanked by well-stocked bookcases, representing the two stores of knowledge upon which whiteness and blackness were seen to rest. The "white" side the bookcase is stacked with classic and contemporary

FIGURE 5. "One Time My Eyes Were Shadowed and I Couldn't See the Light—But Now the Veil is Lifted I Can Take the Course That's Right." Back cover of *Grassroots* 1, no. 4 (1971). Early schoolboy illustration from Shakka Dedi. © Shakka Dedi.

Anglo-American literature, history and religion, with no fewer than three copies of the Bible. The "black" side, topped with a copy of *Grassroots* itself, holds the texts of U.S. Black Power—*Malcolm X Speaks, Soledad Brother, Soul on Ice*, Carmichael and Hamilton's *Black Power*, and, perhaps reflecting James Baldwin's increasing sympathy with black radical politics in this era, Baldwin's short story collection *Going to Meet the Man* (1965).[20]

This was a typical reading list for Black Power activists. Most black radical groups had reading groups and set reading lists. "We were told we had to read certain texts," Lewis recalled. "We had to understand. We had to discuss with each other. We had to learn differently, in order to free ourselves and everyone."[21] At Fasimbas meetings on Sundays and Thursdays, Winston Trew discussed "books I had read on African history and the Slave Trade," not only allowing him to meet "new 'brothers' and 'sisters,'" but to learn "to develop a new language with my new vision."[22] Neil Kenlock, a member of the Black Panther Movement (BPM)'s youth wing, remembers their drive "to educate the community about [...] where they are from and their culture, and they also wanted to tell us about capitalism, and communism, and socialism, and why we were brought from Africa to the Caribbean as black people, why we work as slaves, why slavery was abolished."[23] Linton Kwesi Johnson, also a BPM youth-wing member in the early 1970s, recalls that the reading list included *Soul on Ice*, *The Autobiography of Malcolm X*, *Seize the Time*, W. E. B. Du Bois's classic *The Souls of Black Folk* (1903), and James Baldwin's books.[24] Fellow Panther Farrukh Dhondy remembers *Soledad Brother* and Angela Davis's *If They Come in the Morning* (1971) being discussed regularly.[25] The Black Eagles, in their newsletter, recommended a "Reading List in Black: History, Liberation, Literature, Power," which, along with the above, also included Carmichael and Hamilton's *Black Power*, Du Bois's *Black Reconstruction* (1935), and Elijah Muhammad's *Message to the Black Man* (1965), and recommended the work of Frantz Fanon, Kwame Nkrumah and C. L. R. James.[26] At the meetings of a black radical group in Bristol, Ken Pryce recorded copies of Carmichael and Hamilton's *Black Power*, a volume of the *Philosophy and Opinions of Marcus Garvey* (1968), and a copy of *The Times*'s investigative series *The Black Man in Search of Power* (1968).[27]

Black activists worked to make such readings a common part of black lives. The most famous texts of U.S. civil rights and Black Power were readily available in Britain. But a wider literature of black radical politics—particularly journals and magazines, and lesser-known books by smaller publishers—were harder to come by. In the Lambeth library, as *Race Today* reported in 1973,

the magazine of the local Black Panther Party is kept only in the reference library—presumably for its interest to local historians of the future! But to get in black journals and display them for the black community to use is a totally different matter, which despite the efforts of the Working Party on Services to Immigrants and the fact that most of these journals are extremely inexpensive in relation to the library authority's budget, still has not happened.[28]

Lambeth was "considered one of the more progressive authorities" in this area. At Lewisham library, a commercial library used largely by black students, the librarian was a National Front parliamentary candidate. The library in nearby Bromley, where Kureishi would read *Life* magazine articles about the U.S. Black Panther Party, served as the meeting place for the local National Front branch.[29] As the Organisation of Women of Asian and African Descent (OWAAD)'s magazine *Fowaad!* complained in 1980, "racist attitudes pervade the bookshops and libraries. Few of them (apart from black bookshops with a third world section) stock books by black writers and books by black women are a real rarity."[30] In a cartoon accompanying the article, when a dread-locked black woman visits her public library looking for black writers, she is greeted with a hesitant " . . . er, let me see . . . I remember we did have *one* novel by a knee-grow writer . . . that *lovely* story about those slaves . . . er, what was it called again?"[31]

Confronting this difficulty of accessing black literature, community activists established black resource centers as radical alternatives to public libraries. At the Institute of Race Relations (IRR), Ambalavanar Sivanandan opened its library to the public and brought in new radical titles. "The important thing," as he later recalled, was to encourage people to read—"these were not kids who would read." The library's purpose, as Sivanandan saw it, was "to seduce people into reading."[32] Creating library displays to encourage new readers, Sivanandan's library aimed "to move away from abstracted studies and address itself to fundamental issues of justice and freedom," gathering together "books, manuscripts, pamphlets, press cuttings and over a thousand periodicals [. . .] relevant to the struggles of black people." He recruited volunteers to open the library on evenings and weekends to increase access to its holdings.[33] "Because this body of black thinking could be found only in the IRR's library," Sivanandan later recalled, "we began to attract a whole lot of Black activists and thinkers—from, say, members of the Black Unity and Freedom Party and *Grassroots* to Third World liberation groups."[34]

Similar resource centers sprang up across London in the 1960s and 1970s. Michael de Freitas's Black House in Holloway, opened in 1969, also stocked a library of black radical literature alongside a small museum of slavery and African artefacts.[35] Further west, Notting Hill's Backayard Café and the nearby Black People's Information Centre both offered a public reference library for black radical literature, politics and history, as did the WISC in Earl's Court and north London's Keskidee Arts Centre, where Linton Kwesi Johnson ran the library. In Brixton, the Afro-Caribbean Education

Resources Project (ACER), established by Len Garrison in the mid-1970s, would grow to become one of Britain's largest resources on black history and culture, in a collection that would eventually transmute into the Black Cultural Archives in 1981.[36]

Britain's black bookshops also arrived in this moment, with their heyday being from the early 1970s to the mid-1980s. John La Rose and Sarah White's New Beacon Books in London's Finsbury Park, the first black bookshop to open in Britain, began trading in 1967. It served as the home for New Beacon Books's publishing house, established in 1966 and dedicated to publishing Caribbean and black Atlantic literature, criticism, and political analysis—including a short-lived plan to republish hard-to-come-by U.S. Black Power materials in a black political series.[37] A host of other bookshops joined New Beacon from the early 1970s, concentrated in London but spreading out into a national network. In north London, the BLF established Headstart Books in Tottenham. This joined their Grassroots Storefront bookshop in Notting Hill, while further west was Bogle-L'Ouverture in Ealing—also serving as a black radical publishing house since 1969—and Shakti in Southall.[38] In south London, the Brixton Black Women's Group established the Sabarr Bookshop in Brixton, joining the BPM's Unity Books, and Soma Books in nearby Kennington. Bookshops also sprang up in other metropolitan centers. In Sheffield, I & I Bookshop Trust, Ujammaa, and Unity Books all operated from the 1970s on. Leicester's Raddle Bookstore opened in the early 1970s. In Birmingham, the Harriet Tubman Bookshop opened in the 1970s, later joined by Third World Books, remembered by Paul Warmington, who worked there in the 1980s, as "a second university and a first-rate library [holding] what seemed to be a boundless compendium of black writing."[39] Nottingham's first black bookshop, Ujamma, opened in the early 1980s. From 1982, New Beacon Books, Bogle-L'Ouverture and Race Today Publications brought many of these enterprises, together with radical publishing houses, into an international exchange at the annual International Book Fair of Radical Black & Third World Books, which took place in London, Manchester, Bradford, Leeds, and Glasgow.[40]

Like the feminist bookshops also enjoying a rapid expansion in this period, black bookshops were integral as sites for both cultivating reading cultures and encouraging political debate.[41] These bookshops, Colin A. Beckles has argued, provided an everyday forum for "Passionate debates between patrons, staff and [. . .] passers-by."[42] As Dada of the Grassroots Storefront told Beckles, "bookshops were ideal places [. . .] people could reach out and pick up books, booklets, information and quote other people from across the world on that." Here arguments could rage about "the concept of what is it to be Black, is Black a mental or a physical thing, is it that you were Black or that you were African?"[43] Activists prized bookshops for their potentially formative role in building a radical black politics. "Bookshops and publishers," *Race Today* insisted in 1978, stood as "a major conveyor belt" within the movement to bridge "the hiatus, created by the middle passage, and the long crossings we have made as immigrants from our countries of origin to Britain." "We are given a sense of self with increasing revelations from our past and from reflections of our present, which connect generations. [. . .] All these are formidable constituents in consolidating and generating the political power we have at hand here in Britain."[44]

Alongside the rapidly expanding network of resource centers and bookshops was a rapid expansion of the black political press in Britain.[45] The black radical political groups founded across many of Britain's major cities in the late 1960s and early 1970s were quick to establish newsletters as the mouthpieces of their organizations, an alternative to what the Black Unity and Freedom Party (BUFP)'s Obi Egbuna called "the Fleet Street distractionists."[46] Black organizations, the IRR's Jenny Bourne remembers, produced a torrent of "small cyclostyled and folded occasional broadsheets [. . .] clandestinely produced in someone's front room."[47] These were irregular affairs, often short-lived. They "happened when cash was in hand."[48] They were, however, widely available in black bookshops and resource centers, as well as in the wider network of British radical bookshops. The Black Eagles's *Black Dimension* recommended that readers visit John La Rose's New Beacon Books, while *TriContinental Outpost* provided a list of fifteen London locations at which it could be bought, ranging from Backayard and the IRR to Camden's Compendium bookshop, Collets bookshop in Charing Cross Road, and even local barber shops and South Asian food stores in Notting Hill, Hackney, and Hornsey.[49] Outside, street sellers also hawked the papers in "black" neighborhoods, "at tube stations and street markets."[50] Winston Trew, a member of the Fasimbas, sold *Black Voice* and *Grassroots* on Saturdays at stalls "set up outside black businesses, including a Grocery shop in New Cross, a black Bakery in Brockley and a Barber shop in Brixton."[51] The BUFP's Leila Hassan sold *Black Voice* "at markets all over London," where she "would talk to individuals, try and persuade them."[52] Street sellers, also active at demonstrations, and patrolling Hyde Park's Speakers' Corner on Sundays as black radicals addressed the crowds from their soapboxes, provided one of the chief sources of distribution for these newsletters throughout the first half of the 1970s, until police harassment of the sellers reduced their numbers.[53] Selling these newspapers, as Farukh Dhondy drily remembers of his days street-selling for the BPM, was conceived as a "discipline," a practice of community outreach for building "black consciousness."[54]

Black activists worked hard to make reading materials on black radical politics available in Britain, and to cultivate black reading cultures. They created significant, enduring networks of new institutions geared to this, encompassing resource centers, reading groups, bookshops, publishing houses and newsletters. As the lists of books used in these enterprises reveals, though, the texts of U.S. Black Power frequently dominated. This created problems of translation for those aligning themselves with a politics of blackness through such reading. The dynamics of race in the United States of America did not map easily onto Britain, nor onto the experiences of racialization that many brought with them to Britain. The following sections turn to how such texts were taken up within Britain and negotiated across differences of gender and ethnicity.

SOLEDAD SISTERS AND THE BLACK WOMEN'S MOVEMENT

The texts of black liberation were readily available in Britain, but they often came with problems of translation. George Jackson's *Soledad Brother*, the most popular of such texts, is a case in point. Black radical reading clubs, resource centers, and bookshops worked to make such texts a common point of reference for becoming black in Britain, but these texts often spoke in languages and of worlds some distance from their readers. How, then, did books like Jackson's find resonance in Britain? As Roger Chartier has proposed, making sense of such processes requires a "social history of the uses and understanding of texts by communities of readers who successively take possession of them."[55] We need to look both at and beyond Jackson's book, not only to consider its narrative and argument, its formal properties, and even its materiality, but also to consider how his case was brought to Britain, and what Britons did with it.[56] By asking about the popularity of George Jackson's *Soledad Brother* among black women in Britain, this section reads the formation of black women's politics as it occurred simultaneously through and in tension with the diasporic resources of a masculinized, U.S.-centric Black Power.

George Jackson's was a dramatic, complicated case. Jackson was an inmate in California's Soledad State Prison. He had been convicted in 1960, aged eighteen, of involvement in the theft of seventy dollars from a petrol station. On legal advice, he pleaded guilty, told that he would receive a light sentence, but instead he was given an indefinite one-year-to-life sentence that saw him still in prison for the same offense ten years on, when his case came to international attention.[57] Of those ten years, Jackson spent seven in solitary confinement. Like other prisoners converting to black radical politics before him, he spent many hours reading, and he became part of a group of black inmates connected with the Black Panther Party. For their audacity, as he later wrote, each of those in that group were "subjected to years of the most vicious reactionary violence" by prison guards.[58]

Jackson's case came to international attention in January 1970. On January 13, a prison guard shot dead three of Jackson's fellow inmates involved with the Black Panther Party. The shooter was swiftly exonerated. Four days later, another prison guard was found dying in Jackson's wing. Jackson and two other Soledad inmates—Fleeta Drumgo and John Clutchette—were charged with his murder in what became known as the Soledad Brothers case, which called international attention to the racism in U.S. prisons. The Panthers arranged their legal representation, and Angela Davis, a Panther associate and professor of philosophy, who was fighting her own dismissal from the University of California for Communist Party membership, came to their aid. Davis's connection to the case became pivotal when, seven months later, Jonathan Jackson, George's brother, stormed a California courthouse trying to negotiate the Soledad Brothers' freedom, and was killed in a bloody shootout with police. The guns he used were registered in Davis's name, and Davis was placed on the FBI's Most Wanted list, an invitation, as she understood it, to shoot her on sight. Fearing for her safety Davis went underground, but was caught two months later and imprisoned facing capital charges of conspiracy and murder.

These tumultuous events made the cases of Davis and the Soledad Brothers international cause célèbre, and their supporters launched an international, interconnected campaign to fight for their freedom. *Soledad Brother* was published as part of this campaign. The book was a series of Jackson's prison letters, written between 1964 and 1970 to his family, to Angela Davis, and to his lawyers and campaign leaders. Veering between love and anger, and showing, as Jean Genet noted in the book's preface, "a kind of joy in anger,"[59] the letters revealed Jackson's developing political philosophy, his critique of the

American racial state and its links to imperialism, old and new, and his conception of a kind of revolutionary black subjectivity that, in the end, his brother Jonathan came to embody. It was an international bestseller. For British readers, however, much of Jackson's letters spoke of a world some distance from their own. Institutional racism in British courts could be brutal, but Jackson's sentence had no parallel in Britain. Reports from British jails did not reach the same level of horror as those found in Jackson's Soledad Prison, where he was regularly beaten by guards and white prisoners, received his food mixed with bits of glass and the urine of his captors, and where he was eventually shot dead in an escape attempt in August 1971.[60] The Black Panther Party, of which Jackson was a member, was also a very different organization in the United States, where it advocated armed resistance and engaged in bloody shoot-outs with the police. In Britain, with few armed police, and without a gun culture, such conflicts took a different path.[61]

Why, then, could Jackson's text resonate so in Britain? Why could a reader like Gail Lewis, growing up in a mixed-race family in north London, find the book so "formative"? The attraction of the text could be both ideological and formal. Ideologically, Lewis welcomed how Jackson "laid out the terrain of black struggle and its links to wider anti-imperialist struggles." This link made European and American histories of race, and decolonization projects against Europe and against America, intimately connected—as Lewis noted, Angela Davis's education in Germany resonated with her for similar reasons. When U.S. texts held such symbolic authority, in the uneven power relations of diaspora moves like this helped put Britain also on the map. At a different level, Lewis was also taken by the way that Jackson spoke in these letters, particularly to his family. This was a formal determination. As an epistolary, *Soledad Brother* consists only of Jackson's letters. His appeals and admonishments are met with no reply, and the reader is left to fill in these blank spaces, to inhabit the empty space of the letters' interlocutor. Because the dialogue is incomplete, the reader must imaginatively enter the world of the text, and is positioned directly in the middle of a high-stakes family drama. The text demands, in other words, that its reader imagine the answers to Jackson's urgent letters and take the place of the imagined student of what Lewis remembered as the "political-moral sensibility" Jackson laid out.

The text also offered more individual moments of connection for Lewis, caught up in the psycho-drama of her own family, which she saw refracted now through Jackson's. For Lewis, *Soledad Brother* resonated on a deeply personal level because of George Jackson's relationship to his brother

Jonathan. Jonathan was fair skinned, green eyed, and fair haired. This was, George reveals, a source of constant pain for Jonathan, who was both "forced to beat on some of the blacks because of the big green eyes (used to be blue!) and gold hair" and "had to beat on the whites because he was a nigger."[62] In *Soledad Brother*, George repeatedly urges his friends to be careful around Jonathan's discomforts over his racial identity, even while in letters to family he berates them for their own lack of black zeal, and charges that Jonathan is the only family member sufficiently "black" to see America's racist project for what it is. By the end of the book, when Jonathan has committed his final, fatal act, he becomes the story's hero, resolving the tensions of both the family and the nation, and providing a model of revolutionary blackness for others to follow.[63] Like Jonathan Jackson, Gail Lewis was a fair-skinned adolescent. Her heritage marked her acutely at a time when racism and anti-immigration politics were often hooked around the question of the assumed unbelonging of children of mixed-race unions.[64] Though she has no memory of it, her mother told her that as a young girl she would often question why they lived in a house full of black people, with her mother the only white. More vividly, she remembers the "pre-occupation with complexion" among black people in Britain that, particularly with the rise of Black Power, often cast her outside blackness. "George spoke directly to his young brother in that," Lewis remembers, "and I remember thinking this is so important. It was so important to me translated across the Atlantic into the London landscape." *Soledad Brother* finally allowed her to *feel* "that I was among the black communities of the world, and that was fine, and was still with my mum and my nan as my beloved ones, and with part of my family and heritage as white."[65] This was an individual consequence both of the text's content and its formal properties. But it was a consequence that may well have had wider traction in Britain, where mixed-race families were common but controversial, and where the politics of blackness brought together so many different ethnicities and histories.

Both textual and family dynamics allowed a reader like Lewis to find a way to be radically black in Jackson's *Soledad Brother* despite what Lewis called its "masculine voice" and its African American particularities.[66] But finding this place was also made possible by the dynamics of the Soledad and Angela Davis campaigns in Britain. In early 1971, Lewis saw Penny Jackson speak at the WISC, describing it as her "entry into black politics."[67] Penny Jackson was George Jackson's younger sister, and it was she who took his case to an international audience. Penny had worked full-time on George's defense campaign since 1969. In April 1971, with George Jackson's impending court case, Jonathan's fatal courthouse incursion, and the hunt for and imprisonment of Angela Davis making the case international headline news, she joined Jackson and Davis's lawyers in traveling to Britain to raise money and support.[68] Women, indeed, were at the forefront of the push to internationalize these cases. Six months after Penny Jackson's visit, Angela Davis's sister Fania Jordan also traveled to London to campaign on her behalf, soon joined by their mother. The following year, Fleeta Drumgo's mother, Inez Williams, made the journey to campaign for the remaining Soledad Brothers. Two years later still, Angela Davis herself visited Britain, thanking her supporters there, and meeting with black radical activists who sustained the campaign.[69]

This is a second moment in the internationalization of U.S. Black Power, led by women and remarkably different from the earlier 1960s moment. It was a political moment led by sisters and mothers, who launched their campaigns in their roles as sisters and mothers. But they did not present themselves as peripheral or secondary black radicals. George Jackson may have written that his sisters were "not supposed to hold any opinions other than those of [their] menfolk," and that Penny Jackson's best quality was that she would "sit and listen and try to understand" when men were talking, but Penny's own politics displayed little such passivity.[70] Rather than projecting her love for her brother only as a domestic practice of nurture and support, she introduced a language of love into revolutionary politics that made militancy the measure of love. "All revolutionaries love each other," she told *Race Today*, pressed on the familial and romantic dimensions of the Soledad Brothers and Angela Davis cases.[71] But, as she told *Frendz* on the same occasion, "sisters don't sit around at home while the men are out fighting, their place is out among the people. We should fight and die together."[72] Penny Jackson was an inspiring force for black Britons. She spoke at large rallies at London's Mermaid Theatre and Westminster Central Hall. She spoke at Notting Hill's Metro Youth Club, just weeks before a police siege of the club would turn it into a center of black political mobilization. And at the WISC, where Gail Lewis saw her, five hundred came to hear her speak.[73] *Soledad Brother* may have been a paean to black masculinity, but in the ways that the Soledad campaign was brought to and taken up in Britain, new models of black revolutionary feminism were forged.

Many of the women who were instrumental in facilitating Penny Jackson's visit were at the same time busy forging new black women's politics. Despite the dominance of masculine chauvinism in many Black Power groups, women played active and often decisive roles within them, making up over half the membership of the Fasimbas, and playing important roles in several other organizations.[74] Leila Hassan, who interviewed Penny Jackson for *Race Today*, was a leading member of the BUFP, and later went on to play a key role in the *Race Today* journal and Race Today Collective, where, joined by Barbara Beese and Akua Rugg, women's voices were often at the forefront. Gerlin Bean, who organized Penny Jackson's London tour, was also an early member of the BUFP, and went on to co-found the Brixton Black Women's Group (BBWG) in 1973, which Gail Lewis also soon joined. The BBWG attracted women from across the Black Power groups active in London in the early 1970s, while groups established at the same time in Liverpool and Manchester likely had similar origins.[75] By the end of the 1970s, several of these groups came together to form the Organisation of Women of Asian and African Descent (OWAAD), a national umbrella group for the black women's movement.[76]

These groups, as their chroniclers have made clear, seldom organized completely separately from black men, and many would work jointly on the key campaigns of the 1970s and 1980s, particularly around policing and education.[77] However, they also redrew the map of black radical politics, bringing to the forefront issues that specifically affected women. Britain's National Health Service often recruited nurses of African and Asian descent into the lowest, least-skilled positions, and OWAAD campaigned on behalf of black nurses. They also campaigned against the use of the contraceptive drug Depo-Provera, believed by some to have a long-term impact on fertility, which was used disproportionately on women of Asian and African descent in the 1970s and 1980s. They campaigned, alongside the South Asian–dominated Southall Black Sisters and Awaz, against the "virginity testing" at British airports of South Asian women entering Britain to marry fiancés, and against repatriation cases launched against migrant South Asian women who had left their British husbands.[78] Each of these issues, as the literature of the black women's movement often emphasized, spoke directly to the ways that British racism constructed women of Asian and African descent as various kinds of "problems," as poorly skilled workers, as too fecund and sexually irresponsible, as simultaneously meek and cunning.[79]

In a political culture in which reading was placed at such a premium, and for which the foundational texts were African American and usually steeped in the politics of masculinity, black women in these ways nonetheless carved out a political subjectivity that refused to be limited by the subject positions texts like Jackson's *Soledad Brother* might seem to offer them. If black radical politics in Britain was organized around thinking black, and thinking black was organized around print culture, then these women found ways around the male chauvinism of some of the most prominent texts in that print culture. The rise of Angela Davis, of course, helped this issue. Davis was one of the most prominent international figures of black liberation in the 1970s, and hugely popular in Britain, particularly among black women. Her essays and autobiography, and even more so her image, on badges and posters, became ubiquitous in black British political culture, and in black expressive culture more widely.[80] But it is worth remembering that Davis was just one of the African Americans in whose writings and lives black women in Britain found purpose. This was about how these texts were used.

As well as using existing texts, though, women also worked to transform the renaissance in black print culture that their work was both built around and sustained. They did not always find themselves reflected in the public cultures of black radical politics, particularly in the literature which black groups went to such lengths to make available. "It is not that Black women do not rebel; it is not that they do not say loud and clear and repeatedly what their experience is," Gary Burton, president of the radicalized WISC, wrote in a response to a 1974 *Race Today* article on race, sex, and class. "They do every day in all sorts of ways." But these rebellions were seldom foregrounded in print. "Their statements, their actions, their definitions, their perspectives and resistance are all drowned in the overwhelming tide of the Movement's exclusive concern to highlight the relationship of the Black male working class to capital and the relationship of the Black and White male working class."[81] As one Liverpool woman, Paulette McCulloch, also complained to *Race Today* in 1975, "In Liverpool, a city which is the epitome of exploitation and social control, I find that while there is a growing awareness of the history, struggles and victories of the black people for males, there is particularly in the North a lack of any such progress for British born black women."[82] In their influential 1985 book on black feminist politics, Beverley Bryan, Stella Dadzie, and Suzanne Scafe proposed that this task to "take stock of our experiences, assess our responses—and learn from them" would, in part, "be done by listening to the voices of the mothers, sisters, grandmothers and aunts who established our presence here. And by listening to our own voices."[83] McCulloch, however, urged the need for a print culture for black women who might be cut off from such intergenerational familial modes of women's knowledge. "In the case of a mixed marriage," she pointed out, black women had "little or no opportunity to learn an aunt's, mother's or grandmother's tales of the strategy and struggles of black women against their situation."[84] Gail Lewis might well have felt similarly about having to turn to *Soledad Brother* for guidance.

The black women's movement addressed itself to this absence. Recording and making accessible the history of black women's organization was long a priority for the women in the BPM.[85] As many of these Panthers made their way into the BBWG in the mid-1970s, they used their newsletter *Speak Out* to prioritize such activity. "We have brought to this country a history of exploitation and a tradition of struggle which has never been documented," argued the editorial to the first edition of *Speak Out*.[86] The newsletter's cover, under hand-drawn images of the Triangle Trade, a gun-toting Harriet Tubman, female industrial laborers, and African women in guerrilla liberation armies, proclaimed:

> We planted tobacco cotton and soya beans. We sweated with our men to make profits for the Industrial Revolution.
> We led slave rebellions.
> We are a cheap source of labour. We do degrading domestic work. Many of us bring up our children when alone on social security.
> In Africa and everywhere, we are fighting to build a new society. Unite against racism and sexism to defeat capitalism. Join us to build a new socialist society.[87]

While these historical articles were not in the end that prevalent in *Speak Out*, other journals and publications—notably *Fowaad!* and the hugely successful book *The Heart of the Race* (1985) placed a priority on recovering such histories as a means of locating black feminist politics.[88] Black women were also prominent in educational activism and bookselling. As OWAAD's Mia Morris remembers, "if you didn't have a black women's group and you had a black bookshop, then that's what held the community."[89] Alongside the familiar run of works by African American, Caribbean and African men, these bookshops also prioritized the work of African American women writers, joined, by the mid-1980s, by the boom in black British women's writing.

Black women sometimes struggled to define a place for themselves, and an identity, in a political field dominated by men. And yet, while this often meant the production of new resources for blackness, and other narratives of blackness—new magazines and newsletters, different histories—the cultural-political formation of blackness to which so many divergent groups articulated themselves was made up substantially of a culture in which "diasporic resources," to borrow Jacqueline Nassy Brown's useful term, were widely shared and used to locate oneself—culturally, politically—against the circumstances of their production.[90] George Jackson's *Soledad Brother* is a useful case study here. A classically masculine text of U.S. Black Power, it was nonetheless among the most popular books read by black women in Britain. This fact does not override its masculinism, or the obvious points of disconnection that reading it might emphasize, but it does draw our attention to how such texts became part of new political cultures skilled in taking what they needed from these texts, and building alternative resources to complement them, and give them new meanings.

BLACK ASIANS

People of both Asian and African descent in Britain readily described themselves and their politics as "black." As Thomlinson notes of the black women's movement, this makes it hard to know from the titles alone of their political organizations to what extent these comprised of women of any one ethnicity, and to what extent they were mixed.[91] The ambiguity, though, is instructive. For these women, "black" was not, or not only, a description of skin color or ethnic origin. It was a political label, "bringing together," as Avtar Brah wrote, "diverse groups of people in associative solidarity."[92] Brah's own political life was "inextricably linked with the movement that mobilised around the political subject 'black.'"[93] Born in the Punjab, she moved with her family to Uganda at a young age, before studying in the United States—at the height of the Black Power movement there—and then moving to Britain to rejoin her family, who had been expelled from Uganda under Idi Amin. Her experience was, she proposed, representative of the "entangled racialized colonial histories of Britain's African, Asian and Caribbean descended populations."[94] For Brah, this entanglement meant that the political needs of these populations, while always diverse, would always also hold commonalities, particularly when all faced a racialized exclusion, placed outside the nation and targeted by many arms of the state. "Black" spoke to that commonality of oppression, and named the political solidarity emerging from it. She joined the Southall Black Sisters and a similar organization in Leicester and was a member of OWAAD.[95] Black, as the Southall Black Sisters, a predominantly British Asian group, argued, was "a political term, as a point of unity."[96]

This positioning of blackness as "a political colour," usually glossed in the term "political blackness," is most commonly associated with the work of Ambalavanar Sivanandan and the IRR.[97] A Sri Lankan Tamil, Sivanandan had moved to Britain in 1958, escaping, as he later recounted, the first of the Sinhalese government's pogroms against the island's Tamil population, but arriving in Notting Hill just as the white riots against local West Indians began. As he tells the story of his arrival in England, he was with Sri Lankan friends in a pub in Bayswater, on the south-east edge of Notting Hill, when the riots broke out. On voicing his alarm, he was reassured that "this is nothing to do with us, they are only attacking the Negroes," a response that, coming straight from the violence of the pogroms, he found impossible to stomach—it was his "moment of truth."[98] He quit a career in banking at this time to embark on one as a librarian, eventually working at the Institute of Race Relations, where from the mid-1960s on he regularly wrote articles in response to those in the many civil rights, Black Power, and anticolonial liberation periodicals to which he subscribed its library.

To return to Sivanandan's early essays, his obsession with U.S. civil rights and Black Power writings is evident. He reviewed assiduously: Eldridge Cleaver, George Jackson, Angela Davis, and he had a particular fondness for Baldwin's work.[99] In his essays, though, he would move quickly across the contexts of various struggles of race, from the United States to Africa, South Asia, the Caribbean, and Britain. Explaining the politics of blackness that tore apart CARD in 1967, he would insist that the varied group of activists advocating Black Power in CARD were bound together by a commonality of colonial oppression, something which was, he proposed, "total and pervasive." "In their pain and their purpose," he proposed, "they have found an identity with each other that makes them not many countries but one people."[100] As Sivanandan had it, finding commonality in a political blackness both refused colonialism's "divide and rule" tactics, and recognized the ease with which British racism shifted between various racializing designations, often offering little differentiation between "a no-good nigger, a bleeding wog or just a plain black bastard."[101] His position was at the heart of the IRR's journal *Race & Class*, established in 1974 when Sivanandan and a group of IRR workers broke with their management to remake the institute as a resource center, anti-racist think tank, and political hub.[102] By the 1980s, the idea of political blackness was firmly associated with the IRR's work, particularly as *Race & Class* took on a campaign against government funding initiatives that allocated funding along ethnic lines, and prioritized cultural enterprises over political ones—moves that Sivanandan saw as undermining understandings of blackness as a unifying political concept.[103] In the IRR's conception, as he recounted in the late 1990s, black was "the colour of our politics not the colour of our skin, the colour of the fight." This was a position based on "the common experience of racism and colonialism that bound us—something unique to Britain."[104]

This conception of political blackness as a label bridging ethnic difference was embraced far more widely than Sivanandan's work alone. Indeed, black radical groups often framed their blackness as an inclusive politics. At the National Conference on the Rights of Black People in Britain, a weekend event at London's Alexandra Palace on May 22–23, 1971, the conference program depicted a circle of men and women of African, Caribbean, South Asian, and South East Asian descent, arm in arm under the strap line "Towards Black Unity," and included a banner in the Gurmukhi Sikh script used by many of Britain's South Asian migrants from the Punjab (fig. 6). Organized through a collaboration between London's multi-ethnic BPM and BUFP, Birmingham's Afro Carib Self Help, Wolverhampton's Afro Carib Circle, Leeds's United Caribbean Association, and Huddersfield's West Indian Association, the event also brought a coach-load of twenty-one delegates from Birmingham's Indian Workers' Association.[105] The BPM's newsletter began, in 1971, to print its banner in Gurmukhi, too. The first issue to do so was published in May of that year, with a headline report on a demonstration against the Immigration Bill then before Parliament, recording a multi-ethnic march of "ten thousand Asians, Africans, and West Indians" through London.[106]

Though activists of African descent certainly dominated black radical politics in this era, South Asians and Indo-Caribbeans were always a part of it. Stokely Carmichael, recalling his tour around London in July 1967, noted his surprise "to hear Black Power resonating and to see the raised fists in the Asian communities, especially among Pakistani youth."[107] A television documentary on British Black Power filmed the following year also recorded this impact, finding several young British Asians willing to give their views on and claim themselves a part of the Black Power phenomena.[108] Surveying the rise of Black Power in Britain three years later, Derek Humphry and Gus John would note that with "its powerful appeal to the young, Black Pantherism is growing in this country and it would be a mistake to think, as many do, that only West Indian immigrants and their offspring join the movement. A fair number of Asians are observable at Panther meetings."[109] This appeal of blackness to British Asians certainly cannot be divorced from

FIGURE 6. Conference program for the National Conference on the Rights of Black People in Britain: Towards Black Unity, held at Alexandra Palace, north London, on May 22–23, 1971.

the attraction of its aesthetics of opposition, and as it operated as a youth style culture the blackness desired was often routed through African American or Caribbean coordinates.[110] But, like Sivanandan at the IRR, South Asians also held key roles in black political organizations. In 1967, at least seventeen of the seventy-six members of the Universal Coloured People's Association (UCPA), a predecessor of many later Black Power groups, were South Asians or Indo-Caribbean.[111] One of these, the Indo-Guyanese activist Roy Sawh, became one of the most familiar faces of British Black Power, from his rise to prominence alongside Michael de Freitas in the mid-1960s to his eventual return to Guyana in the mid-1970s.[112] The Indian Ajoy Shankar Ghose, also a founding member of the UCPA, edited *TriContinental Outpost*, a "black consciousness" journal forged very much in the Bandung spirit, which moved freely between the many points of the anticolonial and black liberation struggle. Farukh Dhondy, an Indian from Poona, and Mala Sen, later Mala Dhondy, played pivotal roles in *Race Today*. Tony Soares, born in Portuguese Goa in the mid-1940s and active as a teenager in anticolonial politics in Mozambique, went on to lead the BLF in the 1970s, where he was joined by Ansel Wong, a Trinidadian of mixed African and Chinese descent, who edited the group's *Grassroots* newsletter.[113] In the black women's movements of the 1970s, Asian women often played a significant part.[114] And while the political struggles of Britain's Asian communities, particularly the labor and housing struggles of the 1970s, were not always expressed in the languages of blackness, the leading theoreticians, newsletters, and journals of black radical politics repeatedly identified them within these terms, and lent their support to them.[115] Moreover, there were significant convergences between Black Power and Asian radical groups. Jagmohan Joshi, the Punjabi Sikh general secretary of the Birmingham Indian Workers' Association, was the driving force behind the Black People's Alliance (BPA), founded in Leamington Spa in April 1968 as a "militant front for Black Consciousness and against racialism."[116] The alliance was between representatives of over fifty political organizations, bringing together South Asians, Caribbeans, and Africans, and the BPA would often boost numbers at UCPA and BPM marches, using Indian Workers' Association members. In one BPA march organized to coincide with the meeting of twenty-eight Commonwealth heads of government at the Commonwealth Prime Ministers' Conference in London in January 1969, of the eight thousand who took to the streets, two-thirds were of South Asian descent.[117]

South Asian radicalism was often, however, only ambivalently accommodated within the representational strategies of many black radical groups in this period. Reporting on the Commonwealth Prime Ministers' Conference march, *Black Dimension* noted the multi-ethnic make-up of the demonstration, describing "a truly beautiful sight to witness [. . .] ten thousand MILITANT black people—Africans, Indians, Pakistanis and West Indians" who had "come out on to the streets and place[d] themselves firmly upon the stage of REVOLUTIONARY POLITICAL ACTIVITY here in Britain."[118] Here Britain's various nonwhite populations were united, "in our struggle

FIGURE 7. Una Howe illustration depicting a January 1969 demonstration against immigration legislation, printed in *Black Dimension*, 1 (February 1969). © Una Howe.

against the racist white power structure." However, in the newsletter's accompanying illustration (fig. 7), black men of African descent, fists in the air, dominate the foreground. A few white protestors, identifiable by their long, straight pale hair, are pushed to the margins, excluded from the throng of black humanity, and with their faces obscured. They hunch and run as the black protestors march. But whites are not the only ones conspicuously absent from the thrust of the demonstration. It is hard to identify many women in the crowd, and the one identifiably Asian man, distinguished by his turban, is partially obscured, his arms are by his sides, and his eyes downcast. Black militancy was defined here in opposition to a passivity frequently defined as characteristically Asian.

The BPM's report on its march against the 1971 Immigration Bill was similarly ambivalent in its representation of South Asian participation and black political culture. Their paper reported "ten thousand Asians, Africans, and West Indians" marching in London, arguing that the experience of colonialism and anticolonial resistance gave these protestors a unique insight into contemporary Britain that extended beyond immigration politics alone to have "wider repercussions on British society as a whole."[119] In the *Black People's News Service*, however, this past of colonial resistance was bifurcated, and it was in the African past (though, on other occasions, this could equally be the African Caribbean past) that a politics closest to that advocated by the Panthers was found: "It was within this fierce struggle against British colonialism that we discovered the nature of the world in which we live. We were schooled in the politics of resistance, sometimes violent (the Mau Mau in Kenya), sometimes passive (Gandhi in India)." Anticolonialism in India, of course, never operated only through passive resistance tactics, even if Gandhian nonviolence has since dominated public memories and histories of the independence struggle.[120] Similarly, African and Caribbean colonial history was not uniquely a story of violence and violent resistance. Nevertheless, such perspectives structured both the languages of white racism and, frequently, of radical blackness. Writing in *Black Liberator* in 1971, A. X. Cambridge contended that West Indians had "a far greater understanding of capitalist brutality than the Asians," and that "this whole business of passive resistance, non-violence" limited the potential of South Asian radicalism. "Our history is free from that," Cambridge argued. "We have not thrown up a Gandhi. Nor are we pressed under by a caste system of duty and respect allied to, and substantiated or nourished by [. . .] passive and anachronistic religious forms one finds in India and Pakistan." In contrast, "we've always rebelled. We're mostly a transported people, whereas the Indians have remained fundamentally indigenous[,] and that to a certain extent accounts for our violence."[121]

In conceptions like Cambridge's, African Caribbean blackness was characteristically modern, beginning with the experience of the Middle Passage that both created African Caribbeans as global subjects ("transported people") and placed them in modern relations of capitalist production. Asians, by contrast, were in thrall to "anachronistic" passive religions, the anachronism presumably realized in the unsuitability of passive resistance to the modern world with which African Caribbean peoples had wrestled. Radical blackness here was firmly tied to an African Caribbean history. Similar positions can be found in the BUFP's *Black Voice*, which in 1970 reflected on the reaction of Asians in Britain and the subcontinent to the rise of Powellism.

"It seems to us that perhaps owing to the particular nature of British colonialism, the concept of 'racism' has been on the whole an alien one for the Indo-Pak people," *Black Voice* proposed. "Indeed, when recently some attacks were made on the Pakistani community in this country, it became quite apparent that, although the Caribbean and African communities were quick to perceive the 'racist' nature of these attacks and come quickly to the support of the Pakistanis, the victims themselves found it difficult to locate the nature of these onslaughts."[122] If the blackness of political blackness was a unity through the experience of racism, then clearly for these writers some could perceive (and so act against) that racism more easily than others. Britain's black radical organizations frequently articulated the basis of a black radical tradition, which they understood themselves to be the inheritors of, in New World experiences of slavery. These were experiences they understood to be constituted first-and-foremost through modern violence and violent resistance.[123]

Despite such marginalization, many South Asian radicals in Britain would locate themselves within a conception of political blackness in which they expressed their own blackness as a blend of British, South Asian, and black Atlantic cultures. This was most evident in the Asian Youth Movements (AYMs) of the second half of the 1970s. AYMs were concentrated in the midlands and the north of England, but also founded in London, Luton, and Watford. Emerging often from defensive politics of British Asian schoolchildren against the violence of local National Front organizations in the first half of the 1970s, they were provided a major catalyst by the racist murder of Gurdip Singh Chaggar in Southall on June 4, 1976.[124] These groups laid claim to radical, revolutionary South Asian inheritances, refusing what they saw as the complicity of some Caribbean-led black radical papers in perpetuating racist stereotypes of traditional Asian passivity. Mohsin Zulfiqar of the Manchester AYM recalled that when *Race Today* headed a report on the growth of AYMs with the question "Are Asian Youth Breaking the Mould?" (of traditional South Asian culture's alleged passivity), members "took exception to that [...] it was not a question of us breaking the mould, we had always said there have been two kinds of movements within the South Asian community in this country, one is revolutionary, one is compromising and moderate."[125] Indeed, as Anandi Ramamurthy has shown, there was frequently reverence in AYM literature for "martyrs of the anti-colonial struggles of India, including Bhagat Singh, Udham Singh, Tipu Sultan and the Rani of Jhansi."[126]

In these ways, British Asian black radicalism offered a black radical political subject routed through a South Asian tradition of anticolonial resistance, but not conceived of as separate from other articulations of blackness dominant in the wider black radical political movement in Britain. The language of blackness was key to how AYMs conceived their politics. Though the United Black Youth League, founded in 1981, was the only AYM that explicitly used the anglicized "black" in its title, others used the Urdu term *kala* (black), with newsletters titled *Kala Tara* (Black Star), *Kala Mazdoor* (Black Worker), and *Kala Shoor* (Black Outcry, translated also as Black Consciousness).[127] The iconography of Black Power was also adopted in the badges, membership cards, banners, magazines, and leaflets of these groups, where the clenched fist salute, in particular, predominated.[128] Their politics extended across the black Atlantic world, South Asia, and beyond, encompassing particularly South Africa and Rhodesia, but also Palestine and, closer to home, Northern Ireland and the miners' strikes.[129] Reflecting their emphasis on political blackness, Bhupinder Bassi of the Birmingham AYM recalled, Sivanandan's writing was particularly popular because of how "he invites the black intellectual home," and "we used the words of Siva at meetings."[130] However, alongside Sivanandan, these groups would also embrace Linton Kwesi Johnson's poetry—firmly Caribbean in its expression, though also premised on the establishment of a unified black identity—as well as Bob Marley's music. Such presences vied for space alongside South Asian inheritances that were rarely present in the Caribbean-dominated domains of black radical activism. The anti-imperialist poetry of Faiz Ahmed Faiz, as well as of British-based Urdu and Punjabi poets such as Mahmood Jamal, Bedi, and Mumtaz Awan, was frequently read at AYM meetings.[131] *Samaj in'a Babylon*, a London-based journal founded in 1976, printed in both English and Urdu, and using both anglicized Urdu and the language of Rastafari and reggae culture in its title, made this merger of South Asian and Caribbean culture more explicit.

While South Asian radicals identifying as "black" worked to include South Asian cultural and political inheritances into their narratives of blackness, the readiness with which they might also engage the languages and cultures of Rastafarianism or reggae, or of African America, suggests not only that the "blackness" articulated in this moment was not recognized, by them, as ethnically exclusive, but also that the models of history, memory, and inheritance at play here were open. The memories of anti-racist and anti-colonial politics that made up a black radical inheritance operated, to borrow Michael Rothberg's terminology, "multidirectionally," "subject to ongoing negotiation, cross-referencing, and borrowing."[132] Indeed, the multidirectionality of memories of slavery—crucial to the politics of blackness in this period—appeared able to hold wide social traction. To take just one example, a Pakistani shopkeeper interviewed by the black social worker Chris Mullard in the early 1970s complained that his former boss had expected him "to grovel at the feet of some stupid white chargehand who thinks he's an overseer back in the slave days."[133] As Paul Gilroy observes, "Those of us whose ancestors were property shouldn't relate to this history as if it were now somebody's private cultural property. It doesn't belong to anybody."[134] Since the radical politics of black Britain was unevenly spliced together, multidirectionality was essential, but when South Asian black political subjectivity was articulated, this was often threatened. However, as with Gail Lewis's appropriation of George Jackson's masculinist text to further a black feminist project, the "diasporic resources" of Black Power, as they were passed around and reused in unequal relations of exchange, allowed for new conceptions of blackness.

Again, George Jackson's is a case in point. The Soledad Brothers rally at Westminster's Central Hall in April 1971, at which George's sister Penny Jackson spoke, with three thousand in attendance and another thousand at the doors, was an event that brought together black political London at a key moment of international Black Power politics. Here, blackness was redirected in many new ways, and most successfully by Jagmohan Joshi. Friends of Soledad, Afro-American Solidarity Committee, and the Angela Davis Defence Committee called the meeting both "to rally support for the Soledad Brothers" and to "draw attention to the similarities between their plight and that of black people in this country." In this, they were joined by the BLF, the BPM, the BUFP, and the WISC.[135] Both Penny Jackson and the BPM's David Udo, a Nigerian, proclaimed a universal blackness uninterrupted by national borders. "These people are black people, not just Americans," declared Udo. "They are our brothers and sisters; it means that we black people here in Britain have every right, every moral duty to support them and to identify ourselves with them."[136] "Black people," echoed Penny Jackson, "black people in Harlem, black people in Watts, black people in Fillmore, black people in Brixton, black people in Manchester, black people in London, black people in Liverpool, have *no* chance under the present system."[137] The politics here was based, as *Race Today*'s editor Alexander Kirby noted, on "the indivisibility of black resistance to a racist *status quo*, and the unity of the revolution which ignores national boundaries."[138] Joshi's inclusion on the rostrum pointed to how the national boundaries in question were conceived here beyond their familiar black Atlantic coordinates, and the blackness articulated held British particularities distinctly different from its meaning in the United States.

Speaking in the name of Black Power, Joshi explicitly located this as a politics embracing all former colonials who found themselves now in the heart of the imperial metropole. Anticipating Sivanandan's famous aphorism "We are here because you were there," Joshi told his audience, "We are not here because of our choice, we are here because of the exploitation by the capitalist economies, because of the territorial possession that took place in other parts of the world, because of the East India Company, because of the transportation of African slaves against their will."[139] In this rendition of their commonality, all were "transported people" through some aspect of Britain's imperial project and its aftermath. Moreover, Joshi suggested, a common perspective, and so a common knowledge, bound them all together. When it came to immigration policy, as Joshi reminded his audience, "We know from our own experience that there is no difference between the Labour Party and the Tory Party, just as there is no difference between a cut throat and a burglar!" Significantly, his speech distinguishing blackness and black politics in Britain from the predominantly black Atlantic frameworks of North American Black Power received the most applause of the evening.[140]

It would be possible to read this extending-outwards of blackness from the particular conditions of George Jackson's case, or more widely of North American race politics, as a flattening process, each new inclusion working only by the suppression of yet another point of difference. Certainly, the points of difference are significant, as are the locations of power—we need to keep in mind those erasures of South Asians, those moments of making-secondary of women's politics.[141] Looking at these as moments of multidirectionality, however, helps to avoid throwing the baby out with the bathwater. Joshi took advantage of the Soledad campaign to rearticulate the terrain of British Black Power, and place South Asian experience as an obvious bedfellow in this movement. Later in the evening, when James Baldwin addressed the crowd, a woman interrupted him from the floor, questioning him about the streaming of black schoolchildren in Britain into "educationally subnormal" schools. "Let me say one thing," Baldwin replied, "that woman's voice, that woman's voice is what you have to hear." This woman's intervention, Alexander Kirby wrote in his account of the evening, was "a complementary point, not a contradictory one."[142] The cheers Baldwin's reply evoked suggest that the audience shared Kirby's view. In this reading, to bring a new issue to the table added new dimensions to the narrative of black suffering and resistance begun by the Soledad case. It neither suggested that each case was equivalent, nor that each was mutually exclusive. Instead, "black" became a terrain here for uniting the many divergent sites of conflict around race confronting that room; it drew together a political formation for which racism and racialization were the key objects of politics. This was black politics at its best, in which blackness was not a site of policing, but of enabling, and in which it was not a moment of closure—finally naming its true constituency—but a point of departure. The issues faced by what Satnam Virdee has called Britain's "racialized outsiders" were certainly different.[143] South Asians were much more likely to be stereotyped as illegal immigrants, for example, while those of African descent were stereotyped as muggers.[144] Young men of African or Asian descent were more likely to face violence from the police and fascist gangs, and young women of African or Asian descent might find their bodies more likely to be targeted for medicalized invasion. But employing a common language of blackness pointed to a multidirectional, complementary politics, with a shared interest in the multifarious ways in which racism worked to dehumanize and violate, as opposed to more closed-down, univocal, and unilinear conceptions of blackness.[145]

"FULFILLINGLY BLACK": BLACK AFFECT

When Tariq Modood critiqued the idea of political blackness in the late 1980s and early 1990s, he did so because he felt that it harmed British Asians. Blackness, he proposed, was "powerfully evocative of people of sub-Saharan African origins, and all other groups, if evoked at all, are secondary." Political blackness was not, he argued, "an empty term." On the contrary, efforts to manufacture a sense of black commonality routinely utilized "Afro-Caribbean history or contemporary experience" and supposed these "to be paradigmatically 'black.'"[146] While there were, as we have seen, many exceptions, there was nonetheless truth in Modood's charge. Modood recognized a slippage commonly made between political blackness and the blackness of "black is beautiful." This, he proposed, conflated blackness as a name for anti-racist politics with blackness as a name for "ethnic pride" originating in and limited to African diasporic cultures. This latter point, as scholarship on black style makes clear, relies in part on a false distinction. Black style cultures *were* anti-racist; they were exercises in asserting bodily integrity and inviolable freedoms in the face of oppressive social and political structures.[147] But Modood's wider point, with some qualifications, still held some water: when blackness was mobilized by people of African descent it offered "a historical depth and a cultural texture" that was less present in South Asian articulations, for whom articulations of blackness were often first and foremost "'a political colour,' a reference to a limited aspect of their being."[148]

Modood even shared assumptions here with those most invested in political blackness. Paul Gilroy, a considerable distance from Modood politically, and a favorite target of Modood's invective, would himself express sorrow at the decline of "political blackness" in terms similar to Modood's when reflecting on changes in the political terrain since the publication of his *There Ain't No Black in the Union Jack* in 1987. Political blackness, as he wrote in a 2002 new edition of the book, was a "bridging term" promoting "synchronized action among the victimised," a framing that, in its choice of metaphor, suggested little substantive content to political blackness itself, beyond its coordinating role.[149] Famously, Gilroy's work in *There Ain't No Black in the Union Jack* was at pains to refuse to reduce blackness to anti-racism, and it emphasized precisely a fullness and reach to cultural and political projects emerging out of conceptions of blackness that if reduced only to their challenges to racism missed much of their depth and liberatory promise. But as Modood noted, Gilroy's exploration of this richness was reserved for African diasporic culture, and South Asian politics and culture were marginal to his book's exposition.[150]

The multidirectionality of political blackness explored above gives us some reason for skepticism about Modood's position. His conviction that, as a name for political analysis and alliance, blackness was really a thin concept, acquiring its depth only when it was shifted from a bridging role to a description of an ethnically specific history or culture, worked by a too-fixed, sealed conception of ethnicity.[151] But in more ways than this, this final section argues, to be "politically black," and to think of blackness as a site of political critique and action, could in fact work in just as full, deep, embodied, affective ways as those cultural practices that many advocates of political blackness, like the anonymous contributor to the BLF's *Grassroots* newsletter cited at the start of this chapter, sought to either replace or to transform and politicize. Far from being simply a hollowed-out political signifier, ill-harnessed to the fuller, more intimate terrains of black culture, political blackness was, to borrow Sara Ahmed's terms, a "sweaty concept," affected by and affecting the body.[152] Indeed, it was the ability of political blackness to create affective, deep relationships that accounts for much of its hold.

As Avtar Brah underlined in narrating her turn to political blackness, the assumption of a politics so bound up with how bodies are read and treated could not but be an embodied politics. Brah had come of age in the United States of America as a student visiting temporarily from Uganda at the turn of the 1970s, just as Black Power was taking hold across U.S. university campuses, and dominating the news media's coverage of the politics of civil rights. She turned fully to black politics, though, when she moved to London and within weeks had been called a "Paki."

> I was so taken aback the first time I was called a racist name that I was struck silent. I now realised, in quite a different way from when I was expressing my solidarity with black Americans, what it felt like to be called a "nigger." [. . .] This is not to suggest that one cannot empathise with those whose experience one does not share. [. . .] But there is a qualitative difference when this changing fiction we call "I" or "Me" is directly *subjected* within specific discursive practices. This *experience* matters.[153]

Her experience is reminiscent of Fanon's famous moment of racialization, when "Look, a Negro!" uttered by a child in Lyon serves as the trigger in a total decomposition and recomposition, not only of Fanon's sense of self, but of how he could inhabit his body.[154] But if politicization worked at a deeper level here because of the embodied experience of the moment of racialization that drove Brah to political blackness, it was equally the case that the experience of black political work could have a deep resonance, as something that was not just done, but "felt." Returning to the *Grassroots* writer with whom this chapter began, we can see the task of creating a political conception of blackness was rooted, for her, in the building up of practices for critical reflection that would replace mere "physical manifestations," and would find its target in a "mental condition." Such activists, attempting to build new practices for a "mental condition" of blackness as the basis for a political formation were often careful to distinguish between black expressive cultures, where affective, embodied experience was readily recognized as the order of the day, and the more rarefied forms of intellectual engagement that they championed. But this distinction meant less in practice. The drive to get people reading as a route into black politics was not a process of diminishing, or overriding, some earlier "felt" state of blackness. Indeed, reading and intellectual work were often deeply *felt* experiences. Early in *Grassroots*'s life, one young reader, Sister Maxine, wrote in to congratulate them on their "right on" paper. It was, she wrote, "magnificent! great! fullfillingly black!"[155] We should take seriously this sense of fulfilment, what Sivanandan would describe as the "living, palpitating reality" of black intellectual work, felt in "very existence."[156]

Social life, as the social anthropologist William Mazarella insists, operates in two simultaneous registers, "on the one hand, a register of affective, embodied intensity and, on the other, a register of symbolic mediation and discursive elaboration."[157] Thinking about the affective register can help us understand the hold of blackness. Several historians, working in the wake of the cultural turn, have become dissatisfied with the ways in which subjective life, after that turn, has often been reduced to what Michael Roper calls an ideological "after-effect." To talk of subjectivity in terms only of the subject positions opened up by ideology, Roper proposes, cuts short the "complex mechanisms that operate and which mediate between individual subjects and cultural formations."[158] The affective turn approaches this question by exploring how "society is inscribed on our nervous system and in our flesh before it appears in our consciousness."[159] Recognizing the porous nature of the world of objects, in which, as Frank Trentmann observes, the "boundaries of things are not as self-evident or fixed as we may wish"—not least "the boundaries between things and humans"—scholars of affect look to how the materiality of the body in society presupposes the moment of cultural inscription, and provides its possibility.[160] For Brian Massumi, the most influential thinker in this tradition, the challenge of understanding the dynamics of social life therefore requires both recognizing the material processes that create affective intensity and recognizing the processes through which this intensity is subjected to "sociolinguistic fixing"—how it is "owned and recognized."[161]

New expressive cultures in the 1960s and 1970s transformed black life in Britain. As Linton Kwesi Johnson had it, there emerged "a bran new breed of blacks," now beautifully documented in the rapidly expanding published visual record of the period.[162] Early work explaining these expressive cultures focused on semiotic analysis, reading it as a *language* of blackness.[163] From the mid-1980s on, however, scholars became ever more attuned to the significance of materiality, looking at how "Afro" hair, for example, positioned the body in new ways, and brought together new "black" assemblages, or looking at the significance of the embodied resonance of the voice in communicating black selfhood and experience.[164] Most recently, Paul Gilroy and Julian Henriques have emphasized the importance of music cultures, not just in communicating and enacting new ideas through their lyrics or social relations, but in physically moving bodies, creating immersive experiences that moved across the entire surface of the skin, and resonated in the body.[165] These expressive cultures, in other words, were made through affective, embodied intensity as much as they were symbolically, or ideologically. The depth of such research on expressive cultures, however, has in some ways served to underline the kind of false distinction made by Modood between a deep, cultural blackness and a thin "political blackness" of organized political activity and alliance. While it has been more usual for style cultures to be read affectively, we can in fact see similar dynamics working in the cultures of books, study, and demonstrations that made up the everyday activities of many of those defining themselves through political blackness.

For a start, the worlds of pleasure, politics and reading were never separate. Black style cultures drew readily on the imagery of Black Power. Not only was the popularity of the Afro haircut hugely boosted by its political associations—most notably with Angela Davis—but those origins were seldom far from its various iterations. Black liberation also informed other adornments, from the "battle dress and combat jackets" Dick Hebdige recorded in mid-1970s Birmingham to the ubiquity of "Angela Davis and Malcolm X badges, and Black Power badges showing the clenched black fist" that Ken Pryce found in Bristol.[166] The black music cultures of the 1970s, too, as Gilroy has repeatedly insisted, were "inseparable from the revolutionary upsurge of that moment."[167]

Political activity was firmly integrated into this world. "Activism, study, personal consciousness-raising and growth and music and festivals were all of a swirling mix," Jan McKenley remembers of her time in BBWG and OWAAD in the 1970s and 1980s. "They intertwined. [. . .] That kind of interplay between those things was very, very powerful."[168] Like McKenley, Gail Lewis remembers running all over London in these years, moving between political meetings, reading groups, and bookshops and the soul clubs of the capital, like the Q Club in Praed Street, where she could dance to "deep, deep, deep soul."[169] Indeed, music played an important role in black political culture. Shaka Downbeat, which became one of London's most popular sound systems in the 1970s, was initially formed by members of Fasimba, and performed at key sites of black intellectual and arts activism, including the WISC.[170] In north London's Hibiscus Club in 1975, Michael and Keith La Rose, sons of New Beacon Books's John La Rose, established the People's War sound system, the go-to sound system for New Beacon's social and political events, and later for fundraisers and events surrounding the George Padmore Supplementary School, the Black Parents Movement, and the Black

Youth Movement. They chose the name "because we wanted to identify with some of the struggles against oppression that were going on around the world, like in South Africa, in the Caribbean, and here in Britain."[171]

Black activists also made selling black style a part of their revenue generation and a method of recruitment. This method is recorded in a memorable scene from Horace Ové's *Pressure* (1975), a film about the conversion to Black Power politics of a young black Londoner, Tony, whose activist brother, Colin, is arrested on trumped up charges following a police invasion of a political meeting in Ladbroke Grove. The scene follows Tony and his friends through Portobello Road market, where they come upon a Black Power stall. Colin, running the stall, complains of Tony that that he "just can't get him to think black." His solution is to press on Tony some Black Power newsletters, which sit beside copies of Malcom X's speeches, Jackson's *Soledad Brother*, and local Black Power pamphlets on the market stall. Beside these, though, Colin also sells posters of Amilcar Cabral's People's War movement and prints of Ras Daniel Hartman's popular Rastafari artwork, as well as dashikis, belts, and cowrie-shell jewelry. His companion on the stall, Sister Louise, presses Colin to recognize the importance of style in delivering politics— "You've been using the wrong approach all the time [. . .] you know, you've got to do a little bit of 'mmm-hmm, ahhh-haaa, you know what I mean?'"

This mix of black reading and black style was common. Winston Trew remembers that an "integral part" of the Fasimbas' "sharing of ideas" was "the selling of black books, posters, carvings, badges, Malcolm X T-shirts, African material" at their market stalls.[172] Newsletters also hawked such merchandize. *TriContinental Outpost*, for example, sold Malcolm X posters and badges for four shillings apiece. In 1978, *Race Today* produced a series of illustrated greetings cards, inscribed with verse from Linton Kwesi Johnson, selling them to readers for twenty pence.[173] Going a step further, *Hustler!* printed one of its issues on a series of reversible single-sheets, "like a pack of playing cards—shuffle each page as you feel like it. You can read it back to front if you want to, or stick up any page you particularly dig on your wall."[174] Such materials plastered the walls of political headquarters, cafés, and bedrooms, as the visual record of this era testifies.[175] The communication technologies of black radical politics were embedded in these cultures in ways that made black reading practices a part of wider black expressive culture. The radical press carried advertisements for record stores and music venues, and *Grassroots* even initiated a "Revolutionary Reggae Top Ten" chart. Music and style cultures not only offered sources for revenue or means of political interpellation. When Trew remembers beginning his collection of black literature, it is in the same breath as recalling the wider material cultures of a burgeoning black commodity culture supported by, and supporting, the black activist press. "At home in Peckham," he writes, "I adopted new cultural practices: wearing black, plaiting and then combing my hair out in an 'Afro,' adorning my bedroom with Malcolm X, Marcus Garvey and American Black Panther posters. As well as continuing to collect records, I started a collection of books on Black history."[176]

In Menelik Shabazz's 1981 film *Burning an Illusion*, a story of young black woman Pat Williams's movement into black activism, Pat's conversion is signaled simultaneously by her acquisition of new books (*Malcolm X Speaks, The Wretched of the Earth, Soledad Brother*), new posters (Marcus Garvey, Ras Daniel Hartman prints), and African arts and crafts ornaments. These style cultures are key to showing Pat's transformation into radical politics, as she replaces a love of soft furnishings and makeup with radical posters, music, and plaited hair. The detail was picked up by Akua Rugg, reviewing the film for *Race Today*, who commended the "meticulous attention paid to details of dialogue, dress and décor."[177] Books, though, play a role no less totemic than dress and décor. Pat is a regular shopper at the Grassroots Storefront bookshop, and in her letters to her boyfriend, imprisoned for a fight with a police officer, she records how "the books I've been reading [. . .] really opened my eyes to some of the things about black people's conditions I didn't think about before." Replacing her bookshelf comes to stand as the final gesture into the new kind of blackness that Pat is moving toward in this film. In the penultimate scene, she fondles her new black books, smiling wistfully as she places a copy of Fanon's *Wretched of the Earth* on her coffee table, and removes her previous obsession—a Barbara Cartland novel that used to serve as her bedtime reading. As she bins the Cartland novel in the waste chute, together with a box full of her old bedtime reading, she delivers a closing monologue: "I never believed that my life and dreams could have changed so much. Now like others, I am part of the struggle for equal rights and justice." The symbolic transformation, getting rid of one stack of books, and bringing in another, closes the film. As the credits roll, Pat joins a bus of women, singing on their way to a protest.

Not only were books symbols of radicalization, they were affective objects that allowed that radicalization to be felt. When Pryce recorded the books studied by black radicals in Bristol, he noted that they "clutched" these books in their hands. Neil Kenlock's photograph of BPM members at their

FIGURE 8. Inside the Black Panther Movement's headquarters, London. © Neil Kenlock.

headquarters in Brixton provides a similar scene (fig. 8), in which one Panther holds up a copy of Angela Davis's *If They Come in the Morning* and gives a raised-fist salute, while her companion, in a Malcolm X T-shirt that matches the poster just above his head, joins her in saluting. As well as vehicles for intellectual work, books and newsletters worked as affective objects for new assemblages of blackness. Their materiality comes often into reminiscences of activist lives. Judith Lockhart, active in the BBWG, describes fellow member Olive Morris's house as "laden down with books."[178] Emil Wilson, in a homage to his deceased companion and mentor Peter Moses, a radical activist and educator based in Shepherd's Bush, described the electrifying effect of books on their friendship and politics, in which Eldridge Cleaver "introduced himself to me from the library shelf." These books, Wilson wrote, were consumed "greedily," powering the pair for hours through the night.[179] Books, in this sense, were both style objects and affective objects. Holding books, or being with books, was a way both of becoming black, and of feeling that process of becoming.

As we have seen in the case of George Jackson's *Soledad Brother*, however, these books were also objects in, and ways into, new political campaigns, and a wider political formation. If books became part—perhaps a particularly fetishized part—of the materiality of black political culture in these years, they represented only one of the structured sites through which people became politically black. Another other key site was the political rally, where the affective dimensions of this politics were actively encouraged. As Alan Brien wrote in the *New Statesman* in 1971, reflecting on the Soledad rally at Westminster's Central Hall, "The atmosphere they clearly intended to evoke, and often overwhelmingly succeeded in arousing, was a huge, family get-together, a clan gathering, where the people discussed were all familiar figures, distant relatives about whom news was sought."[180] In describing George Jackson as a Soledad Brother, or in Gail Lewis experiencing herself as a Soledad sister, black politics offered a kind of solidarity that went beyond the bonds of sympathy, empathy or interest that often hold together political formations. Political movements often worked through calls to familial belonging, but as Brien noted, this had a particular resonance at the Soledad rally, where "'Brothers and sisters' was the form of address used by almost all the speakers," and it was an address "uttered with a kind of unselfconscious conviction so different from the ritual invocation to comradeship and fraternity of the Trade Union Congress or the Labour Party conference."

Like any family, the brothers and sisters pulled together as black people in such pieces of political theatre were united by their siblingship, but often uncomfortably so. A part of this, as we have seen, was about the problems of translation involved in the transnational articulation of black liberation between places with often very different experiences and understandings of what blackness, race, or racism might mean. The closeness of the "fit" of black political subjectivity offered in this political formation often came down to differences of gender or ethnicity. Finding a home in blackness in Britain meant forcing the language of blackness into new positions and carving out new spaces within a radical project of thinking black that was not limited to African American particularities, and that often attempted to break away from the image and concerns of masculinity—as, in different ways, Lewis, Sivanandan, or Joshi had done. This process, I have proposed, involved the making of new black political subjectivities, but it also involved processes based less in language, discourse, and ideology than in building up new assemblages of blackness.

The politics of blackness that Brien witnessed in the Soledad rally was, he averred, one that relied on "emotion, not argument, the deep rumbling voice of the gut, rather than the thin impartial pronouncements of the brain."[181] Readers might well be wary of such characterizations of black politics. As Martin Francis has noted, in late twentieth-century British politics—and of course with a long history prior to that—emotional expression and control have been constructed along racial lines in order to dismiss the political claims and activities of people of color.[182] But Brien, in noting this deeper resonance of the experience of becoming a "brother" or "sister"—something he found to be a particularly intimate, felt process of political formation— was recognizing an important dimension of how blackness held together in these years even with its instabilities. The deep rumbling of the gut returns us to the affective dimensions of black politics that were necessary for the rally's efficacy. The rally was about creating and coordinating affective intensities. The embodied materialities of the black cultural renaissance of the 1960s were everywhere in abundance. Ushers walked the isles "with official armbands and acres of badges."[183] Photographs of the rally show a wealth of Afros, sunglasses and dashikis, each differently postured as their wearers posed in various statues of defiance, with raised-fist salutes.[184] Recreating the dialogic soundscapes of soul, audiences responded to speeches with antiphonal cries of "Right on!"[185] Indeed, Penny Jackson delivered her speech, as Brien wrote, with "arms outspread, her bushy Afro-cut head thrown back, caught in the follow-spot like a soloist hitting her high C." This was "an evening for spoken jazz, a jam session of revolutionary arias, angry improvisations, eloquent variations, bitter funny outbreaks of frustrated feeling." The audience rose in sections, fists clenched, cheering, "to spur on the performers, releasing an occasional individual, ecstatic 'yippee' and an approving 'right on,' or a low, breathy, long-drawn 'yeeeeeeh.'"[186] What Roland Barthes would call "the body in the voice" was here as important as the content of the speeches or responses.[187] This was an evening of political ritual in which each message was communicated through the embodied cultural registers of an ascendant black cultural repertoire.

Describing the events in *Race Today*, Alexander Kirby referred to "the sacramentalism of the Soledad rally," noting that this was "doubly useful, not only for focusing direct attention on the problem of immediate concern, but also for screwing up the courage—and raising the consciousness—of the participants." This was an event, as *Frendz* noted, in which "as it progressed the audience became more and more actively involved." As Courtney Tulloch noted in *Race Today*, this built a sense of each spectator as also an actor, bringing the whole audience into the performance of the event—"for the lowly street activist selling revolutionary pamphlets knew that he was a part of something history will remember."[188] Social ritual worked here not only as the necessary medium of the rally's efficacy, but as a process that simultaneously directed affect *and* left that moment of direction "necessarily incomplete, unstable, and provisional," open to other articulations.[189] In these moments of transnational encounter, through a shared blackness created at once through rhetoric, through style, through cadence, through dialogic communication structures, through imagery—"acres of badges"—through the movements of the body, each pronouncement could work multidirectionally, at once both confirming the commitment to the stated political goal, and implying commitment to much more—complementarity not contradiction, as Kirby had it.

In the Soledad rally, we can see engagements with black radical politics as an emotionally loaded, affectively rich encounter. Certainly, the narratives of blackness made available through the new texts that activists insisted were the necessary conduits to a black consciousness offered new frames for understanding life in Britain. And as the different dynamics of racialization and racism within Britain were brought to these texts, they were forced into new meanings, accommodating difference, even if unstably so. Encountering these texts might also be emotional work, as Gail Lewis found when George Jackson's letters to his brother became some form of substitute for the missing intimate interlocutor she needed to reconcile her own racial family drama as a mixed-race woman, living with a white mother while also encountering the sharp end of racism and beginning to identify with the transnational politics of black liberation. The psychodynamics of such encounters are, of course, peculiarly individual, even if we might imagine the structural similarities between Lewis's childhood and others of her generation to have made her experiences far from singular. But to the extent that we can read the role of black politics and culture as affectively resonant, we can also afford to be a little formalist. The black cultural renaissance of the 1960s provided possibilities for new black assemblages to be formed, in which the process of becoming black was both a discursive and a material one, the materiality underpinning and anchoring the discursive. Becoming a black "sister" or "brother" not only meant commitment to the Soledad campaign and the associated black subjectivities. It was also a process of managed affect by which those present could *feel* themselves becoming politically black.

CONCLUSION

The previous chapter explained the politics of thinking black as produced through a particular historical conjuncture—of the U.S. civil rights movement, Caribbean and African decolonization, and the politics of race relations and immigration. The rise of a new politics of blackness in Britain from the mid-1960s on came out of disaffection with the state politics of immigration and race relations, and loss of faith in any of the parliamentary parties' supporting the citizenship and integrity of nonwhite Britons against a rising tide of popular racism given added encouragement by Enoch Powell's anti-immigration platform. Many Caribbean, African, and South Asian Britons with long histories of anticolonial activism in Britain and the former colonies reframed their politics now in alliance with the confrontational politics of black liberation emerging from North America, and from the movements for secondary decolonization gaining pace in much of the formerly colonized world. This chapter has shown how activists attempted to build a cultural-political formation of blackness, premised on a demand to "think black" as the basis of cultural and political, individual and social renewal. The dominant languages of black identity and politics active in this moment were often hooked around African diasporic experiences, and often primarily concerned with the experiences of men, but many different people nonetheless found a sense of home in this politics, despite the displacements this might involve. They did this at an ideological level, by making claims upon blackness from different gendered and ethnic positions, forcing it into new meanings, or expanding its reach. But it was also a consequence of their participation in the expressive and affective cultures of blackness that underwrote this political movement. By becoming black through the array of cultural practices and material cultures claimed under the name of blackness in this era, many were able to *feel* black, even though the movement's politics might not always neatly align with their own concerns and experiences.

THREE

Radical Blackness and the Post-imperial State

THE MANGROVE NINE TRIAL

The Mangrove Nine
Eyes Edward Clarke
Court rises
God Save the Queen?
Power to the People!
Power to the People!
Right On! Right On!

SHABAZZ,
"The Trial of the Mangrove Nine" (1971)[1]

BLACK ACTIVISTS, AS WE SAW in the previous chapter, developed strategies to build a wide political formation. In doing this they worked to construct imagined communities of blackness in their newspapers and literature, and to cultivate reading cultures through which these could be popularized. However, these activists were not only interested in defining and producing communities of blackness, but in defining and confronting the object of their political critique—the British state and racist politics—and in mobilizing a broad front against both the state's immigration and race relations politics and its modes of harassment and brutality. They organized countless marches, pickets, and demonstrations, and were also ready to turn out to protest for others' causes, just as they came to expect support when they protested themselves. This chapter looks at the arrest, trial, and campaign for the Mangrove Nine as a watershed in black political history in Britain, when critiques of the racist state gained substantial ground, black politics made important alliances across the Left, and thinking black became part of a wider public culture.

The trial of the Mangrove Nine—nine men and women tried on charges of riot arising from a 1970 demonstration against police harassment—was the high-water mark of Black Power in Britain, and a key turning point toward greater confrontation between blacks and the police.[2] Both the demonstration and trial attracted widespread attention from the media, politicians, political and community groups and the government and intelligence services. It generated reams of debate in the press, worried police chiefs and Home Office officials, and instigated a decisive victory for black protest when all defendants were acquitted of the most serious charges they faced. The unfolding of the trial revealed how fantasies of black insurrection played into legitimizing and organizing the rise of an authoritarian state in the early 1970s. But the defendants and their campaign team also lost no opportunities to court the media, and to make their case against the state. In doing so, they mobilized significant support across sections of both the Old and New Left.

This chapter shows how and why black activism and experience in the Mangrove Nine case offered a wider form of decolonization for Britain, and how this perspective was embraced beyond black Britain. Arrested and tried at a time when British courts hosted a series of trials against, in Stuart Hall's words, "labour, political dissent and alternative life-styles,"[3] the Mangrove Nine launched a sustained critique of the police and the judicial system, providing a critique of the court machinery, and of the authoritarian turn of the state in the early 1970s. Bringing the long history of slavery and colonial exploitation into the courtroom, the defendants asked white Britons to see the current turn of British politics from this perspective, gathering support, as they did so, across sections of the left-libertarian political formation of post-1968 Britain. In such moves, and as the following two chapters explore further still, thinking black expanded outward across the social formation, taken up by many and divergent groups.

THE MANGROVE DEMONSTRATION

The Mangrove Nine were seven black men and two black women prosecuted in a three-month trial in late 1971 on thirty-one charges arising from a conflict with the police at a demonstration against police harassment of the Mangrove Restaurant in Notting Hill. Darcus Howe, Frank Critchlow, Rhodan Gordon, Althea Jones-Lecointe, Barbara Beese, Godfrey Millet, Rupert Glasgow Boyce, Anthony Carlisle Innis, and Rothwell Kentish stood trial at the Old Bailey on charges of riot and affray, numerous counts of actual bodily harm of policemen, and possession of offensive weapons. The nine included members of the Black Panther Movement (BPM) and those sympathetic to the organization, and many were important figures in black British politics. Jones-Lecointe was the leader of the Panthers at the time, and was at the forefront of anti-racist organization in London. Howe, a former leader of the short-lived Black Eagles group, also joined the Panthers following the Mangrove demonstration. He later became editor, from 1973 to 1988, of *Race Today* magazine, where Barbara Beese would also work. Rhodan Gordan, a race relations worker, was the owner of the Backayard, a café, bookshop, and black cultural center in Notting Hill. Rothwell (Roddy) Kentish was a community organizer, at the time of the demonstration involved in a campaign against the displacement of families in North Kensington caused by the construction of the Westway flyover. Frank Critchlow was the owner of the Mangrove Restaurant, a gathering place that remained at the center of political and cultural life in Notting Hill until its closure in 1992.

Local tensions had long simmered in London's Notting Hill, where problems of overcrowding, dilapidation, and poverty were exacerbated by rapid demographic change and a tradition of heavy policing of the often-shifting local migrant and minority populations.[4] The northern end of the area, squeezed between the metropolitan center of the West End and the Victorian inner suburbs, had a reputation for vice and criminality stretching back to the era of its incorporation into London in the second half of the nineteenth century. The formerly grand mid-Victorian villas to the south had been redesigned since the 1870s as multiple-occupancy flats for a largely transient population.[5] Previously an area of large Irish settlement, from the early 1950s West Indians began to settle in large numbers, often in cramped bed-sitters and rooming houses, in close proximity both to the area's large numbers of prostitutes and to its local white working-class population.[6] Some of these newcomers, indeed, took over parts of the local economy in gambling and prostitution—a small but visible minority, who attracted significant local attention and press coverage.[7] The expansion of multi-ethnic settlement in an area of the city most famed for its illicit economy was a cause for celebration and excitement for some—most notably the English novelist Colin MacInnes, for whom it offered deliverance from the staid, stolid lives of mid-century "respectable" Englishness that he found so suffocating.[8] More often, though, black migrants were blamed for the degradation of the area, condemned as hustlers and pimps. A housing crisis in the late 1950s and early 1960s, driven by both restricted housing stock and the liberalization of rent control in 1957, increased local tensions, particularly as unscrupulous landlords used white fears of black newcomers to pressure sitting tenants to move, and owners to sell.[9] These tensions spilled over in 1958, with a week of racist violence against the area's black population.[10] Oswald Mosley was sufficiently convinced of the strength of anti-black animus in North Kensington to choose to contest the parliamentary seat in the 1959 General Election.[11] Despite a burgeoning industry in local race relations philanthropy and social work, and a small but growing cosmopolitan culture, white hostility toward black neighbors remained a stubborn feature of Notting Hill's politics into the 1960s.[12]

From the late 1950s, Notting Hill was also at the forefront of a burgeoning black political culture concerned with fighting racism at a local and national level, establishing new sites of black community and organization. This was driven, in part, by the riots of 1958. As the Mangrove's Frank Critchlow recalled, the riots "changed our attitudes. [...] People decided to have their own thing. We used to meet in blues dances at the weekend, socialising, getting to know folks from different Caribbean islands."[13] In the wake of the riots Baron Baker, a Jamaican former RAF pilot who had lived in Notting Hill since the mid-1940s, established the United Africa-Asia League, holding weekly open-air meetings in Blenheim Crescent. Nearby, Amy Ashwood Garvey, widow of Marcus Garvey, founded the Association for the Advancement of Coloured People, while Frances Ezzrecco, an English woman of Polynesian descent, married to a West Indian jazz singer, founded the Coloured People's Progressive Association, with Michael de Freitas as vice-president.[14] The Notting Hill Carnival, established in 1965, became increasingly Caribbean-focused by the late 1960s, feeding the area's popularity with Caribbean migrants and their children, as well as its reputation as the Caribbean cultural capital of London.[15] Notting Hill remained the base for much black political activism in the later 1960s, too, home to the Racial Adjustment Action Society, Roy Sawh's various organizations, and the Black Eagles. By the late 1960s, Notting Hill's visibility as a burgeoning black political center was increasing apace. The "front line" of this increasingly visible new black politics and style was All Saints Road, where the Mangrove, a cosmopolitan restaurant attracting a wide clientele, opened in 1969. Rhodan Gordon's Backayard Restaurant on nearby Portobello Road also drew a steady stream of visitors inspired by the new black politics.[16]

Alongside seasoned Caribbean radicals such as C. L. R. James and Walter Rodney, regulars at the Mangrove included the Labour MP for North Kensington, Bruce Douglas-Mann; Lord Gifford, a vocal supporter of the

Soledad Brothers and Angela Davis, who later went on to chair the Broadwater Farm Inquiry; the actress and activist Vanessa Redgrave; and Richard Neville, the editor of the magazine *OZ*.[17] The restaurant itself was equally a homage to the black cultural and political renaissance of the 1960s and a celebration of swinging London's pop culture and hippiedom. The walls sported not just African figurines and posters decrying police brutality, but pictures of John Lennon and psychedelic advertisements for countercultural "happenings."

In the hardening anti-permissive and "law and order" politics of the late 1960s, the Mangrove as a site of vernacular and visceral cosmopolitanism, and its reputation as a hub for the area's political organizers, attracted the attention of the local police.[18] The Notting Hill police conducted their first drug raid on the Mangrove in February 1969, shortly after the restaurant's opening. Despite finding no evidence of drugs, they raided it again in June 1969 and May 1970, both times also unsuccessfully. Because of the raids, the restaurant attracted fewer customers, and business fell by over half. But despite lodging complaints with both the Home Office and the Race Relations Board, Critchlow was unable to launch any action against the police, and indeed soon found himself charged with assaulting the officer conducting the May raid, receiving a four-month jail sentence, later reduced to a fine on appeal.[19] The restaurant, accused of trading after hours, also lost its late-night license following the May raid, and it was subject to numerous visits by health inspectors, which Critchlow believed to have been instigated at the behest of the police.[20] In the face of this apparent police determination to close the restaurant, *Grassroots* reported, it was "rumoured in the Grove that the Mangrove management is being harassed because it refused to toe the line and pay protection and/or inform on customers."[21] Whatever the truth of such rumors, the relationship of the Mangrove's owner and customers with the police was sour, and this reflected a wider discontent with the local police among the black community of Notting Hill and Ladbroke Grove. Indeed, the officer leading the campaign against Mangrove—Police Constable Frank Pulley—was long hated by many of the local population.[22]

Following the third raid on the Mangrove on May 30, 1970, Selma James and Tony Mohipp formed the Mangrove Defence Committee at Selma and C. L. R. James's Willesden house. Selma James was a former member of the Brent chapter of CARD, and founder, in 1969, of the Black Regional Action Movement. Together with Mohipp, a lawyer and head of legal advice at the Black People's Information Centre, James planned a demonstration to protest the Mangrove raids. James and Mohipp sent letters to the prime minister, home secretary, leader of the Opposition, and the high commissioners of Guyana, Barbados and Trinidad and Tobago, notifying them of the planned demonstration and the reasons they had called it. The plan was to march past the police stations at Notting Hill, Notting Dale, and Ladbroke Grove, before returning for a rally at the Mangrove. Seeing Althea Jones-Lecointe speak at the West Indian Students Centre, James was "impressed by her forceful style," and asked her to speak at the demonstration.[23]

One hundred and fifty turned out for the demonstration on Sunday August 9, 1970. Before the march began, Jones-Lecointe and Howe mounted a car outside the restaurant to address the crowd. Jones-Lecointe's speech has not survived, but Howe's was biting in its critique and its hope for the beginning of a new political moment. "It has been for some time now that black people have been caught up in complaining to police about police, [. . .] complaining to judges about judges, complaining to politicians about politicians," he announced. "We have become the own shapers of our destiny as of today." Referring to a recent incident in which one hundred black people, mostly teenagers, had marched on nearby Caledonian Road police station in protest at the arrest of five of their peers after a funfair at Islington's Market Road, Howe suggested to his audience that this set a precedent for how black politics should proceed. "Young kids have committed the greatest revolutionary action that has been known in this country for some time. They walked into a police station and took it over." This, he suggested, was a "fight to prevent any infringement on our rights," and it was being furthered that day in the Mangrove demonstration.[24]

The Mangrove demonstrators started as planned, marching first to Notting Dale police station, and then to Notting Hill police station. Carrying a pig's head and banners of the Black Panther Movement, they waved placards declaring "Slavery is Still Alive," "Stop Police Brutality or Start Oinking," "The Fire This Time" and "Black Power Is Gonna Get Your Mamma!" As the demonstrators marched, chants of "Black Power!—People's Power!" relayed in call-and-response between the leaders of the march and the crowd behind them. For all its confrontational rhetoric, though, this was a peaceful march. Two hours in, this changed. As the marchers left Notting Hill police station to move to Ladbroke Grove, they were confronted, as Howe later related, with "a whole host of constables lined in military formation" on Portnall Road.[25] Violence broke out between police and protestors, leading to a prolonged conflict. At the end of the confrontation, nineteen people had been arrested, between seventeen and twenty-four police officers and thirty protesters injured, and six officers and an unknown number of demonstrators admitted to hospital.

Coverage of the demonstration revealed the continued traction of long-ingrained tensions over the area's reputation as a center of black criminality, as well as increasing concern about the rise of a more confrontational black politics. In a widely reported statement, Constable Pulley described the Mangrove as "a den of iniquity" frequented by "pimps, prostitutes and criminals," a charge he had previously made against the nearby Africa Shop on Portobello Road in 1969.[26] Suggesting that anybody who went to the Mangrove was "corrupted," he also claimed that its posters, "sometimes violent, sometimes obscene, would render it unacceptable to most people who go out for an evening meal."[27] Iniquity here stood alongside political violence. Indeed, as well as claiming expertise on the vices of Notting Hill, Pulley was regarded by Detective Inspector Stockwell of Notting Hill police station as the officer "most conversant with the identities of the Black Power supporters" of London.[28] Local residents also made these associations between street criminality and Black Power violence. One blamed the violence on "the undesirable blacks, the drug-takers, prostitutes and villains who stir up race hatred and try to take it out on the police," but refused to be named for "fear of reprisals from Black Power henchmen."[29] Another resident identified the troublemakers as "Black Power organisers and 'hustlers.'"[30] Journalists were also quick to point to signs of Black Power to explain the violence. The *Daily Telegraph*, reporting from inside the Mangrove, recorded African paintings and "heathen gods," alongside a "sinister" poster decrying police brutality, a "Black is Beautiful" slogan, and a "blown-up photograph of Cassius Clay, alias Mohammed Ali, the American Black Power figurehead."[31]

In the aftermath of the demonstration, the press began further reports on the possibilities of black political violence. The Black Panthers, in the words of a contemporary study, were associated with "ugly, aggressive violence [. . .] in the public mind."[32] In Notting Hill, one paper reported, "violence is simmering under the surface and could erupt at any moment—there is a black panther under your bed."[33] The *Telegraph* reported Special Branch investigations into the alleged "quasi-military style training" of the Black Panther Movement. The Panthers were "believed to have a 'military wing,'" funded by the African American entertainer Sammy Davis Jr. and supported by

Kwame Nkrumah, Ghana's ex-president, "which carries out drill practice in the London area."[34] The *Daily Sketch* added to this image with a report on Vince Hines, press officer to Michael de Freitas's Black House, in which Hines was interviewed in his office before a map of London with pins marking "areas of possible confrontation." Here the disorganized violence of the confrontation was reframed as an attack on authority planned with military precision: "Portnall Road is at the centre of a cluster of red drawing-pins—the zones where Negro militants expect bloody conflict to erupt [...], with a score of blue markers where tension between coloureds and the police is mounting towards violence."[35] Reports such as these insinuated that the area's decaying inner-city streets, long seen as a threat to morality, now also threatened political violence.

Following the demonstration, when eighteen of those arrested were brought before Marylebone Magistrates' Court, it became clear that the political affiliations of some of the protestors were a concern for the government. "Special Branch has had the movement under observation for more than a year," Home Secretary Reginald Maudling announced. "Police now regard Black Power as, at least, worthy of tight surveillance." Home Office intelligence reports reveal that this surveillance extended at least as far back as September 1967.[36] Maudling pressed for a tough response to the demonstration. Correspondence between the Home Office and Scotland Yard discussed whether prosecution under the Race Relations Acts was a possibility, and following the dismissal of the charge of riot at the initial Marylebone Magistrates' Court hearing, the director of public prosecutions (DPP) stepped in to reintroduce the charges, and the case went to the Old Bailey Central Criminal Court.[37] "As a result of the Black Power inquiry carried out by Special Branch Police Officers," the Black People's Information Service suggested, "nine people were selected as likely candidates because they were believed to have certain political views. [...] It is the intention of those who are responsible for governing our lives to duck their responsibility for the conflict in Portnall Rd. and instead to place it on the backs of the Mangrove 9. An inquiry into Black Power provided ample cover for this conspiracy."[38] The state in this way escalated the conflict, framing the Mangrove Nine as evidence not only of local tensions with the police, but of a growing challenge to the state's authority. Bringing the defendants to the Old Bailey and charging them with riot and affray, the DPP used the Mangrove case as an opportunity to discredit black politics as a threat to the stability of the polity.

DECOLONIZING THE COURTROOM: THE TRIAL AND
THE PUBLICITY CAMPAIGN

If the Mangrove trial offered an arena in which radical blackness could effectively be put on trial in Britain, it also provided a venue in which important new readings of the British state of the early 1970s could be publicly articulated. For the Mangrove defendants, this was conceptualized as a process of decolonizing the courtroom, demystifying its modes of operation, and demonstrating its present and historical links with racialized forms of state power and terror.

A major strategy of the Mangrove defendants was bringing the experiences of black oppression in Britain and globally into the courtroom, to contest the reading of racial violence provided by the police. The Mangrove Nine trial began at the Old Bailey on October 4, 1971, and lasted ten weeks, with significant media attention throughout. The defendants, recognizing the media interest, played to the gallery, using the trial to publicly criticize the judicial system. As their first move, they asked for an all-black jury, claiming that this was the only way they could defend their rights "against the deeply entrenched racist mentalities of white jurors." White jurors, they suggested, were "unrepresentative of the background from which we come" and "completely out of touch with the issues that affect our daily lives."[39] Judge Edward Clarke refused the request, but it gained significant press coverage. For Howe, the attempt "served to establish that we were prepared to attack all the worn out and repressive bourgeois legal procedures."[40] For similar reasons, both Jones-Lecointe and Howe chose to defend themselves, and they were later joined by Rhodan Gordon in this move. They used the license this afforded them to catalogue police harassment and brutality in Notting Hill for the jury, building a picture of a local black community beset by racist abuse, police violence, planted evidence, and unjustified raids on homes and businesses. Their speeches certainly carried a charge. The *Kensington Post*, which provided weekly updates on the trial, called Gordon's closing speech to the jury "dramatic," saying that it held the courtroom "spellbound for four hours." Howe's closing address—"the second 'blockbuster' defence closing speech"—was equally theatrical. Delivering his speech dressed all in black and standing, he said, "black and proud" in the dock, he "punctuat[ed] his three-hour speech with emphatic gestures," telling the court that the case "has opened issues, has seared the consciences of black people, to such an extent that history would not be written without it."[41]

In these "blockbuster" speeches, the Mangrove Nine aimed to launch a public critique of the post-imperial British state's authoritarian turn that could gain traction across left, radical, and libertarian politics. Unifying police and media readings of the demonstration was the suggestion that the violence of the Mangrove protest was the natural consequence of the criminality of the area and—intimately linked to this—the Black Power affiliations of the marchers. The Mangrove defendants offered a different reading of the violence. Black political organizations had long provided distinct readings of the social environment of the modern city as a space of state violence and oppression against the black subject, with a long colonial history behind it. In the Mangrove trial, these perspectives found their way into the courtroom.

The black radical press catalogued the abuses of the British police. The BPM *Black People's News Service*'s monthly forum enumerated the day-to-day encounters of black Britons with racism and exposed a world of police violence inconsistent with police and media accounts. Black pedestrians were bundled into police vans. Knives and drugs were planted in police stations. Heads were smashed against walls. Doctors denied signs of injury.[42] The brutality that followed the arrival of the police is accentuated by the mundane settings of so many of these encounters—en route to the barber; returning from the tailor; shopping; hanging out with friends. Snatched from the street and deposited in police cells, black people were transformed from ordinary pedestrians into objects of state oppression. For black activists, this was the face of the state, and it was some distance from the state-managed multicultural harmony promised in the race relations acts. The "community relations experts" of the 1970s, *Grassroots* would joke, satirizing the language of the race relations settlement, were not do-gooding social workers or youth club leaders, but helmeted, truncheon-wielding police (fig. 9).

These experiences and histories were brought into the courtroom during the Mangrove trial, where alternative readings of racism and the state were at the forefront of the case for the defense. In the testimonies of the Mangrove defendants, the marker of violence in the street came to be the police station, in which police violated and brutalized blacks, and from which police came to bring violence to the streets. Darcus Howe's claim during the demonstration that Notting Hill police station "was the station from which police officers went out to plant drugs on black people and where black people were beaten up"[43] shifted the locus of violence from the demonstrating crowd to the object of their demonstration. In court, Howe expanded on this, noting that following the demonstration, no fewer than fifty police officers had gone

FIGURE 9. "Your Community Relations Expert, 1971," cartoon in *Grassroots* 1, no. 4 (1971).

to the Mangrove Restaurant with the express aim of arresting Rupert Boyce. "I am suggesting to you that during the demonstration this heavy, organised, disciplined force led to the incidents in Portnall Road," Howe said.[44] The demonstrators, living under the constant threat of police violence, were "terrified," he told the court. Rhodan Gordon seconded this reading of events. Rejecting Judge Clarke's demand that the evidence of the defense refer only to the incidents of the demonstration itself, Gordon gave the court an account of black life in Notting Hill in which all aspects of black lives—from workplaces to homes and private parties—were open to the constant threat of police intervention and violence. In Gordon's testimony, it was the police who transgressed boundaries, entering black homes to break up gatherings and smash sound systems.[45]

In indicting British policing, Mangrove campaigners sought also to link it to a wider, global assault on black life. Certainly, the tensions present in Notting Hill expanded beyond the immediate district, and brought together the points of the black Atlantic. "The struggle of black people all over the world exploded on Portnall Road," Howe insisted in an interview following the demonstration.[46] The recent Black Power uprisings in Jamaica and Trinidad and Tobago, Howe recounted, were at the forefront of many minds. Another immediate context, as Howe also suggested, was the upsurge in state prosecutions of and violence against black radical leaders in the United States. Jonathan Jackson's tragic death at a California courthouse had happened only two days before the Mangrove demonstration. Black Panther Chairman Bobby Seale's 1969 trial as part of the Chicago 8 conspiracy also resonated. The Mangrove defense lawyer Ian MacDonald, a former CARD lawyer, used the image of Seale bound and gagged in a Chicago court in an attack on "naked judicial tyranny" at the Mangrove trial.[47]

In the lead-up to the trial, George Jackson's death and Angela Davis's arrest provided further points for comparison. At a London meeting commemorating George Jackson in September 1971, one month before the Mangrove Nine trial began, *Time Out* recorded that "the crowd's greatest response was reserved for an unidentified black woman who spoke on behalf of the Mangrove Nine."[48] At the opening of the trial, the BPM organized a "Freedom Meeting for Angela Davis and the Mangrove 9" in Brixton, with flyers reproducing a famous photograph of Davis in glasses and Afro alongside one of three white policemen holding a black demonstrator at the Mangrove demonstration.[49] The London-based Soledad Defence Committee further linked the cases. Their newsletters, reprinting much of the literature on George Jackson from the U.S. Black Panther Party's press, regularly intercalated this material with news of the Mangrove trial. One double-sided flyer presented the case for Angela Davis back to back with that of the Mangrove, adding that the "British power system is like the American and will get worse unless we act in whatever way we can to stop it." Inviting readers to see "how 'British justice' manifests itself," it described being "jostled by police in the specially restricted public gallery" at the Mangrove trial, seeing "the sterile unreality of a typical courtroom," and watching "Judge Clarke's antics." Charging Judge Clarke with adopting a patronizing tone, attempting to humiliate the defendants, deliberately obstructing the defense lawyers, aiding police witnesses, and leading the jury, they suggested that, as for Angela Davis in America, "British 'justice' does not exist."[50]

If the Mangrove Nine attempted to link British injustices synchronically to the experiences of black liberation in the United States and the Caribbean, they also sought to locate the racism of the British state diachronically in the long history of British colonialism. This, indeed, was crucial to their argument in court. "The judge says he has 35 years of legal experience," Howe told the court, in a remark declared by the *Guardian* to be "probably the most memorable comment on the confrontation made by any of those on trial." "Well, I have 400 years of colonial experience."[51] Howe set the tone for many of the Mangrove Nine's claims. By bringing the colonial past into the courtroom, he claimed a continuation from (neo)colonial periphery to metropolitan center and from colonial past to postcolonial present. It was an argument made often in the black radical press, and here the colonialism remembered was remembered as violence. "Why are we, Black people, here in Britain in the first place?" one BPM newsletter asked in a typical formulation. "We are in Britain not by choice or by chance but because of the historical fact that Britain first came to our countries." This was an experience of "plunder" and "ruthless violence," of "inhuman torture" from "Africa and Asia to the Caribbean and the Americas." Significantly, it was a history that did not stop in Britain. "Having been induced by Britain to make our homes here, Black people now face mounting Racism and Exploitation in Immigration, Employment, Housing, Education as well as increasing persecution and brutality by the police."[52] Confrontations with racism in Britain here became the last stage in a conflict four hundred years old. Colonialism, violence, and anticolonial struggle were "historical experiences which we brought to Britain in the depth of our consciousness."[53]

These forms for remembering the colonial past were also deployed in appeals to solidarity across racial lines. In a film made by the Mangrove defendants in the year following the trial, Althea Jones-Lecointe suggested that recognizing the British state as a colonial formation opened up anti-authoritarianism for white as well as black.

They say things like in *our* country and in *our* law it's been so for hundreds of years. They even fooling those white people because it hasn't been so for hundreds of years. Their men used to be sent off to the colonies. It used to be "off-with-their-heads" and they gone. They used to be hung drawn and quartered for stealing sheep and all kinds of things. So this whole thing [...] where its "hundreds of years" and "our law" and "you have these rights" and "nobody's saying you don't have no right to demonstrate"—that is a whole farce. What they fail to say is that it's not a question of "this law exists for hundreds of years." Black people were slaves by that same laws. Them same Old Bailey used to enslave black people and uphold that.[54]

For Jones-Lecointe, the claim to authority made by the courts—and, indeed, the claim to Britain as a modern liberal society—only worked by obscuring the position of the courts within a historic network of state violence that controlled the population in Britain and in the colonies. Here, Jones-Lecointe was contesting the narratives of liberal modernity through which British history was most readily publicly spoken. By highlighting the links between slavery and the historic control of populations within Britain through state terror and transportation, she was suggested that race had become a means of obscuring the wider coercive moves of a state that continued to erode freedoms across the polity. Indeed, she asserted that it was the white people whom the state was "fooling."

Policing in Britain often seemed close to its colonial precedents. In a raid on Notting Hill's Metro Youth Club in 1970, as *Black Voice* reminded its readers at the time, the police officer in charge had previously served in Anguilla "as one of those who led the suppression there" when British police and paratroopers were dispatched to the island in 1969. The arrest of four Fasimbas members at Oval station in 1972 was led by Detective Sergeant Ridgewell, a former officer in the Rhodesian police force.[55] Blacks might well thus claim to have a better perspective on policing in Britain than whites. Defending what he saw as their inevitable antagonism to the rising authoritarian measures of the British state in the early 1970s, one Panther claimed: "We are coming from a group of countries which agitated for Independence, which agitated for the overthrow of the Commonwealth, which agitated for the removal of colonialism; and therefore there is this fundamental difference between us and the workers coming from Europe."[56] It was a line the Panthers would often take, and in his later role as editor of *Race Today*, Darcus Howe made such readings central to the journal's editorial stance. Writing in early 1974, in the context of "the military presence in Northern Ireland, frigates on their way to Grenada, [and] troops and police mobilised to attack the miners" in Britain, he commented that "not since 1926 has the white section of the British working class faced such a test of strength." But, he added,

> We make the distinction between white and black because to the immigrant sections of the working class, the violence and brutality of imperial rule are not new experiences. [...] Much of what has gone down in the colonies—Africa, the Caribbean, Brixton, Handsworth and Notting Hill—has been concealed from the indigenous working class. [...] This in turn has led to a dangerous misconception of the nature of the police and the army. Somehow

the British police are different (the myth of the nice bobby); the army is the repository of good British gentlemanship; the courts, if carefully handled, can administer impartial British justice. [. . .] the white working class [. . .] have not for decades had to face the full implications of naked State power.[57]

For Howe, the British state was thus correctly viewed as a colonial formation, and black residents who had experienced de facto colonialism in the empire or Commonwealth, or whose near relations had, were best equipped to see this.

For the defendants and for some commentators both within and outside black radical organizations, the Mangrove trial was not only a means of clarifying the processes by which racial terror operated through the state, it also offered potential for this wider form of decolonization hinted at by Jones-Lecointe and Howe. As the *Sunday Times* journalist Derek Humphry commented, the defendants aimed to "cut through the jungle of court rules and niceties to say whatever [they] please[d], regardless of whether the judge thinks it relevant or admissible."[58] "The judge came with his orders from his masters which is this case is about a real situation involving people who are prepared to come and say what that situation is," Howe later noted, explaining the decision to defend himself at the Mangrove trial. "His responsibility is [. . .] to camouflage the entire situation of police brutality in this country."[59] *Grassroots* thus celebrated the Mangrove victory as the ability of the defendants "to shit-talk and bamboozle the police conspiracy." In an editorial celebrating the vernacular and carnivalesque qualities of black culture, the paper praised "the easy wit and ability to play around with the 'Man''s language, which characterised the excellent performance of the Mangrove defendants." "The Mangrove defendants," the editorial proposed, "did a remarkable thing, they managed to take the bla[c]k man's experience on the street with 'pig' troops into the clean law courts. They managed to take evidence that is usually classed as irrelevant to the legal presentation of cases, and to force the court to take recognition of that evidence."[60] Here, the "law of the law courts, which is mainly written down in books and tries to pretend to understand how a man performs a so-called 'criminal' act" was replaced with "the law of the streets and everyday living."[61]

Key to the Mangrove defense, and the aim of Jones-Lecointe, Howe, and Gordon in defending themselves and demanding an all-black jury, was this ability to bypass the restrictions of the court and to show how these regulated admissible evidence in a way that hid the structures and histories of institutional racism. This was also dramatized in Ian MacDonald's speeches. MacDonald "attacked the whole structure of the court," Jones-Lecointe recalled. "He tell the jury how the judge keep them under control. He tell the jury how the judge keep us under control. He tell the jury how the judge sit on high. [...] He exposed that whole structure and how it meant to psychologically terrorize ordinary people."[62] For the *Guardian* columnist John Heilpern, the trial marked a move toward the modernization of the court itself. In a biting commentary, Heilpern saw the archaism of the court broken by the intervention of these smiling, "brightly dressed" defendants.

> Judge Clarke, president of Staines Amateur Regatta, pink-faced with the corners of his mouth permanently downwards [...] yawns occasionally, jotting down notes, smiling only at the jury or barristers and ushers when they exit from the courtroom bowing low, shoes squeaking.
>
> The nine defendants look relaxed at this stage, a mixed bunch, brightly dressed, smiling at friends and conferring with advisers in the well of the court. At times, when the evidence is lengthy and complex, they seem to have dropped in on a gentlemanly debate which has little to do with them. On such occasions, they are like the rest of us. The judge rebukes a barrister in the manner of an Oxbridge tutor: the days drift by.
>
> But when the urbane and thoroughly English atmosphere of the court changes suddenly, as it has done when police officers have been called liars, the majesty of the court proceedings falters enough for a greater sense of reality to emerge.
>
> On these occasions, as the police officers look resolute and reply: "No, sir!" the gallery stirs and the black faces in the dock harden.[63]

Here, "black" experience provided a means for decolonizing both the formerly colonized and the former colonizers alike. In these readings, it was in fact only through the actions of the country's black communities that Britain could be finally brought into modernity. Heilpern contrasted the stuffy, old-fashioned, uptight representation of the court with the vibrant, vernacular, and direct voices of the defendants, voices whose intervention could provide "a greater sense of reality" than was accommodated by the archaism of the court.

Linking decolonization to changing social relations in the former imperial metropole, David Cannadine has suggested that "as the [British] imperial hierarchy faltered and fell abroad, the domestic hierarchy, which the empire had both replicated and reinforced, also began to lose credibility and conviction." Historical processes here sound like suspiciously passive phenomenon, but Cannadine's emphasis on "lessened respect for established institutions" as a "significant domestic consequence of the loss of empire," certainly carries some weight.[64] What Cannadine misses, however, and what the Mangrove trial highlighted, is how far this fraught struggle for domestic decolonization, and the limits to it, turned, not on forgetting class, but on remembering race. The Mangrove defendants contested police and judicial power by centering experiences of racial terror and racial violence. Becoming postcolonial, for white and black, turned on the recognizing this.

ESCALATING THE CONFLICT: CRISIS,
CONFRONTATION AND THE BRITISH STATE'S
AUTHORITARIAN TURN

In the Mangrove trial, the courtroom became a site from which the police and judiciary articulated discourses of race and criminality, and from which black activists sought to confront and challenge these. The courtroom's key place in the politics of race of the 1970s has long been noted, though the role of black defendants in the court has received less attention.[65] To understand the significance of the black challenge to the court in the Mangrove trial, however, we need to also see how it was knitted into a wider clash with the state for which the theatrical didacticism of the courtroom was key. In the escalating conflict between black politics and the state, the repressive arms of the state took increasingly dramatic measures to identify and arrest presumed political militants, and in the process near-criminalized *any* potential marker of affiliation to the cultures of blackness unleashed or given sustenance by the black liberation movements of the 1960s. This conflict was itself part of a wider historical shift under way in Britain since the mid-1960s, which gathered pace in the 1970s and culminated in the Thatcherite victory of 1979. These years, as E. P. Thompson would write in 1980, reflecting on the changes of the previous two decades, witnessed "the steady increment in the powers and presence of the state, the closure of 'consensual' political life, the incorporation of democratic process or the diversion of this into harmless ritual forms: in short, the advance of authoritarianism not only as ideology but as fact."[66]

For black politics, the Mangrove trial was only the latest episode in a longer state campaign marked by heavy-handed policing and police raids, high-profile trials and harsh sentences, the intervention of the government in the judicial process, and the criminalization of sections of the population and of cultural and political practices. This was often played out as a dimension of local campaigns against black community gatherings, but it was given saliency by the presumed threat that black political activity posed to the security of the state and the stability of the polity. In the months following Stokely Carmichael's visit in July 1967, as we saw in chapter 1, all the new Black Power leaders who had risen to prominence following Carmichael found themselves the objects of state attention. This continued through the late 1960s. "Black Activists are being accused of such violation of laws as inciting riots, creating affrays, behaving riotously, using insulting and obscene words and causing grievous bodily harm," *TriContinental Outpost* observed, reflecting on five years of state persecution and prosecution following the Mangrove Nine trial.[67] Its list of such prosecutions included the September 1967 trials of the Universal Coloured People's Association (UCPA)'s Alton Alexander Watson, Roy Sawh, Ajoy Ghose, and Michael Ezekiel, under the Race Relations Act, for speeches in Hyde Park; the November 1967 trial of the Racial Adjustment Action Society's Michael de Freitas, under the Race Relations Act, for a speech in Nottingham; the July 1968 trial of UCPA's Obi Egbuna, Peter Martin, and Gideon Dolo, under the Offences against the Person Act, for speeches in Hyde Park; the October 1968 trial of UCPA's Tony Soares for inciting people to riotous assembly during anti-Vietnam War protests; and the March 1970 charging of twenty-one protestors with threatening behavior, obstruction, using insulting words, and assault on the police at a demonstration against the imprisonment of the U.S. Black Panther leader Bobby Seale.[68]

Arrests and prosecutions of black activists continued apace in the early 1970s. The Caledonian Road Police Station affair occurred on July 27, 1970, after four young black men and a woman were arrested at an amusement park on Islington's Market Road. One hundred people marched on the police station where the young people were being held. The crowd, led by Michael de Freitas, demanded entry, and following a brief scuffle, eight were arrested, and five police officers and several of the crowd were treated for minor injuries.[69] Three months later, and only three weeks after the clash with police at the Mangrove demonstration, a police raid on a Black Panther dance at London's Oval House led to the arrest of several partygoers and the conviction of three BPM leaders on charges of assault on police, possession of weapons, and incitement to murder.[70] Two months after that, the police raided the Backayard Restaurant and the Metro Youth Club—a popular Notting Hill dance venue with a growing reputation for black "militancy." They also regularly harassed black mechanics at the garages where the Mangrove defendant Roddy Kentish worked.[71] At a further raid on the Metro Club in May 1971, ten were arrested, and four—the Metro 4—placed on trial at the Old Bailey on charges of causing grievous bodily harm and affray, only later to be acquitted in June 1972, following a widespread campaign by black activists.[72] In March 1972, only three months after the end of the Mangrove trial, four young Fasimbas members were arrested at London's Oval Underground Station on charges of pick-pocketing, soon instigating a prolonged campaign in their defense in the black radical press and *Race Today*. In April of the same year, Tony Soares, now leader of the Black Liberation Front (BLF), was again put on trial, this time for reprinting the recipe for a Molotov cocktail from the U.S. Black Panther Party's newspaper in the BLF's *Grassroots*.[73] By May 1972, prosecutions had been brought against members of all the main Black Power groups in London. When Detective Sergeant Westacott of the Special Branch was asked during Soares's trial whether it was his duty to investigate black political organizations, he confirmed that it was.[74]

While it was often the country's black populations who bore the brunt of it, authoritarian statecraft, and the rise of what Stuart Hall would term "authoritarian populism," extended beyond just the politics of race, launched on several fronts at once, as the embryonic new social and political movements of the 1960s were met with a conservative backlash.[75] Black activists took a lead in pointing to this wider authoritarian turn and calling for a wide alliance to combat it. Situating the Mangrove trial within its wider contexts, the *Black Liberator* took stock in September 1971:

> Is it not true that against the peoples of the five continents, against every weak nation and nationality, world fascism moves on the offensive? Take Britain alone since January. An incomplete picture of growing fascism is this: the continued suppressions of the Irish people, introduction of the Immigration and Industrial Relations Bills, the proposed thirty per cent pay rise for the pigs (as further incentive to repress the working people), suppression of the GPO, Pilkingtons and Ford strikes, the Sunderland Road bombing incident, the BUFP, BPM, Oval House, Mangrove, Metro, Oz and now the Jake Prescott and Ian Purdie arrests and trials.[76]

As the *Black Liberator* reminded its readers, it was not just in the field of racism and black politics—"the BUFP, BPM, Oval House, Mangrove, Metro [. . . and] the Sunderland Road bombing"[77]—that the current crisis was playing out. Since the Royal Ulster Constabulary's attack on a civil rights march in Derry in October 1968, the civil rights struggle in Northern Ireland had become a significantly bloodier affair, escalating further with the joint loyalist and police attack on protestors at the so-called Battle of Bogside in August

1969, and increasing paramilitary action on both sides. In 1971, the passage of the Emergency Powers Act allowed for the mass internment of people suspected of being involved with the Irish Republican Army, a process begun in August of that year. This ramping-up of the state's repressive powers through new legislation was also occurring in mainland Britain in 1971. The 1971 Immigration Act gave police and immigration officers new powers of arrest (without warrant) and detention, which were used extensively once the Act came into effect; the original Immigration Bill had also proposed requiring migrating Commonwealth citizens to register with the police, though this clause was defeated.[78] The 1971 Industrial Relations Act required the official registration of unions, established a National Industrial Relations Court to judge "unfair practices," including sympathy striking, and gave ministers a right to suspend any strike, and to impose a sixty-day pause and compulsory postal ballot.[79] Meanwhile, the 1971 Misuse of Drugs Act substantially increased sentences for drug offenses, while the 1971 New Criminal Damages Act widened the scope of acts that could be prosecuted under the offense of "damage," and allowed for harsher sentences for such prosecutions.[80]

As the *Black Liberator* signaled, this creeping authoritarianism in parliamentary legislation was matched by a series of defeated strikes, with the defeats often blamed on collusion among union leaders, industrialists, and the government. The General Post Office (GPO) workers' strike in early 1970 ended, after six bitter weeks, with a pay deal well below the 13 percent initially demanded, in a climb-down that many rank-and-file strikers attributed to an undemocratic union leadership in league with the government.[81] A strike by glassworkers at the St Helen's Pilkingtons factory in Lancashire in the spring of 1970 led to similar dissatisfaction with union leaders, and thousands broke ranks with their union to continue the strike unofficially. From the picket line, many strikers were picked up by police for minor offenses and summarily sentenced to prison by local magistrates.[82] In early 1971, 42,000 Ford workers came out on strike, demanding parity of pay with Midlands car workers. The strikers faced the wrath of Henry Ford II, who threatened to pull his investments from Britain if the government did not act to prevent such strikes. In the eventual settlement reached, in which workers lost their demand for parity, secret negotiations between trade union leaders, the government, and Ford management were again accused of bypassing the rank and file.[83]

These various moves by which some aspects of the rising economic and political crisis were managed by the state, introducing new disciplinary powers and trying out new tactics in fighting rising industrial unrest, went along with a concerted effort in the courts to prosecute people identified as responsible for the social and political crisis engulfing Britain. Running concurrently to the Mangrove Nine trial was the trial of Jake Prescott and Ian Purdie, also held at the Old Bailey in November and December 1971. This trial was part of a wider public campaign to identify and prosecute the Angry Brigade—a left-libertarian group formed in the late 1960s and responsible for a series of bombings of government and commercial properties in 1970–72. Led by Detective Chief Superintendent Roy Habershon, the high-profile campaign against the Angry Brigade often relied on the theatre of state power. Habershon conducted numerous police raids against hundreds of people, including well-known pop music and counterculture figures. His heavy-handed tactics at one point led to twenty-five people being arrested without charge at Barnett police station, with two men being held for a total of seventy-two hours without charge, and many denied access to a solicitor. The eventual questioning and charging of those alleged to be involved with the group was plagued by accusations of police brutality and forced confessions. Eventually Prescott and Purdie were identified as members of the Angry Brigade and put on trial for conspiring to carry out the bombings. Five months later, eight further suspected Angry Brigade members were put on trial at the Old Bailey, in what would become the longest trial in British legal history.[84]

But while the Angry Brigade posed an undeniable threat, if not to public safety then certainly to the credibility of state security,[85] Habershon's tactics found echoes, too, in far less likely places. In the summer of 1971, as the Mangrove defendants and Prescott and Purdie awaited their appearance at the Old Bailey, other equally landmark trials were occurring. Following a raid on the offices of Stage One—the publishers of controversial Danish pamphlet *The Little Red Schoolbook*, which offered advice on drugs, sex, and contraception to school children—the publisher Richard Handyside was prosecuted in Lambeth Magistrates' Court and convicted of publishing obscene material. The case generated much media attention and the campaign against *The Little Red Schoolbook*, spearheaded by Mary Whitehouse, succeeded in having the book banned following the trial.[86] Barely three weeks after Handyside's conviction, an obscenity trial began against the counterculture magazine *OZ*. Like *The Little Red Schoolbook* trial, the *OZ* trial had begun with police raids. The countercultural press of the late 1960s was subject to continued raids throughout its existence, most relating to obscenity charges, drug searches, or, as the Angry Brigade saga reached its peak, suspected terrorism conspiracies. After a series of raids over two years, *OZ*'s sister publication *International Times (IT)* was prosecuted in 1969 for publishing contact ads for gay men. However, it was the raiding of *OZ*'s office by Detective Inspector Luff and the Obscene Publications Squad in the summer of 1970 that had the most tumultuous outcome. The trial often bordered on the farcical, but the sentences—though later revoked—were punitive.[87]

The Mangrove trial was part of this wider series of high-profile trials of the early 1970s in which the traditions of libertarianism, New Left politics, and labor disputes of the 1960s were challenged by an ascendant politics of law and order. The reams of press debate generated by these high-profile public trials saw them functioning in a similar mode to those public trials of the 1950s that Frank Mort has proposed as "major interpretative devices," dramatizing contemporary anxieties and leading to significant changes in social mood.[88] Through draconian powers granted to the police and the judiciary, these cases mapped out those who were on the side of "society" against those seen to be conspiring for its downfall.[89] The set-piece courtroom battles of the early 1970s dramatized this growing crisis on a public stage and through public spectacle. This created the conditions for new alliances, and black activists worked to give their critique of the postcolonial British state wider public traction.

BUILDING ALLIANCES

The blacks are in the front ranks of the battlefield. But the rest of us will be there soon.

ALAN BRIEN,
"Soledad Brothers and Sisters"[90]

In the Mangrove trial and its aftermath, thinking black meant reading the current and historical experiences of racial state violence to retell the 1970s British state as a colonial formation, and to point to how its techniques of racial division served to mask its wider authoritarian moves. The final section of this chapter traces the wider support for the Mangrove Nine and British black radical politics, and shows how their critiques of the state translated out across sections of the social formation. These translations out were limited and partial, and in some cases involved others appropriating the capital of black politics for their own purposes. In this respect, black activists fought both with and against a wider left and libertarian formation that they hoped to rework through the promise of thinking black. Despite the challenges involved, the Mangrove trial and its effects significantly influenced the way radical libertarian and left politics in Britain were reworked through black politics.

Black activists often made appeals for alliance, but these frequently fell on deaf ears. As Satnam Virdee has noted, in the rising tide of class politics of the late 1960s and early 1970s, there was no concomitant rise of anti-racist politics. "In fact, in those early years of intensifying class confrontation between 1968 and 1972, the white working class and its institutions remained resolutely indifferent to the struggles being waged by black workers against discriminatory practices."[91] Indeed, Powellism drew much of its support from the white working class, and the most dramatic immediate crisis provoked by Powell in 1968 was a nationwide series of blue-collar strikes in support of his "Rivers of Blood" speech. Within the labor movement, apart from a few belated critical statements focusing on Powell's anti-union credentials, there was little organized opposition to Powellism.[92] When the Heath government sought to further racialize the conditions of British citizenship in the 1971 Immigration Bill, there were again few campaigns from within the organized trade union movement. While black radicals consistently campaigned on two fronts, linking the Immigration Bill with the Industrial Relations Bill, which they saw to be its natural counterpart, the Trades Union Congress (TUC), as Robert Miles and Annie Phizacklea observed, "had nothing to say" on the Immigration Act.[93] As Virdee notes, it was not until the later 1970s that mass solidarity campaigns against racism became a reality with the Grunwick strike, Rock against Racism, and the Anti-Nazi League.[94]

There were pockets of sympathy for black radical and anti-racist politics on the wider British Left. Jodi Burkett's study of largely middle-class left-wing pressure groups of the 1960s shows growing support for anti-racist politics over the course of this decade, though this often remained a side issue among predominantly white groups.[95] The radical Left of the labor movement, gaining ground in the late 1960s and early 1970s, as the postwar labor settlement was eroding, was also home to some important anti-racist campaigns.[96] The *Morning Star* newspaper (formerly the *Daily Worker*) consistently supported Angela Davis throughout her period of incarceration. When Davis's sister Fania Jordan arrived in Britain in October 1971 for a speaking tour, the paper gave daily updates on her movements and implored its readers to attend her rallies. Among these was a rally held on the picket of the striking

Ford Dagenham workers, at which she collected hundreds of signatures of support, and sold copies of Davis's *If They Come in the Morning* (1971) and "dozens of badges and photographs."[97] And while Davis, a communist, might expect the ready support of the *Morning Star* and some of the Ford picketers, this also provided a platform for the campaigns of and for British black radicals. As the *Morning Star* also reported, when Jordan spoke in support of Davis at a rally at Westminster's Central Hall, she readily connected Davis's incarceration to "the bloody repression of the Irish Civil Rights Movement, the imminent passage of the racist Immigration Bill, the proposed entrance into the Common Market, and the new Industrial Relations Bill, directed against the working people."[98] Appearing on stage beside her, too, were figures representing this coalition of radical politics: Sid Harraway, a Ford Dagenham shop steward convener, Jack Woddis of the Communist Party's International Department (a late stand-in for Jimmy Reid, shop steward of the Upper Clyde Shipbuilders), Mike Terry of the National Union of Students, Tennyson Makawane of the African National Congress, and the Manchester black radical leader Ron Phillips. Indeed, the Communist Party had aimed to link these struggles before, organizing a march on the U.S. Embassy and Downing Street in the month previous, which aimed to "protest against racialism, linking the shooting of George Jackson and the trial of Angela Davis in the United States with the Tories' haste to pass their Immigration Bill [. . .] which is 'openly racialist and based on colour discrimination.'"[99]

Black radical activists, however, accused the Communist Party of opportunism. The Communist Party's "familiar pattern of instinctive racialism," the *Black Liberator*'s Cecil Gutzmore argued, writing on their Angela Davis Campaign, made "a mockery of its participation in the struggle to free a black revolutionary."[100] Also writing in *Black Liberator*, Gary Burton, president of the radicalized West Indian Students Union, complained that "the British Communist Party have both passed resolutions and indulged in empty rhetoric about racism in England. But they have [. . .] evaded their duty to throw the whole of their organisation and resources into a public and sustained attack on racist oppression in England."[101] Despite the wealth of funds plowed into the Angela Davis Campaign by the Communist Party, Burton noted, the Party had never "set up a real, not paper, campaign against British racism (to say nothing of its own organic racism, paternalism and chauvinism)." His charge held water: as he also noted, at the Westminster Central Hall rally for Angela Davis, "Members of black revolutionary groups and of the Mangrove Nine who spoke did so as a result of a private unofficial arrangement with myself." And Burton, despite his membership to the Communist Party–funded Angela Davis Campaign and his role as chair at the Central Hall rally, was repeatedly frozen out of the campaign's strategizing, and his suggestions only ever reluctantly conceded. The Angela Davis Campaign, for Burton, was not about joining or supporting anti-racism and black politics, but about "containing black liberation," and aiming to win over the energy of an emergent independent black political movement to boost their own cause.[102] Crucially, Burton also doubted that the Communist Party was really listening to Davis when she urged recognition of how race stratified class or emphasized the significance of black and anti-racist politics for the success of socialism.

Others on the Left, however, were readier, not only to support black radical activists, but to reorientate their own politics through a black radical perspective. The Mangrove demonstration and trial were crucial here. In October 1970, the Black Defence Committee (BDC) formed in London as "a militant group to counter racist and fascist activities."[103] Formed in response to the Mangrove affair and headed by the Mangrove regular Tariq Ali, the Committee was based in the offices of the Trotskyist International Marxist Group (IMG). Its initial march, on October 31, 1971, followed the route of the Mangrove protest, passing the Harrow Road, Notting Hill, and Notting Dale police stations, and "the major targets of police repression in the area"—the Mangrove, the Backayard, and the Metro. The march of a few hundred protestors brought together a wide radical Left alliance, including representatives from the IMG, the Revolutionary Marxist-Leninist League, Goldsmiths College Socialist Society, Essex University Socialist Society, and the People's Association (a broad-based Notting Hill organization for community action), as well as individual members of the Communist Party, the Young Communist League, International Socialism, and the Irish Solidarity Campaign.[104]

The BDC aimed to work with black radical groups and build a broad alliance, seeking "to demonstrate to the authorities that if they attempted to strike against the militant black organizations they would meet not just resistance from that quarter but from the whole of the revolutionary left, from the student movement, from Irish militants in England and from the vanguard of the working class itself."[105] From January 1971, the BDC established a Black Defence and Aid Fund, "to raise funds to assist black people and organisations faced with mounting legal bills and fines," targeting "white sympathisers," trade unions and political groups for donations.[106] At a campaign later that year against the 1971 Immigration Bill, the platform included Tariq Ali, the Northern Irish civil rights campaigner Bernadette Devlin MP, the anti-apartheid activist Peter Hain, Tony Polan of the International Socialists, and speakers from the Indian Workers' Association, the Black Panther Movement, and the Black Liberation Front.[107] The group also worked with black radicals as it grew, with new branches beyond London established on the back of Black Panther Movement's speaking tours—a detail that also suggests the commitment the Panthers had to sustaining the alliance. Soon they were campaigning on a raft of cases championed by the black radical press, including not only the police campaign against the Mangrove, but harassment of Backayard and the Metro and the police beating of Joshua Francis in Brixton, a campaign that was central to the early growth of the Black Panthers in that neighborhood.[108]

The IMG, both working through the BDC and independent of it, was the most active of the radical Left groups fighting for justice for blacks along with black radical activists. In contrast to the Communist Party, it was also outspoken on the need to reorientate class politics in Britain in recognition of the insights of black radicalism. *Red Mole*, a paper put out by the IMG activists and BDC founders Tariq Ali and Robin Blackburn, criticized those "Left groups who put out propaganda aimed at recruiting blacks directly to their own organisation" and urged them, not only to recognize many black activists' suspicion of the white radical Left—not least because of its lack of engagement with anti-racist politics—but to recognize the particular vantage point open to black people on the state's authoritarian turn.[109] "It is this constant process of what Huey Newton calls 'learning through direct experience' which quickly radicalizes black people and leads them towards acquiring a revolutionary consciousness generally ahead of the white working class," Lucy Gray contended in *Red Mole*. [110] The Mangrove Nine trial had done more than any of the other show trials of the early 1970s to highlight the growing politicization of the justice system, Steve Cohen argued in the same publication; the Left, he thought, could learn from it.[111]

The Mangrove demonstration also achieved wide support from the countercultural press.[112] The counterculture had long engaged with black radicalism in Britain. Not only had the Dialectics of Liberation congress in July 1967 hosted Stokely Carmichael as one of its most vocal and controversial participants, but the Anti-University, established in London's Shoreditch in 1968 under the direction of Allen Krebs, both reprinted literature of the U.S.

Black Power movement for its classes and boasted Obi Egbuna and Roy Sawh among its staff.[113] Michael de Freitas, meanwhile, was not only appointed an early director of Alexander Trocchi's Project Sigma, but became involved with the photographer and journalist John Hopkins in the London Free School in Notting Hill, and was a regular contributor to the various counter-culture publications.[114] Sebastian Clarke, a young black poet closely involved with the radicalized West Indian Students' Centre, began, in 1969, to write for *Friends*, *International Times (IT)*, and *Time Out*, as did *Hustler!*'s founder, Courtney Tulloch, while Darcus Howe wrote for the magazine *Seven Days*. Funding for black radical ventures was also drawn from important countercultural and libertarian figures. John Lennon and Yoko Ono funded de Freitas's Black House, and John Berger had financed the purchase of a Black Panther Movement headquarters in Finsbury Park. The Mangrove, as we have seen, was also regularly patronized by counterculture celebrities.

This is an important history of intellectual exchange. The networks and publications of the counterculture and black radicalism in London became steadily interconnected. Studies on the formation of the counterculture in Britain have been curiously reticent in addressing the position of black political and cultural developments and their place in this history,[115] and yet in the back of the countercultural newspapers can be found advertisements for black radical materials; in the pages of the same papers black radical figures are interviewed, provide their own copy, and even edited editions. Such connections are visible in the black radical press as well. The libertarianism of the counterculture—Jim Haynes, editor of *IT*, saw its politics. for example, as "extreme libertarianism and the bias towards an individual's right to do with his or her mind and body what he or she wanted to do"[116]—dovetailed well with a black political culture that also put a premium on liberty of the body.[117] Shared also was an emphasis on style and pleasure. However, it was in the flip side to this, in the critique of the state developed in both cultures of radical blackness and the counterculture, that the most significant convergences occurred.

The state crackdown on "permissiveness" gained in strength in 1967 with the high-profile trial of Mick Jagger for drug possession in June and the establishment of Regional Drug Squads in July, realizing a routinized victimization through which, as Caroline Coon noted, "young people with long hair may be stopped and searched for really no other reason than they are perceived as being of a suspect generation."[118] Coon's reaction was to establish Release, an organization with its headquarters in *OZ*'s office, which provided legal advice and support for those arrested on drug charges. She was influenced by a similar outfit, Defence, established in 1966 by Michael de Freitas, Colin MacInnes, Frank Critchlow, and Courtney Tulloch in response to the police harassment and framing of blacks in North Kensington on charges of living off immoral earnings and possession of marijuana.[119] Convergences such as this were the outcome of the counterculture springing up in those neighborhoods in which black Britons had already faced years of police brutality, particularly as black activists became involved in counterculture projects. The British counterculture was also influenced directly by African American politics. *IT*, as the magazine's editor Tom McGrath recalled, had itself been influenced by the literature of the U.S. Civil Rights movement, while *Friends* began reprinting the literature of the U.S. Black Panthers after a friend of the editor returned from the United States newly acquainted with the black radical literature there.[120] It was in such countercultural publications—which, as one contemporary journalist commented, necessarily had a "sharper eye on the index of oppression"—that the Mangrove trial and the Prescott-Purdie and *Oz* trials received the most extensive coverage.[121] The lexicon of radical blackness became a central vocabulary for these periodicals through which political opposition to the rise of an authoritarian state could be expressed.

Within the countercultural press of the late 1960s and early 1970s, one symbol, above all, was ubiquitous: the pig. In tracing the life of the word "pig" in the underground press, we can gain some sense of how far the politics of the counterculture borrowed from and reworked a black radical inheritance. The U.S. Black Panther Party promoted the derogatory application of the word to its enemies in the late 1960s as part of an effort to create a new political vocabulary. "We have to have some terms that adequately define the police and fascist bigots who commit murder, brutalize, and violate people's constitutional rights," said Huey Newton.[122] Through the U.S. Black Panthers, "pig" became a keyword of black radical cultures, a term capable of carrying "particular formations of meaning—ways not only of discussing but of seeing many of our central experiences."[123] It crystallized, in the late 1960s, as a "significant, indicative word [that] bound together certain ways of seeing culture and society" that could articulate a whole politics.[124]

In the pages of the underground press, "pig" became a common sign from the late 1960s on, initially appearing most frequently in reference to U.S. politics, and in the reproduction of U.S. Black Power material, through which the cartoon images of pigs in police uniforms became familiar copy.[125] The Mangrove demonstration hastened the reproduction of this language in coverage of British black politics, both as statements of the British Black Panthers were afforded column space, and as editorials and opinion pieces offered their own coverage.[126] The term was also quickly expanded in its reference beyond just police confrontations with Britain's black communities. In the months following the Mangrove trial, we see the language of "pigs" used variously to describe the police reaction to the "Garden House" protest of fifteen Cambridge students against Greek colonels, Tower Hamlets Council's efforts to evict squatters, and the Labour government's legislation on drugs and immigration; and to link the police and government's reactions to the Angry Brigade with the Mangrove case and with police confrontations at the Metro.[127]

Police assaults on black political and cultural centers were connected to a wider stepping up of state power. *Frendz*, for example, drew connections between the Prescott-Purdie trial, the *OZ* trial, the *Little Red Schoolbook* trial, and the "Oval House riot" ("which the pigs caused and the Black Panthers were convicted of"), naming the latest instance as just "another political trial, another attack on the alternative society and our style."[128] On August 22, 1970, just weeks after the Mangrove demonstration, a group calling themselves the Community Liberation Front held a "Pig of the Month" rally at Trafalgar Square, and *Frendz* magazine made this an annual event, holding competitions inviting readers to vote for their Pig of the Year. The January 1972 "Pig of the Year Contest" elected candidates from Police Constable Pulley (chief witness in Mangrove trial), to Commander Bond and Detective Superintendent Habershon (pursuing the Angry Brigade), Chief Inspector Kelaher (of the Drugs Squad, and recently charged with corruption), Police Sergeant Kitching (a Leeds police officer convicted of the murder of the homeless Nigerian David Oluwale), and Detective Inspector Luff (who led the raids on *OZ*).[129] Here a cross-section of police officers from across the country, all with rumors or convictions of misconduct surrounding them, were presented as evidence of a concerted attack on personal liberties.

In these various incarnations the symbol of the "pig" was used to link up the terrains of state oppression. Assessing the Mangrove fallout, *Ink*, which marketed itself as an alternative political broadsheet, took the opportunity to emphasize the importance of understanding the new political lexicon such events popularized if the current historical moment was to be viewed for what it was. "It shows no awareness to call the police pigs while secretly believing that they're just ordinary people doing a job dictated by the law of the land which they are as powerless to change as you or I," read the editorial.

"That this is untrue should, by now, be terrifyingly obvious to everyone whose head is not completely buried in the sand of apathy. The police force is the front line of repression, and the army waits only paces behind."[130] This new keyword of the counterculture, then, demanded not just a substitution ("police" to be replaced with "pig"), but an overhaul of how the role of the police in British society should be viewed. We thus cannot fully appreciate the politics and thought of the counterculture without recognizing the importance of this cultural vocabulary in organizing its ways of seeing.

Crucial to the observations of the *Ink* editorial was that the ascendancy of "pig" as a keyword was a redefinition of policing in Britain. Inscribed onto the body of the police officer were two competing narratives: the "indulgent tradition" of the "English Bobby,"[131] and the Black Power image of the "pig." "Unfortunately we live in a country [with] an unparalleled faith in the honesty and incorruptibility of the police," *Friends* lamented. [132] Richard Neville likewise predicted that although "discrepancies have emerged from police evidence" in the Mangrove and Angry Brigade cases, "one suspects its impact on the jury will be dulled by the persisting, although declining, myth of the honest Bobby struggling daily on low pay to help old ladies cross the road."[133] *OZ* concurred that the production of such myths "succeeds in obscuring from us the real role of the police. It obscures from us and makes it very difficult for many people to believe that the police tell lies, take bribes, frame people, employ crude forms of torture and have set up a special branch to spy on you, if you are critical of society and have the audacity to do something about it." For *OZ*, this dissociated the image of the British bobby "from all that police brutality which foreigners have to suffer."[134]

The inscription of the image of the "pig" policeman, borrowed from the readily visible history of racial violence and police brutality in the United States and disseminated through the culture of black protest in Britain, was an attempt to reject the myths of the exceptional fairness and good conduct of the British police. Countercultural attempts to read "pig" assaults on the counterculture as equivalent to racist police brutality were, of course, problematic. Richard Neville and his co-defendants at the *OZ* trial, for example, were forced to cut their hair for their Old Bailey appearances, but they did not report the same levels of violence that were evident in the BPM's carefully compiled accounts of policing in Brixton and Notting Hill. In this respect, as in the appropriations of the Angela Davis and Mangrove case by sections of the Communist Party, reworking thinking black into new contexts always carried the risk of subsuming some of the themes that were closest to the hearts of those activists who worked to make such ways of thinking common currency. These, though, are the risks of any political project as it expands, making a bid to become part of a wider public culture. The Mangrove Nine case is significant for how, occurring at a moment of heightened conflict in the shift toward the law-and-order politics of the 1970s and drawing in a diverse crowd of actors, black campaigners managed to stage its narrative as an interpretative device for understanding the wider structures and shifts of British society at that time.

CONCLUSION

The Mangrove Nine built up a coalition of support from their connections to the cosmopolitan cultures of Notting Hill, from those sympathetic to their position because they were experiencing assaults on their own liberties, from those sympathetic to the widely publicized cases of state persecution of black political leaders in the United States, particularly of the Soledad Brothers and Angela Davis—to whom the Mangrove activists lost no opportunity to compare themselves—and from those hoping to build broad radical Left alliances in the context of a postcolonial New Left politics. The concerted publicity campaign of the Mangrove Nine and their supporters brought the case to a national audience. In this, as we have seen, many critical of the state, on the lookout for a new political solution to the current crisis, were ready to ask how far black experience in Britain, and the colonial histories that tied black Britons to a wider global conjuncture, might be necessary to formulating this new politics.

The ambition and reach of black radical politics, in this respect, was far beyond the numbers of those active in various campaigns or organizations. In this era of "third world" revolution and seismic changes in the politics of decolonization, many on the Left, as Ian Birchall notes, were ready to believe "that the locus of revolutionary change had shifted," away from the old imperial metropolitan centers.[135] Black radical activists sought to demonstrate their own politics as the locus of this change within the metropole itself, connected up to these wider, global movements, offering their politics as the route out of what was an increasingly entrenched political crisis. In stressing the significance of race, colonialism, and the politics of decolonization, thinking black showed how blackness, both in the colonies and in the metropole, marked the limits of state accountability and the rule of law.

"History has placed us on the right side of the barricade," the *Black Liberator* insisted.[136]

It would be easy to overstate the reach of such thinking. Certainly, as we have seen, even within the broad Left of this period there was much disagreement, and perhaps even a failure to recognize that this tradition of thinking black existed at all, let alone that it might have something to say to them. Nonetheless, the Mangrove Nine trial marked a significant turning point in the expansion of the political-cultural formation of radical blackness that this book traces, bringing in many groups who might previously have been distanced both from the protests and political causes of black radicals and from their ways of seeing. In the next chapter, we turn to another form of black radical critique of the state, in the black education movement of the 1960s–1980s, and look at its connections to a wider radical Left and libertarian spectrum, and the ways in which it foregrounded "thinking black" as the solution to the growing political crisis of this era.

FOUR

Black Studies

"IN THE STAFFROOM OF THE SCHOOL at which I first taught," Farukh Dhondy remembered in 1978 of his first teaching appointment in Clapham, South London, "nobody talked about 'class.' It was as though the word didn't exist in the vocabulary. All the teachers talked about was blacks."[1] Class was the watchword of the education politics of the postwar settlement. When Dhondy began teaching in the late 1960s, "comprehensivization" of the British educational system—a policy that, drawing on the language of the U.S. civil rights movement, advocated the abandonment of grammar schools as "desegregation"—was at its height under Harold Wilson's Labour Party government. Dhondy's first appointment was at a school undergoing precisely this process of comprehensivization: the grammar school was merging with two local comprehensives, which had closed down. He had expected to confront a politics of class. When studying at Cambridge in the mid-1960s, in all the education journals he read, "The problem was a class problem, and [. . .] the Labour Party would sort all that out." Instead, he found a crisis of race: "It was panic." The headmaster responded to comprehensivization by dividing the school into eleven classes, the top of which were "exclusively white," the bottom of which "were black." Reflecting on his experiences teaching, Dhondy agreed that schooling in Britain was in crisis. For him, however, this was a crisis of the school as a "political institution," and race— or, more precisely, blackness—was not its cause, but its solution. "Black pupils are an active force in the politics of schooling," Dhondy proposed. This was the opportunity for the "decolonisation [of] British schooling."

In the Mangrove Nine trial, explored in the previous chapter, critiques of the British state's authoritarian turn were channeled through the experiences of black Britons on the front line of conflict with the police and judicial system. Many people, across the New Left and counterculture and beyond, used the Mangrove Nine trial to take stock of the relations of state and society in Britain at the beginning of the 1970s, and to think about Britain's role as a postimperial, multicultural formation. This chapter turns to another terrain in which the political crises of the 1970s were refracted through apprehensions of blackness: the education system. The education system, as historians have long noted, was an institution at the heart of postwar social democracy. But by the late 1960s, the settlement that had prevailed since the 1944 Butler Education Act, first under the tripartite system and later under comprehensivization, was fracturing. Despite a public cross-party consensus on comprehensivization, many in the Conservative Party were never reconciled to the comprehensive drive. Emboldened by panics around the student unrest of the late 1960s, this rump in the Conservative Party revived criticism of comprehensivization by publishing an influential series of education Black Papers between 1969 and 1975 that attacked "progressive" education, teacher control of the curriculum, and the lack of parental choice. The case made in these was furthered by the 1975 Bullock report on reading abilities; the 1976 report by Neville Bennett and his colleagues on *Teaching Styles and Pupil Progress;* the controversy over the radically "child-centred" William Tyndale Junior School in the mid-1970s; and successive press reports of failing schools. In 1976, conceding many of these criticisms, Labour Prime Minister James Callaghan's "great debate" on education made the case for slashing school funding. With the consensus on comprehensivization breaking down, support for "progressive" education in question, and schools evidently unable to redress the problems of the reproduction of class inequalities, education was in crisis.[2]

For all the many contradictions bound up in this crisis, Dhondy's experience in his Clapham staffroom suggests that race played a key role in how the crisis was lived on the ground. The crisis may have been brought about, as critics at the time noted, by the strains of the postwar social democratic settlement. The education settlement promised the impossible, and this impossibility became acute with the economic decline and political turmoil of the 1970s. It promoted education to a central place in the provision of a new social democratic order, investing in it the possibilities of a social change that in reality it could never effect.[3] But as this promise failed, Dhondy and many of his contemporaries argued, black students often got the blame. And as schools struggled to negotiate tightening budgets, increased student numbers, and the ruptures caused by reorganization, black students were often the first casualties of the crisis. At the same time, though, in a new black education movement and in a rising radical education politics—the one often a part of the other—black children became the focus for a reformulation of education itself, and the locus of a promise for pursuing the possibilities failed in the postwar education settlement. In this, radical educationalists placed their hopes for resolving the crisis of the education system in those same black children blamed by others for that crisis. Advocates of the black education movement saw their attempts to set free the radical potential of these black children—indeed, to make them *black* children—as at the heart of a new conception of what education in Britain might become.

This chapter uses a study of autobiographical writing practices in the black education movement as a way into showing why the education of black schoolchildren assumed a particular significance in debates over the future of education in this crisis. Autobiographical writing played a major part in the development of postwar "progressive" education, embraced as a route to realizing the democratic promise of the 1944 Butler Act.[4] The initial promise of such writing was that it would allow working-class children, newly welcomed as social-democratic citizens, to develop a sense of their self-worth and their stake in society. It was, in this respect, a fairly anodyne pursuit, and the writing involved was geared to the mundane. As it was revived by radical educators in the 1970s, however, autobiographical writing took on a more directly confrontational bent, geared to the political struggles of the day. In the black education movement, this brought a different tradition of democratizing writing practices to the forefront, with its history not in the extension of the franchise or the implementation of a social democratic state, but the struggle for decolonization and the challenging of a racialized social and political order. Black children came to hold a symbolically significant place in the education crisis in large part because they combined the two most overloaded sites of contemporary political conflict: the school and multiculturalism. This also led radical educators vigorously to take up the issues of black writing, black studies, and the role of black children and black culture in reformulating schooling. We can trace this history of how questions of black experience, culture, and politics reformulated the politics of education through following the development of writing practices in the black education movement, and through the ways in which the question of black studies as it was first articulated within this movement was fed back into discussions of the multicultural school in the 1970s and 1980s.

Dhondy was not alone in finding that both the blame for and the consequences of a strained and failing education system fell on the heads of black pupils. Certainly, the difficulties of managing working-class children was a common complaint among schoolteachers, particularly as comprehensivization led to significant changes in the makeup of most schools. In teachers' complaints about teaching working-class children, we can see how far the crisis of the education settlement was determined also from below, on the ground among the teachers, and not only among party strategists and campaigners. But insofar as these teachers experienced and explained this as a crisis of class, it was one refracted frequently through race. Marina Maxwell, a Jamaican teacher working, in the late 1960s at schools in Brent, ten miles north of Dhondy, found staffrooms fixated on their black pupils. Offering a "Sample of staffroom fare" for readers of *Race Today* in 1969, Maxwell reported a constant "general refrain about this one or that black," and a torrent of abusive language: "the bastards—blockheads—black-faced bastards [. . .] in the staffrooms [. . .] the children are being attacked, slandered, denigrated."[5] Staffroom ire was not exclusively reserved, in Maxwell's experience, for black children—"teachers, middle class and climbing, care little for the 'children of navvies.'" And yet, Maxwell observed, "There is a built-in class prejudice to start with, and multiply that by BLACK. Multiply that by all the black children in schools, be they from Africa, India, Pakistan or the West Indies."[6] The Guyanese teacher Beryl Gilroy, teaching in North London schools—and confronting periodic racism from children and fellow teachers—since the mid-1950s, similarly noticed a change in teachers' attitudes toward black children in the 1960s. "Some of the women teachers were repelled by the situation in which they found themselves. Their whole concept of teaching lay in dealing with a familiar situation—a white, working-class school. But now, a new situation had been wished upon them." For these teachers, Britain's expanding multicultural schools portended a shift in their whole professional self-understanding. "They were no longer teachers but child-minders, child-care officers and social workers."[7] Such attitudes continued into the 1970s. Speaking to the Select Committee on Race Relations and Immigration in 1976, one young black Londoner suggested that her headmistress was "frightened of black pupils."[8] In an article by a black schoolgirl published in *Spare Rib* in 1977, the author reports how a teacher had confided in her why she was quitting the school: "it was better before they let all the coloureds in."[9] The Jamaican teacher Carlton Duncan, applying for a job at a Brent comprehensive, was asked, incredulously, "I don't know why you all want to come and work here anyway. Did you notice the school is full of niggers?"[10]

The situation for black students in British schools in this era was not good. Examples of teacher racism toward pupils were ubiquitous. Hanif Kureishi, for example, remembers how at school "one teacher spoke to me always in a 'Peter Sellers' Indian accent. Another refused to call me by my name, calling me Pakistani Pete instead." ("Thank God for Peter Sellers," Beryl Gilroy remembers a fellow teacher saying to her, "he takes liberties with them. Good luck to him.")[11] A teenage girl interviewed by activists of the Organisation of Women of Asian and African Descent (OWAAD) recalled how at school "this teacher pulled me up in front of the class and said I was dirty and that she was going to make sure that my neck was cleaned—and she proceeded to do it, with Vim." (Her father, hearing of this, set off for the school with a machete.)[12] Another remembers one teacher referring to her as "blackie";[13] another, that her teacher had told her "to go home to the jungle."[14] Racism could also work in more insidious ways. Chris Mullard remembers the "extremely subtle way school taught me to consider the colour of my skin as ugly. My teachers never mentioned my colour. Instead they mentioned the customs of black people in far off lands, Britain's former role in civilizing the natives, making them acceptable to the white man and in turn to themselves." His curriculum was steeped in the traces of empire. For Mullard, this subtle racism functioned as an existential threat, a form of erasure. "I was a little white boy in a black skin. Everything about me was shrouded in whiteness."[15]

Coupled to the racism of teachers or the curriculum were wider structural and policy issues that often left black schoolchildren vulnerable, side-lined, or without support. From 1963, several local authorities, motivated by the concerns of white parents at the changing ethnic makeup of their children's schools, began a policy of dispersing nonwhite children to schools outside their local area. The practice began in Ealing and was soon copied by LEAs in Blackburn, Bradford, Hounslow, Huddersfield, Luton, Walsall, and West Bromwich. By 1973, four thousand black students, mostly British Asians, were being bused every day.[16] These students faced long journeys, often in unfit vehicles, arrived late to class, and could not attend after-school activities. They often found themselves the targets of racist attacks from white students at their new schools, particularly as the National Front's popularity rose in many of the areas where busing was used. In Ealing in 1974, fifteen-year-old

Mohammed Malik was murdered in such an attack. Despite a prolonged and widespread campaign against the practice—a campaign that won support from the Race Relations Board and the Department of Education and Science in 1975—busing continued until 1981.[17] Comprehensivization also had significant effects on the dispersal of black children and damaged their educational opportunities. In 1968, Caribbean parents in north London found that the comprehensivization of schools in the borough of Haringey, initially welcomed as an opportunity to allow their children into schools previously dominated by children of the middle classes, was being managed as a policy of dispersing black children between schools, and often streaming them into the lowest ability bands. Forming the North London West Indian Association (NLWIA), these parents led the campaign against this policy of "banding," publishing internal memos from Haringey LEA which exposed the racist premise of the actions.[18] Trevor Carter, working in a London school which had undergone this process of "banding," remembers his first school as a "snow-capped mountain." At the top, a white head teacher and staff. Immediately below, white children. "Then the black children, concentrated at the base of the mountain, a long way from the snow."[19]

The NLWIA also became concerned with the number of black children—particularly of African-Caribbean descent—being placed in schools for educationally subnormal (ESN) children. By 1967, African-Caribbean children made up 15 percent of the Inner London Education Authority's (ILEA) primary and secondary school pupils, but comprised 28 percent of the pupils in ESN schools.[20] John La Rose, a prominent member of NLWIA, led the campaign against ESN. In 1970, he formed the Caribbean Education and Community Workers' Association (CECWA), initiating a research project into the concentration of black students in ESN schools, and appointing the young Grenadian teacher Bernard Coard to head the research. When La Rose published Coard's findings as *How The West Indian Child Is Made Educationally Subnormal in the British Education System* (1971), the book sold ten thousand copies, attracting substantial interest from the mainstream media, and leading Coard to organize a nationwide speaking tour.[21] Coard reported the overrepresentation of black students in ESN schools and showed that they had been wrongly placed there, that the majority never returned to mainstream schools, and that they suffered academically and in their job prospects as a result.[22] His book launched an extensive campaign, which achieved some success in reducing the flow of black students into these

FIGURE 10. "ESN," illustration in *Black Liberator* 1, no. 1 (September–October 1971).

schools, and allowing many students in these schools to take their O-level and A-level examinations there, or to return to a mainstream school. The parents of those black students who remained in mainstream schools also had to fight against suspensions and exclusions, or the streaming of black students into vocational courses. In 1979, Haringey LEA introduced disruptive units, quickly labeled "sin bins" by black education activists, where many black students were placed on accusation of misbehavior.[23]

Supplementary schools were a solution to this deliberate failing of black students. These schools, as Barbara Beese and Leila Hassan wrote in 1975, were "the major weapon with which the West Indian Community fought back" against racism in the British education system.[24] Migrants from the

Caribbean had hoped to provide a better education for their children. Oral histories of Windrush migrants repeatedly emphasize this hope, and the shock of realizing that it was not guaranteed.[25] As the number of children moving to or born in Britain increased in the 1960s, many parents proposed supplementary education, a tradition that they brought with them from the Caribbean, as a means of redressing that failure.[26] From the late 1960s to the mid-1980s, local black political groups established supplementary schools across Britain. In Greater London, where the largest concentration of these schools were, the Barbadian anti-racist campaigner Reverend Wilfred Wood established the earliest supplementary school in Shepherd's Bush in 1967, with John La Rose founding the second, the George Padmore Supplementary School, two years later, with links to Wood's school.[27] By 1981, a report on British Caribbean supplementary schools in London listed forty-one schools, but did not claim to be comprehensive.[28] By 1987, supplementary schools had been established in at least thirty separate districts, from Leyton in the east to Southall in the west, and from Brockley in the south to Tottenham in the north.[29] Beyond London, by the mid-1970s there were schools in Birmingham's Handsworth and Liverpool's Toxteth, and by the early 1980s in Braford, Leeds, Manchester, Nottingham, and Wolverhampton.[30] Jessica Huntley, who with her husband Eric established a Saturday school at her house in Ealing in the early 1970s, and who took children to the West Indian Students Centre for events on black history and culture, remembers a network of supplementary schools stretching across Britain. One school in Leeds, Huntley claims, hosted "hundreds of children" on Saturday mornings.[31]

Women's activism was crucial. Even though men led these schools as often, women took on much of the work, and it was mothers who often sent their children to these schools. "Caring for children has always been seen as 'women's work,' and since we bear and rear the children, overseeing the institutionalized care provided by the schools—an extension of child-rearing—has also been seen as our responsibility," Beverley Bryan, Stella Dadzie, and Suzanne Scafe write. "Many a Black mother has had to confront, challenge and counteract the second-class, no hope provision we have been offered, either alone or with the support of friends and the wider community."[32] Women made up the majority of the campaigners against banding in Haringey in 1968, and in 1973 black mothers in Leeds led a boycott of Cowper Street School in protest against its racist headmaster.[33] As Race Today Women noted in May 1975, "much of the militant activity by women" from the Caribbean had been around education politics. "When they saw that the schools their children were attending were 'dustbin' schools they were instrumental in setting up supplementary schools in black communities up and down the country."[34] Judith Lockhart, active with the Black Women's Collective, the Brixton Black Women's Group, and OWAAD from the mid-1970s on, remembers that supplementary schooling was always central to the politics of these groups.[35]

The immediate concern of those parents and activists involved in setting up supplementary schools was extra instruction, usually in English and mathematics—a means of combating the undereducation in state schools, and the streaming and banding of black children that saw them placed in classes where expectations were low and tuition often basic. However, supplementary schools were rarely only concerned with extra tuition within the established curriculum. As one parent who moved her daughter to a supplementary school to combat the low level of education she was receiving in her ESN school remembered, "My daughter really got a lot out of those sessions, because it wasn't just about reading and writing. They taught the kids about Black history and showed them that they had nothing to be ashamed of because Black people are as good as anyone else."[36] Many schools offered teaching in black history and culture. In Handsworth, for example, the West Indian Parent Teacher Association ran one school, focusing "mainly on school subjects," while the Afro-Caribbean Self Help Organisation's school offered "black history as well as the usual school subjects."[37] Sometimes, the project of "blackening of the curriculum," as Ansel Wong, founder of the supplementary school Ahfiwe, named it, was a case of giving different contexts to established critical practices. "As I would say to people," Wong recalls, "you have a mathematical problem, contextualising with train travel from Kings Cross to Glasgow, why can't it be a train from San Fernando to Port of Spain? Or Kingston to Montego Bay, or something like that."[38] However, as we shall see, more often the process of cultivating a "black" identity in students was understood to encompass broader political questions. This commitment to a black politics is evident in the names chosen for some of the earliest schools. The schools took names of anticolonial and black liberation politicians, activists and educators from the Caribbean (C. L. R. James, George Padmore, Marcus Garvey), Africa (Kwame Nkrumah, Josina Machel), and the United States (George Washington Carver, Queen Mother Moore, Malcolm X).[39]

Many supplementary school founders conceived of the schools as a part of a wider black political formation. Trevor Phillips, who ran a self-help center with Vince Hines in Notting Hill from the early 1970s remembers,

> the projects were like safe houses where African and Caribbean history could be taught and discussed, where information, gossip and rumour could be dispensed, and where demonstrations and campaigns could be planned. At their best moments they formed a loose network of activists throughout the country who supported each other in the inevitable battles against the police or the local authorities.[40]

The role of schools in political networks could make them the targets of police and local racist groups. In May 1973, when *Race Today* reported on the Afro-Caribbean Self Help Organisation's school in Handsworth, twelve of the staff were on trial following clashes with the police, and the school had recently been firebombed with gasoline.[41] However, this embeddedness within a wider project of black radical politics was, for many, the biggest promise of the supplementary school movement. Trevor Carter, who hoped that black supplementary schools might be the route into a revived socialist education movement, suggested that it was this embeddedness in the local community and political networks that allowed for such a possibility. If, Carter suggested, "the failure to capture the parents along with their children" was one of the shortcomings of the British socialist Sunday schools of the late-nineteenth century, then "the unity, trust and co-operation between the generations within our own black supplementary school movement could be, by contrast, its lasting strength."[42] His hopes were certainly borne out in the accounts of some of the women interviewed by Bryan, Dadzie, and Scafe. "We started running a school on Saturdays [...] and we all worked as volunteers, contributing whatever time we could," one interviewee recalled. "I worked in the school for over a year, and what it did for me was to make me more aware, more conscious." "Black consciousness," Carter proposed, "welded to socialist commitment could just be the historic catalyst which could bring about the 'opportunity of a healthy and happy life for all' dreamed of at the turn of the century by our predecessors in supplementary education."[43] This sense of black supplementary schooling bringing together a political formation, connecting what was happening in the school to what was happening beyond it, was central in the challenge and new direction that critics like Carter saw the black education movement offering. We can see this most vividly in the way that activists reformulated autobiographical and other writing practices for the education movement.

Autobiographical writing was a central pillar in postwar social-democratic education policy and practice. As Carolyn Steedman has shown, "progressive" educationalists promoted autobiographical writing in primary schools since the early 1950s, and the 1967 Plowden Report of the Central Advisory Council for Education gave the practice unqualified support. By the early 1970s, auto-biographical writing had also made significant inroads in secondary school teaching.[44] Telling the story of the self was an educational method deemed particularly important for working-class children. It was understood to have significant "psychological benefits," and to offer a form of "recuperative self-hood."[45] Its role in the cultivation of a sense of selfhood and self-worth matched state efforts on other fronts, from providing free orange juice and milk to free school dinners, which told children like Steedman, growing up in 1950s Britain, that they "had a right to exist" and were "worth something."[46]

The failure of the education system to fulfill the promises of social democracy, however, led some to question the progressive possibilities of autobiographical practices as they stood. In his 1977 study *Learning to Labour*, written as an indictment of the failure of the school system to tackle ingrained processes in the reproduction of a class-bound, stratified society, Paul Willis found creative writing to be just about the only remaining mark of "the era of progressivism and relevance" left. But revealing something of the selfhood constituted in this practice, and some of the roots of his skepticism over its efficacy, Willis printed the harrowing opening line of one boy's story of his weekend escapades: "We couldn't go out Paki bashing with only four."[47] And if Willis was skeptical of the value of invitations to autobiography alone to challenge the existing socioeconomic structure, black teachers and parents had perhaps even more reason for suspicion. Beryl Gilroy recalls how, when she asked a class of primary schoolchildren to paint themselves, "The black children made the most unrealistic pictures of themselves, showing features and characteristics they did not and could never possess." This was the late 1950s, but when Gilroy returned to teaching again in 1965, she found that "if anything, the children had become even more colour-conscious. There was much talk of 'foreigners.'" Attempting to persuade a Nigerian student to paint his self-portrait in black, "he wailed, 'Stop it! I don't want all that blackness on me.'"[48] Bernard Coard, who taught in East London schools in the late 1960s, tells an almost identical story. Asking his students to draw each other, Coard found that his five black pupils "got painted white by all the white children! What's worse [they] had painted each other white also!" An Indian student, Coard reported, denied that she was Indian when asked by her English friends; a Jamaican student pretended not to know where Jamaica was, "and stated indignantly that she was not from 'there.'"[49] Through personal experience and through the publicized writings of Coard, Gilroy, Maxwell and others, black teachers and parents recognized the limits of current educational practice in realizing the career ambitions, self-integrity, and democratic citizenship of black schoolchildren. Rather than abandoning autobiographical practices, though, they reimagined them, drawing on the politics of decolonization and black liberation.

The state's implementation of creative writing in education drew on a wider democratic movement celebrating "ordinary" writing that had been gaining significant pace since the 1930s. This democratization of writing is often told as a national story, but it is also an imperial one. Following the trajectories that led to the black writing projects of the 1970s reveals the long project of decolonization as the major moment of divergence in that story, which left black writing the more politically charged activity. Before turning to the development of black writing within the black education movement in the next section, this section explores the politics of writing as a decolonization project, showing the energies invested in black writing and the promises that many believed this held for remaking blackness and challenging racial subordination.

The Britain to which many New Commonwealth migrants traveled in the 1950s was particularly invested in celebrating the "everyday" and the "ordinary" in public life. This was no doubt encouraged by the Labour Party's overwhelming victory in the 1945 general election, but it was a cultural tendency of longer duration, dating back to the late nineteenth century, consolidated in the 1930s, and evident since then, as Christopher Hilliard notes, across a wide range of popular forms, in "novels that deal with a single day, uneventful short stories, newspaper features on 'a day in the life' of a particular profession, [and] Mass-Observation's surveys."[50] With postwar planning scattering historic working-class communities, and revived fears about Americanization causing many to worry about the erosion of these traditional cultures, such projects took on a heightened significance in the 1950s, evident equally in the popularity of the humdrum working-class television soap opera *Coronation Street* and the nostalgic reminiscences that open Richard Hoggart's *The Uses of Literacy* (1957).[51] As critics have also long noted, however, this was overwhelmingly an ethnically homogeneous "everyday" into which nonwhite Britons intruded as intruders, if they did so at all. West Indians and South Asians lobbied hard against such exclusions, particularly from television, the iconic postwar democratic technology.[52] They also, though, became writers themselves, challenging their exclusion and offering other representations of everyday life, paralleling those found in the mainstream press and television. West Indian magazines and newspapers, most notably the *West Indian Gazette* and *Flamingo*, provided analogous profiles of "ordinary" migrant lives and creative writing focused on the everyday experiences of life in Britain, while the careers of several West Indian writers were launched in books exploring the everyday lives of black Britons—usually Londoners.[53] South Asian migrants also adapted traditional story-telling forms to quotidian tales of new lives in Britain.[54]

Becoming a writer held a different meaning in the contexts of imperialism and decolonization, particularly for writers of color. The desire to become a writer has a long history in struggles for a democratic culture in Britain. The claim that writing could be an ordinary activity was a democratic one, an articulation of "a shared sense of entitlement to participate in cultural activities," tied up with struggles for political democracy in its various imaginings.[55] It was a claim underwritten by the expansion, since the late nineteenth century, of writing magazines, correspondence courses, writers' clubs, and an institutional publishing infrastructure geared to "ordinary voices."[56] But this national story also had an imperial dimension, most pronounced in the relationship between Britain and the West Indies. As V. S. Naipaul famously depicts in his 1963 novel *A House for Mr Biswas*, the writers' clubs and correspondence courses that sustained the rise of ordinary writing cultures in Britain held similar promises of democratic inclusion, modern citizenship, and movement toward the center of things for aspiring writers in the West Indies in the 1920s and 1930s.[57] If the BBC's Light and Third Programmes offered "ordinary" writers in Britain a national platform in the 1940s,[58] its Colonial Service offered West Indians a comparable one in its popular *Caribbean Voices* show. The democratic claims implicit in having one's work included in a BBC broadcast were, however, complicated by decolonization. The BBC developed *Caribbean Voices* to win support in the West Indies for the war effort in the wake of the anticolonial and labor unrest of the 1930s, but in the postwar years, the program also became integral to the formation of new nationalist sentiments, fueling calls for independence.[59] The BBC's symbolic authority retained a strong pull, and there is evidence of real *pleasure* among West Indian writers in getting their work commissioned there.[60]

But this was a vitiated pleasure. As George Lamming reminded his readers in *The Pleasures of Exile* (1960), the BBC was a deeply segregated institution: the Colonial Section was seen, when it was seen at all, "as the arse-hole of the Corporation."[61] If this was an imperial project of democratic inclusion, it was, like so many others, one structured in hierarchies of race in ways that undermined its own claims to universality.

Rising anger over the failed promises of decolonization in the later 1960s made untenable the already uneasy relationships that Caribbean writers had maintained with the institutions of cultural authority in Britain and their Caribbean counterparts in the early years of independence. In the 1950s, the literary cultures of Caribbean writing were closely bound with the literary cultures of postwar Britain. Caribbean writing was published primarily in Britain, reviewed often in British literary periodicals, and printed and sold in Britain. Indeed, it was tied to end-of-empire liberal-imperial designs to foster new Commonwealth literary cultures along metropolitan lines.[62] The major break with this model came with the rise of Caribbean Black Power. As black radicals launched multipronged campaigns against the racialized order of the postcolonial Caribbean, artists and writers sought to resituate cultural production and consumption as communal projects, prioritizing the voices and communication networks of a "blacker" Caribbean. This shift, led in Britain and the Caribbean by the Caribbean Artists Movement, a group that brought together many of those previously associated with *Caribbean Voices*, transformed the politics of writing both in Britain and the Caribbean. In the Caribbean, the post-1968 era saw a wealth of new initiatives aiming to amplify vernacular oral and writing traditions, to place the aesthetics and ideals of these traditions at the heart of new artistic projects, and to restage artistic production and consumption in those spaces most marginalized by the traditional arts establishment.[63] This was matched in Britain by an effluence of new writing programs and publishing initiatives, and an effort to involve black youth—usually understood as the most put-upon of black Britons—in these. In each instance, advocates of black writing created space for new voices and encouraged new writers to write in those popular modes least accommodated within the ideas about literature and writing inherited from imperial schooling, and continuing in much Caribbean education in the post-independence period. Writing held a promise of decolonization. It held a promise of recognizing the lives and validity of those marginalized in the colonial and neocolonial order, and carrying forward the radical spirit of black liberation. Edward Brathwaite, a founding member, with John La Rose and Andrew Salkey, of the Caribbean Artists Movement, wrote in praise of this recent turn in Caribbean letters by suggesting how it actively channeled memories of the guerrilla insurgencies that fought for liberation across Africa and the Caribbean. This was writing "in English: but often it is in an English which is like a howl, or a shout or a machine gun."[64]

The drive to publish the voices of those most marginalized by racism in Britain led to a renaissance in black British writing in the 1970s. The Jamaican poet James Berry, reflecting on these changes in the mid-1980s, noted a "new obsession with the written word" sustained and developed by supplementary schooling, the black studies movement, cultural centers, theatres and workshops, and independent publishing. "In a new spirit and drive, people whose families for generations had never written a single creative word began to buckle down to the business of expressing themselves through writing."[65] Writing was seen here both as a process of personal liberation and as a practice that connected one up to a political collective, as more and more writers came to express "blackness," and articulate a collective experience. As Berry suggested, people "had only to sit and write to find that their work was regarded as part of a tradition called 'political' or 'protest literature.'"[66]

An array of new institutions sustained this drive. Independent publishing houses played an important role in supporting writing by young black men and women. In London, Dalston's Centerprise bookshop, established by the African American publisher Glenn Thompson, began publishing young black writers from the early 1970s, initially with the encouragement of local teachers. Ken Worpole, who taught at the nearby Hackney Downs School and began working at Centerprise in 1970, described the bookshop's commitment to publishing local voices as rooted in a conviction "that the encouragement of self-expression, the description and analysis of everyday life, our present history, was not a diversion from the 'real' struggle to change society, but an integral part of a wider dynamic for change." An early collection published by Centerprise, a book of poems by a local black schoolboy, Vivian Usherwood, sold thousands of copies on its publication in 1972 and continued to sell well into the 1980s.[67] A similar project in Ealing, Commonplace Workshop, launched in 1976 with the publication of an anthology of writing by local children of African, Caribbean, and South Asian descent, continuing to publish these works throughout the 1970s and early 1980s.[68] Bogle-L'Ouverture, also based in Ealing, joined this publication of children's writing with Accabre Huntley's *At School Today* in 1977. The book was greeted by *Race Today* as a poetry collection that "speaks for a generation of British born blacks who are confident about who they are and what they are about."[69] In 1978, the Black Ink Collective established itself in Brixton, described by Berry as "one of the life-saving small presses of the area." Its first publication was sixteen-year-old Michael McMillan's play *The School Leaver*, which was soon followed by an anthology of writing by local black youth.[70] In Manchester, from the early 1980s on, the adult literacy project Gatehouse Publications published the writing of several black teenagers and adults.[71] Founded in 1984, the Asian Women's Collective—internally divided over whether they should describe themselves or their writing as "black"—published the work of young writers from across Britain.[72] Collections of poems from younger black writers were also published by the older generation associated with the Caribbean Artists Movement, first in their journal *Savacou* in 1974, and then in a collection emerging from a nationwide tour of young poets engaged in school, community, and adult education workshops arranged by James Berry in 1975.[73]

Black cultural centers also played an important role. The Keskidee Centre, established in Kings Cross in 1968 by Oscar Abrams, an ex-CARD official and vice-chair of the West Indian Students Centre, was just one—though a particularly important one—of a network of black youth and cultural centers established across several British cities since the late 1960s, teaching art and sculpture, and encouraging young poets and playwrights. Hosting Linton Kwesi Johnson as a librarian and writer-in-residence in the mid-1970s, the Keskidee Centre held collaborative writing sessions and competitions, with the winners getting their work published in *Race Today*.[74] Spaces such as the Keskidee were also part of a network of national and international institutions encouraging young black writers. Edgar White, whose play *Matura* was written and first performed at the Keskidee in 1976, was later taken up by the Royal Court Theatre, whose Gerald Chapman, director of the Young People's Theatre Scheme, promoted a series of women's plays, gay plays, and black plays in this era.[75] Michael McMillan, also adopted by Chapman's scheme, gained his first exposure as part of Festac '77, a festival of international black arts and culture held in Lagos in 1977.[76] Other institutions, such as South London's Oval House, Brixton's Black Writer's Workshop, and the weekly Black Voices open mic slot, running from 1973 at the Troubadour in London's Earl's Court, proved indispensable in encouraging black writing. The Black Writer's Workshop, described by Berry as a "keen, intense, committed" workshop where "young men and women often worked on well after midnight, producing work," provided much of the content for the Black Ink

Collective's publications.[77] Alongside this, black feminist organizations emerging in this period provided crucial spaces for creative expression. These institutions were crucial in offering new black subjectivities, encouraging and sustaining the identity of a "black writer." As one OWAAD member recalls of reciting her poetry at the OWAAD 1980 conference, "I had a really great sense of people wanting me, and wanting to hear from me. I felt nervous at first, but in a way I also felt safe because I knew I was around sisters and had nothing to worry about. For the first time in my life—and no one had ever said this before—people started telling me, 'You're a writer.'"[78]

The process of writing was both politically and affectively loaded. For black writers and activists, encounters with the written word carried a particular weight. Reading at school was often described as an emotionally intense, fraught, and potentially alienating experience. "I had always liked reading, and could have really enjoyed literature at school," one black woman told interviewers from OWAAD.

> I suppose I liked the strange and different world I found in books, especially the ones about life as it was supposed to have been like in Britain. This couldn't last, though, because reading often became a nasty, personal experience. You would be getting deep into a story and suddenly it would hit you—a reference to Black people as savages or something. It was so offensive. And so wounding. And sometimes you would sit in class and wait, all tensed up, for the next derogatory remark to come tripping off the teacher's tongue.[79]

In this context, writing could not be other than affectively loaded. The practice of writing was usually welcomed as allowing a means of "laying claim to our selfhood, making bold to assert ourselves" against the racist logics of the texts encountered in day-to-day life.[80] However, to the extent that writing was cathartic, this was as often for the way in which it offered a process of recognizing and articulating pain and protest as it was for its soothing promises of a less contradictory, less alienating presence in text. Chris Mullard, reflecting on the process of writing his book *Black Britain* (1973), recalled "all the time I spent writing [. . .], I found not solace, comfort, or tolerance, but tension, a disturbing desire to break, smash and riot, to bellow: 'Whitey! One day you'll have to pay!'"[81]

Writing offered a means of interpellation into a black community and a black politics formed in the drive for decolonization. This was particularly the case for writing in nonstandard English, in the vernacular Englishes of the Caribbean, referred to at the time often as "patois" or "creole." As Rachael Gilmour has demonstrated, against the fraught language politics of the 1970s and 1980s, in which such speech was often stigmatized as "broken language" or "jungle talk," language became established as "a privileged locus of resistance, and individual and collective self-determination."[82] Black writing practices asserted the expressive and intellectual depth offered by creole writing, and its capacity to bear the weight of black experiences. As Berry noted, black writers' workshops "offered liberty to write in oral language—'Nation Language.' A new freedom, this!"[83] New writing experiments in creole, or—borrowing from the influential work of Edward Kamau Brathwaite—"Nation Language,"[84] were practiced in a variety of forms. This range, from essays, short stories, and plays to poetry, can be found in the writing produced, for example, in the supplementary school projects discussed below, or in any number of the publications produced by black and community presses. Poetry, however, became the privileged medium for black written communication, particularly with the seismic impact of Linton Kwesi Johnson's poetry from the mid-1970s on.[85] As one OWAAD member wrote, "I used to write in standard English, but later on, when I met people like Linton Kwesi Johnson I liked the way he was using the language and decided that if he was using it that way then I could too."[86] Berry, writing in the mid-1980s, noted that it was "not surprising that schoolchildren—and adult English poets too—should write and perform poetry in his style. Among young blacks his influence has prompted the mushrooming of new poets." In turn, as Berry also noted, these new poets were supported and sustained through institutions like the ACER Penmanship Awards, discussed below.[87]

Vernacular writing as a *youth* practice was particularly important at a time when young black people faced discrimination in schooling, by the police, and in employment, and when many were rebelling against this discrimination.[88] For Ansel Wong, who sponsored such writing throughout his career as an educationalist, "these young lions [. . .] have invested Creole with new dimensions and meanings, for it is around these young people that the ethos of resistance is developing. One of the principal features of this resistance is the ability to communicate in a unique form of language, invariably described as Creole, Patois, Jamaica Talk, dialect, 'Backayard' lingo."[89] Lauretta Ngcobo, introducing a volume of black women's poetry after the series of urban uprisings in British cities in the early 1980s, suggested that writing played an active part in constituting political identities and challenging white racial common sense.

There is a parallel between such poetry and the so-called riots in Brixton, Toxteth, Handsworth and other inner-city areas. [...] Out of our acrid neighbourhoods [...] springs this rioting literature. It is not art for art's sake; its vibrancy and immediacy are intended to forge unity and wrench a new identity. It is unavoidable that we as Black writers at times displease our white readership. Our writing is seldom genteel since it springs from our experiences which in real life have none of the trimmings of gentility. If the truth be told, it cannot titillate the aesthetic palate of many white people, for deep down it is a criticism of their values and their treatment of us throughout history.[90]

In these contexts, the cultivation of "black voices" was not simply about developing a sense of identity in the face of racist exclusion. It involved an active challenge to that racism, confronting the ways in which language embodied racial meaning, and from this, challenging the culture underpinning the distribution of power in Britain. This worked both on a public political stage, where the devaluation of creole was challenged and its expressive potential confirmed, and in the most intimate dimensions of personal experience, where one could find now, not alienation, but community with others resisting racism. Chris Waters has described the "ordinary" writing practices of working-class literature in these decades as almost devoid of "an explicit sense of politics," spurning critique, and invested in nostalgia.[91] Such a characterization does not stand for black writing, which was deeply bound up with the politics of secondary decolonization. It was *this* politics of writing that black educationalists saw as a potential savior in the education crisis that black schoolchildren faced.

BLACK WRITING AND BLACK EDUCATION

As a frontline service where black activists could work with put-upon black youth, supplementary schools were central to the drive to establish Brathwaite's "machine gun" tradition of black writing in Britain, and to reimagining the role of writing in education as a disruptive—rather than merely inclusive—activity. It was through supplementary schooling, and then through the wider black education movement, that the politics of writing explored in the previous section came to transform the politics of education in its moment of crisis.

John La Rose's George Padmore Supplementary School (GPSS) in Finsbury Park is an early example of this investment in cultivating radical black writing. The school was among the first supplementary schools to open in Britain, setting up in 1969. La Rose had first begun teaching a year earlier. With other members of the North London West Indian Association, he founded the Paul Bogle Youth Club in 1968, named after the leader of the 1865 Morant Bay Rebellion. Lecturing on Caribbean and African history and culture to young black men and women at the center, he discovered that many felt embarrassment about or contempt for these subjects. He founded GPSS on deciding that a permanent home for black education was required. As with many supplementary schools, a key concern at GPSS was additional tuition in English, science, and mathematics. However, La Rose additionally emphasized the importance of African history, as well as teaching lessons in world geography and Caribbean cuisine.[92] La Rose, who became a key figure in the renaissance of Caribbean letters in the late 1960s, ran the school from his home, which also served as the base for his New Beacon Books bookshop and publishing enterprise. Students had ready access to a wide range of literature. While much of the set reading utilized the burgeoning children's literature being published in the Caribbean, and by Caribbean publishers in Britain, there were also black radical and Marxist texts. A class reading list from the mid-1970s included Vic Reid's *The Young Warriors* (1967), Louise Bennett's *Anancy Stories and Dialect Verse* (1973), and Bernard and Phyllis Coard's illustrated children's story *Getting to Know Ourselves* (1972), alongside *Malcolm X Talks to Young People* (1969), and *Lenin and the Bolsheviks* (1967). Reflecting links with the wider radical education drive of the early 1970s, discussed below, students also read Chris Searle's *Ferndale Fires: A Children's Story* (1974), an experimental volume of poetry from Searle's students at Brixton's Santley Junior School.[93] The GPSS encouraged students "to take their books home and to ask parents to read the same books that they are studying."[94]

Many lessons centered on writing composition and reading comprehension exercises. These were undertaken in dialogue, with reading comprehension classes exploring key texts of a radical black tradition, and writing exercises often using these explorations as springboards. Roxy Harris, a teacher at the school, noted how in his classes "young black students showed a strong desire for reading material with which they could make some connection, and which would enable them to explore their own experience."[95] In many British classrooms of the 1960s and 1970s, this need would have been met by Valerie Avery's childhood memoir *London Morning* (1964), a text Avery wrote for a school exercise in 1955, which was later widely used as a model for other children to begin their own autobiographical and creative writing pursuits. It was a book deeply tied up in the tradition of recovering working-class community to which the "ordinary" writing drive in schools cleaved.[96] Harris, however, provided students with extracts from Eldridge Cleaver's *Soul on Ice* (1968) and George Jackson's *Soledad Brother* (1970), along with a list of reading comprehension questions. The questions, Harris noted, "were framed in an open-ended way so that they could be answered by people at different levels," but they ultimately served "a deeper motivation [. . .] to give black readers an opportunity for self-definition." In this thinking, there was no contradiction between advocating a practice self-reflection intended to cultivate "man's [. . .] ability to define himself for himself," and offering an inherited literary model within which this definition could be found. There was no dislocation either in offering, for this purpose, the writings of two African Americans. Indeed, for Harris, Jackson and Cleaver proved the ideal choice for black British youth: "*Soledad Brother* and *Soul on Ice* are particularly relevant to the British situation in that they highlight many of the issues confronting blacks when they are a minority in a white, advanced urban society."[97]

To "find" one's own "voice" as a young black man or woman was, simultaneously, to become one with the voice of a wider community defined through a shared experience of blackness, an experience also understood as necessarily political, finding its coordinates in the literature of black liberation politics. In Harris's lesson plans for *Soledad Brother* and *Soul on Ice*, alongside more straightforward interpretative questions ("Why does George think that it is no use trying to be 'more English than the English'?"), and political questions leading from these interpretations ("Do you think that black people should take action to improve their conditions or is it up to white people to start treating blacks better?"), the prompts for self-expression focused on allowing individual experiences to join this collective narrative of black politics: "Try to describe any time when you have been scared of white people"; "Some prisoners spend most of their time in prison fighting the guards, others just read books. What would you do with your time if you were in jail?"; "Give examples of times when you or your friends have deliberately done things against what you have been taught is right." Each prompt anticipated a dialogue on the issues raised, so these exercises were tied into a wider process of political education, particularly in the politics of race. At the core of Harris's exercises was the process of learning what it meant to be black, how to speak blackness, and, indeed, how one might begin to "think black." To reach a wider audience, New Beacon published his lesson plans in 1981 under the title *Being Black*.[98]

This drive to encourage a more combative, critical students' writing was also embraced by other parts of the radical education movement in Britain, beyond black supplementary schools, but here, again, the politics secondary decolonization was important in transforming the politics of writing. As Matthew Thomson has shown, radical educators in Britain used writing projects to involve local citizens in taking control of their communities—evident, for example, in Hackney's Centerprise, and West London's Notting Dale Urban Studies Centre, or in the various community arts projects that thrived across London in the 1970s and early 1980s.[99] The 1970s saw a rise in radical education initiatives, which previously, since the socialist Sunday schools of the late nineteenth century, had been only a minor presence in British education.[100] The establishment of "free schools" was a means for accommodating those students failed by the mainstream school system—excluded or truanting children, and underachieving children. In schools like Camden's Freightliners Free School, or Angel's famous White Lion Free School, new teaching models, centered on communal participation and undisciplined, nonhierarchical learning environments, attempted to undo the authority of the traditional school environment in an implicit—and often explicit—critique of its social and political role.[101] Encouraging children's self-expression was central to this radical education politics, in which the earlier progressive politics of self-narration were reworked in a challenge to the failures of the social-democratic education policies of the postwar settlement. And central to this drive was Chris Searle, a man who had cut his teeth teaching in Berkeley at the height of its radical activism in 1968, and then in Trinidad on the eve of the 1970 Black Power revolution.

Chris Searle was a young English teacher at Sir John Cass School in London's East End. At Sir John Cass School in the early 1970s Searle encouraged his students to write about their own lives, and to make connections between the struggles that they faced and broader political struggles of the day. When he published the results of this experiment as *Stepney Words* in 1971 he was promptly dismissed by Sir John Cass School, only to be reinstated following a strike by his former pupils.[102] He went on to publish numerous additional volumes of children's writing throughout the 1970s, acting, in Sam Wetherell's estimation, as the tone-setter for "the next decade and a half of community-arts projects in the East End."[103] Influenced by his time in Berkeley and Tobago, Searle's radical politics were centrally concerned with race. After his time at Sir John Cass, he taught from 1976 to 1979 in FRELIMO's Mozambique, and between 1980 and 1983 he helped establish the new education system in the New Jewel Movement's Grenada, also helping to establish the revolutionary government's publishing house, Fedon. In these years he became closely involved with the group of radical intellectuals associated with the Institute of Race Relations and *Race & Class*.[104]

From his earliest interventions in children's writing and publishing, Searle was determined to challenge racialized language, to cultivate new senses of blackness, and to transform the school and its role through this process. Writing for *Race Today* in 1972, he pointed to the ways in which the connotations of "blackness" in the English language were being reworked through "West Indian voices like those of Marcus Garvey, Frantz Fanon, and Walter Rodney, and the black presses in this country like New Beacon Books and Bogle L'Ouverture," challenging the ways in which dominant uses of the English language "still reflect and give support to a colonial, racist world." In the children's poetry he published in *Stepney Words*, he suggested, there was evidence of this "new meaning in the English language for the word 'black'. 'Black man' is 'one who struggles, one who fights oppression.'" "In this sense, with this meaning," Searle argued, "we should all be black"—a point he underlined by publishing a poem by Imtiaz, a fourteen-year-old British Asian, calling to "Black the humans."[105] Following black radical reformulations of the role of education in this era, Searle proposed that the school was "the institution of state which condones and promotes racism for its own economic interest and survival." However, he suggested, at the same time there existed within schools "a growing power of resistance and commitment to transform the state and transform the school as a servant institution of the state."[106] Through strategies of self-expression, these antagonisms to the current order, he thought, might be cultivated and turned against it.

This process of the cultivation of black political self-expression was taken furthest in Ansel Wong's Ahfiwe, established in Brixton in 1974 and drawing on both the black supplementary school traditions of activists like La Rose, and the radical education movement of the free schools. Wong's involvement in the politics of education began when he was a student at the University of Hull. He had moved to England from Trinidad in 1965 for university, and chose Hull for its teaching provision in Caribbean and American literature. There he was quickly drawn into student politics, joining the Radical Student Alliance and soon playing a central role in its activities. On university holidays he began to visit the West Indian Students Centre and soon also became a key player in the radicalization of that space, helping to establish the C. L. R. James Supplementary School there in 1969.[107] Wong's career reveals the connections between the black education movement and a wider radical education politics alive in Britain—and globally—in this period. His ambition, later abandoned, was to become a Jesuit priest, and when he began teaching, his touchstone was the Brazilian educator Paulo Freire's *Pedagogy of the Oppressed* (1968). Freire's radical pedagogy, drawing on Marx, Fanon, and Catholic liberation theology, advocated a reconceptualization of the learning environment to conceive of students as co-creators of knowledge, and to democratize the languages and tools of knowledge production. More locally, Wong was also influenced by the libertarian experiments at A. S. Neill's Summer Hill School and the White Lion Free School in Islington.[108] In Ahfiwe, these influences were manifested in Wong's efforts to involve older pupils in teaching younger ones and in building a school magazine driven by a collective ethos and that allowed space for self-expression and debate.

Black self-narration was central to the project of empowering pupils at Ahfiwe. Wong's teaching practices echoed Roxy Harris's in conceiving the process of narrating the black self as a dialogic one, in which black radical literature would play a formative role. A poem by the Ahfiwe student Susan Chin, "To My Black Teacher," published in Ahfiwe's journal, narrated this dialogue:

> Malcolm, Angela, Mao and Lenin,
> And all the rest. [...]
> Rap Brown, Lester,
> Fanon, Cleaver,
> All this reading going round my head.
> The poems are constantly forming:
> In my sleep, in my head,
> Walking around, shopping,
> When I'm awake, when I'm in bed.
> There is a new me
> Screaming to get out. [...]
> The poems are getting longer,
> More aggressively black.
> Now I'm running
> I can't go back.
> Thank you for showing me
> The person inside.
> I'm more a black woman
> Studious, Cultural
> Militant and Free.[109]

WHEN BRAIN MEET BOOK—
IT DREAD
join one of our classes today

AHFIWE SCHOOL, GRESHAM
ROAD, BRIXTON SW9
Tel: 733 0690

FIGURE 11. Advertisement for Ahfiwe School, c. 1974, *Ahfiwe* 2 (n.d.).

In Wong's ambition "not only to provide supplementary assistance but also to support and counter the more harmful aspects of their education and debilitating social environment," cultivating a "black" identity was crucial.[110] Ahfiwe based its politics around the articulation of a communal black identity. The banner of its journal was "The Inseparable Tie Is Our Blackness." As can be seen in Chin's poem, Ahfiwe drew heavily on African American writers in its exploration of blackness—though it also brought in a familiar triumvirate of radical liberation politics, Mao, Lenin, and Fanon. However, it was in students' writing in response to this reading, and in response to their own experiences, that Ahfiwe's emphasis lay.

Like Chris Searle earlier in the decade, Ahfiwe soon began publishing its pupils' writing. The school's journal teems with writing by the students and co-teachers—Wong recruited sixth formers from the local girls' school at which he taught to help in the delivery of the classes. Echoing Searle's approach, Wong's editorials were kept to a minimum, and the majority of the page space was given over to the voices of the pupils. Publishing the writing of these students was, as Wong later reflected, a practice aimed at allowing students an "understanding of their own sense of worth."[111] However, this sense of self-worth was also understood to be the articulation of a challenge. The writings, Wong wrote, "represent the feelings and perceptions of black youths in Brixton—a voice that is becoming increasingly clear, loud and uncompromising."[112] Indeed, as a short piece in the journal titled "Black Youth Speaks," by a student, Clive Robertson, demanded, "What is happening to black youths today? [. . .] We are all black brothers and sisters and so we all have to join the struggle in order to overcome police brutality, not with words but with action."[113]

The *Ahfiwe* journal aimed to help the process of recognizing oneself as a black "brother" or a black "sister," and knowing what "is happening to black youths today." The range of writing found in the journal is remarkably broad. Several poems are directed at the figure of the black woman, either as "Mother of humanity," or as a force "subdued and suppressed by her man and the system" and in need of "her voice to be heard." Ahfiwe had a majority female studentship and staff, and they discussed these questions with urgency. Domestic violence and domestic labor were also touchstones of the writing. However, the poems also frequently narrated a form of revolutionary black violence, often in explicitly masculine terms, celebrating black "fighting sons." The legacy of slavery was ever present. "Black is a black man / From slavery born," one poet wrote. In another poem, this enslaved past was brought into the present: "Stacked, crammed, chained / Whipped to make them go / Filth, stench, hunger, pain. / Nothing here has changed / The problems here are still the same." The experience of blackness was often narrated as a conversion, a process of becoming. As one poem described: "Eyes had sight / But these eyes were blind / [. . .] / The light became clear / The blur was gone / The eyes saw." The experiences of the school and its associated institutions—youth clubs and dances—drove this process of becoming black. The writing emphasized the role of the school in allowing this process of transformation into blackness, a process that, without the school, would be conducted on the more ephemeral terrain of mass-mediated culture:

"Unfortunately I was born in England but when they put a black documentary on T.V. I watched it and wrote down as much as I could," wrote Evelyn G. Christie. "And now I attend the Black Studies class at Ahfiwe School and hope to learn more to pass on to others."[114]

Alongside the growth in supplementary schools, several other projects emerged to encourage self-expression and self-narration by black children. One of the most influential of these was Len Garrison's Afro-Caribbean Education Resources (ACER) Project, which aimed at reformulating black creative expression in British schools. Garrison had come to Britain from Jamaica in 1954, aged eleven, to join his parents. Educated at Kingsley Grammar School in Chelsea, he remembered a school life in which, as one of only two black students at the school, he faced a daily racism that, he felt, he had "no language to explain."[115] In the 1960s he became involved in youth work in Brixton, teaching classes in black history. This interest continued as he studied for a diploma in development studies at the University of Oxford's Ruskin College in 1971, researching the Rastafarian movement in Jamaica, before completing a BA in African and Caribbean history at the University of Sussex in 1976. Garrison established the ACER Project in the autumn of 1976, bringing together his twin interests in education and black history and culture. Aiming "to collect and disseminate material drawn from the African and Afro-Caribbean sources related to the black child's cultural background for use in the multi-cultural classroom," it was funded by the ILEA, and housed at its Centre for Urban Education Studies.[116] Garrison was ACER's director, and the project also brought together several significant activists and educators, including Ansel Wong, Roxy Harris, and the future Labour MP and then peer Paul Boateng, at that time a solicitor, fighting the campaign against police abuses of stop and search powers. ACER pursued a three-pronged strategy. First, it collated the details of black and anti-racist educators, writers, publishers, and campaigners in London and around Britain, for publication as a resource list for teachers wanting to make contact. Second, it reproduced extensive amounts of work on race and education, as well as commissioning new work, and organized these reproductions into booklets for teachers and schools, based around themes such as racism in children's books, parents' and children's experiences, and short stories and images featuring positive representations of black children. Finally, it encouraged, and later sponsored, black creative writing by children and young adults, publishing the results.

These various strategies were interrelated, and the creative writing project, which went on to become ACER's biggest intervention into black education, was supported by its other programs of reading and reflection. The ACER Project was concerned to foster a clear sense of black history among black schoolchildren. As with other contemporary narrations of black history, histories of slavery and rebellion were foregrounded. One ACER report on the North Lewisham Supplementary School, reprinted as part of a portfolio of successful projects, recorded how "children were encouraged to challenge preconceptions which they seemed to hold about themselves and their history and forebears, e.g. indicating that the slaves rebelled from their first encounter with the white man in Africa, that many died because they bravely rebelled, that they participated in their own emancipation."[117] At the same time, ACER's own projects also encouraged critical reading by schoolchildren, so that they might "examine how images of people or groups, both visual and written, can influence our comprehension and how they can also lead to distortion and obscurity," so that they could "critically analyse the ways in which some groups have evolved stereotyped or obscure views about others."[118] These exercises were integrated into the process of self-narration, and ACER provided a series of writing prompts to encourage students to reflect on their learning and their understanding of themselves. One ACER writing prompt, for example, linking critical reading to self-consciousness, asked writers to respond to the title, "The book or experience that made me conscious of my blackness is/was."[119]

This aspect of ACER's work developed into the Black Youth Annual Penmanship Awards, which began in 1978 and became, over the following decade, "one of the major celebrations in the calendar of Britain's Black community."[120] The Penmanship Award was an essay competition for black youth, established by ACER and dedicated to the memories of two black radical activists, Peter Moses, a member of the Black Liberation Front and teacher at the Marcus Garvey Supplementary School in Shepherd's Bush, and Olive Morris, a former Black Panther and a founding member of OWAAD.[121] A Penmanship Award panel judged the entries to the competition each year and issued prizes for the best entries in each age category in an annual ceremony at Lambeth Town Hall.[122] The Penmanship Award, ACER reported, "reveals the extent to which the children themselves are aware of their plight and the conditions in which they find themselves. We feel that they are the best persons to express their own experiences."[123]

The students' essays were certainly understood to display a raw authenticity, but they responded to prompts provided by ACER's judges. The suggested titles for the 1983 competition give a sense of the flavor of the politics of blackness in the Penmanship Awards. The list included the essay titles "Blackness is not only a skin colour, it is culture and consciousness," "They took me out of Africa, but they can't take Africa out of me," "'Education' rather than 'schooling' is the key to liberation," and "Let the pen speak for I."[124] The last title, in particular, was used repeatedly as a prompt, and commented upon by the editors of Penmanship Awards booklets. ACER's essayists understood the act of writing as integral to a process of both personal and political "arrival" into blackness. They repeatedly emphasized publicly *writing* black experience. "I only want the world to know / What hell I've been through / The sound of my soul / It must be told," wrote one young man. This act of writing, though, was also understood to express truths about blackness in Britain more widely. "[T]his story will use but one child, but will encompass (see how me use a long word) the life generally of Black children," wrote another. "The child's name was Enoch (what else!) and he resided in Brixton, in Handsworth, Toxteth, Chapeltown and all over Babylon."[125] This sense of blackness as a shared experience was inextricably tied to the possibilities of its articulation as such. Essayists frequently expressed and enacted the process of composition as dialogic. Alongside the writing prompts provided by ACER, future essay titles were drawn from the essays of previous years' competitions. Moreover, the drive to *write* these experiences was bolstered by the knowledge that so many others might do the same. "Although Black British experience is examined in many different ways by individual writers," Paul McGilchrist wrote in *Black Voices*, an anthology of Penmanship writing, "even the most personal of them is resonant with the knowledge that others have felt similar pains, pleasures and indignities."[126] Again, we can see the development of a black writing culture here as closely tied to the development of the subjective position of the "black writer," as well as the politics it entailed—radical, critical, bound up with the colonial past and means of overcoming it.

For these writers, the act of writing was a process of coming into history. Ngũgĩ wa Thiong'o, who contributed the introduction to the *Black Voices* collection, had long championed the importance of creative self-expression and communal cultural production for new forms of revolutionary postcolonial politics in his native Kenya.[127] For Ngũgĩ, the *Black Voices* essays evidenced the writers' "struggle to acquire a positive consciousness of who they are; their place in the economy; their real place in history; and their real friends and their real enemies." Historical consciousness was particularly important: these were "attempts by the young people to define themselves and their history," and this was a history defined by "legacies of slavery; colonialism."[128] ACER's Penmanship Awards celebrated the idea that these young writers could, should, and did "recover" their pasts, and that these pasts allowed new, more defiant senses of self. The act of writing was also celebrated, however, as a historic act in itself. "So often, a person enters a competition, and if he/she does not win, that person will feel disillusioned and discouraged," the competition judge Martin Glynn wrote in an introduction to the 1985 winning essays. "While it is not very easy to gain recognition or win a prize for work done, it is important that all writers realise their contributions are vital to the survival of documenting our existence and lives at moments through our history."[129] There is an important doubling of temporality in Glynn's understanding of the essay competition. While commending the essays for how they recreated "Echoes of the past," Glynn simultaneously invited readers to imagine the present moment of the essays—the act of their composition—as itself the object of a future memory, "documenting our existence." This transformation of the present into the past by anticipating its memory revealed the double logic of this drive to get young black Britons writing their lives. With increasing intensity through the 1970s and 1980s, as we shall see in greater detail in the next chapter, black radicals invested their hopes in black youth not only as the repository of past struggle, but also as the agents of history themselves. Writing did not merely record politics and history: it was a historical moment of political formation. Through establishing new writing practices, the black education movement sought to build this political formation at the heart of schooling in Britain.

REFORMING THE SCHOOL: BLACK STUDIES, ANTI-RACISM, MULTICULTURALISM, AND THE STATE

If black supplementary education and its associated practices of learning and self-narration were seen to promise the cultivation of a radical black political formation, this was in part because of the close ties between black education and the institutions of a radical black civil society—publishers, youth and cultural centers, bookshops, and political headquarters. Indeed, the promise of black self-expression through the black education movement was often that it brought the raw energy of black youth rebellion on the streets into contact with these institutions and offered the means of translating these experiences into a wider collective experience of blackness.[130] The self-narration practices of the black education movement, in this thinking, could be both sustained by and a reinvigorating force for a wider black political formation. However, the drive for black self-narration also gained ground within mainstream education—as the editor of *Oral History*, another important organ in this revolution in self-narration practices in the postwar era, noted in 1980, "in a number of London schools, teachers have been encouraging black children to write their own life stories as a means of gaining confidence in self-expression."[131] Here, black radical activists were far more circumspect about its radical potential and alive to the possibility that it might be compromised into a soporific. In the protracted debates and controversies over the introduction of multicultural schooling in Britain in the 1970s and 1980s, we can see both the diversity of positions on how to introduce black culture, history, and, sometimes, politics into the curriculum, and the manner in which such debates drew attention to the different understandings of "blackness" in play between the black education movement and the wider project of multicultural schooling.

In the 1970s, black studies became a significant presence in adult and further and higher education. In part, this was an organic dimension of college life, where the influence of black radical politics led to invited talks and students established reading groups. The Black Student Society at Ferdinand Dennis's further education college in London's King's Cross area included many with experience in the Black Panther Movement. They invited regular guest speakers, including Darcus Howe, Cecil Gutzmore, John La Rose, and Linton Kwesi Johnson, and held "intense, lengthy discussions on the 'Black experience,'" swopping books by Stokely Carmichael, Bobby Seale, Malcolm X, Frantz Fanon, and Eldridge Cleaver. "These heady books," Dennis recalls, "gave me a language which helped to make sense of my situation which seemed to lack historical precedent and about which no books had been written."[132] At the same time as these organic developments, however, courses in black studies were being put together across London, and further afield. "These studies," James Berry observed of the many courses begun in the 1970s, "were usually intense experiences."[133] The Organisation for Black Unity ran a black studies module at the University of Birmingham in 1970.[134] From 1974 to 1976, the Polytechnic of Central London Centre for Extramural Studies offered a "Black Culture and Political Liberation" module. Run by the Nigeria-born Dapo Ladimeji, the module featured lectures by Edward Brathwaite, John La Rose, Wole Soyinka, and Jessica Huntley and included study of Fanon, George Jackson, and black women's politics.[135] Further education colleges in Hammersmith and Tottenham also provided courses in black studies.[136] Independent institutions offered additional provision. At the Holloway Institute, Winston Pinder, a postal worker from Barbados who became active in youth work in the early 1970s, established a National Institute for Black Studies.[137] Also in London, Roy Sawh, who taught black studies with Notting Hill's short-lived Anti-University in early 1968, that same year established the Free University for Black Studies, whose stated aims were "the need for affirmation of dignity and to combat the problem of self-identity" and "politicisation in terms of increasing awareness of the necessity to participate actively in a struggle against oppression, on the immediate level against racism; and, in the ultimate analysis, against the capitalist system." Echoing many of the models of black studies courses in the black supplementary education movement, the Free University emphasized the interconnection between autonomous learning and autonomous political action, convinced that "consciousness" of oppression by "the oppressed" was the necessary route to "liberating and humanising not just themselves but their de-humanised oppressors."[138] Sawh's Free University lasted until 1974, and attracted significant attendance, as well as joining the protracted campaign to introduce black studies into school curriculums.[139]

The introduction of black studies into school curriculums, however, was far more controversial. In the early 1970s, several schools began to organize black studies programs. The initial drive was led by Teachers against Racism (TAR), a group formed in 1971 and in regular dialogue with black radical educators, including Bernard Coard and Gus John. With bases in London, Liverpool, Leeds, and Birmingham, TAR campaigned for black literature in school libraries and for black studies as a new subject in state school curricula. In September 1972, it produced a black studies program for radio, broadcast on Radio London after school hours.[140] TAR's flagship successes were two south London schools, Tulse Hill Comprehensive and Dulwich's William Penn Comprehensive, both of which introduced Black Studies as their General Studies O-level qualification. These programs were self-consciously radical in design, teaching African history and geography, and African American history "right up to the Black Panther Party, Angela Davis, George Jackson, and the Attica massacre," as well as "the black immigrant in Britain." After a decade of teaching the syllabus, the teachers behind the Tulse Hill experiment went on to publish on the black British dimensions of their project, with learning materials for other teachers to use.[141] In Birmingham's Handsworth area, the William Murdoch School incorporated black studies into a Community Studies course in 1971, although the move brought several complaints from teachers and parents, and the course was ended after the chief education officer intervened. A concerted campaign in the local press, in which black studies was accused of stoking racism and tension, effectively blocked any revival of the initiative at William Murdoch. However, the incident led to the formation of a local TAR branch, and the curriculums of several Handsworth schools included black studies in 1973, according to *Race Today*.[142]

This drive to incorporate black studies into the curriculum was matched by a drive, centered on campaigning organization of radical teachers, and facilitated by bodies like Garrison's ACER Project, to confront racism and sexism in the school curriculum, and in the teaching tools used in schools. TAR, a prominent body in this campaign, aimed "to expel from school libraries and curricula as much of the old racially biased material as we can."[143] This aim was taken up by many campaigning groups in the 1970s.[144] As racist texts were slowly removed from school libraries and curriculums, they were often replaced by the new writing for black children, which was booming in the 1970s, supported by black publishers. Len Garrison's ACER Project promoted such resources tirelessly, with considerable success. Smaller operations also contributed. The Brixton Black Women's Group's Sabarr Books aimed, in the words of its journal, to "keep in contact with schools and other institutions with whom we discuss educational material available in the bookshop for their use."[145] The Institute of Race Relations's radical transformation under Sivanandan in 1973 also saw it launch a children's section in its library, aiming in particular to provide resources for supplementary school-teachers.[146] These books found a ready market in state schools as well as supplementary schools. Writing in late 1973, Mike Phillips observed that "it is difficult to avoid the army of earnest teachers and students scouring London for the correct 'multi-racial' texts. It may be that the picture is different outside London, but it should only be a short time before these attitudes are also reflected in the provinces."[147]

As the concern with black studies became more prevalent in mainstream schooling, however, many in the black education movement became wary of selective appropriations of black cultures and the self-narration strategies of black studies, which removed these from the context of anti-racist critical thinking, crucial to how engagements with blackness in supplementary schools were initially conceived. The Tulse Hill and William Penn projects acted as test cases for a black radical project in the mainstream education system. For Nigel File, architect of black studies at Tulse Hill, the logic of the module was: "Our society is a multicultural, multiracial one and all of us need to understand it better." For this reason, he advocated black studies for white children, too, and considered it "especially important that those living in areas where there are at present few black people should have access to this sort of information."[148] Such a position became more firmly entrenched as pedagogical orthodoxy following the 1985 Swann Report, *Education for All.* Indeed by 1989, despite the Thatcher government's recent introduction of what was widely perceived to be an ethnically exclusive national curriculum, Suzanne Scafe, then working as a teacher in London, could suggest that "most students at schools or colleges in inner-city areas have had some encounters with Black literary texts" and histories, the result, she noted, of "long and hard" struggle.[149] However, facing what she saw to be the continued undervaluing of these materials on black culture and history, Scafe also "came to the conclusion that a far more radical approach was needed than one which merely argued for a parallel canon of Black literary works. The whole white, male, literary tradition and the criteria by which texts enter that tradition had to be challenged."[150]

For Barbara Beese and Leila Hassan, writing in *Race Today* in 1975, the presence of black studies in schools was an appropriation of a radical initiative, designed for the removal of its radical content and to pacify the radical potential of black pupils. "School authorities latched on to the concept of Black Studies like a drowning man clutching at straws," Beese and Hassan opined. "They saw immediately that here was a not-to-be-missed opportunity to channel the chaos being created daily by black children in the classrooms."[151] Tulse Hill, for Scafe, and for Beese and Hassan, confirmed both the danger of the appropriation of black studies by teaching staff in schools, and its radical potential if wrestled back into the control of students. For Scafe, the black studies presence at Tulse Hill, initiated through the campaigns of black students, was incorporated into the curriculum by teachers "because of its threat to the authority and control of the school." Refusing to allow teachers to "hijack" the program, however, black students demanded, and won, control of content, inviting speakers from local black political groups—predominantly the Black Panther Movement—and also using their regular meetings to campaign against police harassment of local black youth.[152] As Beese and Hassan noted, in this assertion of control at Tulse Hill "the black studies class became a forum for the critique of problems faced by the black community, and in so doing became a potential political platform."[153]

Behind these critiques of black studies as a dimension of the school curriculum was a seemingly paradoxical claim that, on the one hand, studying black history and culture was in itself and inevitably politically radical, and yet on the other that there were, nonetheless, strategies used by schools to remove this radical potential. The task, then, was preserving the assumed radical potential of black studies. For Hazel Carby, a former teacher of Jamaican and Welsh descent beginning a research project on race and education in Britain at the Birmingham Centre for Contemporary Cultural Studies in the late 1970s, there was a "curious silence about, avoidance of, or inadequacy in, addressing Racism" in the manner in which state schools incorporated aspects of black studies into the curriculum. As Carby characterized it, the dialogue between the demands of black students and the school went thus:

SCHOOLS: We're all equal here.

BLACK STUDENTS: We KNOW we are second-class citizens, in housing, employment and education.

SCHOOLS: Oh, dear. Negative self-image. We must order some books with Blacks in them.

BLACK STUDENTS: Can't we talk about the Immigration Laws or the National Front?

SCHOOLS: No, that's politics. We'll arrange some Asian and West Indian Cultural Evenings.[154]

For Carby, concerns with "self-image" as they appeared in the state politics of multiculturalism were turned into a strategy for diverting, rather than cultivating, the radical energy of black students. In making this argument, Carby followed Farukh Dhondy, who proposed that "if the state, the educational authorities and inspectors of schools are serious about what they say," about incorporating black studies into the curriculum, this would necessarily mean starting "from the fact that young blacks fight the police, they refuse dirty jobs; their forms of culture gathering always brings them into conflict with the rulers of this society. Their very music, professed philosophies and life-styles contain in them an antagonism to school and to society as it is."[155]

Like Beese and Hassan before them, Dhondy and Carby were proposing that a proper incorporation of black experience into the curriculum necessarily challenged the dominant organization of society, because black experience was an experience of living in a racist society, under a racist state—whether in immigration laws, employment, education, policing, or popular racism.

Challenges such as these meant that Beese, Hassan, Dhondy, or Carby could at once bemoan the version of the black education movement which had made it into state school practice and policy in the 1970s and early 1980s, and simultaneously deny that this *was* a properly "black" move in education, citing how it erased the fundamental aspects that made up black life, constituted black culture, and so gave an oppositional, necessarily radical bent to black politics.

In this context, black radicals often interpreted black studies in state schools as a practice of social control. Bryan, Dadzie and Scafe complained that black studies continued the educational disadvantaging of black children. It was "used by some schools as a convenient means of social control, enabling 'non-examinable' Black pupils to be pacified and controlled, while white pupils got on with their 'O' levels and CSEs."[156] This was, for Carby, also an attempt to neutralize black political agency. Black movements' insistence on "an awareness of black history and culture, formed in the struggle against imperialism and colonialism, and essential in the struggle against contemporary forms of racism," were turned by the state into "a superficial gesture in an attempt to control the rising level of politicized black consciousness."[157] In 1980, as the Rampton Committee on Education was preparing its findings for its interim report of the following year, several black organizations waded into this debate about anti-racism and multiculturalism in education. Submitting a report to the Rampton Inquiry, the Institute of Race Relations (IRR) proposed that while "the differences in language, customs, values, etc. of different ethnic groups" might "be mediated by the educational system and even help to change attitudes," such mediation "is content to tinker with educational techniques and methods and leaves unaltered the racist fabric of the educational system. And education itself comes to be seen in terms of an adjustment process within a racialist society and not as a force for changing the values that make that society racialist." Offering a way forward, the IRR revealed that it planned "to produce, in pamphlet form, materials which will radically re-examine white society and history in the light of the black experience."[158]

In this debate on anti-racism, multiculturalism and black studies, Hazel Carby and her colleagues at the Centre for Contemporary Cultural Studies are most often remembered for their critique of focuses on black culture undertaken at the expense of identifying and attacking racism.[159] However, echoing the IRR, Carby's concern was not that a concentration on black culture should be replaced by a critique of white racism, but that the version of black culture endorsed by the politics of multiculturalism served to evacuate the political content of that culture, a content that she, in accordance with so many of her contemporaries in the black education movement, understood to be fundamentally anti-racist, and fundamentally interested in restructuring social and political relations according to this critique of racism. Noting the coincidence of the Rampton Report with the urban uprisings of 1981, Carby—in a comment echoing Dhondy—proposed that "the forms of resistances of black youths that these schemes have been attempting to manage and control are not about merely entering a hierarchy and leaving it untouched, but transforming that hierarchy and the sets of social relations that are oppressive."[160]

There were, of course, exceptions among black educationalists in Britain to this assumption of the inevitable radical potential of black studies. In 1973, Sam Morris, a Grenadian long involved in anti-racist, anticolonial and Pan-African politics in London and Ghana, presented his essay *The Case and the Course: A Treatise on Black Studies* at a conference at the West Indian Students Centre, launching a widespread debate on what black studies meant in Britain, and leading to the formation of a Black Studies Committee, which published his essay soon afterward.[161] Morris's course was wide-ranging, beginning in ancient Egypt and ending with Black Power, Pan-Africanism, and British race relations. However, Morris framed black studies in terms of social cohesion, good governance, and training in good citizenship—an emphasis some distance from what would gain popularity with a later generation of activists.[162] Morris proposed that government-funded black studies courses could offer both tuition in the necessary political rights required to live in a democratic society and a reminder of the "responsibilities and obligations" of this commitment. This would, he suggested, give "a tremendous saving all round, it would constitute at the same time the soundest investment the people and government could ever make. It would more than repay itself in less Borstal and prison expenditure, as well as in less payment for Social Security funds."[163]

Morris's black studies vision was some distance from those others we have looked at in this chapter. Morris, who had come to London at the age of thirty-one in 1939, was of a different generation to Beese, Hassan, Dhondy, and Carby. He had initially been active in Harold Moody's League of Coloured Peoples, later working in the Ministry of Labour with Learie Constantine. After a spell working for Nkrumah's government in Ghana in the 1950s and 1960s, he returned to Britain in 1967 to work first with the National Committee for Commonwealth Immigrants (NCCI), and later with its successor organizations, the Community Relations Commission

(CRC) and the Commission for Racial Equality (CRE), publishing his black studies proposals also in the CRC's journal *New Community*.[164] The institutions in which Morris worked might well have attracted the ire of some black radicals. At the IRR, Sivanandan launched a protracted critique of governmental race relations policy as managed by institutions like the NCCI, CRC, and CRE. He was characteristically scathing about the CRC, whose "black self-help groups, youth clubs, supplementary schools, cultural centres, homes and hostels" and program for "black studies" and "black curricula," were, in effect, containing measures designed "to stop black militancy from infecting the body politic."[165] Those who worked with the CRC, Sivanandan would describe as "black" only in inverted commas. They had, he implied, sacrificed their blackness. John La Rose and the group running the GPSS in Finsbury Park were equally suspicious of government financing and involvement, and believed that the political possibilities engendered through these projects could only be maintained if they kept their distance from the state. Trevor Carter, in his account of supplementary schooling written in the mid-1980s, reported similar concerns from a black education activist, who was "worried that the supplementary school movement has been colonised by the state." Access to grants, this educationalist worried, had lost independence and autonomy. "I'm suspicious of strings being attached—a certain level of attendance, this or that curriculum. [. . .] It's too easy to sit back and not bother with consciousness-raising anymore, with the result that our supplementary schools become passive rather than active instruments for change."[166]

Sivanandan's justly famous critiques have since provided the impression of a black political movement split along these lines of independence or collaboration with the state,, but the course of the black education movement was in reality never so clear-cut.[167] The Black Parents Movement, headed by La Rose and Bogle-L'Ouverture's Eric and Jessica Huntley, condemned the CRC as "a kind of colonial office for the black community in this country," and yet they continued to support and maintain communication with several schools receiving government funds.[168] Umbrella organizations like the Caribbean Teachers Association, which brought together black educators from across a wide political spectrum, were funded by the CRC, and later by Urban Aid programs. And radical supplementary schools often received funding. Ansel Wong's Ahfiwe was funded through a CRC grant, though his funding was later in jeopardy when he faced accusations of politicizing his pupils.[169] The Black Liberation Front's Headstart school in Tottenham, funded by the CRC and condemned by the Black Parent's Movement's sister organization, the

Black Youth Movement, as a place "to contain the unemployed and [. . .] for the police to pick up and harass the youth," was nonetheless opened by La Rose in 1976, and maintained cordial relations with him.[170] And the GPSS's Roxy Harris was closely involved with Len Garrison's government-funded ACER Project. The black education movement was always inevitably bound up with the designs of the state, and while some institutions remained steadfastly independent of state funding, many required that funding to survive. However, as Wong's experience shows, in the instances of the black education movement working with the state, it was frequently over the question of the nature of black studies, and the meaning of blackness, that relations were most strained, and liable to break down. In these strained relations, we can see the manner in which the black education movement was built around a notion of blackness that, while sometimes loosely defined and open to shifts and reinterpretations, was continually routed through ideas of a radical, transformative anti-racism: that learning to be black was a political process of becoming.

CONCLUSION

"Secondary Modern students never got the credit they deserved for making their schools such hot potatoes that education authorities hastily dropped them in favour of at least the notions of 'going comprehensive,'" Ken Forge, a teacher at the William Penn school, wrote in a letter to *Race Today* in 1974. In the mid-1970s, Forge felt that this mantle had now passed to a new generation of black students, who were "forcing our establishment to think very hard about the restructuring of our whole school system—a restructuring which is urgently needed in the interests of the great majority of all students, black and white, female and male."[171] For radicals like Forge, the new crisis in the British education system opened the possibility of new radical futures, a contribution to a new society. The education crisis came about through a breaking of the postwar settlement from many angles—disgruntled Tories, a hostile press, parents' activism, progressive education scandals, and reports of the failure of social mobility, all put under pressure by economic recession.[172] If children were not receiving the social equality nominally promised in the social-democratic education settlement, though, for many radical educators it was by turning to the insights of those children that a solution to the problems they faced might best be gleaned. This ideal was common across the radical education movement of the 1970s and 1980s, but it was the peculiar force of black creativity in the era of secondary decolonization, and the availability of that creative energy through the international black writing infrastructure developed in that era, that brought black students to the forefront. If children themselves held the key to challenging the failures of the school system and making school a better vehicle for social justice, then black children appeared, to many, to be particularly suited to this role.

By the early 1980s, the British state had begun to address the question of racism and education, first with the Rampton Report (1981) and then the Swann Report (1985). However, this was a question that had concerned black educators and political activists since the 1960s, when they read the much-discussed "crisis" of the education system as a crisis lived through race, the victims of which were black schoolchildren, consistently failed by their schools, bullied by teachers and fellow-students, and erased from the curriculum. The black education movement, born in the late 1960s at a time of secondary decolonization, aimed to combat racism in education. But unlike the politics of multicultural education that would come to dominate the political discourse on race and education over the following two decades, the black education movement was not so much concerned with liberal pluralism and cultural diversity as with anti-racism, challenging the school as a social and political institution and empowering students to lead this challenge. The black education movement, Farukh Dhondy claimed, was about the "decolonization" of British schooling, and this meant challenging the school's role in reproducing hierarchies of class and race.

Radical educators took up black self-narration as the starting point for this potential transformation of the education system and, by extension, of society. As a process of self-empowerment, through which black schoolchildren could recognize themselves as political subjects, part of a wider black community understood in terms of its transformative potential, black self-narration promised to cultivate a new cultural-political formation of blackness, capable of confronting the British state with the challenge of decolonization. This was not, of course, the only terrain of struggle, and as we shall see in the next chapter, in the late 1970s and early 1980s, it was increasingly activities beyond the school gates that attracted the most interest and investment by black radicals. "While it is clear that the main struggle for change goes on outside the schools," Forge wrote to *Race Today*, however, "we inside do not have to wait for the revolution." Black self-narration offered the possibility of beginning this struggle from within, armed only with a pen.

———

FIVE

Thinking about Race in a Time of Rebellion

ON JUNE 9, 1973, a white teenager was stabbed in a fight among young men at a crowded fish-and-chip shop in south London. The affray was not in itself unusual, but it quickly escalated. The stabbing occurred as revelers made their way home after the firework display at the annual Brockwell Park fair in Brixton. By the time the police arrived, a large crowd leaving the park had already pressed in to see what was happening. Claiming to have spotted those responsible for the stabbing, police drew their truncheons on two young black men, Horace Parkinson, a nineteen-year-old youth worker, and eighteen-year-old Lloyd James, an attendee at Parkinson's youth club. The police were met by a volley of bottles and stones from the crowd in protest to their treatment of Parkinson and James. After police reinforcements arrived, a larger skirmish developed, leading to injuries on both sides. Parkinson and James were arrested, along with fourteen-year-old Robin Sterling, a pupil at the local Tulse Hill Comprehensive. All three reportedly received severe beatings at Brixton police station. Although none of them were charged with the stabbing that triggered the incident, they were charged with assaulting police officers and carrying offensive weapons, and following a trial at the Old Bailey in early March 1974, each received a sentence of three years' imprisonment.

The defense campaign for the Brockwell 3, as Parkinson, James, and Sterling came to be known, mobilized traditional organs of black local politics established in the Brixton area over the previous two decades. The case was first taken up by the Jamaican Courtney Laws, a community relations worker active in Brixton since 1958, and founder of the St John's Inter-Racial Club, later renamed the Brixton Neighbourhood Association. Laws, in turn, appointed an Indo-Guyanese solicitor, Rudy Narayan, to handle the case. However, after the sentence was passed on the Brockwell 3, a new organization, engaging in a different form of politics, emerged to challenge the ruling. On March 27, 1974, students at Tulse Hill Comprehensive—one of the first British schools to implement a black studies program—called a meeting for black students at the Gresham Centre, home of Ansel Wong's Ahfiwe school. Over seventy students attended and founded the Black Students Action Collective (Black Sac), organizing a march of five hundred people from Brockwell Park to Railton Road, one of the centers of black settlement in Brixton. On the success of this march, Black Sac organized a student strike for April 3, attracting the support of the National Union of School Students. Across London, 1,000 students came out on strike to join a rally organized by Black Sac in Kennington Park, before marching, via Camberwell Green Magistrate Court, Brixton police station and Tulse Hill Comprehensive, to Brockwell Park. At the park, the marchers were met by Paul Stephenson, the former leader of the 1963 Bristol bus boycott, now working as a governor of Tulse Hill Comprehensive and a youth officer with the Community Relations Council. Stephenson left with two representatives from Black Sac to deliver a letter of protest to the House of Commons, and to speak about the case with David Ennals, Labour's new minister of state for the Foreign and Commonwealth Office.[1]

This chapter argues that the escalating urban conflicts between youth and the police in areas of black settlement came to define black politics in the 1970s and early 1980s. Many saw the key to the future of racial politics in Britain to lie in the fate and actions of urban black British youth, who had the potential, it was thought, to transform the nation's current political setup. The issues of black schooling and relations with the police converged in the Brockwell 3 case. "For black young people," the Grenadian youth worker Gus John wrote in 1981, "the school and the police are the two major institutions in this society that are posed against them, and, as such, are at the interface between the black working class and the society. It has come as no surprise, therefore, that over the years, both these institutions have joined forces together to do battle with young blacks."[2] Chapter 4 focused on why schooling was so important to black activists, and how the relationship between black children and the school came to assume such political weight in this era. The politics of the school, though, were overtaken by the politics of policing for many activists. As Farukh Dhondy wrote, the Brockwell 3 case proved "that the black students in schools will more readily concentrate on the interference of police in their lives and educational institutions, than they will on the quality of the curriculum."[3] If part of the promise of black children in schools was that they could reveal the contradictions and tensions of a racialized society in the classrooms, it was on the streets that they first encountered these contradictions and tensions. As conflicts between youth and the police escalated, the practice of thinking black that had developed over the previous decade was realigned with the question of youth rebellion, while youth cultural practices were reinterpreted as the new focus of black social and political thought and action. Black radical intellectuals were not alone in focusing their attention on black youth in these years. Social scientists, government officials, journalists, philanthropists, and politicians all took it upon themselves to explain the escalating conflicts between black youth and the police—their fate, on all sides, became tied up with the fate of the nation. For black radical intellectuals, however, this was all the more reason to understand, to speak for, or to attempt to allow the voices of black youth to be heard. Against a hardening "new racism" on the right that frequently cast black youth—particularly young black men—as the central threat to the coherence and stability of the nation and state, these intellectuals looked to black youth's cultural and political practices for the promise of an alternative solution to the deepening crisis of the long 1970s.[4]

BLACK YOUTH AND THE POLICE IN THE 1970S AND 1980S

... from your skin is black dem have to stop you.

—BIRMINGHAM JAMAICAN MAN[5]

In the 1970s and early 1980s, police action against and confrontations with black communities, and particularly black youth, increased dramatically. This led to what had been one among many of the political concerns of Britain's black communities in the 1960s becoming the central political issue for many black Britons by the early 1980s. The charge of police mistreatment of black and immigrant groups was nothing new in the 1960s, and debates on police relationships with black communities became increasingly common from the middle of that decade on. In 1965, Joseph Hunte, the secretary of West Indian Standing Conference, published a report on the police harassment of West Indians in Lambeth, a practice that, Hunte recorded, was referred to by police as "nigger hunting."[6] Complaints against the police by black Britons were becoming ever more frequent in the late 1960s, as police harassment became, according to the *Sunday Times* journalist Derek

Humphry, "a way of life."[7] The National Council for Civil Liberties reported in 1971 that based on a recent survey, "the alleged harassment of immigrants far outweighs the proportion they represent in this country," and a National Opinion Polls survey conducted the same year reported that "West Indians [...] were particularly critical in thinking that the police generally pick on coloured people and did not deal with them fairly in their locality." The report's author deemed this criticism "too widespread to be a figment of imagination."[8] A widely publicized investigation, also in 1971, into the death two years previously of a Nigerian, David Oluwale, in Leeds showed that significant police violence and brutality were involved and led to charges of manslaughter against two Leeds police officers. The deterioration of relations between police and the black community by 1971 was sufficient for the issue to be included in the evidence-gathering sessions of the parliamentary Select Committee on Race Relations and Immigration of that year. Evidence collected from West Indian community leaders included allegations of blackmail, drug planting, false charges, and assault, particularly against the young.[9] In 1979, the Institute of Race Relations produced a sixty-eight-page document on policing abuses and racist police practices for the Royal Commission on Criminal Procedure.[10]

The increased policing and criminalization of black Britons was key to the race politics of this era. The 1970s and 1980s, as Paul Gilroy observed, were decades of "increasingly vivid images of the particular crimes and criminals that [were] understood to be the anti-social effects of black settlement."[11] While the policing of Britain's black communities involved the harassment and arrest of individuals irrespective of age or gender, it focused on black youth, perceived as a criminal class. Stuart Hall and his colleagues at the Birmingham Centre for Contemporary Cultural Studies famously followed one important dimension of this criminalization of black youth in their study of the "moral panic" around "mugging" that developed in Britain in the early 1970s. "Mugging," Hall proposed, was a new label, imported from the United States, to describe an old practice of street robbery, a racially coded term that came to be read by the press and politicians in this era as a specific form of black youth criminality, the policing of which became a central process in the consolidation of a "law and order" state, reinforced by harsh sentencing, and condoned through media campaigns. In the context of the political crises brought about through economic decline, the erosion of the postwar consensus and the perceived polarization of social and moral values brought about through the social changes of the 1960s, policing the crisis,

Hall argued, meant "policing the blacks." The effects of this for black Britons were multiple: it provided a political justification for anti-immigration and repatriation rhetoric and policy; it provided an apparent legitimacy to every-day expressions of racist sentiments; and, in the arena of policing and the courts, it led to heightened police activity against black people, and a readi-ness of the judiciary to use the criminal justice system as a mechanism for the disciplining of this supposedly deviant population.[12]

The consequence of this on the ground was that being arrested on the street on charges of having committed or being about to commit a robbery became a common occurrence for young black men and women. With the arrival of the moral panic around mugging, police divisions began to form new Anti-Mugging Squads, performing sweeps of areas presumed to be mug-ging hotspots—usually shopping precincts, areas of black settlement, and the transport network. Detective Inspector Sergeant Ridgewell, in charge of one such squad in south London, revealed that these officers targeted "coloured young men."[13] In the later 1970s, similar sweeps targeting black youths in British cities were part of the widespread practice of "sus" (i.e., "suspected person") policing. Under section four of the 1824 Vagrancy Act, any person could be arrested on suspicion of loitering with the intent to commit an arre-stable offense. Those charged could only be tried before a magistrate, not a jury. All that was required for conviction was the evidence of two police officers that the accused had acted suspiciously on two separate occasions, though these could be only minutes apart. "Sus" arrests were used dispropor-tionately against black youths, with one study of London in 1977 finding that this group, who made up less than 3 percent of the population, accounted for 44 percent of such arrests. With the burden of proof for conviction resting only on police testimony, the charge was near impossible to rebut, and con-viction rates were high. A study by Waltham Forest Community Relations Council between January 1977 and October 1978 found that out of thirty-four cases brought before the local magistrates' court, only one defendant was acquitted.[14] By the later 1970s, as the solicitor Paul Boateng, a leading figure in the anti-sus campaign, observed, "sus" policing practices were increasingly relying on the charge of conspiracy against larger groups, leading to mass trials.[15] As with the "sus" law, the charge of conspiracy required no proof that a crime had been committed or attempted, only that there had been an agreement to commit a crime. Charges of conspiracy led straight to trial at the Old Bailey and carried heavier sentences than charges under sec-tion four of the Vagrancy Act. In 1976, eighteen young men were arrested by police in Islington under such a charge.[16] A similar case in Lewisham in 1977 saw twenty-one young men arrested in dawn raids on their homes, charged with conspiracy to steal.[17]

Meeting places, particularly youth clubs and dance halls, were also a common target for the police. In the early 1970s, Metropolitan Police Commissioner Sir Robert Mark introduced what he termed "fire-brigade policing," a strategy for urban centers in which officers would patrol in cars backed by a central mobile reserve of reinforcements. Numerous court cases arose from confrontations with the police triggered after these reinforcements were called in when officers, entering youth clubs or dance halls on the pretext of looking for an alleged offender, met resistance from the attendees.[18] In May 1971, police raided the Metro Youth Club in Notting Hill, after two officers entered the club to arrest a suspected robber. The resulting fight with the police ended in the arrest of at least ten people, and the subsequent trial of the four of these in what came to be termed the Metro 4 trial.[19] Another North London youth club, the Carib Club in Cricklewood, was raided by police with dogs and riot shields on October 12, 1974. The raid began on the pretext of chasing a suspect who had abandoned a stolen vehicle nearby, but hostility to the raid by the crowd led to 140 police officers entering the club with six Alsatians. Following mass arrests, charges were brought against twelve of those present—the Cricklewood 12.[20] A month earlier, in Brixton, two coachloads of police had stormed the Swann disco, arresting seven, while the following year in Hackney a raid on the Four Aces Club, on the pretext of searching for four youths who had stolen a purse, ended with eighteen arrested. As the Institute of Race Relations commented on these cases, the charges that were finally brought often bore no relation to the original enquiry, "but to the 'incident' provoked, in the first place, by police tactics."[21]

The resistance to police incursions on meeting places and dance halls was repeated, in more dramatic and public events, in rising instances of mass confrontations between black youth and the police on the streets of British cities, often as people gathered to protest these earlier spontaneous assaults. Following mass arrests at an amusement park in Islington in May 1971, a hundred protestors, headed by Michael Abdul Malik, marched on the Caledonian Road Police Station. Following another mass arrest at Peckham Rye fair a few months later, the Black Unity and Freedom Party organized a similar protest march. Both ended in further arrests.[22] Two years later, the events leading to the Brockwell 3 trial followed a similar trajectory. Outside London, larger outdoor confrontations were also becoming more common.

In a Liverpool neighborhood in July 1975, a retaliation attack by local black youths on white men led to police from across Merseyside cordoning the area off with roadblocks, imposing a curfew, and arresting those who did not vacate the street. The events led to a running battle with the police and mass arrests.[23] Four months on, three hundred clashed with police in Leeds's Chapeltown after the police, in breach of an agreement they had with community leaders, sent a convoy of officers to the local fireworks display. Twelve were arrested on charges of assault, possession of offensive weapons, criminal damage, and affray. This confrontation was followed by similar smaller-scale events in Wood Green, Brixton, Harlesden, and Manchester's Moss Side in the early summer of 1976.[24] These, however, were themselves quickly overshadowed by the violent clash at London's Notting Hill Carnival in August 1976, where 1,598 officers had been brought in to police the street festival, a twenty-six-fold increase from the sixty deployed the previous year.

In the 1970s the Notting Hill Carnival became an increasing source of concern for the local council and police. As early as 1971, as Courtney Tulloch noted, the council's support for the Carnival was waning "since large numbers of black kids started beating Shango drums and expressing pent-up ghetto feelings which an on-looker would find alien."[25] From 1974, the number of black youth attending the Carnival increased as static reggae sound systems were introduced, and this increase, in the context of the police and media criminalization of young blacks in the early 1970s, quickly led to an effort by the police and some local residents and councilors to close the event down. The officer in charge of coordinating policing of the 1976 Carnival, Chief Superintendent Ron Patterson—his previous achievement, as many black newsletters and Carnival revelers noted, had been to suppress the 1969 Anguillan revolution—argued the need for "not hundreds of police but thousands," and adopted an aggressive policing strategy that sparked mass confrontations.[26] Sixty-eight arrests and 250 injured, including 120 police, resulted.[27]

In the 1970s, the Carnival became a politicized event, bringing together local and national experiences of oppression and resistance, and dramatizing these through the global politics of Black Power and decolonization. A 1971 masque included a ten-foot statue of Police Constable Pulley, the officer leading the case against the Mangrove restaurant in the Mangrove Nine trial, with the words "I'm right behind you" glued to his chest. The 1973 Carnival included masques on the theme of black youth incarcerations and "ghetto" life.[28] Later in the 1970s, masques were staged acting out contemporary

African liberation struggles and celebrating past anticolonial struggles in Africa and Latin America. Political activists from local black radical organizations also used the Carnival as an opportunity to distribute their literature and posters.[29] "We were now into our Black Power and Rastafari," Cheddar, a young member of the Metro Youth Club present at the 1976 Carnival, recalled, "and we were going to stand our ground."[30] *Race Today* commissioned a report of the event from a young man arrested on the day of the 1976 Carnival. In the Paddington police station in which he was held, he reported a "spirit of jubilation" as those arrested exchanged stories of the confrontation, and reveled in the "licks" they had given to the police. The cellmates were not only from Notting Hill, but Brixton, Harlesden, Birmingham, and Leicester, and the conversations the young man reported ranged over other confrontations, in other places. "Last week it was Soweto, this week it's Notting Hill," one cellmate announced, recalling the bloody suppression of South African students of June 1976. For others, the story was a national one.

> "The police come there to war," one of the brothers said. He was clutching his head, rubbing it, smiling thoughtfully. "Yeah, they catch a licking in Leeds, Stockwell, Cricklewood. We deal them some heavy blows in the past few months. In the streets, in the courts and all."
> "Yeah, sight"—everyone is familiar with the incidents we are referring to—"and they get a good warring too."[31]

Soweto, Anguilla, Leeds, Cricklewood: the Notting Hill Carnival provided a venue in which the local and global sites of racial violence and black liberation could be thought through each other.

Conversations at youth clubs and other meeting places, and the exchange of posters detailing the events, helped cement these confrontations in what Gilroy terms "the folk memory of black Britain."[32] A 1971 report on one such space—the Church Hall at Farraway Road, Notting Hill—records walls "covered with posters listing the battle honours of the last year . . . the Metro Youth Club (sixteen arrested), Harlesdon (eight), Acton Park (ten), Peckham Rye Fair (over fifty), Lisson Grove; and so the list reads on."[33] The clashes also enjoyed national media coverage. Keith Piper, a schoolboy in Birmingham at the time, remembers seeing the front page of the *Observer Review* in the wake of the 1976 Carnival, and the image acting "for me, as it must have done for a whole range of my peers and contemporaries, to aid in the crystallization of a whole body of unfocussed but romantic assumptions around what it was to be young, Black and male in the Britain of the 1970s." "What was symbolically crystallized at that moment," Piper remembers, "was that to aspire to become the Black of heroic defiance, was 'where it was at.'"[34] In Piper's remembrance, we can see how an image of confrontational youth was reproduced and learned in this era across a range of communication technologies, as well as the gendering of that image—black men predominated.

Police stepped up their presence even further in the Notting Hill carnivals of the later 1970s, and launched a broader offensive against black youth. In the wake of the 1976 Carnival, despite widespread press criticism of the policing of the event, Sir Robert Mark was defiant in supporting the actions of his officers, blaming the violence on pickpockets, and promising there "are not going to be any 'no go' areas in Metropolitan Police districts."[35] Following the Carnival, seventy further arrests were made in Notting Hill, and the subsequent arrest and trial of the Islington 18 on conspiracy charges relating to allegations of pickpocketing in Notting Hill was also a direct response to the Carnival.[36] The Black Parents Movement reported that youth across London were being picked up, asked if they were at Notting Hill Carnival, and "told that if they were there they would be taken to Notting Hill police station and the officers there would know how to deal with them." Those with previous convictions reported being warned by police to stay away from future carnivals, while a magistrate in Camberwell took the step of banning Lewisham youths from attending Carnival in 1977.[37] At that year's Carnival, and for the following two years, police were deployed in full riot gear—a spectacle previously associated primarily with the conflicts of Northern Ireland. They policed the event on the offensive, cordoning off and clearing roads in advance of anticipated confrontations and quickly moving in to make arrests in the clashes that inevitably followed.

While the Notting Hill Carnival—an event that drew in revelers from across the country and beyond—became the set-piece stage for annual confrontations with the police in the late 1970s, relations with the police continued to deteriorate at the local level in cities across Britain. On April 2, 1980, in the St Paul's district of Bristol, this spilled over in the first of a series of urban riots that erupted throughout the first half of the 1980s, largely consisting of pitched battles between the police and black and, to a lesser extent, white youth. St Paul's had been a site of tense relations between police and the local black community for many years.[38] Following police closures of other black social spaces in the area, the Bristol disorders began when police raided the Black and White Café on accusations of illegal drinking and drug use. Customers at the café and local residents resisted, and the conflict escalated into a six-hour confrontation between the police and three hundred youths, in which twenty-one buildings were damaged or destroyed by fire and fifty police injured. Interviews with some of those involved revealed the depth of animosity between black youth and the police, as well as the role of politicized black expressive cultures in articulating and directing this animosity. Referring to the police force, in the language of Rastafarianism, as "Babylon," one young man explained, "We associate Babylon in our history as a place of repression and suffering. The Babylon is always harassing us and this time we kicked back."[39] Another young man, Patrick, told *Westindian World* that "this incident is just the start of an all-out war against the police in Bristol." The paper also, without giving sources but with surprising prescience, reported that "Black youths from Birmingham, Manchester, Liverpool and London have shown their solidarity with their Bristol brothers and are planning to confront the police in numbers if their grievances against the police are not given serious consideration by the authorities."[40]

Nine months later in London, on January 18, 1981, a fire at a party in London's New Cross, widely believed to be the result of a racist arson attack, resulted in the deaths of thirteen young black people and injury of twenty-six more. The incident was largely overlooked by the national media, mishandled by the police—who quickly blamed the fire on a fight between partygoers—and drew little response from the government, despite a similar event in Dublin three weeks later prompting messages of sympathy from Margaret Thatcher and the Queen. *Westindian World*, reporting the reactions of New Cross's black residents, noted that the "incident has, overnight, made them a bitterly angry people, who no more worry about restraining those who talk about hitting back, and hitting hard at the racist death squads, which they believe can only operate with their present effrontery because they enjoy powerful support in top police and political circles."[41] A letter to the paper argued that the black community should follow the example set by "our friends in the Jewish community" and "invite commandos over from Africa [...] for special instructions in self-defence."[42]

John La Rose and Darcus Howe channeled community anger. Responding to the police, government and media indifference, and seeking an inquest for the families of the deceased, they organized the New Cross Massacre Action Committee, drawing together an alliance of community groups and organizations. The alliance was a broad church, encompassing the Black Parents Movement, the Black Youth Movement, the Race Today Collective, the Black Unity and Freedom Party, Headstart and the Socialist Workers' Party. After six weeks of campaigning, the Action Committee organized the Black People's Day of Action for March 2, 1981, a march of between fifteen and twenty thousand from New Cross to Hyde Park, via Fleet Street.[43] Marchers came to London from across Britain—Gus John, reviewing the events surrounding an urban uprising in Manchester's Moss Side four months later, recorded six coachloads leaving from there to join the march.[44] Though the media made much of some minor confrontations, resulting in seventeen police injured and twenty-three arrests, the march was peaceful. One of the most popular slogans of the marchers, though—"Blood Ah Go Run If Justice Nah Come"—revealed some of the depths of the tension recorded by *Westindian World*.[45]

Later that year, more urban confrontations broke out, first in London but soon followed by similar events across the country. On the weekend of April 10–12, 1981, large-scale civil unrest broke out in Brixton. Four days earlier, police had launched operation "Swamp '81," involving the saturation of the Brixton neighborhood with plainclothes police officers tasked with tackling street crime by, as the instructions given to officers demanded, "a concentrated effort of 'stops' [. . .] proceeded by persistent and astute questioning."[46] Swamp '81 began with raids on premises and mass arrests, followed by 943 stops over the six-day operation; at the end of the operation, 118 had been arrested. Several skirmishes broke out with the police over the early course of Swamp '81, but wider unrest erupted on the evening of April 10, when local youths intervened as police were giving first aid to a young black man who had been stabbed, the youths being under the impression that the police were responsible for his injury. As the standoff escalated, the crowd confronting the police grew to around one hundred people, and some began to throw bricks and bottles. The conflict was relatively minor, but when nearly a hundred additional police were drafted in to patrol the neighborhood the following day, a further incident that afternoon, triggered by a Swamp '81 stop of a taxi driver wrongly suspected of hiding drugs, quickly led to a far larger conflict involving crowds in their hundreds, and riot police reinforcements. The destruction was dramatic. Rioters overturned and torched cars, and threw missiles at the police—bottles, bricks, and stones, but also, to much alarm in the press, petrol bombs. Police conduct was often brutal and indiscriminate. By the end of the weekend, 279 police and 45 members of the public had been injured, 56 police vehicles and 61 private vehicles damaged, many overturned and burned, and 145 properties damaged, 28 by fire.[47]

Three months later, in July, another series of disturbances occurred. On July 3, Southall in suburban west London witnessed a pitched battle between hundreds of skinheads and local Asian people. Clashes with police erupted in Liverpool's "Liverpool 8" district that same day, lasting three days.[48] A similar conflict erupted the following day in Manchester's Moss Side, and black youth involved cited the Liverpool 8 confrontation as a trigger.[49] On July 15, following early-morning raids by 176 police on eleven houses on Brixton's Railton Road—raids conducted on the premise of unlawful drinking and petrol bombs, evidence of neither of which was found—rioting again broke out in Brixton. The following weeks saw smaller-scale incidents occur in Birmingham's Handsworth, Sheffield, Nottingham, Hull, Slough, Leeds, Bradford, Newcastle, Huddersfield, Halifax, Knaresborough, Stoke on Trent, Southampton, Aldershot, Portsmouth, High Wycombe, Leicester, Nottingham, Fleetwood, Derby, Blackpool, Birmingham, Wolverhampton, Maidstone, Cirencester, and Luton.[50] Urban conflicts between black and white youth and the police occurred again in 1982 and 1983 in London and Liverpool. In 1984, the Metropolitan Police Commissioner reported "many mini-riots which had the potential to escalate to Brixton 1981 proportions," adding that "London is nowadays a very volatile city."[51]

The major conflicts of the following year occurred first in Handsworth, however. Small-scale confrontations with the police began in July 1985, but quickly died down. However, on September 9 a dispute between a black man and the police over a parking ticket quickly escalated into a mass confrontation, involving local black youths, of Asian and African descent, and local whites, pitched against the police. The disorder resulted in 122 injured, mainly on the police side, many buildings looted, and 45 burnt down, including a post office owned by two Asian men, who died in the fire.[52] Smaller conflicts broke out in other West Midlands cities and towns, including Moseley, Wolverhampton, and Coventry, and again in St Paul's, Bristol, in the following weeks.

The summer ended with two large-scale confrontations in London. On September 28, armed police in Brixton shot a Jamaican, Cherry Groce, in her home after they raided the house looking for her sons. Police refused to meet with a deputation of protestors, and later that evening the Brixton police station was petrol-bombed, sparking a conflict that lasted for two days, and drew in the local white and black population.[53] Immediately following the end of disturbances in Bristol, on September 30 conflicts arose again in the Liverpool 8 district, after four young black men, part of a community of young people who claimed to have been subjected to a summer of harassment by local police, were refused bail at Liverpool Magistrate's Court.[54] A week later, on October 6, when police raided a home on Tottenham's Broadwater Farm Estate looking for Floyd Jarrett, a youth worker at the Broadwater Farm Youth Association, Jarrett's mother, Cynthia Jarrett, collapsed and died. Rioting broke out as residents on the mainly black Broadwater Farm Estate confronted police, and ended with 20 members of public and 223 police injured, and one police officer killed in the riot. Further, smaller-scale disorders erupted again in 1986, in Notting Hill and Plymouth, but the Broadwater Farm affair marked the last instance of large-scale urban unrest in 1980s Britain, with similar levels of unrest not occurring on the streets of mainland Britain for another twenty-six years, in the riots of 2011.

This section has outlined the escalating policing of black Britain in the 1970s and 1980s, and the protests that this sparked. These were the conflicts that underwrote the explosion of black intellectual activity around policing, youth, race, and the state that occupies the remainder of the chapter. The following subdivided section looks in detail at the responses of four leading black institutions to the police brutality and black resistance of the 1970s and 1980s. It shows how, in various ways, each insisted on the centrality of race to the dynamics of British politics in this era. The above section has derived some of its argument from the readings of race politics in late-twentieth-century Britain provided in Stuart Hall and Paul Gilroy's work. The following section, however, makes the argument that these more familiar interpretations of race and politics in Hall and Gilroy's work make more sense when we see how they drew on and were in dialogue with this far wider radical intellectual conversation emerging out of two decades of black radical activism in Britain, and with its connections to a wider black Atlantic world, particularly the Caribbean and the United States of America.

BLACK INTELLECTUALS, YOUTH RESISTANCE, AND RACE POLITICS

Riots are the voices of the unheard.
—MARTIN LUTHER KING JR.[55]

Within days of the Brixton uprisings, Home Secretary William Whitelaw appointed the judge and barrister Leslie Scarman, Baron Scarman, to undertake an inquiry into the disorders. The liberal press praised Lord Scarman's appointment—his previous inquiries, into the 1969 civil rights conflicts in Northern Ireland and the 1974 clash between fascists and anti-fascists in Red

Lion Square, earned him many accolades for his open-mindedness and independence.[56] However, a campaign by black groups in Brixton called on Brixtonians and local political groups to boycott the inquiry. The Brixton Defence Campaign accused the inquiry of prejudicing the rights to a fair trial of those still to come before the courts on charges arising from the events. More than this, they proposed that the ostensive basis of the inquiry—to uncover the causes of the riots—was disingenuous. Noting that over the previous five years there had been "repeated requests to the Home Secretary for a public inquiry into police brutality and malpractice," the Campaign argued that "where the black communities' grievances over the racist, brutal, lawless and uncontrolled policing-methods used against them are concerned the state has no basis for even claiming to be ignorant. A mountain of evidence has been 'submitted' and ignored."[57] Backing this argument, *Westindian World* called for the boycott to be supported "throughout the black community." When requested to submit their own evidence to the inquiry, the paper responded that they would not do so "because we have written everything we have to say, and they are quite welcome to read it." This "Scarman tendency of asking reporters who have written at great length to go before them and repeat what they have already put down on paper," the *World* complained, was "just typical of the whole method."[58]

The Scarman boycott had some impact locally, though Scarman brushed aside its importance in his final report noting that despite these efforts the inquiry received nineteen applications for representation from local organizations.[59] The campaign, however, draws our attention to the existence of this marginalized tradition of black political reporting and analysis, which had consistently offered critiques of the state and race relations policy, but felt itself frozen out of mainstream public debate on these matters. As *Westindian World* repeatedly bemoaned of the Scarman Inquiry: "What on earth can Scarman find out that black people haven't been saying for years and years?"[60] When Scarman published his report in November 1981, focusing the public debate on new policies of community policing and the possibilities of an independent police complaints commission, *Race Today* protested that this, again, diverted attention away from the real issues fleshed out in black critiques of the state. Characteristically, in a lament made often by black journals in this period, *Race Today* read the post-Scarman debate as an attempt to shift attention away from those who had broken onto the national stage in the events of 1981: "the public are being trained to take their eyes off the central protagonists, the black youth."[61] The Scarman Inquiry, instead, as the

Black Liberator's Cecil Gutzmore would argue, took "the police line on 'black crime.'"[62]

This section reads this alternative, marginalized body of writing on the politics of race, offered by *Race Today, Race & Class,* or *Black Liberator,* as a domain of "thinking black" centered on attempts to privilege and interpret the voices and actions of black youth. In this body of writing, the debate about the position of black youth in relation to the state had been ongoing for a decade. The discussion was led by four central institutions: the Institute of Race Relations (IRR)'s *Race & Class;* the Race Today Collective (RTC)'s *Race Today;* the *Black Liberator* journal; and, joining these discussions by the mid-1970s, a group of academics at the University of Birmingham's Centre for Contemporary Cultural Studies (CCCS). It was often a fraught debate, though there was also much intellectual and personal exchange. What united the intellectual efforts of these institutions, however, was their concerted effort to place race at the center of critical analysis of the British state and British society, and their commitment to orientate themselves toward the expressive cultures and political interests of those black young people deemed to be on the front line of confrontation with the state. In the aftermath of the successive clashes between young black men and women and the police in the 1970s and early 1980s, sociologists, the press, and government initiatives—most substantially through the Community Relations Commission and the Urban Aid program—articulated a reading of "black youth" that framed them, primarily, as a social problem caused by inadequate family lives, conflicted or wanting social identities, and poor integration.[63] These intellectuals challenged these meanings of "black youth," and used this challenge to launch a wholesale rereading of British politics and the state in this conjuncture.

They engaged with and mobilized the category of "black youth" to launch three related critiques of the state, and of the meaning of "black" politics. First, they situated black youth in the context of British class relations as a means of exploring the place of race in structural unemployment during economic recession. Second, they situated black youth in relation to other aspects of the "black community," both within Britain and transnationally, rejecting the isolation of "youth" politics from a wider politics of resistance and arguing that the fetishization of this category aimed at dividing black political unity. Third, they interrogated the question of what the "blackness" of "black youth" meant, and how a politics of blackness could be elaborated from the cultural and political practices associated with that term. In this final move, black intellectuals also questioned where "thinking black" occurred, finding an organic intellectual life on this front line of confrontations with the state.

This intellectual project was deeply embedded, though often uncomfortably, in the intellectual history Marxism. Geoff Eley has noted the extent to which the radical debates on race at the CCCS occurred in the context of "the very particular preoccupations of British Marxist debates" of the 1970s and early 1980s.[64] At the CCCS, this hinged on the protracted and fraught debates over the work of Louis Althusser that marked the theoretical direction of the so-called "second" New Left of intellectuals associated with the post-1964 *New Left Review*.[65] The extent to which radical thinking on race was engaged with and through Marxism was not limited to this New Left; Eley's point stands equally when considering the Althusserian Marxism of *Black Liberator*, the Jamesian Marxism of *Race Today*, or the various engagements with anticolonial Marxism at the IRR. Marxist thought was central to black politics and intellectual work in this era. Indeed, *all* of the black political thinkers and organizations whom we have encountered in this book were, to varying but substantial degrees, part of a socialist politics, often coming to black radical politics through earlier commitments to Marxism and Marxist or communist versions of anticolonial nationalism, and often understanding black radical politics as necessarily socialist in form. Indeed, socialism, more broadly understood, overdetermined what black meant in this period. The vocabulary of blackness, as we have seen, sprang from political struggles in North America, the Caribbean, and Africa, most of which were heavily invested in some form of socialist transformation.[66]

Eley suggests that in the thinking on race emerging out of this conjunction of black politics and Marxism in 1970s and 1980s Britain, the continuing pull of class as an explanatory framework was a distortion of how "race" works, and one which would happily fade as Marxist analysis lost its hold in the later 1980s. His focus on the limitations of Marxist frameworks, however, risks underplaying the degree to which, for radical intellectuals in this period, Marxism was largely the only game in town, and certainly an intellectual tradition with which any serious political thinker had to engage. In the long history of black and anticolonial Marxism, Marxism was at once claimed and forced into new analytical positions. This was a Marxism that displaced the centrality of European metropolitan development, emphasized the significance of imperialism, and often insisted on the place of race as the organizing social experience in the modern life of global late capitalism.[67] Though infrequently recognized as such outside of Stuart Hall's work, this black Marxism was a component of—and a radical point of departure within—a wider tradition of New Left thought in Britain, but the intellectual and political energy that drove it was that of individuals and institutions often forgotten in histories of the British New Left.[68] Returning to the conjunction of Marxism and black politics offers us not only a fresh perspective on the transnational permutations of late twentieth-century Marxism, but an understanding also of how blackness was then defined. What kept these various thinkers in dialogue with one another, and focused on understanding young black people, was a shared sense that blackness both had something to offer a socialist future and embodied important lessons for rethinking Marxism.

The Race Today Collective

In 1974, *Race Today* journalists and political activists formed the Race Today Collective. *Race Today*, founded in 1969 as the IRR's magazine, had become a central vehicle in the IRR's radicalization, first under Alexander Kirby's editorship and then, from 1973 on, under Darcus Howe's. Taking over the editorship of the paper when it was under the auspices of the new, radicalized IRR, Howe's intention was "to steer the magazine yet further from its quasi-academic origins forwards to the front lines of racial politics."[69] In an early editorial, he promised "to give theoretical clarification to independent grass roots self-activity with a view to its further development," and supporting grass-roots political struggles became *Race Today*'s chief objective for the duration of its existence, until the late 1980s.[70] Splitting with the IRR in August 1974 as a means of maintaining the IRR's charitable status, *Race Today* moved to Brixton's center of radical politics—the squatting networks around Railton Road, a district also known, informally, as the "front line."[71] Here, Howe founded the Race Today Collective with Farukh Dhondy and Leila Hassan, soon also bringing in Mala Sen, Jean Ambrose, Patricia Dick, Barbara Beese, Akua Rugg, and Linton Kwesi Johnson. The Collective, as Howe's biographers note, was an eclectic mix. Dhondy and Sen were ex–Black Panthers; Hassan and Ambrose, former members of the Black Unity and Freedom Party; Dick was a one-time member of the IRR; Beese was a former member of Release and one of the Mangrove Nine; and Johnson was a member of the Black Panther Movement's youth wing, steadily making a name for himself as a poet.[72] While *Race Today* reported on various black grass-roots struggles in Britain and black liberation struggles, particularly in

Africa and the Caribbean, the Race Today Collective spent time on the ground offering organizational support and speaking at demonstrations and pickets.

For the Race Today Collective, the key to understanding the significance of young black men and women as a challenge to the British state lay in one word: shitwork. The term, which first gained popularity as a description of the drudgery of women's labor through second-wave feminism in the late 1960s, had become thoroughly sedimented in black popular culture by the mid-1970s.[73] In a 1975 *Race Today* editorial, Howe suggested it was the "overwhelming refusal of shitwork" that defined a "distinct group of unemployed young men and women which increases at the end of every school year." The refusal of shitwork by these young men and women meant, Howe proposed, that traditional Marxist theories for explaining the structuring of class by capital did not apply. This was not the "disposable industrial reserve army, that belongs to capital quite as absolutely as if the latter had bred it at its own cost," no "mass of human material always ready for exploitation."[74] A class who were expected to wait "to be called upon at the will of London Transport, Fords, night cleaning agencies, hospitals and all other employers of black immigrant labour," Howe proposed, were now refusing. "Call as they might, the youths have uncompromisingly refused to budge."[75] Howe was writing at the height of the mugging panic of the mid-1970s. In Brixton, the community activist Courtney Laws had established a Parents against Muggings group, while in Haringey, the record store owner Len Dyke formed a similar organization, the Black People and Youth Action Committee. Howe's editorial was published as a response to these actions, and called for the older generation to rally in support of the younger. The Race Today Collective published the editorial as a pamphlet, which was, according to John La Rose, "circulating widely."[76]

Howe's position, La Rose noted, marked "a sharp break with previous formulations and discussions about black youth" by emphasizing the ideological significance of their refusal. The positions of "liberal race professionals and community relations workers" had previously "floundered in lagoons of attitudinal psychology: claimed that the youth were only reacting to the illiberal and vicious operations of the education and social system; so if they were behaving as they were, they were not to blame in the circumstances." This, La Rose argued, easily tipped into blaming parents for lack of firmness and working too much overtime, and was obfuscation. The refusal of shitwork not only rejected the disciplining structure of capital, it undid the ideology of the work ethic. "The black youth have withdrawn from the work ethic," La Rose proposed. "No ruling class is welded to the work ethic. The British did the Grand Tour, besported themselves in the South of France, the Bahamas, or their spacious country homes and estates." By also withdrawing from the work ethic, black youth, La Rose suggested, exposed its unevenness. The police, as *Race Today* insisted, were charged with breaking this refusal. "Since the late 1950s," Ian MacDonald proposed in an earlier article, "the state's strategy has been to isolate the unemployed from the rest of the class, and to crack down on institutions like shebeens which were subversive of the work ethic." Repeating arguments familiar from the feminist movement that the community was the site for the reproduction of labor, MacDonald suggested that

> Home, school and pubs which shut at 11.00 p.m. are all geared into this need. The police are a key part of the power which capital wields in the community to ensure that its requirements are not subverted by people asserting their own needs above capital's. It is in fulfilment of this role that the police hound unemployed youth standing at street corners, arrest drunks and invade shebeens.[77]

For the Race Today Collective, then, black youth were strategic to the undermining of capital in two respects: they refused their role as a reserve army of labor, and they undermined the ideology of the work ethic that disciplined the sites for the reproduction of labor.

In these moves, the Race Today Collective argued, black youth held a strategic centrality in the battle against capitalism in Britain. "The sharpness of the break with mundane social conceptions," La Rose argued, "is likely to open up the whole political spectrum to a serious consideration of where the live revolutionary forces are and what new alignments need to be made."[78] This role of throwing into relief wider social antagonisms was, for *Race Today*, the crucial political significance of the action these young black people. In mobilizing other workers to refuse the discipline of the work ethic, and to withdraw themselves from the logic of the reserve army of labor, Howe agreed, there lay the possibility that "the rebels" might "incite by their own activities the imagination of political activists who in turn will place their skills at the disposal of the rebels," and, ultimately, might "split the bourgeoisie and win over the liberal element."[79]

The Race Today Collective assumed a special historical role for black youth, whose open politics of refusal offered the possibility of reordering the political landscape. As the everyday culture of refusing shitwork became punctuated by the increasing incidence of open battles with the police, the Collective suggested that a new phase in the history of black struggle in Britain had begun. Reflecting on the 1973 Brockwell Park confrontation, Howe drew attention to how young friends and supporters built a popular campaign on the arrests. While conflicts with the police were usually "closed, private affairs, known only to the immediate participants," the Brockwell case brought tensions with the police into an open confrontation through a mass struggle with the police, followed by strikes and marches. This coordinated action, for Howe, was expected. It was a waiting-to-happen spilling over of "a history of accumulated wrath" that all those involved had carried within them—*Race Today* had spent a long time reporting the opinions of young blacks, laying out these collective grievances that became public in such confrontations. Such cases could potentially make "white people... aware of the opposing forces within the British nation, and, in particular, of the strength and power of the black community."[80] Three years later, when Carnival revelers clashed with the police in Notting Hill, *Race Today* proposed that the "open defiance to our rulers and their representatives, which young blacks displayed on the streets of Notting Hill, shows that a whole period in the history of our presence here in Britain has come to an end. A new stage is about to emerge."[81] For *Race Today*, the refusal of shitwork as an open, defiant act marked the moment when private histories of conflict and refusal were transformed into public ritual.

A. X. Cambridge, Cecil Gutzmore, and the Black Liberator

Two years after *Race Today* was established, and just as it was turning to a more radical politics, Alrick (Ricky) Xavier Cambridge, a founding member of the Black Unity and Freedom Party (BUFP), launched the *Black Liberator*. He was soon joined by Cecil Gutzmore, founder, with the former Mangrove Nine defendant Rhodan Gordon, of Notting Hill's Black People's Information Centre (BPIC). Together, Gutzmore and Cambridge, both Althusserian Marxists, developed the *Black Liberator* as the theoretical arm of black radicalism in Britain. In the 1970s, the former BUFP member Harry Goulbourne remembers, *Black Liberator* became "the leading black and Caribbean journal in Britain."[82] Indeed, the journal enjoyed international circulation. Stella Dadzie, later a leading figure in the Brixton Black Women's Group and a founding member of OWAAD, remembers her entry into black politics beginning when she read a copy of *Black Liberator* as a student in Heidelberg in 1972 and began correspondence with the editors.[83]

Like *Race Today*, *Black Liberator* was particularly concerned with interpreting the position and actions of black youth. Cambridge, though, refused Howe's reading of the immediate political significance of the refusal of "shitwork," and of the police's role in disciplining this struggle. Noting the centralization of capital, the reduction of labor needs through technological development, and the increasing globalization of industry, which relocated production to the underdeveloped territories of the former colonial world, Cambridge suggested that those who refused work were merely making a virtue of necessity. Drawing on Althusserian structuralism, moreover, he also refused to read the police as the defenders of capital, suggesting the reduction of the various arms of the state to the direct imperative of the economic structure was an overly simplistic form of economic determinism. The state might have many racist functions, he suggested, but these were all relatively autonomous, moving by their own logics; they could not be collapsed together, nor read simply as functions of and for capital.[84]

The *Black Liberator* nonetheless invested increasing political potential in the actions of young blacks against the police. They praised what they saw as their expansive conception of political change. This view was significantly backed by the *Black Liberator*'s early involvement with the Metro 4 case, with which the paper, through their connections to the BPIC, was closely involved. The Metro club had long been a site on the radical map, attracting Black Power speakers, and even receiving a visit from Penny Jackson when she toured London in 1971. It had first been raided by police in October 1970, shortly after the Mangrove demonstration. In May 1971, it was raided again. On this occasion, youth leaders at the club had offered sanctuary to two young men fleeing the police, and on the police's arrival refused them entry, initially blocking the doors. When police reinforcements arrived and raided the club, a mass confrontation broke out. The four young men tried for those events had their case heard at the Old Bailey in 1972, in what many took as a repeat of the Mangrove trial of the previous year. As in the Mangrove trial, the defendants were outspoken in their criticisms of the police, "accusatory rather than defensive and apologetic," as Rudy Narayan observed. Also as in the Mangrove trial, the defendants were exonerated of the charges in court.[85] Only weeks later, the Metro's leaders got into a sustained battle with the Inner London Education Authority after the club was threatened with closure, apparently for its hosting of political events. This, for *Black Liberator*, was evidence of a newly militant youth, willing to turn their meeting places into political sites, and to challenge the state on many fronts at once. In a feature praising the case, Cambridge and Tony Mohipp, BPIC's director, celebrated the Metro's rejection of the more limited "parliamentary road" that they saw the older generation advocating. For Mohipp, the Metro case showed "youths [. . .] demanding real and definite change. They are thinking seriously about ideas concerning the *State, Law and Order,* democracy, socialism, capitalism and its institutionalised and oppressive agencies, like racism, unemployment, *mal*-education, bad housing, police brutality and harassment."[86]

Black Liberator, in a move that shared ground with *Race Today,* also proposed that such actions by black youth would lay bare wider antagonisms within British society. Reflecting on the rising incidence of clashes with the police throughout the 1970s, Cambridge, writing in 1978, reminded readers of the murder of David Oluwale, the march on Caledonian Road police station, the Mangrove demonstration and trial, the Cricklewood 12 and Islington 18 cases, and the widespread police offensive launched following the 1976 Notting Hill Carnival. In this context, Cambridge proposed, black experience provided a vantage point on the unfolding of authoritarian statecraft in the 1970s. "No group of people in British society knows more than we do the severities of police harassment: or knows the distance which exists between the claim made for our 'civil liberties' and their denial by wicked state and police practices" he argued. "These are our daily experiences in our communities."[87] For the *Black Liberator,* the dramatization of this authoritarian turn in the experiences and actions of young blacks was a means of allowing others to see the direction in which Britain seemed to be headed. Colin Prescod, furthering Cambridge's argument, proposed that the critical insight that the experience of young blacks offered was into the speed and intensity of the state's authoritarian turn. Anti-racism, he proposed, was too often reduced to the anti-fascism directed against the National Front. But this missed the dimensions in which black Britons confronted "physical, economic, political, cultural and psychological attacks" from the state. It was here, he proposed, that their experiences offered the basis for building a broader oppositional politics. This involved recognizing the prescience of black voices diagnosing the current crisis. Like George Jackson's letters from Soledad, Prescod proposed, the voices of black youth could throw into relief "the historical climax (the flash point) of the totalitarian period." The "leaders of popular opinion" in Britain, Prescod thought, "must look at the incidence of state repression of black people, and the growth and expansion of state repressive powers, more particularly, to be used against the entire working class."[88]

Finally, the *Black Liberator* made the argument that the refusal to be disciplined was symbolically significant for black youth politics, and this was a refusal that they inherited from the antagonisms of the colonial past. Despite disagreements with *Race Today* over the issue of the refusal of shit-work, *Black Liberator* shared much common ground when it came to reading the importance of black youth's apparent insistence on displays of leisure and pleasure in the face of hostility to these. Again, this conviction increased as the 1970s progressed. In 1978, Cecil Gutzmore, echoing members of the Race Today Collective, was convinced of the symbolic importance of black youth rebellion for shifting the balance of power against the state. Speaking on the clashes at the Notting Hill Carnival of the late 1970s, he noted that this "violence and open confrontation between what I call the black masses in the United Kingdom and the British state" was the only arena in which such violence and open confrontation presently existed, and that this was because in other domains, such as work, there were mechanisms of control already in place, mediating conflicts. For Gutzmore, it was in the threat *through leisure* to the disciplining arms of the state that black youth offered hope. He noted that confrontations with the police had occurred often in the domain of "culture," in police attacks on events such as Brockwell Park fair and Leeds Bonfire night, youth clubs and night clubs, and even on "cultural practices," from walking "jauntily," to walking in groups and even "choosing to walk on the street at all." In sum, this meant "state repression of what is perceived to be dangerous, or potentially dangerous, or disruptive, or undisciplined culture on the part of the black masses." Gutzmore's gambit was that these were evidence that Caribbean people carried a historic refusal of having their leisure time and activities restricted or disciplined. Invoking Hogarth's chaotic sketches of Southwark Fair, Gutzmore argued that such events were occasions of "mass jollity" that were "systematically suppressed by the British state." But the attempts by the colonial government in Trinidad to similarly suppress the carnival tradition there in the early nineteenth century, he noted, were unsuccessful. As the Caribbean traditions of mass jollity in defiance of the disciplining arms of the state reappeared, now, on the streets of Notting Hill, Gutzmore was suggesting, here was the return of the repressed, bringing the disorder of the periphery to the heart of the metropole to disrupt the centuries of order imposed there by the ruling class.[89] While *Black*

Liberator was unwilling to subscribe to the Race Today Collective's reading of the significance of black youth's refusal of shitwork as a disruption of the structure of the reserve army of labor, in Gutzmore's estimation the libertarian possibilities of black culture, led by the actions of young black men and women, retained a central place in keeping alive a culture of refusing authority, contesting the law and order ideology through which the authoritarian state was consolidating.

Ambalavaner Sivanandan and Race & Class

Following the takeover of the Institute of Race Relations by its staff, the Sri Lankan writer Ambalavaner Sivanandan's new IRR assumed control of both its magazine *Race Today* (soon to move to Brixton under Darcus Howe) and its quarterly journal *Race*, renamed *Race & Class* in October 1974. From July 1974 on, the IRR also published a series of pamphlets with extended essays on anti-racism, the politics of race relations sociology, anti-racist feminism, the state, British fascism, and neocolonialism, as well as a series of critiques of policing. Sivanandan considered himself primarily "a pamphleteer" in this period, using these pamphlets and essays in *Race & Class* as a forum through which to respond to the ongoing political crises of the day.[90] He elaborated a critique of contemporary thinking on race and politics that insisted, first, that to understand contemporary socioeconomic and political life in Britain, and Britain's place in the world, required placing race at the center of the analysis, and, second, that the means of doing this were offered through the writings, actions, and cultural and political practices of black men and women.

Sivanandan's work in the 1970s, as Stuart Hall noted, "inserted the black question into the very centre of a growing and wide-ranging concern—novel at the time—with shifts in the strategy of the state."[91] The most significant of his early essays in this regard was "Race, Class and the State," published in *Race & Class* in Spring 1976 as a response to the imprisonment of Wesley Dick, one of three young men who held up a Spaghetti House restaurant in Knightsbridge in 1975 in a plan to finance black supplementary schools and support African liberation struggles.[92] Reading Dick's actions as a part of the rising rebelliousness of the "second generation," Sivanandan used the essay to analyze the political landscape and propose strategies for challenges to the state. He proposed, first, that reading the relationship of black people to the state would work "like a barium meal" to reveal "the whole organism of the state" in its wider project of managing the new processes of capital accumulation in the transition to a postimperial global economy; and, second, that through this analysis, the political strategies for anti-racist anti-capitalism could be thought out.[93] In a move that has since become commonplace, Sivanandan argued that Britain was faced with a chronic shortage of labor after World War II, and that the demand for labor was met by encouraging migration from the underdeveloped economies of the Empire and Commonwealth. These migrants, settling in Britain, were forced into the lowest-skilled, lowest-paid jobs and the worst housing and neighborhoods; the result, he suggested, was that "the economic profit from immigration had gone to capital, the social cost had gone to labour, but the resulting conflict between the two had been mediated by a common 'ideology' of racism."[94] In the late 1950s, Sivanandan argued, automation and new technology helped British industry compete with Europe for the markets freed up by decolonization, while at the same time this technology reduced the need for unskilled migrant labor, and decolonization allowed Britain the diplomatic space to begin regulating the free movement of labor in the Commonwealth from which it had previously benefitted. From an intake of Commonwealth migrant settlers regulated by skill sets in the 1962 Immigration Act to the removal of the automatic right of settlement for Commonwealth migrant workers in the 1971 Immigration Act, the British state shifted its immigration laws in line with the demands of capital.

If one side of this story was the regulation of international labor to the shifting demands of capital, the other side, Sivanandan proposed, was the management of the social consequences in the prevention of political challenges. With discrimination in education and employment and harassment by the police, and as immigration legislation gave a fillip to popular racism, organized black resistance challenged state and society. Increasingly assertive black communities in the post–Black Power era "posed a problem from within British society—they posed the problems of it."[95] The state's solution, Sivanandan argued, was "domestic neocolonialism." Through the Community Relations Commission's financing and support of self-help, youth clubs, supplementary schools, and black studies, the state "has taught the white power structure to accept the blacks and it has taught the blacks to accept the white power structure. It has successfully taken politics out of the black struggle and returned it to rhetoric and nationalism on the one hand and to the state on the other. It has [. . .] created a black bourgeoisie [. . .] to which the state can now hand over control of black dissidents in general and black youth in particular."[96]

It was in this last quantity—black youth—that Sivanandan found the most potential for an alternative political settlement, and the largest focus of the state's neutralizing functions. "As though to confirm the dialectics of history they, the British born, carry the politics of their slave ancestry. And so it is to them that the state now turns its attention."[97] Sivanandan wrote "Race, Class and the State" in early 1976, before the mass confrontations at Notting Hill Carnival; the image of politicized black youth foremost in his mind was the doomed politics of the Spaghetti House Siege, which had ended in lengthy prison sentences for the three men involved. Nonetheless it was the possibility of a future "mass politics" through youth rebellions, potentially drawing in not just other racialized sections of the population, but the wider "working class as a whole," that Sivanandan and, he felt, the state anticipated. The contours of that politics, and its revolutionary potential, for Sivanandan, lay in the historical experiences of race that it brought to the table. Race, as he wrote in an early essay on this issue, was "a revolutionary experience." It was all-pervasive, forcing all social institutions and ideas—"the State, the Church, power, people, love, sex, society—ourselves"—to be read "in terms of the categories that it has thrown up."[98] While one side of Sivanandan's work, then, was concerned with articulating a critique of the changing relations of labor, capital, and the state that placed race and racism at the center of the story, the other side was an attempt to locate and narrate the historical forces that exposed this dynamic and offered alternatives to the current political settlement.

In the wake of the 1981 uprisings, Sivanandan dedicated a special issue of *Race & Class* to their interpretation. His essay "From Resistance to Rebellion: Asian and Afro-Caribbean Struggles in Britain"[99] opened the issue. This essay, as Sivanandan recalled, was a riposte to interpretations of the uprisings which either blamed the events on "a handful of troublemakers," or saw them, in a "sort of 'victim historiography,'" as "a result of unemployment, and not as the culmination of years of resistance to the double bind of poverty and racism that black youth had been cast into." The essay was, Sivanandan claimed, "the first history of blacks in Britain written from a subaltern point of view." Since its republication in 1982, it has become one of the most frequently cited accounts of the development of black politics in postwar Britain.[100] The familiarity of Sivanandan's narrative today, however, obscures more than it reveals. This essay was an attempt to *define* the "black" of resistance, and to force new historical experiences into a public debate on the uprisings for which, as Paul Gilroy had complained in a *Race Today* review of what he termed the "riotology" literature of the early 1980s, history was either entirely absent, or deemed to have begun with first bottle thrown in St Paul's, Bristol, on April 2, 1980.[101]

Sivanandan's account of black resistance in Britain began with the hanging of Udham Singh, who shot Sir Michael O'Dwyer in London in 1940 in retaliation for his role in the 1919 Amritsar Massacre. For the opening paragraph of a special edition journal on the events of 1981, this move certainly offered the "sense of history [that] has been lacking in analyses of the rebellions."[102] In contrast to those explanations of youth rebellion that dominated the pages of *Black Liberator* and *Race Today*, this was also an opening that firmly reclaimed blackness as a politics that included South Asians. Sivanandan not only insisted that there was a history behind the events of 1981, but that this history took us back beyond the large-scale postwar, postcolonial migration, and beyond Britain's shores, too, linking modern Britain with its imperial past. This sense of history, he maintained, was popular and organic. When New Zealand–born teacher and anti-racist campaigner Blair Peach was killed at the hands of the police Special Patrol Group at a demonstration against the National Front in Southall in April 1979, as Sivanandan reported, "Asian newspapers recalled the Amritsar massacre of another April in 1919." These histories, he insisted, were present in 1981: "Southall, Southall knew, would not be lightly invaded again, as 3 July 1981 was to prove."[103] Sivanandan's essay spanned across Britain's former colonial territories, but also insisted on the long presence of anticolonial and anti-racist politics in the metropole. Beginning with Udham Singh in London, it moved from there back to the founding of the West African Students' Union in 1925 and the League of Coloured Peoples in 1931, and forward to the 1945 Manchester Pan-African Congress, the Indian Workers' Associations of the 1950s and their West Indian counterparts, the defense campaigns of the 1958 riots, the *West Indian Gazette*, the Bristol bus boycott of 1963, and then on to the numerous more documented struggles of the 1970s. It was a history of black politics as a politics of resistance, but it was also an insistence on the historicity of this politics, and its gathering momentum as it rushed toward the present. For Sivanandan, this process reached a new apex in the actions of a new generation who, jobless, avoided the "discipline" of work and the trade union discipline of "a labour aristocracy," and who had "a hunger to retain their freedom, the lifestyle, the dignity which they have carved out from the stone of their lives." The young black generation of 1981, he proposed in concluding the essay, represented the consolidation of "a new society that waits in the wings of the new industrial revolution."[104]

Beginning in the mid-1970s, the University of Birmingham's Centre for Contemporary Cultural Studies (CCCS) developed into an important space for anti-racist debate. Although the Race Today Collective, *Black Liberator*, and Institute of Race Relations had longer, firmer links to organized black radical politics in Britain, and have often been considered its central institutions in the 1970s and 1980s, relations between CCCS and this wider black radical network were significant. From the mid-1970s to the early 1980s, CCCS researchers called for a wholesale realignment of thinking about British history and politics. Greater weight need to be accorded to race, and especially to the way the historical experience of former colonial territories was remaking the politics of the metropole, they argued. In short, working toward a new political future required investing in the contemporary politics of blackness.

These arguments were first formed through a CCCS project on the politics of mugging, published as *Policing the Crisis* in 1978, which began in response to the arrest and trial in 1972 of three young mixed-race men in Handsworth, charged with a violent "mugging," for which they received lengthy prison sentences. Asking why the sentences handed down to these men were so punitive, the researchers—Stuart Hall, the CCCS director, and four postgraduate students, Chas Critcher, Tony Jefferson, John Clarke, and Brian Roberts—proposed that the answer lay in the ways in which various tensions and crises were displaced into concerns about and policing of black youths, a process working through the mutually reinforcing actions of the police, the judiciary, and the media. They suggested that the period from the mid-1960s on marked the beginning of a crisis of hegemony. Confronted with a deepening economic crisis and heightened class conflict, reflected in the turmoil of 1968, the postwar social-democratic consensus was exhausted, and the state adopted a more authoritarian mode, seeking popular approval of a "law and order politics" that attributed the woes of British society to abandonment of ideals of community, responsibility, and sobriety. Youth subcultures, moral permissiveness, irresponsible trade unionism, and militant leftism were all held responsible, but the image of societal disarray was most condensed in the panic around the "mugging epidemic" as a scourge of black criminality. In this reading, spearheaded by Enoch Powell, Britain's current crisis could be explained as a consequence of postcolonial immigration.[105] In the post-Powellite moment, as Hall argued in an essay published contemporaneously to *Policing the Crisis*, "an 'official' racist politics [formed] at the heart of British political culture." Through this political culture, he proposed, "Race is the lens through which people come to perceive that a crisis is developing. It is the framework through which the crisis is experienced. It is the means by which the crisis is to be resolved—'send it away.'"[106]

In the four decades since its publication, *Policing the Crisis* has become a foundational text in the fields of cultural studies, sociology, politics, and criminology, and it is increasingly finding an audience among historians seeking to understand the rightward turn of the British state in the run-up to the electoral victory of Margaret Thatcher's Conservative Party in 1979.[107] The prescience of the text in anticipating the rise of what Hall came to term "Thatcherism"[108] has helped it become best known for its Gramscian conjunctural analysis of the crisis of the postwar consensus and its Althusserian interrogation of the mechanisms of the state and the media in the production of consent. Often forgotten, however, is that the book finishes, not with its anticipation of the Thatcherite project, but with an extended analysis of black politics, an insistence on the necessity *of* black politics, and an invested discussion of the kind of black politics needed to challenge the New Right. Powellism and the mugging panic had fueled a politics of law and order, racism, and repatriation, the authors proposed, and the racist policing of young black men and women, the black consciousness movements of U.S. and Caribbean politics, and black popular culture, had politicized blackness. Young black school-leavers, heavily policed and with least access to employment, had begun to constitute "an *ethnically distinct class fraction*," and come to a consciousness of themselves as a social fraction through race. Independent, radical, activist black politics developed appeals to this group through a language of blackness, paralleled by "a loss of credibility, confidence and legitimacy in the professional race-relations agencies."[109]

Drawing on Sivanandan's writing, the CCCS researchers proposed that, however much the crisis of the 1970s might be grounded in economics and class relations, it was managed through race, in the organization of capital and labor and in the policies of the state.[110] Moreover, this form of class subordination, structured through race, was also "lived" through the languages and experiences of blackness. "Race," they proposed, was the modality through which "blacks comprehend, handle and then begin to resist that exploitation which is an objective feature of their class situation." Particularly in the case of "black youth," blackness served as the central interpretative framework through which "the black working class becomes conscious of the contradictions of its objective situation and organises to 'fight it through.'"[111] This was a radical move to make. It insisted that the conditions of Britain's transformation to a postcolonial society had placed race at the center of how political and social life was organized. As the psychic and political energy generated in the various crises in the collapse postwar settlement were displaced onto the fate of "black youth" in Britain's inner cities, so the resources that these young people had for thinking about blackness assumed a new intensity, moving to the center of how they understood their predicament. Blackness became *the* resource for their politics.

In the final section of *Policing the Crisis*, the authors offered a sustained engagement with the ideas put forward by the Race Today Collective and *Black Liberator*. This section was prepared with substantial input from Darcus Howe and Alrick Cambridge, including through two "very long interviews with them about the emerging argument."[112] Though Hall and his colleagues ultimately disagreed with *Race Today* on the imminence of political transformation engendered by the black youths' refusal of "shitwork," they used Howe's work to insist that "the black working class as a whole belongs to two, different, though intersecting, histories: the history of Caribbean labour and the history of the British working class." And they used this analysis to argue that this Caribbean colonial and postcolonial history, given meaning through the popularity of the writing of anticolonial intellectuals like Fanon, had assumed a new weight in 1970s Britain, perhaps with the future potential to organize the refusal of "shitwork" by black youth into a political challenge to the state.[113] Drawing on the experiences of the U.S. Black Panther Party as the most successful example of such a transformation—though also one subsequently obliterated by the state—they insisted that, though the solutions were not easily available, one fact had become clear about how the conflicts of British society in the 1970s, particularly around class, might be resolved: whatever solutions were posed, they could not ignore the ways in which race structured economic life, subjective experience, and political possibility. Black politics was not going to disappear, and the duty of politically committed academics, as the CCCS researchers considered themselves to be, was to therefore think about where it might lead.[114]

The same year that *Policing the Crisis* was published, the Race and Politics Group was established at the Centre for Contemporary Cultural Studies, bringing together researchers who argued for the centrality of race to political and cultural life in modern Britain, and aiming to challenge the dominant academic frameworks through which race was currently researched and written about. This group—Paul Gilroy, Errol Lawrence, Hazel Carby, Pratibha Parmar, John Solomos, Bob Findlay, and Simon Jones—published their collective work as *The Empire Strikes Back* in 1982, a collection of essays exploring race and capitalism, "commonsense" racism, sociology, policing, education, feminism, Asian women's resistance, and class politics. Whereas Hall was the only black writer on the *Policing* project—and Hall has himself talked often about his complicated relationship to the kinds of black subjectivities emerging in the 1970s—*The Empire Strikes Back* brought together five black writers, one of South Asian descent and four of African-Caribbean descent. It was couched in a language of "black sufferings" and "Babylon" which immediately identified it with a politics of blackness.[115] The book's central contention, explicitly following the lead of *Policing the Crisis*, Sivanandan's work, and *Race Today*, was that "the construction of an authoritarian state in Britain is fundamentally intertwined with the elaboration of popular racism in the 1970s."[116] Particularly in Errol Lawrence's contributions, *The Empire Strikes Back* was strident in its critique of existing academic discussion on race, particularly in race relations sociology, for its pathologizing accounts of black culture, its lack of engagement with racism and the state, and its frequent co-optation by the repressive arms of the state. This critique was sufficiently influential over the following decades that, as Michael Keith proposed, reviewing the volume thirty years on, "for a generation of researchers [. . .] projects directed at bringing to the academic public portrayals of British Black life" were treated with much circumspection, and research agendas shifted from black life and culture to white racism and the state. The consequence, Keith proposed, was that, following *The Empire Strikes Back*, "the valorization of the creativity, productivities and political power of everyday cultures of the oppressed" that were so central to earlier work at the CCCS fell from discussion, an ironic silence in the context of the urban unrest of 1981, in which "the voices of the unheard were on the streets of the UK."[117]

Keith's critique, however, downplays how the Race and Politics Group, particularly through Paul Gilroy's work, was deeply invested in the politics of black expressive cultures, and especially black youth culture. Indeed, Gilroy's final chapter in *The Empire Strikes Back* drew significantly on an earlier essay he had published in *Race & Class* in response to the 1981 uprisings, in which the energy and political possibility offered by black culture was paramount. He would develop these positions significantly in his work of the late 1980s. Gilroy began the essay by rehearsing an argument that drew on *Policing the Crisis*, and would become central to *The Empire Strikes Back*: "It is precisely because race binds the processes by which ethico-political hegemony is presently reproduced that focussing analysis around it offers a privileged view of unfolding state authoritarianism, the stage of capital accumulation and the balance of forces in political struggle."[118] Condemning the eurocentrism of the British Left, and particularly its readiness to refuse any real structural depth to how "race" works in class formation, Gilroy insisted that to take stock of the central role of race in the reproduction of ethico-political hegemony involved turning, instead, to a black radical tradition, to the "sixty years of black critical dialogue with Marxism" presented in the work of Marcus Garvey, George Padmore, C. L. R. James, and Richard Wright.[119] However, while a black intellectual tradition of this nature would animate his later work of the early 1990s,[120] it was in black vernacular youth culture that Gilroy found the most immediate challenge to existing thought on race, and to the existing racialized order, at this point. "The mass of black people, who arrived here as fugitives from colonial underdevelopment," he proposed, "brought with them legacies of their political, ideological and economic struggles in Africa, the Caribbean and the Indian subcontinent, as well as the scars of imperialist violence." In the black cultures of the metropole could be found a continuation of the struggles of the former anticolonial periphery:

> Though their new struggles at the centre are diffused throughout a different structure in dominance, the lingering bile of slavery, indenture and colonialism remains, not in the supposedly pathological forms in which black households are organised, but in the forms of struggle, political philosophies and revolutionary perspectives of non-European radical traditions, and the "good sense" of their practical ideologies.[121]

As with Hall's caution in reading these as any natural or inevitable inheritance, so too Gilroy was keen to propose that, insofar as these cultures were part of black Britain's present moment, this was through their reproduction in present practices, rather than some essential characteristic of blackness. But while this present reproduction was hypothesized for Hall as the consequence of the popularity of writers like Frantz Fanon, through whom young black Britons could rethink the anticolonial pasts of their parents' generation, for Gilroy these cultures were preeminently reproduced through everyday cultural transmission in domestic and community spaces, "organic links, in their kitchens and temples—in their communities."[122]

Emphasizing the existence of black community offered a means "to re-establish the unity of black people in answer to the divisions which state policy, race relations sociology and common-sense racism have visited on their experience of domination." Refusing the divisions of black workers versus black unemployed, black politics versus black culture, and first genera-tion ("respectable and hard-working") versus second generation ("whose 'identity crises' and precarious position 'between two cultures' impel them into deviant behavior"), Gilroy sought to establish a commonality in "cul-tures of resistance" that spanned the various domains of black experience, and offered the possibility of a united power bloc. However, revealing the hold that the actions and cultures of black youth had on the imagination of black intellectuals in this era, his argument returned repeatedly to youth culture when locating the driving force of potential political transformation in this moment. In a nod to the work of an earlier CCCS postgraduate, Dick Hebdige, Gilroy suggested that black cultures "may have had a profound impact on the racism of young Britons who were not, like their parents, weaned on an unadulterated diet of Empire." The "catalyst and inspiration" provided by large-scale black settlement offered an "inspiration to the grand-children of jingoism who were quick to ape, absorb and adapt the styles and cultural practices which were black relics of a distant colonial engagement with their foreparents."[123]

The most significant black oppositional cultures, for Gilroy, derived from Rastafarianism and, most substantially, music. In his monograph *There Ain't No Black in the Union Jack: The Cultural Politics of Race and Nation* (1987), an outgrowth of his CCCS doctoral thesis, he devoted a long chapter, now famous, to the cultural forms of the "autonomous institutions" of black British youth culture, concentrating in particular on dance halls and music production. This work, coming late in the period under study in this book, is nonetheless emblematic of the practices of "thinking black" that I have been tracing here, and it played a crucial role in bringing such intellectual proposi-tions into academic debate. For Gilroy, the cultures he explored were defined by their black particularity, but were not limited to it—they offered a rich-ness of expression, a depth of political and cultural critique. These were cul-tures that derived from a particular historical experience and cultural inher-itance. Enlisting James Baldwin, he insisted that there "is a very great deal in the world which Europe does not or cannot see."[124] However, the possibility of *making these things visible*, for Gilroy, offered wider redemptive possibilities, beyond the confines of "race." Black cultures, he proposed, were not "reducible to the narrow idea of anti-racism," and they were not reducible to *race*. Nor were they simply variations on some universal form of "radical" politics:

> Nor are these cultures mere aggregations of oppositional statements [...], which once decoded will be easily translated into the political vocabularies of other historically specific traditions of radicalism. Their protests are synchronized with an affirmation of particularity. Afro-centric spirituality and conjure [...] as well as the linguistic tropes which negotiate the boundaries of insubordination and insolence in slave cultures denied legitimate access to literacy, have all bequeathed distinctive political legacies which may not, for example, have immediate equivalents in the epistemological repertoire of contemporary Marxism or social democracy.[125]

Gilroy's extended discussion of diasporic black cultures in *There Ain't No Black in the Union Jack*, which laid out much of the conceptual blueprint for his later work *The Black Atlantic* (1993), is more complex than the brief summary here can do justice to. Significantly, though, when he turned to the ways in which these forms "comprise a radical politics capable of universalizing the issue of emancipation beyond the primary question of racial or ethnic particularity," it was in youth culture, particularly music, that he formed a critique of capitalism mobilized through a "denunciation of capitalist social relations for which the memory of slavery serves as an enduring metaphor, and [...] a critique of the commodity form to which black humanity was reduced during the slave period."[126]

•   •   •

The various individuals and institutions explored above constituted a black radical formation in British intellectual life. Certainly, this formation could be as much a site of dispute as consensus, and egotism also had its place in creating ruptures and discord. Sivanandan would famously denounce Hall in the early 1990s over Hall's involvement with *Marxism Today*, and what Sivanandan claimed was Hall's turn toward postmodernism and identity politics, and away from the struggle against racism.[127] However, the two had publicly supported each other's work throughout the 1970s and 1980s, and researchers at the CCCS were regular visitors to the IRR.[128] *Policing the Crisis*, as we have seen, was written with what Hall described as "a lot of help from, on the one hand Darcus Howe from the *Race Today* collective, and on the other hand Ricky Cambridge and the *Black Liberator*."[129] Paul Gilroy contributed to both *Race Today* and *Race & Class* in the early 1980s, and was involved in frequent dialogue with Cambridge and Gutzmore, as well as Sivanandan, Jenny Bourne, and Colin Prescod of the IRR.[130] Prescod had himself previously written for the *Black Liberator* before he joined the IRR. *Race Today*, by contrast, began life with the IRR before splitting and moving to Brixton, and while relations between the two became more strained, particularly between Howe and Sivanandan, there was still much affection between many of the writers and activists associated with each institution.[131] This was an intellectual formation held together, for all its disputes, by a common set of interests, particularly in black youth politics and their potential for socialist transformation. It was also an intellectual formation that, in this interest, consistently worked closely with young black people in their struggles, and often attempted to position its own political arguments as elaborations on the organic politics formed in those struggles.

The IRR, *Race Today, Black Liberator*, and the CCCS had in common several key arguments about race in modern Britain. Firstly, they insisted that the current political moment could only be properly understood, and only be properly addressed and resolved, by recognizing the formative role of the politics of race. In this, they recognized race as a central force in British politics, which mediated and organized social, economic, political, and cultural relations. Secondly, they responded to the political and cultural challenges that they found articulated and advanced in various domains of black British life, and particularly in the actions and cultures of young black men and women. They consistently framed their responses in opposition to the dominant readings of this constituency in the mainstream media by politicians and by the wider "race relations industry." Thirdly, they shared, to varying degrees, the conviction that the cultural and political challenges offered by black youth were one of the necessary forms that black oppositional politics must take at this point, but also that the form of this politics had a significant role to play in the reformulation of a wider radical politics in Britain, led by those who might recreate the decolonization struggles of the colonial periphery now in the old metropolitan center. Black youth, in this reading, became both the inheritors of a particular historical tradition of anticolonial struggle and the basis for the potential generation of a future mass politics, whether this was through their refusal of the work ethic, their exposure of the authoritarian turn of the state, or the new models for social relations and new critiques of commodity culture and capital that their cultural practices offered.

The intellectuals at the IRR, *Race Today, Black Liberator,* and the CCCS were always concerned to define their relationship to the "black youth" whose cause they often championed, not least because this was in part a measure of their own blackness. Affirmations of the richness of the expressive cultures and actions of young black people were common. Gilroy's work suggested that black intellectual production happened within popular cultures of blackness, primarily among young black working-class men and women; it was the job of public intellectuals and black critical institutions to listen and respond to them. The black intellectual, as Sivanandan would similarly write, "understands with Gramsci and George Jackson that 'all men are intellectuals' or with Angela Davis that no one is."[132] Not only was there a demand to recognize this democratization of intellectual work, but there was a demand that intellectual work and other domains of political engagement could not be separate, and that black intellectual work must connect up the sites of black struggle as a part of the political interventions for and with those seen to be on the front lines of racism in Britain. Prescod, indeed, had abandoned *Black Liberator* on the grounds that it failed to "make the language and analysis that it used intelligible to the people it was struggling for and very much alongside."[133] This was a primary measure of its fidelity to the cause. Similarly, when *Race & Class* reviewed *The Empire Strikes Back,* its major initial criticism—though one quickly retracted in a follow-up review in the subsequent issue—was that it represented "an anti-racism that is [. . .] confined to intellectual activity."[134]

The previous section of this chapter concentrated on the arguments of a handful of significant black intellectuals who used the public spaces they had created as venues in which to discuss the meanings of black politics and the significance of race in response to the growing upheavals and conflicts of the era. They placed the question of blackness at the forefront of their analysis, and they argued for the central importance of black intellectual work. At the same time, though, these intellectuals were concerned with how *others* were also prioritizing "blackness" as a dominant interpretative frame. Intellectuals connected with these various institutions repeatedly spent time identifying and analyzing the significance of black popular culture and political activity, which they understood to be centrally directed by ideas about race, and specifically about blackness. It is not my argument that "thinking black" must be understood *either* as a description of what these intellectuals did *or* as a description of what they saw those whom they studied to be doing; for all that there were, at times, ruptures and distances between these two practices, the two existed in dialogue, and the one was not cut off from the other. If we are today perhaps more familiar with ideas of blackness as it was conceived of and produced in black popular culture, this is in part a testament to the success of those intellectuals discussed in the previous section in making these cultures visible—recording and discussing them as they occurred. In this, indeed, they were a part of a much wider array of artists, photographers, journalists, film makers, and writers who aimed to capture the contours of black popular culture and black politics in this era. This closing section explores the ways and sites by which these various practices connected up.

The Race Today Collective (RTC) played a central role in black politics in this period. Its offices in Brixton, as Leila Hassan later convincingly claimed, were "the centre, in England, of black liberation."[135] As Robin Bunce and Paul Field have shown, *Race Today* was "a campaigning journal. The Collective helped foster self-organization, while the magazine recorded the struggles."[136] In the summer of 1974, the RTC supported the strike of Asian workers at Imperial Typewriters in Leicester, Howe moving in with one of the strikers and speaking regularly at the picket line. In 1976, Farukh Dhondy and Mala Sen, who had campaigned against "Paki-bashing" by skinheads in London's East End since the early 1970s, lent RTC resources to help fight the Greater London Council's efforts to evict Bengali families, drafting in lawyers to advise the campaign, and later helping to establish the Bengali Housing Action Group. Campaign groups also approached the RTC for their support. The Bradford Black Collective made contact in 1976, and soon enlisted the RTC's support in the defense of George Lindo, arrested in Bradford in 1977 on charges of armed robbery and wrongfully convicted and imprisoned for two years before the joint campaign secured his freedom.[137] The Leeds black group formed around the journal *Chapeltown News* also enlisted the RTC's support in a campaign defending young people arrested over conflicts with the police at a Bonfire Night celebration in 1976. Two years later, the RTC allied with Gus John's Manchester-based Black Parent's Movement, and with a smaller group based in Sheffield.[138] In the later 1970s, it established alliances with parts of the white Left, facilitated through a close relationship with Max Farrar.[139] This growing list of alliances and contacts would prove crucial when the RTC took a leading role in the New Cross Massacre Action Committee, and later in organizing and leading the Black People's Day of Action, in early 1981. Its embeddedness in the local community in Brixton also put the RTC at the center of political responses to the Brixton uprising later that year. After hosting leaders of the uprising at a meeting in its offices to "debrief" them on the events, it helped set up the Brixton Defence Committee, which campaigned for amnesty for those arrested during the uprising.[140]

The RTC's politics and public profile were also popularized through its political alliances and communications network, especially its journal *Race Today*, which enjoyed wide distribution. The collective also published a series of pamphlets between 1974 and 1982, covering questions of feminism, education, and Caribbean politics. Linton Kwesi Johnson's poetry was, however, most successful in the popularization of the journal's politics—his words were conferred an authenticity that went beyond what was possible by other channels. "No amount of comment by journalists or sociologists could speak of our experience quite as these poems do," Bogle-L'Ouverture declared in 1975. His poems were conceived of as, and certainly became, popular scripts for articulating black experience in Britain. "He means the poems to be read aloud and not confined to the page. They are statements to be used when we talk among ourselves."[141] Such claims spoke to a wider faith, prevalent at this time, in the ability of poetry as a vehicle for the expression of black community and protest—as Lauretta Ngcobo would write, black poetry, written in "the language of the ghetto," encouraged audiences "to embrace this poetry as their own. In it they see themselves and laugh, for it gives vent to humour as well as to social protest."[142] There is reason to give credence to such claims. Johnson's poetry was hugely successful. Initially performing his poems with African drum backing, in the late 1970s, he teamed up with Dennis Bovell to record his poems and to perform live with a dub reggae band. Bovell, heading the reggae band Matumbi, was one of the most popular British reggae musicians of the era, as well as one thoroughly caught up in the politics of the day—indeed, he was the central defendant of the Cricklewood 12 trial of 1974.[143] Through live shows and, from 1978 on, a series of highly successful records, Johnson's collaboration with Bovell helped him carve out a career that won him international acclaim and made him a local hero in Brixton, where he was known to local black residents simply as "the poet." He performed his poetry in local community centers, spoke at local schools, and worked as a librarian and community worker for the Keskidee Arts Centre in North London.[144]

Not only did Johnson's poems offer an articulation of blackness, and an affirmation of black presence, they were also repeatedly concerned with recording and contributing to black political events. Gathering much of his material from his involvement in the RTC, Johnson in this way also popularized the collective's work. As James Procter has noted, Johnson's poetry was often written for and delivered at political events "as they unfolded." During the George Lindo campaign, Johnson performed his poem "It Dread Inna Inglan," composed in defense of Lindo, on the steps outside the police station in which Lindo was held. He then incorporated the crowd's chants at this rally into the subsequent recording of the poem. He repeated this strategy when Darcus Howe was arrested following an altercation at Notting Hill Gate underground station in 1977, performing his poem "Man Free" outside the court where Howe was on trial.[145] In these public performances, for which Johnson invited his audience to repeat the central refrains, public poetic performance became a means of chronicling black history in the making, and doing so as a dialogic process, interpellating performer and audience into the narrative as the bearers of this history. This strategy of composing poems in response to, and in remembrance of, black political campaigns and events recurs throughout Johnson's oeuvre, and his four records released between 1978 and 1984, as well as numerous pieces published by *Race Today* and Bogle-L'Ouverture, include poems on the killing of Clement Blair Peach by the Special Patrol Group (SPG) of the Metropolitan Police, the battle for the Notting Hill Carnival, the anti-"sus" campaign, the New Cross Massacre, the Black People's Day of Action, and the urban uprisings of 1981. It is perhaps in these poems, and the recordings made of them, that popular memory of these events lives on at its most vibrant.

The *Black Liberator*, despite its reputation in some quarters for a theoretical abstraction thought to be removed from the immediate (or privileged) language of black struggle, was equally embedded in wider political and social communities. A. X. Cambridge, who established the journal in 1971, had previously worked closely with Claudia Jones, and wrote for the *West Indian Gazette*. As founding member and first leader of the Black Unity and Freedom Party, he coordinated a persistent campaign against police racism in south London, where the organization was based, and his skills as a journalist also allowed him to win the organization significant column space.[146] Gutzmore, who joined the editorial board of *Black Liberator* in 1972, ran the Black People's Information Centre in Notting Hill in the 1970s and through this organization was active in Carnival throughout this period. He also participated in the black education movement in this period, speaking for the "Black Culture" course organized at the Central London Polytechnic.[147]

In April 1981, following the Brixton uprising, Gutzmore was a leading figure in the Brixton Defence Campaign, where he worked with the Brixton Black Women's Group, OWAAD, and local youth clubs, and he was also active in building connections between campaigns in Brixton and in Liverpool, Bristol, and Tottenham.[148]

The Institute of Race Relations, as we have seen throughout this book, was firmly embedded in radical networks, offering a space for researchers and activists to meet and debate, and often intervening in political debates on policing, immigration legislation, and race relations policy. The IRR's intellectual output also played a significant role in shaping black politics in this era. As "a pamphleteer," Sivanandan wrote many of his essays in response to developing political situations, to offer clarification or argument about these.[149] The impact of these interventions is widely recognized. Chris Mullard, a former IRR employee, reflecting on its impact in 1985, said that

> there can be little doubt that the way in which many of the more recent struggles have exhibited a consciousness of purpose and a deep understanding of the social and material relations of racism can be almost directly attributed to [the IRR's] involvement in both the national and the international struggle for black liberation—publishing, researching, politically intervening and organising alternative alliances, debates and forms of politics.[150]

Sivanandan's essays, as Hall had also noted three years earlier, enjoyed a significant "underground reputation."[151] "Photocopies of his articles from *Race & Class* and well-worn copies of his IRR pamphlets were circulated amongst those who read," Prescod remembered.[152] Balvinder Bassi of Birmingham's Asian Youth Movement recalled how Sivanandan's pamphlet *From Resistance to Rebellion* (a reprinting of his 1981–82 essay in *Race & Class*) would be carried around "almost like a campaigning manual": "I remember it cost £1 and we would sell it at our meetings."[153]

The landmark texts on race to emerge from the CCCS were also a part of wider political projects. The project on policing and race that would eventually be published as *Policing the Crisis* first came about through Chas Critcher's involvement in a support committee for the three Handsworth youths whose "mugging" case framed the later book. Although the book itself would not be published until five years after the Handsworth case, and it was not conceived of as a direct political intervention, Critcher had produced a pamphlet on the case early on, published through his "action centre" in Handsworth and designed to be accessible to a general reader.[154] The group of young CCCS researchers who produced *The Empire Strikes Back* in 1982 were also closely involved in local politics. Paul Gilroy had long-standing links with Big Flame and Rock against Racism, and his decision to come to the CCCS was as much determined by his politics as it was by the underground reputation of the Centre. "I went to the Centre to be with Stuart [Hall] and to be a part of the 'Handsworth Revolution,'" he remembered.[155] Errol Lawrence had previously worked as a youth worker with the Community Relations Commission and been deeply influenced by black nationalist politics.[156] The subsequent canonization of *Policing the Crisis* and *The Empire Strikes Back* makes these texts appear inevitable, and makes the politics of their constitution, and even the significance of their intervention in the life of the CCCS, less visible. But, as Hall has emphasized, both books were "only accomplished as the result of a long, and sometimes bitter—certainly bitterly contested—internal struggle against a resounding but unconscious silence" within the CCCS.[157] Neither text appears to have enjoyed quite the popularity of Sivanandan's essays or Linton Kwesi Johnson's poems among black activists—a point readily (perhaps too readily) conceded by Hall, who would later claim that the CCCS "never produced organic intellectuals (would that we had) at the Centre. We never connected with that rising historic movement."[158] Both texts, however, had a significant influence on black intellectual discourse, and CCCS academics—particularly Gilroy—continued to contribute to a range of other, less "academic" political magazines, journals, and pamphlets in this era, including, of course, *Race & Class* and *Race Today*.

CONCLUSION

This chapter has traced the dominant contours of "thinking black" in British politics of the 1970s and 1980s, as these cohered around the question of racist policing, clashes with police, and the increasing incidence of urban rebellion. "Thinking black," as I use it here, is not a description only of what the intellectuals of the Race Today Collective, *Black Liberator*, Institute of Race Relations, or Centre for Contemporary Cultural Studies did; nor is it a description only of the epistemic structures or content of black vernacular cultures described by them. Though many of the former may have deferred to the latter, the two always existed in dialogue: the one was not cut off from the other.

The effect of this concerted effort to listen to, interpret, and use the action of black youth rebelling in Britain's inner cities in the late 1970s and early 1980s, however, had an effect on those who found themselves the objects of this discussion, and the willed subjects of history. John Akomfrah has discussed how, for him and so many of his contemporaries who were, in Dennis Morris's phrase, growing up black in the 1970s, there was a "primal moment" of recognition in which "you think, 'oh, so I'm that person they're talking about. I'm a black person.'" "That realisation is a slightly shocking one, because you [. . .] suddenly become aware, [. . .] that you were now about to carry an additional weight. And it's either a weight of expectation, or [. . .] accusation," Akomfrah remembered. "Basically, *the spotlight was going to be on you.*" For Akomfrah, son of an upper-middle-class Ghanaian politician, "I didn't know race. I had no interest in race. I didn't even know I was black." And yet, growing up in the 1970s, with all eyes trained on "black youth," "we went through the [. . .] baptism as kids growing up in the 70s."[159] This is an experience remembered most readily as it relates to the demonization of black youth by politicians and the media as criminals and delinquents. But it was not only by white journalists, politicians, or sociologists that young black men and women were appealed to for information, or in whose writing they found themselves reframed in the public eye. The "weight of expectation" Akomfrah describes came from those invested in radical black politics for whom the youths were now at the forefront of political change in Britain, the promising historical repository of the far-flung resistances against colonial oppression of an older generation, ready to bring that history back now to the metropolitan center.

This weight of expectation was the result of a concerted effort by black radical intellectuals and activists. These activists, acting in response to and often in concert with an increasingly harried, brutalized, and restless section of the population, sought to seize hold of the energy of youth urban resistances of the 1970s and 1980s, and to see in them, not the end of society, but its new beginnings. By publicly supporting these young men and women, challenging those in the government, academia, and the news media who sought to frame their actions in terms of "integration," "alienation," "race relations," or "law and order," and finding instead in them a critique of the current political crisis and the solutions being offered to it, the public cultures and practices of thinking black cultivated in the years since the eruption of Black Power on the political scene in the mid-1960s fought a continual war of position against the New Right. Searching for where divisions between old and young, working class and middle class, or black and white might be bridged, they argued that it was through the politics and cultures of black youth that bridges might best be built. This politics could easily trip off radical tongues in the 1970s and early 1980s, as urban rebellions increased apace, spreading across British cities and drawing more and more people into the fray. In 1984, Cedric Robinson, surveying the field of British race politics, could insist on the "special historical part" that black people were bound to play "in the ending of these horrors."[160] But this was also, as we shall see in the epilogue, a formation on the brink of collapse and reorganization.

Epilogue: Black Futures Past

"IN YEARS TO COME WHEN RESEARCHERS are digging into our thing, it will be documents like these that will really be the evidence of Britain's racism and fascism," the Jamaican British writer Andrew Salkey wrote to the Guyanese-born activist and publisher Jessica Huntley in July 1978.[1] The documents to which Salkey referred were photographs of the vandalized frontage to Huntley's Bogle-L'Ouverture Bookshop, in London's Ealing district. Britain's black bookshops were subjected to a campaign of abuse throughout the 1970s. They were firebombed, defaced with racist graffiti, and targeted by stickering and leafleting campaigns. Their windows were smashed, and there were threatening phone calls. Huntley, whose shop bore the brunt of a concerted attack by the National Front, Ku Klux Klan, and other local racists, founded the Bookshop Joint Action committee in September 1977, together with New Beacon Books and the Race Today Collective. The photographs of Bogle-L'Ouverture's destroyed frontage were part of their campaign to highlight the frequency of such attacks, and to pressure the police and government to act to defend the bookshops and bring the perpetrators to justice.[2] They are harrowing documents.

Salkey was right to point to the future historical usefulness of such an archive. Such attacks, as Colin A. Beckles notes, were rarely covered in the press and received little recognition from the police. It was the work of organizations like Bookshop Joint Action that made this otherwise submerged world of racist violence visible.[3] Without the efforts of black activists to archive their struggles, this book would not have been possible. But Salkey's eye on the future speaks also to the sense of history *and futurity* that pervaded black radical politics in these years—a sense, not only that black politics inherited particular histories, but that it was, as Linton Kwesi

Johnson's 1983 LP had it, *making history*.[4] "I wanted you to know how the documents hit me, at this distance," Salkey's letter continued, "both as present time factual records and as material for history." Salkey's friend John La Rose had been busy since the mid-1960s collecting an archive of black political and cultural activity in Britain, storing countless boxes of letters, journals, newspaper clippings, and flyers. His collection became the basis of the George Padmore Institute's archive, housed above New Beacon Books in Finsbury Park's Stroud Green Road since 1991. Across the Thames in Brixton, Len Garrison, an avid collector of African and black British historical arte-facts, established the Black Cultural Archives ten years earlier in 1981, and the archive has in recent years become a hub for the personal papers of several leading black activists active in the period explored in this book. I am that researcher "digging into" their "thing." Salkey, Huntley, La Rose, Garrison, and countless others, worked tirelessly to make this future digging possible. They were driven by a desire to record history in the making.

Beginning in the 1960s and gathering pace in the 1970s and 1980s, there was a determined effort by black writers, publishers, and activists to narrate a history of black resistance in Britain. While a good part of the focus here was on recognizing the historical longevity of Britain's black communities, it is also remarkable how many efforts were made to record the contemporary history of black political struggle.[5] "Already the first skirmishes have been written into black history," Chris Mullard wrote in his 1973 book *Black Britain*, "the stabbings in Liverpool and London in the 1930s, Notting Hill, Nottingham, Leeds, Kelso Cochrane, the Peckham riots, David Oluwale, Stephen McCarthy, Andreas Sava, Aseta Simms, the hundreds of cases of police brutality, 'Paki-bashing' and nigger hunting."[6] In the 1970s, the pages of *Race Today, Race & Class, Grassroots, Black Voice*, and the *Black People's News Service* often reminded readers of the recent history of black struggle. These usually recounted instances of racist violence and murder—most infa-mously, as Mullard noted, the murders of Kelso Cochrane and David Oluwale—alongside accounts of court trials such as the Mangrove Nine and the series of trials centered round black youth clubs in the early 1970s, or set-piece confrontations with the police, at demonstrations, fairs, or carni-vals. In the late 1970s and early 1980s, this practice became all the more pronounced with David Koff's television documentary *Blacks Britannica* (1978), made in close collaboration with Colin Prescod of *Race & Class;* Prescod's *Struggles for Black Community*, broadcast on Channel Four in 1982; Darcus Howe's three-part history of postwar black resistance in Britain published in *Race Today* between 1980 and 1982; and Sivanandan's much-cited essay "From Resistance to Rebellion: Asian and Afro-Caribbean Struggles in Britain," published in *Race & Class* in 1981–82 and reprinted as a pamphlet in 1986.[7] Linton Kwesi Johnson's poetry, again, was equally a part of this process of memorialization of recent struggles:

> when yu fling mi inna prison
> I did warn yu
> when you kill Oluwale
> I did warn yu
> when yu beat Joshua Francis
> I did warn yu
> when you pick pan de Panthers
> I did warn yu
> when yu jack mi up gainst de wall
> ha didnt bawl,
> but I did warn yu.[8]

Cases of police brutality and resistance to it from across the country, as Paul Gilroy noted in 1987, were "passing into the folk memory of black Britain," playing a central role in "the reproduction of black political sensibility."[9]

. . .

Discussing the rising popularity of Stokely Carmichael at the West Indian Students' Centre in 1967, C. L. R. James reminded his audience that history was moving "very fast these days."[10] My question, in this epilogue, is when did historical time begin to slow down again, and why? When did the era of radical blackness that is the subject of this book come to an end in Britain? When did black futures become black futures past?

A sense of historical time sped up pervaded the drive to record every instance of struggle that defined black cultural and intellectual life in Britain in the 1970s and early 1980s. In these articulations of trains of historical abuses and victories, historical time was compressed, one incident piling on top of another. In 1981, the St. Kitts–born director Imruh Caesar's *Riots and Rumours of Riots* provided a narrative of the recent uprisings in British cities intercut with footage from the 1940s and 1950s, of the "colour bar," the

Notting Hill riots, and Kelso Cochrane's funeral. Akua Rugg, reviewing the film for *Race Today*, remarked how, in this "year when 13 West Indian children were massacred in a racist arson attack," footage of Cochrane and the Notting Hill riots "transmits shockwaves of recognition." "The films capture and reflect the spirit of insurrection abroad in the black community, and show that despite their settlement in Britain for three decades and more, blacks cannot be regarded as mere coloured versions of the whites they live alongside."[11] In films, songs, poetry, posters, magazines, newspapers, and popular folklore, the recent history of black life in Britain was recorded as a catalogue of struggle. Certainly, this shows us a black political culture tied up with its pasts—both the long past of slavery and colonialism, and the more recent past of police brutality and racist violence. The drive, noted by Salkey, to record each instance in this history as it unfolded, though, points us also to the sense, signaled in James's prediction of 1967, that Salkey and his companions were at the apex of historical change, that new futures were at hand. Indeed, we can understand the process of the memorialization of the present—gathering the materials of the present as future memories of struggle—as itself a form of futurity.

This dynamic reached its apotheosis in the early 1980s in reactions to the urban unrest of those years, and in the mass political action of the Black People's Day of Action. The Day of Action was itself bound up with anticipations of the future. A chant at the march—"Blood Ah Go Run"—repeated the expectations of impending violence that pervaded Linton Kwesi Johnson's poetry, and that had formed a staple of black radical imaginaries since the late 1960s. Marchers interviewed in Menelik Shabazz's documentary of the Day of Action, *Blood Ah Go Run* (1981), read the unfolding events as the anticipation of a new future. One woman on the march, asked whether she thought the day's events were important, replied resolutely: "important? More than important, brother, this is the beginning, not the end." The event itself can also be understood as a form of future orientation, in which the present was lived as if looked back on, as the past, from the future. From the moment of its inception, the Black People's Day of Action was articulated as a "historic" event, heralded in Shabazz's film as "a truly historic day of action." As Shabazz remembers of his motivations for making the documentary, "I felt impelled to record this moment on film."[12] In the Black People's Day of Action, the memorialization of the past caught up with and overtook the present. The memorialization practices at the Black People's Day of Action— by which the events were understood and recorded as historic events *even as they were occurring*—were an instance of what Jacques Derrida would term "archive fever," described by Mark Currie as "the frenzied archiving and recording of contemporary social life which transforms the present into the past by anticipating its memory. [. . .] The temporal structure of a present lived as if it were the object of a future memory."[13]

Recognizing this sense of time passing quickly, and anticipation of the central role of black cultures and black historical experience in the futures close to hand, is essential to understanding the character of black politics in the era of "thinking black," as well as the distance between that moment and our world of today. "From Tehran to Bangladesh, from Moscow to Brixton, from Grenada to Southall," the Race Today Collective wrote in 1979, "the question is posed: The destruction of the existing world order and the emergence of free workers and peasants in free association throughout the world."[14] "These were years," as the Jamaican scholar David Scott has written of three decades of radical decolonization that followed the Bandung Conference of 1955, "when revolutionary futures were not merely possible but *imminent;* not only imminent, but *possible.*"[15] In 1979, while anti-racist protestors and the police clashed on the streets of Southall, in Iran a broad coalition of socialists, Marxists, and Islamic radicals had overthrown the U.S.–backed government of Mohammad Reza Shah Pahlavi, while in Grenada the New Jewel Movement had seized power from the dictator Eric Gairy, aiming to establish a new socialist state. In Guyana, Walter Rodney's Working People's Alliance formed itself into a popular parliamentary party aiming to challenge the increasingly corrupt regime of Forbes Burnham.

The world described by *Race Today* was to shift decisively, however, over the following four years. The unstable coalition that won the Iranian Revolution was replaced by a deeply conservative Islamic administration, which had successfully consolidated its hold on power by 1982. In June 1980, Walter Rodney was assassinated by a car bomb, a month after returning from independence celebrations in Zimbabwe. In an era of increasing political turmoil in Guyana, Rodney was slain, as Linton Kwesi Johnson wrote, "before di really crucial scene / di really crucial scene / wen di people dem come een."[16] Three years later, the New Jewel Movement's revolutionary government in Grenada came to an end with a U.S. invasion of the island following the toppling of the New Jewel Movement's leader, Prime Minister Maurice Bishop, in a coup led by the deputy prime minister—and former British school teacher active in the early Black Education Movement— Bernard Coard. These events hit black radicals in Britain hard. Many in

Britain were heavily invested in what was happening in Guyana and Grenada. "Grenada," as *Fowaad!* wrote in November 1980, "is a proud example of our efforts to control our future." Noting the "enlightened Black women at the forefront" of Grenada's revolution, the paper welcomed "waking up to a force which is fully activated and is sure to speed up the liberation of our people wherever they may be."[17] While in the United States, Black Power as a radical political movement was largely defeated by the mid-1970s, most significantly in the FBI's concerted and infamous campaign against the Black Panther Party, black radical politics continued to play a significant part in Caribbean politics through the 1970s and into the early 1980s.[18] The defeat of the Grenada revolution, however, marked the end of Black Power as a world-historical phenomenon. The failure of the New Jewel Movement's revolution in Grenada, David Scott observes, was, not merely "the beginning of the end of the particular story of the Grenada Revolution itself," but "the beginning of the end of a whole era of revolutionary socialist expectation—indeed of revolutionary socialist possibility."[19] After Grenada, that global generation of postcolonial radicals formed in the politics of secondary decolonization of the late 1960s found themselves suddenly in the temporal disjuncture of "living on in the wake of past political time, amid the ruins, specifically, of post-socialist or postcolonial futures past."[20]

The articulation of blackness and radicalism ushered in through the 1960s politics of "thinking black" was undermined, also, by the rising influence of alternative radical postcolonial politics, most notably in the rise of radical Islam given a fillip by the success of Iran's Islamic Revolution. In Britain, the urban uprisings of the early 1980s, which had generated so much energy for the politics of blackness, disappeared after 1985. The mass demonstration of the Black People's Day of Action, a pinnacle in the organizing power of black radical activists in Britain, was also not repeated. The next mass demonstration of this scale was the march of 30,000 Muslims through London's Hyde Park on May 27, 1989, in protest against the publication of Salman Rushdie's *The Satanic Verses* (1988), a protest that received £1 million in funding from Tehran. As Kenan Malik who reported on the book burnings in Bradford and London in the winter of 1988–89 remembers, many of the young British Asian men involved in the anti-Rushdie campaign had come out of an earlier engagement with anti-racist organization, "a generation that did not think of itself as 'Muslim' or 'Hindu' or 'Sikh,' or even as 'Asian,' but rather as 'black.'"[21] The visible decline of black radicalism on the world stage by the mid-1980s was matched by the rise of this new international politics of postcolonial radicalism, beginning with the Iranian Revolution, but impacting Britain most substantially with the Rushdie Affair. As anti-imperialist politics became increasingly tied up, in the Muslim world, with Islamic politics, so too radical Islam offered an increasingly appealing form of postcolonial radicalism.[22]

The meanings of blackness in black politics, and its relationship to political change, were also rapidly changing in the 1980s. The mid-1980s was witness to "the demise of the black community" as "a culture of resistance to racism" for Sivanandan.[23] The rise of state multiculturalism in the 1970s through race relations legislation and the founding of the Community Relations Commission created, he warned, "a nursery of comprador blacks" in the "race relations industry," which threatened the independence of black radical politics.[24] Sivanandan's was, in many respects, a misreading of black radical politics in Britain. To imagine that this was a political formation developed always and only in opposition to the institutions of state overlooked the fact that several political initiatives spearheaded by black radical groups who would work closely with Sivanandan's Institute of Race Relations and other black radical centers also received state funding or worked closely with state agencies.[25] Nonetheless, Sivanandan was correct in identifying a growing movement within the state in the 1980s to accommodate black political and cultural initiatives. This was particularly prominent in local government in the 1980s, with a number of local governments across Britain aligning themselves with a political conception of blackness, realized in funding for self-help initiatives, cultural centers and Racism Awareness Training programs for local government officials. In the aftermath of the 1980s uprisings, funding for self-help and community projects increased significantly, with the Urban Aid program—the central driver of this policy—receiving £270 million funding in 1982–83.[26] State multiculturalism, Sivanandan argued, funded self-help in preference over making challenges to the structures of institutional racism, and funded ethnically specific community projects to the detriment of a politics of blackness as a united antiracist front: "Multiculturalism deflected the political concerns of the black community into the cultural concerns of different communities, the struggle against racism to the struggle for culture."[27]

The Black Sections movement within the Labour Party also heralded a new direction for black politics in the mid-1980s. For Sivanandan, again, this was evidence chiefly of a "comprador" class using the language of blackness to achieve higher office for itself. Darcus Howe agreed, chastising the Black

Sections movement as "the quest of the black, professional middle-class for power-sharing with its white counterpart."[28] Many within the Black Sections movement, of course, regarded themselves as fighting primarily an anti-racist battle, and one defined by a politics of blackness inherited from those same traditions that Sivanandan and Howe spoke. Not only did the Black Sections movement understand "blackness" as a political term defined by an anti-racist agenda, but many within it, as the sociologist Sydney Jeffers, active in his local Constituency Labour Party's Black Sections movement in the mid-1980s, argued, "felt that somehow real power lay in the streets and that our section would, or should, be a popular organization trying to bridge the gap between the local black community, which was under-represented in the party, and the local party whose leadership ran the borough."[29] This was, as Jeffers admitted, a tough move, and one often frustrated by the party leadership as well as by the ambitions of various factions within the Black Sections movement. Emerging as a force within the Labour Party in 1985, just when Neil Kinnock denounced the Militant tendency at Labour's Party Conference, and when the Militant-led Liverpool District Labour Party was excluded from the National Executive Committee, the Black Sections movement held little hope of advancing a radical political agenda. "At any election, in order to avoid confusion and get elected, or to prevent being slung out by Neil Kinnock, they have to say they go for the Labour Party manifesto and programme," Farukh Dhondy complained. "There is no danger that Black Sections will bring in their wake the riotous section of the black working-class that fights the police and sets fire to cars and buildings. The most that it can bring to the party and the bureaucracies of the state that it captures is hordes of well-paid advisers and project-runners."[30] The Black Sections movement, for many black radicals, only succeeded in bringing political blackness into the institutions of state power at the expense of its radical promise.

If the early-to-mid-1980s witnessed a disarticulation of blackness from radicalism as political blackness was increasingly taken up within institutions of state, both within the Labour Party and in the policies and practices of a number of left-wing local governments, the latter half of that decade saw the erosion of "black" as a unifying political category *tout court*. Gaining much of its popularity as a cultural and political label through the internationalization U.S. Black Power and soul culture in the 1960s and 1970s, blackness, as we have seen, was always unstably positioned as a signifier of culture, politics, race, and ethnicity. Despite the ostensive openness of blackness as a political signifier uniting various groups experiencing racialized oppression, and as a cultural signifier for those cultural practices born out of histories of racialized oppression, the politics of blackness was often dominated by a definition of blackness that drew heavily on a masculinized reading of African and African Caribbean experience, and marginalized South Asian histories, experiences, and cultural traditions, as well as gender or sexual differences. As it moved into mainstream political discourse, the slippage between blackness as a signifier of a political position and as a signifier of African heritage became pronounced in the Black Sections movement. They were committed to blackness as "a political concept [. . .] used to include all racially-oppressed minorities."[31] But, as political scientist Tariq Modood noted, when Black Sections celebrated winning seats in the June 1987 General Election, many newspapers remained confused as to "how many 'black' MPs were elected," slipping between "black" and "black and Asian" in their description of the cohort.[32] Modood welcomed such confusion, hoping that through it might come a realization that, within the politics of blackness, British Asians were held hostage to a political identity that did not accommodate them, and within the terms of which they could "be only secondary or ambiguous blacks."[33] The campaign by some British Asians against political blackness, in which Modood played a leading role, was largely successful in challenging the use of "black" as a label that either lumped victims of racism together, signified commitment to a certain kind of politics, or both. By the late 1980s, many local councils had dropped the anti-racist use of the term "black," and in December 1988 the Commission for Racial Equality revised its ethnic monitoring categories, removing "Asian" as a subcategory of "black," and introducing a far wider range of ethnicity categories.[34]

While campaigners like Modood hoped to break the hold of "black" as a marker of a political formation, others sought to open up the politics of blackness to difference. The British black arts renaissance of the 1980s, as Stuart Hall famously noted at the time, pushed at the limits of hegemonic discourses of blackness, and fought to establish new subject positions within blackness that recognized, as Hall put it, "the immense diversity and differentiation of the historical and cultural experience of black subjects."[35] Producing new positions in black feminist and queer politics through, for example, the work of Sankofa and the Black Audio Film Collective, the writings of Hanif Kureishi or Jackie Kay, cultural criticism developed by Valerie Amos, David A. Bailey, Hazel Carby, Gail Lewis, Amima Mama, Kobena Mercer, and Pratibha Parmar, or the artwork emerging from the Midlands-based Blk Art Group, this cultural renaissance offered new politics of blackness in the 1980s.[36] It carried the possibility, Hall hoped, of working "with and through difference [. . .] able to build those forms of solidarity and identification which make common struggle and resistance possible but without suppressing the real heterogeneity of interests and identities."[37] In these practices, the hegemonic conception of blackness as a confrontational politics constituted on the frontline of conflicts between blacks and the state was dislodged or openly interrogated. Black writers and artists sought to move, as the title of Ferdinand Dennis's account of his journeys around "Afro-British" neighborhoods in 1987 expressed it, Behind the Frontlines.[38]

The mid-1980s marked a new conjuncture for black politics in Britain, in which global and local political and cultural trends merged to pull apart the articulation of blackness and radicalism that had driven the politics of thinking black of the previous two decades. The failure of Black Power as a revolutionary formation, the rise of radical Islam as a new politics of postcolonial radicalism, the removal of radical political programs as black politics became more fully incorporated into the state, the growing dissatisfaction with "blackness" as a label that appeared to merge political and ethnic identities, and to marginalize some ethnicities at the expense of others, the accommodation of this critique in the reorganization of the state politics of multiculturalism, and the renaissance of black cultural expression geared to challenging the hegemony of masculinized, heteronormative, and frequently Afrocentric, conceptions of blackness and black politics all worked to shift the terrain of blackness in the second half of the 1980s, and to inaugurate a new political moment. This was a conjunctural moment, to be sure. But as Stuart Hall reminds us, the unrolling of a new conjuncture is not about a wholesale replacement of a previous cultural and political order, but about a rearticulation, reorganization, and repositioning. The era of radical blackness that this book has followed still leaves its traces in the political and cultural formations of today.

· · ·

When C. L. R. James spoke at the West Indian Students' Centre in 1967, he predicted that the audience that night might live to see a statue of Stokely Carmichael erected in London. Comparing George III's denunciation of the leaders of American Independence to Harold Wilson's banning of Carmichael from Britain, he reminded his audience that "We have lived to see a statue of George Washington in the heart of London [. . .] and we may yet live to see Stokely, not only welcomed in Britain, but given the honour of a public statue. That, I am sure, is not as extravagant as some of you might think. Remember: history moves very fast these days and can quickly leave the dull behind."[39] Carmichael did return to Britain eventually, in 1983, but not as a statesman.[40] If he were to receive a public statue today—unlikely as that seems—it would no doubt be in a far more sanitized form, representing a more sanitized politics, than James had in mind. But although Carmichael has not received a public statue, this is not to say his presence cannot still be found in Britain today, if we know where to look.

In this epilogue, I have focused on the temporalities of political life. The period covered in this book is book-ended by two conjunctural moments, and I have proposed that between these two moments we can find some unity to the articulation of blackness, politics, and radicalism, and the varied projects devised for and under this articulation. By focusing on what David Scott calls "the lived experiences of time passing," we can account for some of the energy that drove the politics of radical blackness in Britain between the mid-1960s and the mid-1980s. The various projects recounted here were undertaken with a sense of anticipation of new futures at hand, which, today, might seem misguided, or indeed entirely foreign. If, on the one hand, history was experienced at fast pace, so that time itself seemed to be speeding up, driven forward, with each new march or demonstration, with each case of police brutality or civil disobedience, in a tightening dialectic, then, on the other, there was also a sense of the proximity of certain pasts driving that future forward. In Linton Kwesi Johnson's poetry, the current generation of black Britons—understood here in an African Caribbean frame—are "the beginning of the end [. . .] we are black blood screaming flesh / seeking / peace for our dead."[41] And where Johnson's poems anticipated new futures (or apocalypses) at hand, they did so by an articulation of past, present, and future bound together in the black body. In Johnson's poetry, slavery exists both as a historical past still to be appeased and as a lived history accessible through those blacks who found themselves the objects of racial violence today: "Listen to the voice of him who is dead / the echoes are the voices of the far-off dead"; or, "Imprisoned in memory / of whip's sting, / tear in the flesh [. . .] Soon some white one will stroll by, / And strike he will to smash."[42]

The black radical imaginaries that stretched forward into the future, sustained by institutions and practices for narrating the history of blackness as it unfolded in the fast-paced 1960s, 1970s, and 1980s decades, existed also, then, through an articulation of the past that transformed it from the inert time of history-as-a-series-of-dates into an explosive, emotive, lived time, combining memory as a private, relived experience, with a lived form of historical time. One might not only have a sense of history as a part of one's formation, but come to embody, and stand close to, history itself. "[F]or my own part," writes Amitav Ghosh in his wonderful exploration of the intertwining of history and the present in the societies and politics of the modern Middle East, "it was precisely the absoluteness of time and the discreteness of epochs that I always had trouble in imagining."[43] It is precisely the coexistence, indeed the bundling-together, of different historical temporalities that gave black radical politics in Britain the energy that it possessed, that drove its projects, that accounted for its appeal. At a time of acute and deepening social, economic, and political crises, the histories of slavery and colonialism reanimated within Britain, drove a new political formation, and offered new futures.

We are, in many respects, a greater distance from this past (the 1960s–80s) now than merely the years that have passed might indicate. The other pasts alive then—slavery, colonialism, anticolonial liberation—seem equally displaced, not gone by any means, but less direct, more complicated. This is not to suggest that either black politics or racism has disappeared, contrary to the wishful thinking of some. Even as I write, we witness the astounding momentum of the Black Lives Matter movement, spreading from the United States to Europe and Australia, while the Rhodes Must Fall campaign, begun as a challenge to the legacies of colonialism in South Africa, have equally transformed the debate about postcoloniality in Britain, particularly around education and heritage. We have witnessed a revival of Black Power groups in the United States, and attempts in Britain, so far unsuccessful, to plan a new Black People's Day of Action in protest at the continued racism of British policing.

Recently, at a conference at the University of Sussex, I delivered a paper on Peter Fryer's *Staying Power: The History of Black People in Britain* (1984) and his demand that we "think black." An argument broke out between two of those present as to whether they should, or did, "think black" now. The two speakers were a generation apart: one remembered clearly when Fryer's book was published; the other had not yet been born at that time. Interestingly, it was the younger of the two in this argument who saw the greater mileage in Fryer's proposal. She did, she said, "think black." It was how she organized her politics. A year or so earlier, I attended a discussion event at Café Oto in London's Dalston area to celebrate the publication of a new book on the music cultures of U.S. Black Power. John Akomfrah, one of the speakers, remembered attending Malcolm X reading groups at the Portsmouth

Polytechnic in the 1970s. Paul Gilroy, who also spoke, remembered his early engagement with Black Power writers and quoted from Huey P. Newton. A young member of the audience, evidently keen to historicize, rebuked Gilroy, asking us to remember that Newton was not our contemporary, and that we must see him in his historical context. "He may not be your contemporary," Gilroy responded. "He is mine."

Historical time does not stay within discreet epochs, and it seems that today these pasts are being rearranged and reimagined once again, impinging more urgently on the present. Postcolonial critique has been perhaps at its most effective, as Bill Schwarz has argued, when it has been able to demonstrate this refusal of different historical times to stay in place.[44] Colonial empires may have largely come to an end—falteringly, unevenly—in the early part of the second half of the twentieth century, but colonialism continued, in new forms, to organize the time after this end and continues to do so today. The same is true of the politics of anticolonialism and black liberation, which outlasted the end of formal colonialism and challenged its continuation as it structured politics, society, economy, and culture in the former colonial territories, and in the former imperial centers. The demand to "think black" was a demand to recognize a particular organization of this relationship between the colonial and anticolonial past as it animated the present, and to carry forward the promises of anticolonial liberation as these might be realized as new forms of decolonization needed for the late twentieth century. It was a demand sustained by the development of an array of new institutions of cultural and political life, and the production, distribution and redefinition of a wide range of cultural and political practices. It brought together a set of statements about the world, and of representatives of the world of black politics, which were to have a substantial affective hold— Huey P. Newton, George Jackson, Eldridge Cleaver, Angela Davis; and later, home-grown leaders: Linton Kwesi Johnson, Sivanandan, Olive Morris. In today's tumultuous political landscape, we may yet see "thinking black" revived again in some form, though that form will necessarily be different, reorganized, with new articulations. What is certain is that those histories I recount in this book have not yet fully played out. We are, in many ways, still attached to them.

NOTES

INTRODUCTION: HISTORY MOVING FAST

1. C.L.R. James, *Black Power: Its Past, Today, and the Way Ahead* (London: Frank John, 1968), 1.

2. Dick Gregory in *Baldwin's Nigger*, directed by Horace Ové (1969; London: British Film Institute, 2005), DVD.

3. "West Indian Students' Centre: Warden's Report for the Month of February, 1968," West Indian Students' Centre, Book Two, Andrew Salkey Collection (AS), British Library, London. The Trinidadian filmmaker Horace Ové filmed the meeting and produced it as *Baldwin's Nigger*. All subsequent quotations from the evening are taken from that footage.

4. Satnam Virdee, *Racism, Class and the Racialized Outsider* (New York: Palgrave Macmillan, 2014). Hall and Gilroy's work in this area is vast, but see esp. Stuart Hall et al., *Policing the Crisis: Mugging, the State, and Law and Order* (London: Macmillan, 1978); Paul Gilroy, *There Ain't No Black in the Union Jack: The Cultural Politics of Race and Nation* (London: Hutchinson, 1987).

5. Dick Hebdige, "Reggae, Rudeboys and Rastas," in *Resistance through Rituals: Youth Sub-cultures in Post-war Britain*, ed. Stuart Hall and Tony Jefferson (London: Hutchinson, 1976), 126.

6. See David Scott, "On the Very Idea of a Black Radical Tradition," *Small Axe* 17 (2013): 1–6.

7. See Kathleen Paul, *Whitewashing Britain: Race and Citizenship in the Post-war Era* (Ithaca, NY: Cornell University Press, 1997); Zig Layton-Henry, *The Politics of Immigration: Immigration, "Race" and "Race" Relations in Post-war Britain* (Oxford: Blackwell, 1992).

8. For "race relations" policy, see Camilla Schofield, *Enoch Powell and the Making of Postcolonial Britain* (Cambridge: Cambridge University Press, 2013), chap. 4; Gavin Schaffer, *The Vision of a Nation: Making Multiculturalism on British Television, 1960–1980* (New York: Palgrave Macmillan, 2014); John Davis, "Containing Racism? The London Experience, 1957–1968," in *The Other Special Relationship:*

Race, Rights and Riots in Britain and the United States, ed. Robin D. G. Kelley and Stephen Tuck (New York: Palgrave Macmillan, 2015), 125–46.

9. Bill Schwarz first underlined this sense of a collapsing racial order in his "'The Only White Man in There': The Re-Racialisation of England, 1956–1968," *Race and Class* 38 (1996): 65–78. He develops this thesis in Bill Schwarz, *Memories of Empire*, vol. 1: *The White Man's World* (Oxford: Oxford University Press, 2011). See also Schofield, *Enoch Powell*. More widely, as Amy Whipple has demonstrated, the 1960s and 1970s witnessed the steady growth of a new constituency of self-defined "ordinary people" convinced that their ruling elites had abandoned them and were unsympathetic to their concerns, whether on education, housing, welfare, religion and morality, sexuality, crime and punishment, or any number of other issues. See Amy C. Whipple, "'Ordinary People': The Cultural Origins of Popular Thatcherism in Britain, 1964–79" (PhD diss., Northwestern University, 2004). See also Ben Jackson and Robert Saunders, eds., *Making Thatcher's Britain* (Cambridge: Cambridge University Press, 2012).

10. Stuart Hall, "Racism and Reaction," in *Five Views on Multi-Racial Britain*, ed. Commission for Racial Equality (London: Commission for Racial Equality, 1978), 30. Anne Marie Smith proposes that Powellism's language of race was "central to the legitimation of Thatcherism" and the articulation of a specifically postcolonial nationalism. See Anne Marie Smith, *New Right Discourse on Race and Sexuality: Britain, 1968–1990* (Cambridge: Cambridge University Press, 1994), 5, 14.

11. The continuities between 1960s black radicalism and earlier civil rights and anti-imperial politics has been most forcefully argued in the U.S. context. See Jacquelyn Dowd Hall, "The Long Civil Rights Movement and the Political Uses of the Past," *Journal of American History* 91 (2005): 1233–63; Peniel E. Joseph, "Introduction: Toward a Historiography of the Black Power Movement," in *The Black Power Movement: Rethinking the Civil Rights–Black Power Era*, ed. Peniel E. Joseph (London: Routledge, 2006): 1–25; Robert O. Self, "The Black Panther Party and the Long Civil Rights Era," in *In Search of the Black Panther Party: New Perspectives on a Revolutionary Movement*, ed. Jama Lazerow and Yohuru Williams (Durham, NC: Duke University Press, 2006): 15–55. On the black Atlantic, including a discussion of Delany, see Paul Gilroy, *The Black Atlantic: Modernity and Double Consciousness* (London: Verso, 1993). On Garveyism and early twentieth-century black nationalism, see Winston James, *Holding Aloft the Banner of Ethiopia: Caribbean Radicalism in Early Twentieth Century America* (London: Verso, 1998).

12. William Van Deburg, *New Day in Babylon: The Black Power Movement and American Culture, 1965–1975* (Chicago: University of Chicago Press, 1992), 6; Eddie S. Glaude Jr., "Introduction: Black Power Revisited," in *Is It Nation Time? Contemporary Essays on Black Power and Black Nationalism*, ed. Eddie S. Glaude Jr. (Chicago: University of Chicago Press, 2002), 5. As Glaude argues, it was through Black Power that "many young, poor, and middle class blacks made sense of their lives and articulated a political vision for their futures" (1). The role of race thinking in the articulation of political projects is explored in Robert O. Self, *American Babylon: Race and the Struggle for Postwar Oakland* (Princeton, NJ: Princeton University Press, 2003),

and Komozi Woodard, *A Nation within a Nation: Amiri Baraka (LeRoi Jones) and Black Power Politics* (Chapel Hill: University of North Carolina Press, 1999).

13. See David Austin, *Fear of a Black Nation: Race, Sex, and Security and Sixties Montreal* (Toronto: Between the Lines, 2013); Michael L. Clemons and Charles E. Jones, "Global Solidarity: The Black Panther Party in the International Arena," in *Liberation, Imagination, and the Black Panther Party: A New Look at the Black Panthers and Their Legacy*, ed. Kathleen Cleaver and George Katsiaficas (New York: Palgrave Macmillan, 2001): 20–39; Peniel E. Joseph, *Waiting 'Til the Midnight Hour: A Narrative History of Black Power in America* (New York: Holt, 2006); Robin D. G. Kelley, "Stormy Weather: Reconstructing Black (Inter)Nationalism in the Cold War Era," in *Is It Nation Time?* ed. Glaude, 67–90; Kate Quinn, ed., *Black Power in the Caribbean* (Gainesville: University of Florida Press, 2014); Nico Slate, ed., *Black Power Beyond Borders: The Global Dimensions of the Black Power Movement* (New York: Palgrave Macmillan, 2012); Quito Swan, *Black Power in Bermuda: The Struggle for Decolonization* (New York: Palgrave Macmillan, 2009); Michael O. West, William G. Martin and Fanon Che Wilkins, eds., *From Toussaint to Tupac: The Black International since the Age of Revolution* (Chapel Hill: University of North Carolina Press, 2009); Anne-Marie Angelo, *Global Freedom Struggle: The Black Panthers of Israel, the United Kingdom, and the United States* (Chapel Hill: University of North Carolina Press, forthcoming); Lata Murugkar, *Dalit Panther Movement in Maharashtra: A Sociological Appraisal* (Bombay: Popular Prakashan, 1991); Daniel R. Magaziner, *The Law and the Prophets: Black Consciousness in South Africa, 1968–1977* (Athens: Ohio University Press, 2010); Robbie Shilliam, *The Black Pacific: Anticolonial Struggles and Oceanic Connections* (London: Bloomsbury Academic Press, 2015); Emma Hunter, *Political Thought and the Public Sphere in Tanzania: Freedom, Democracy, and Citizenship in the Era of Decolonization* (Cambridge: Cambridge University Press, 2015), chap. 8; Alyssa L. Trometter, "'The Fire in the Belly': Aboriginal Black Power and the Rise of the Australian Black Panther Party, 1967–1972" (PhD diss., University of Melbourne, 2013).

14. Linton Kwesi Johnson, "Time Come," in *Dread, Beat and Blood* (London: Bogle-L'Ouverture, 1975), 24–25.

15. Colin MacInnes, "Calypso Lament," *New Society*, April 6, 1972. Until now, most historical studies have concentrated on this organized politics of Black Power in Britain. These accounts are invaluable for what they can tell us about the ideological diversity of British Black Power, how U.S. political cultures influenced the organization of black groups in Britain, and the character of British black radical political groups. There is, however, little work exploring the ways in which these groups were part of a wider political culture thinking black. While black radical political organizations in Britain were many, their membership was small and many were short-lived. But when black activists called meetings, they could pack a hall; when they called a demonstration, they could expect many hundreds, sometimes thousands, to attend; and much was seen to hang in the balance for such campaigns. Understanding the relationship between black radical political organizations and this wider political culture for thinking black is a central goal of this work. For the

existing explorations of British Black Power, see Anne-Marie Angelo, "The Black Panthers in London, 1967–1972: A Diasporic Struggle Navigates the Black Atlantic," *Radical History Review* 103 (2009): 17–35; Robin Bunce and Paul Field, *Darcus Howe: A Political Biography* (London: Bloomsbury, 2014); Robin Bunce and Paul Field, "Obi B. Egbuna, C. L. R. James and the Birth of the Black Power Movement in Britain," *Twentieth Century British History* 22 (2011): 391–414; Kalbir Shukra, *The Changing Pattern of Black Politics in Britain* (London: Pluto Press, 1998); Winston N. Trew, *Black for a Cause, Not Just Because: The Case of the 'Oval 4' and the Story of Black Power in 1970s Britain* (Derby, England: Derwent Press, 2010); Rosalind Eleanor Wild, "'Black Was the Colour of Our Fight': Black Power in Britain, 1955–1976" (PhD diss., University of Sheffield, 2008). The question of U.S. influences has been particularly well covered in recent literature. See Graeme Abernethy, "'Not Just an American Problem': Malcolm X in Britain," *Atlantic Studies* 7, no. 3 (2010): 285–307; Saladin M. Ambar, *Malcolm X at the Oxford Union: Racial Politics in a Global Era* (Oxford: Oxford University Press, 2014); Kelley and Tuck, eds., *Other Special Relationship;* Mike Sewell, "British Responses to Martin Luther King Jr and the Civil Rights Movement, 1954–68," in *The Making of Martin Luther King and the Civil Rights Movement*, ed. Brian Ward and Tony Badger (New York: Macmillan, 1996): 194–212; Joe Street, "Malcolm X, Smethwick, and the Influence of the African American Freedom Struggle on British Race Relations in the 1960s," *Journal of Black Studies* 38 (2008): 932–50; Stephen Tuck, *The Night Malcolm X Spoke at the Oxford Union: A Transatlantic Story of Antiracist Protest* (Berkeley: University of California Press, 2014); Brian Ward, "A King in Newcastle: Martin Luther King, Jr. and British Race Relations," *Georgia Historical Quarterly* 79, no. 3 (1995): 599–632; Clive Webb, "Britain, the American South, and the Wide Civil Rights Movement," in *The U.S. South and Europe: Transatlantic Relations in the Nineteenth and Twentieth Centuries. New Directions in Southern History*, ed. Cornelis A. van Minnen and Manfred Berg (Lexington: University Press of Kentucky, 2013): 243–63.

16. Quoted in Dilip Hiro, *Black British, White British* (London: Eyre & Spottiswoode, 1971), 103.

17. See Tanisha C. Ford, *Liberated Threads: Black Women, Style, and the Global Politics of Soul* (Chapel Hill: University of North Carolina Press, 2015); Monique Guillory and Richard C. Green, eds., *Soul: Black Power, Politics, and Pleasure* (New York: New York University Press, 1998); Amy Abugo Ongiri, *Spectacular Blackness: The Cultural Politics of the Black Power Movement and the Search for a Black Aesthetic* (Charlottesville: University of Virginia Press, 2010); Kevin Gaines, "Music Is a World: Stevie Wonder and the Sound of Black Power," in *Black Power*, ed. Slate, 191–211; Brian Ward, *Just My Soul Responding: Rhythm and Blues, Black Consciousness and Race Relations* (Berkeley: University of California Press, 1998).

18. Quoted in Ken Pryce, *Endless Pressure: A Study of West Indian Life-Styles in Bristol* (New York: Penguin, 1979), 58. Pryce conducted his research between 1969 and 1974.

19. Norma Walker quoted in Michael McMillan, *The Front Room: Migrant Aesthetics in the Home* (London: Black Dog, 2010), 69. On television and race politics

in Britain, see Rob Waters, "Black Power on the Telly: America, Television, and Race in 1960s and 1970s Britain," *Journal of British Studies* 54, no. 4 (2015): 1–24.

20. I am drawing here on the relations between culture, politics, and affect argued in Sara Ahmed's "Affective Economies," *Social Text* 22, no. 2 (2004): 117–39.

21. On the flexibility of Black Power, compare, for example, Jeffrey O. G. Ogbar, *Black Power: Radical Politics and African American Identity* (Baltimore: John Hopkins University Press, 2004); Joseph, ed., *Black Power Movement;* Tom Adam Davies, *Mainstreaming Black Power* (Oakland: University of California Press, 2017).

22. See "The Threat of 'Black Power,'" *Brixton Advertiser*, August 4, 1967; "West Indians Will Call Mass Meeting," *South London Press*, August 18, 1967; "West Indian Group Deplores 'Race Hatred' Meeting," *South London Press*, August 22, 1967.

23. "Black Power in Britain," *Man Alive* (BBC2, February 27, 1968).

24. Rob Waters, "Student Politics, Teaching Politics, Black Politics: An Interview with Ansel Wong," *Race & Class* 58, no. 1 (2016): 17–33.

25. Brent Hayes Edwards, "The Uses of Diaspora," *Social Text* 19, no. 1 (2001): 66. See also Brent Hayes Edwards, *The Practice of Diaspora: Literature, Translation, and the Rise of Black Internationalism* (Cambridge, MA: Harvard University Press, 2003); Jacqueline Nassy Brown, *Dropping Anchor, Setting Sail: Geographies of Race in Black Liverpool* (Princeton, NJ: Princeton University Press, 2005), 41–42.

26. Edwards, *Practice of Diaspora*, 11. Edwards is drawing here on Stuart Hall's reading of Louis Althusser in "Race, Articulation and Societies Structured in Dominance," in *Black British Cultural Studies: A Reader*, ed. Houston A. Baker Jr., Manthia Diawara, and Ruth H. Lindeborg (Chicago: University of Chicago Press, 1996), 16–60.

27. Salman Rushdie, "The New Empire within Britain," *New Society*, December 9, 1982.

28. See Salman Rushdie, *The Satanic Verses* (London: Penguin, 1988), 413–14.

29. Quoted in Trevor Carter, *Shattering Illusions: West Indians in British Politics* (London: Lawrence & Wishart, 1986), 81.

30. Rushdie's article as annotated in Stella Dadzie Papers, "Anti-Racist," DADZIE/4/22/2, Black Cultural Archives (BCA), London.

31. Gilroy, *Ain't No Black*.

32. Recent studies have explored how imperial links were sustained through migration, familial and friendship networks, a vast traffic of letters, money, and commodities, and the rise of international holiday travel, as well as in film, literature, television, public ceremony, architecture, language, and popular culture. Economic life, too, was significantly affected by Britain's transition from an imperial to a postimperial power, while the development of the postwar welfare state, as Jordanna Bailkin has demonstrated, relied on forms of knowledge and expertise produced in the "colonial laboratory." See Andrew Thompson, ed., *Britain's Experience of Empire in the Twentieth Century* (Oxford: Oxford University Press, 2012): 251–97; Elizabeth Buettner, *Empire Families: Britons and Late Imperial India* (Oxford: Oxford University Press, 2004); Elizabeth Buettner, "'We Don't Grow Coffee and

Bananas in Clapham Junction You Know!': Imperial Britons Back Home," in *Settlers and Expatriates: Britons over the Seas*, ed. Robert Bickers (Oxford: Oxford University Press, 2010): 302–28; Anna Bocking-Welch, "Ghost Hunting: Amateur Film and Travel at the End of Empire," in *The British Abroad since the Eighteenth Century*, ed. Martin Farr and Xavier Guégan, vol. 2: *Experiencing Imperialism*, (New York: Palgrave Macmillan, 2013): 214–31; Stuart Ward, ed., *British Culture and the End of Empire* (Manchester: Manchester University Press, 2001); Wendy Webster, *Englishness and Empire, 1939–1965* (Oxford: Oxford University Press, 2005); Philippa Levine and Susan R. Grayzal, eds., *Gender, Labour, War and Empire: Essays on Modern Britain* (New York: Palgrave Macmillan, 2009); Jodi Burkett, *Constructing Post-Imperial Britain: Britishness, "Race," and the Radical Left in the 1960s* (New York: Palgrave Macmillan, 2013); John Darwin, *The Empire Project: The Rise and Fall of the British World System* (Cambridge: Cambridge University Press, 2009), chaps. 13 and 14; Jordanna Bailkin, *The Afterlife of Empire* (Berkeley: University of California Press, 2012), quotation at 8.

33. Bill Schwarz, ed., *West Indian Intellectuals in Britain* (Manchester: Manchester University Press, 2003); Kennetta Hammond Perry, *London Is the Place for Me: Black Britons, Citizenship, and the Politics of Race* (Oxford: Oxford University Press, 2015); Marc Matera, *Black London: The Imperial Metropolis and Decolonization in the Twentieth Century* (Oakland: University of California Press, 2015). On this concept of "decolonizing" Britain, see also Ruth Craggs and Claire Wintle, eds., *Cultures of Decolonisation: Transnational Productions and Practices* (Manchester: Manchester University Press, 2016); Simon Faulkner and Anandi Ramamurthy, eds., *Visual Culture and Decolonisation in Britain* (Burlington, VT: Ashgate, 2006).

34. Bill Schwarz, "Crossing the Seas," in *West Indian Intellectuals in Britain*, ed. Bill Schwarz, 12. For a perspective on South Asian migrants, see Shompa Lahiri, "South Asians in Post-Imperial Britain: Decolonisation and Imperial Legacy," in *British Culture and the End of Empire*, ed. Ward, 200–216.

35. Bill Schwarz, "Claudia Jones and the West Indian Gazette: Reflections on the Emergence of Post-Colonial Britain," *Twentieth Century British History* 14 (2003): 264–85.

36. John La Rose, "We Did Not Come Alive in Britain," *Race Today*, March 1976, 65.

37. "Thesis in Black," *Bumbo: Special Unity-Week Issue*, July 1970, JOU/7/10, George Padmore Institute (GPI), London.

38. Matera, *Black London*, 3. For a comparative analysis of the French case, see Gary Wilder, *Freedom Time: Negritude, Decolonization, and the Future of the World* (Durham, NC: Duke University Press, 2015). On the interrelation of anticolonial and imperial identities and politics, see also Anne Spry Rush, *Bonds of Empire: West Indians and Britishness from Victoria to Decolonization* (Oxford: Oxford University Press, 2011); Simon Gikandi, "The Embarrassment of Victorianism: Colonial Subjects and the Lure of Englishness," in *Victorian Afterlife: Postmodern Culture Rewrites the Nineteenth Century*, ed. John Kucich and Dianne F. Sardoff (Minneapolis: University of Minnesota Press, 2000): 157–85; Simon Gikandi, "Pan-

Africanism and Cosmopolitanism: The Case of Jomo Kenyatta," *English Studies in Africa* 43 (2000): 3–28.

39. Perry, *London Is the Place for Me.*

40. Keith Piper, "Passing the Cricket Test," March 2015, www.keithpiper.info /crickettest.html.

41. Hanif Kureishi, "London and Karachi," in *Patriotism: The Making and Unmaking of British National Identity*, ed. Raphael Samuel, vol. 2: *Minorities and Outsiders* (London: Routledge, 1989), 284.

42. *Pressure*, directed by Horace Ové (1975; London: British Film Institute, 2005), DVD.

CHAPTER I. BECOMING BLACK IN THE ERA OF
CIVIL RIGHTS AND BLACK POWER

1. See Peniel E. Joseph, *Stokely: A Life* (New York: Basic Civitas, 2016); Stokely Carmichael with Ekwueme Michael Thelwell, *Ready for Revolution: The Life and Struggles of Stokely Carmichael (Kwame Ture)* (New York: Scribner, 2003). More widely, Joseph, *Waiting 'Til the Midnight Hour.*

2. Joseph, *Stokely*, 197.

3. Edward Brathwaite, "Timehri," *Savacou*, no. 2 (September 1970): 40.

4. Susan Craig, "Black Power Groups in London, 1967–1969" (MA thesis, University of Edinburgh, 1970), 35.

5. Ibid., 35. Emphasis added.

6. Mike Phillips, *London Crossings: A Biography of Black Britain* (London: Continuum, 2001).

7. Mike and Trevor Phillips, *Windrush: The Irresistible Rise of Multi-Racial Britain* (London: HarperCollins, 1998), 232. See also Waters, "Black Power on the Telly."

8. Joseph, *Stokely*, 197. For challenges to this reading of global Black Power as an outgrowth of American activism, see Nico Slate, "Introduction: The Borders of Black Power," in id., *Black Power*, 1–10; Kate Quinn, "Introduction: New Perspectives on Black Power in the Caribbean," in id., *Black Power*, 1–24.

9. Carmichael with Thelwell, *Ready for Revolution;* Jan Carew, *Ghosts in Our Blood: With Malcolm X in Africa, England, and the Caribbean* (Chicago: Lawrence Hill, 1994). On the Caribbean roots and routes of early-twentieth-century black internationalism, see Lara Putnam, *Radical Moves: Caribbean Migrants and the Politics of Race in the Jazz Age* (Chapel Hill: University of North Carolina Press, 2013); Winston James, *Holding Aloft the Banner of Ethiopia.*

10. See Hakim Adi, *West Africans in Britain 1900–1960: Nationalism, Pan-Africanism and Communism* (London: Lawrence & Wishart, 1998); Peter Fryer, *Staying Power: The History of Black People in Britain* (London: Pluto Press, 1984); Joshua Guild, *In the Shadows of the Metropolis: Cultural Politics and Black Communities in Postwar New York and London* (Oxford: Oxford University Press,

forthcoming); John McLeod, "A Night at 'the Cosmopolitan': Axes of Transnational Encounter in the 1930s and 1940s," *Interventions* 4, no. 1 (2002): 53–67; Minkah Makalani, *In the Cause of Freedom: Radical Black Internationalism from Harlem to London, 1917–1939* (Chapel Hill: University of North Carolina Press, 2011); Matera, *Black London;* Susan D. Pennybacker, *From Scottsboro to Munich: Race and Political Culture in 1930s Britain* (Princeton, NJ: Princeton University Press, 2009); Perry, *London Is the Place for Me;* Bill Schwarz, "Black Metropolis, White England," in *Modern Times: Reflections on a Century of English Modernity*, ed. Mica Nava and Alan O'Shea (London: Routledge, 1996), 176–207; Laura Tabili, *We Ask for British Justice: Workers and Racial Difference in Late Imperial Britain* (Ithaca, NY: Cornell University Press, 1994).

11. Richard Drayton has usefully described Caribbean Black Power as a politics of "secondary decolonization." See his "Secondary Decolonisation: The Black Power Movement in Barbados, c. 1970," in *Black Power in the Caribbean*, ed. Quinn, 117–35.

12. C. L. R. James, *Black Power*, 1.

13. Stuart Hall, "Gramsci and Us," in *The Hard Road to Renewal: Thatcherism and the Crisis of the Left* (London: Verso, 1988), 162.

14. C. L. R. James, *Black Power*, 3.

15. Brown, *Dropping Anchor*, 41.

16. R. J. M. Blackett, *Building an Antislavery Wall: Black Americans in the Atlantic Abolition Movement, 1830–1860* (Baton Rouge: Louisiana State University Press, 1983); Alan J. Rice and Martin Crawford, *Liberating Sojourn: Frederick Douglass & Transatlantic Reform* (Athens: University of Georgia Press, 1999).

17. Layton-Henry, *Politics of Immigration*, 37; see also Ron Ramdin, *The Making of the Black Working Class in Britain* (Burlington, VT: Ashgate, 1986), 204–10; Edward Pilkington, *Beyond the Mother Country: West Indians and the Notting Hill White Riots* (London: I. B. Tauris, 1988).

18. Pilkington, *Beyond the Mother Country*, 140.

19. George Lamming, *The Pleasures of Exile* (1960; London: Pluto Press, 2005), 79, 76. See also Phillips, *London Crossings*, 25–26.

20. Mark Olden, *Murder in Notting Hill* (Winchester: Zero Books, 2011); Perry, *London Is the Place for Me*, chap. 4.

21. Erik Bleich, *Race Politics in Britain and France: Ideas and Policymaking since the 1960s* (Cambridge: Cambridge University Press, 2003), 41.

22. "Labour Pledge on Colour Bar," *The Times*, September 22, 1958. See also Gavin Schaffer, "Legislating against Hatred: Meaning and Motive in Section Six of the Race Relations Act of 1965," *Twentieth Century British History* 25, no. 2 (2014): 253; Dennis Dean, "The Race Relations Policy of the First Wilson Government," *Twentieth Century British History* 11, no. 3 (2000): 271.

23. Pilkington, *Beyond the Mother Country*, 129–32.

24. Paul, *Whitewashing Britain*, 158.

25. Butler cited in ibid., 166.

26. "Immigration Control," *Flamingo*, January 1962. Cf. "The Lunatic Fringe," *Flamingo*, September 1961.

27. Roy Hattersley, "Immigration: Defending the White Paper," *Spectator*, August 20, 1965. On the race relations settlement, see Mark Bonham-Carter, "The Liberal Hour and Race Relations Law," *Journal of Ethnic and Migration Studies* 14, no. 1–2 (1987): 1–8; Dean, "Race Relations"; Davis, "Containing Racism?"

28. Perry, *London Is the Place for Me*, 156.

29. "Immigrants Main Election Issue at Smethwick," *The Times*, March 9, 1964.

30. Layton-Henry, *Politics of Immigration*, 77–8. In Southall, the British National Party's John Bean secured 9.1 percent of the vote, the largest share of the vote for a minority party in the postwar era. See Satnam Virdee, "Anti-Racism and the Socialist Left, 1968–79," in *Against the Grain: The British Far Left from 1956*, ed. Evan Smith and Matthew Worley (Manchester: Manchester University Press, 2014), 211.

31. Editorial, "Before and after Smethwick," *West Indian Gazette*, November 1964.

32. Quoted in "White Backlash in Leyton?" *Magnet*, February 13, 1965.

33. Clayborne Carson, *The Autobiography of Martin Luther King* (London: Abacus, 2000), 258.

34. As Mike Sewell has shown, in the mid-1960s, comparisons were often drawn between the campaign for Race Relations legislation and King's Civil Rights legislation, and the violence of American race politics was seen as the inevitable future for Britain if race relations was not kept out of popular politics and managed through anti-discrimination legislation. See Sewell, "British Responses."

35. See Webb, "Britain, the American South," 249. Like King, Rustin had visited Britain twice previously, speaking at a Campaign for Nuclear Disarmament (CND) rally in Trafalgar Square in 1958, and meeting the CND leadership again in London in 1963. See H.L. Malchow, *Special Relations: The Americanization of Britain?* (Stanford: Stanford University Press, 2011), 171–72; Burkett, *Constructing Post-Imperial Britain*, 49; *Brother Outsider: The Life of Bayard Rustin*, directed by Nancy D. Kates and Bennett Singer (Boston: PBS, 2003).

36. Carson, *Autobiography*, 258. On Rustin's involvement, see Benjamin W. Heineman Jr., *The Politics of the Powerless: A Study of the Campaign against Racial Discrimination* (London: Institute of Race Relations, 1972), 18.

37. Pearl Connor, interviewed by Anne Walmsley, February 25, 1987, CAM/6/14, GPI; "Dr. Martin Luther King in London," *Flamingo*, June 1962; "Dr King's Racial Warning to Britain," *The Times*, December 7, 1964.

38. See Kevin K. Gaines, *American Africans in Ghana: Black Expatriates and the Civil Rights Era* (Chapel Hill: University of North Carolina Press, 2006).

39. Andrew Salkey, interviewed by Anne Walmsley, March 20, 1986, CAM/6/64, GPI. Salkey interviewed King for the BBC three times during his brief stay, for the Topical Tapes Unit's *Dateline London*, the Caribbean Service's *Calling the Caribbean*, and the West African Service's *Morning with Myers*. Sadly none of these interviews survive. See RCONT 12, Salkey, Andrew, Talks File 8B, Oct–Dec 1964, BBC Written Archives Centre (WAC), Reading.

40. Heineman, *Politics of the Powerless*.

41. Perry, *London Is the Place for Me*, 211.

42. Glean quoted in Heineman, *Politics of the Powerless*, 28.

43. See Marika Sherwood, *Malcolm X: Visits Abroad, April 1964–February 1965* (Oare, Kent, England: Savannah Press, 2010), 50–51, 104, 118–29.

44. See Tuck, *Malcolm X*, 166; Sherwood, *Malcolm X*, 126.

45. See Tuck, *Malcolm X*, 101–41.

46. "Malcolm X's Views Deplored," *The Times*, February 13, 1965.

47. See Street, "Malcolm X," 941–42.

48. Marion Glean, "Whatever Happened to CARD?" *Race Today*, January 1973, 15.

49. Darcus Howe quoted in Bunce and Field, *Darcus Howe*, 25.

50. Carew, *Ghosts*, 10–11.

51. Stuart Hall, *Familiar Stranger: A Life Between Two Islands* (London: Allen Lane, 2017), 37.

52. See Putnam, *Radical Moves*, 72, 126; Carew, *Ghosts*.

53. Kate Darian-Smith, Patricia Grimshaw and Stuart Macintyre, "Introduction: Britishness Abroad," in *Britishness Abroad: Transnational Movements and Imperial Cultures*, ed. Kate Darian-Smith, Patricia Grimshaw and Stuart Macintyre (Melbourne: Melbourne University Press, 2007), 1.

54. Bill Schwarz, "'Shivering in the Noonday Sun': The British World and the Dynamics of 'Nativisation,'" in *Britishness Abroad*, ed. Darian-Smith et al., 23. See also Gikandi, "Embarrassment of Victorianism"; Rush, *Bonds of Empire*. More widely, see David Scott, *Conscripts of Modernity: The Tragedy of Colonial Enlightenment* (Durham, NC: Duke University Press, 2004).

55. Perry, *London Is the Place for Me*, chap. 2.

56. Malcolm X interviewed in *Flamingo*, April 1965, reprinted in *Malcolm X: February 1965. The Final Speeches*, ed. Steve Clark (New York: Pathfinder, 1992), 44.

57. Reproduced in Carew, *Ghosts*, 136–37.

58. Marika Sherwood, with Donald Hinds, Colin Prescod, and the 1996 Claudia Jones Symposium, *Claudia Jones: A Life in Exile* (London: Lawrence & Wishart, 1999), 49.

59. Michael de Freitas, like Carew, spent some time with Malcolm during this visit, and was later to write of this experience in his autobiography, *From Michael de Freitas to Michael X* (London: André Deutsch, 1968). De Freitas met Malcolm X at the Congress of African Unity headquarters in London's Earl's Court and accompanied him on a speaking tour to Birmingham, where newspaper reports named him "Michael X."

60. Bookshops and the reading lists of black radical organizations are discussed in chapter 2.

61. Jan Carew to Andrew Salkey, August 7, 1967, Jan Carew correspondence, AS.

62. Frantz Fanon, *The Wretched of the Earth* (New York: Penguin, 1967), chap. 1.

63. Ibid., 28.

64. See David Cooper, ed., *The Dialectics of Liberation* (London: Penguin, 1968); Stokely Carmichael, "Talk by Stokely Carmichael given at the West Indian Students

Centre," *West Indian Students Union Newsletter*, 1967, JLR/2/5/4, GPI; Anne Walmsley, *The Caribbean Artists Movement, 1966–1972: A Literary and Cultural History* (London: New Beacon Books, 1992) 92–3; "No Converts for Prophet of Hate," *Sunday Telegraph*, July 23, 1967; Universal Coloured People's Association, *Black Power in Britain: A Special Statement* (London: Universal Coloured People's Association, 1967).

65. "The Pattern of Violence," *The Times*, July 25, 1967; "Carmichael Report Is Ordered," ibid.

66. See "Stokely Carmichael's World in Action," *Daily Mirror*, July 31, 1967.

67. See Waters, "Black Power on the Telly."

68. Jessica Huntley and Eric Huntley, interviewed by Harry Goulbourne, May 20, 1992, 4463/F/07/01/001, London Metropolitan Archives (LMA).

69. C. L. R. James, *Black Power*, 4.

70. John La Rose and Stuart Hall in "First Day of Conference: Talks and Discussions," August 1968, transcript, CAM/4/2/2, GPI.

71. Berry and Laws quoted in "The Threat of 'Black Power,'" *Brixton Advertiser*, August 4, 1967, 1.

72. Heineman, *Politics of the Powerless*, 50–52; Perry, *London Is the Place for Me*, 220–21.

73. Heineman, *Politics of the Powerless*, 63.

74. Ibid., 86, 96.

75. Carmichael with Thelwell, *Ready for Revolution*, 573–76; Angela Davis, *An Autobiography* (London: Hutchinson, 1975), 149–50.

76. On Egbuna, de Freitas, and Carmichael, see Waters, "Black Power on the Telly," 962–63.

77. Heineman, *Politics of the Powerless*, 190.

78. *Dialectics of Liberation: Public Meeting and Discussion*, Liberation Records, 1968, LP

79. Audience contributions in *Dialectics of Liberation: Public Meeting*.

80. Stokely Carmichael in *Dialectics of Liberation: Black Power—Address to Black Community*, Liberation Records, 1968, LP.

81. Beryl Foster, interviewed by Margot Farnham, May 14, 1991, Hall-Carpenter Oral History Project, C456/108/01–04, BL.

82. Jessica Huntley and Eric Huntley, interviewed by Harry Goulbourne, May 20, 1992, 4463/F/07/01/001, London Metropolitan Archives (LMA).

83. Craig, "Black Power," 34.

84. Courtney Tulloch, "Revolution and Rhetoric," *Race Today*, June 1971, 184.

85. *Dialectics of Liberation: Public Meeting*.

86. On these gendered sites, see Wendy Webster, *Imagining Home: Gender, 'Race' and National Identity, 1945–64* (London: UCL Press, 1998).

87. *Dialectics of Liberation: Public Meeting*.

88. See Elizabeth Buettner, "'Would You Let Your Daughter Marry a Negro?': Race and Sex in 1950s Britain," in *Gender, Labour, War and Empire: Essays on Modern Britain*, ed. Philippa Levine and Susan R. Grayzel (New York: Palgrave Macmillan, 2009), 219–37.

89. Fanon, *Wretched*, 28.

90. Ongiri, *Spectacular Blackness*, 189.

91. Earl Anthony and Eldridge Cleaver quoted in ibid., 76. See also Jane Rhodes, *Framing the Black Panthers: The Spectacular Rise of a Black Power Icon* (New York: New Press, 2007).

92. Nikhil Pal Singh, "The Black Panthers and the 'Undeveloped Country' of the Left," in *The Black Panther Party (Reconsidered)*, ed. Charles E. Jones (Baltimore: Black Classics, 1998), 83.

93. Stokely Carmichael, "Power and Racism" (1966), in *Stokely Speaks: Black Power Back to Pan-Africanism* (New York: Random House, 1971), 25.

94. Stokely Carmichael and Charles V. Hamilton, *Black Power: The Politics of Liberation* (London: Jonathan Cape, 1968), 54.

95. *Stokely Carmichael at the Dialectics of Liberation, London 1967*, directed by Peter Davies (1967; Villon Films, 2012), DVD.

96. Moïse Tshombe worked with the Belgians and the CIA to overthrow the Congolese independence leader and Prime Minister Patrice Lumumba in a coup in 1960. The case was widely discussed in the black Atlantic world of the early 1960s, and popularized particularly through the efforts of Malcolm X. See Joseph, *Waiting 'Til the Midnight Hour*, 38–44.

97. *Stokely Carmichael* film cited n. 95 above.

98. Ibid. On his Saturday trips to the cinema in Trinidad, see Carmichael, "Power and Racism" in *Stokely Speaks*.

99. Ibid.

100. "Stokely Carmichael Recordings for Sale," *The Times*, August 5, 1967.

101. Obi Egbuna, *Destroy This Temple: The Voice of Black Power in Britain* (London: MacGibbon & Kee, 1971), 10–11.

102. See, e.g., Times News Team, *The Black Man in Search of Power* (London: Nelson, 1968).

103. On black masculinity and Black Power, see Kimberly Springer, "Black Feminists Respond to Black Power Masculinism," in *The Black Power Movement: Rethinking the Civil Rights–Black Power Era*, ed. Peniel E. Joseph (London: Routledge, 2006), 115–18; Rolland Murray, *Our Living Manhood: Literature, Black Power and Masculine Ideology* (Philadelphia: University of Pennsylvania Press, 2007). More widely, Hazel Carby, *Race Men* (Cambridge, MA: Harvard University Press, 1998).

104. The most comprehensive collection of literature for these organizations is held by the Institute of Race Relations. See also *Peter Moses: July 1945–December 1972* (pamphlet, n.d. [1973]), 4463/D/11/02/001, LMA. "Backlash," *Race Today*, October–November 1973, 318; "Afro-Caribbean Liberation Movement," file, 01/04/04/01/04/01/01, Institute of Race Relations (IRR), London; "Black People's Freedom Movement," file, 01/04/04/01/04/01/08, IRR; "Black People's Liberation Party," file, 01/04/04/01/04/01/10, IRR; Black People's Liberation Party, *Visions of Bena Balunda: A Documentary History of the Black Power Movement in Leicester 1970–1972* (Leicester: Raddle Publications, 1990), DADZIE/5/7, BCA.

105. See G. Llewellyn Watson, "The Sociology of Black Nationalism: Identity, Protest and the Concept of 'Black Power' among West Indian Immigrants in Britain" (PhD diss., University of York, 1972), 42; Neil Kenlock, interviewed by Keanna Williams and Lyida Amoabeng, July 15, 2013, in Organised Youth, *The British Black Panthers and Black Power Movement: An Oral History and Photography Project*, ed. Lizzy King (London: Photofusion Education Trust, 2013), 70.

106. Lawrence Black, *Redefining British Politics: Culture, Consumerism and Participation 1954–70* (New York: Palgrave Macmillan, 2010), 7–8.

107. On Whitehouse and moral conservatism, see ibid., chap. 5; Whipple, "Ordinary People," chap. 2. On Powellism, see Schofield, *Enoch Powell*.

108. See Adam Lent, *British Social Movements since 1945: Sex, Colour, Peace and Power* (New York: Palgrave, 2001). On some of the connections between new social movements and race politics, see Burkett, *Constructing Post-Imperial Britain*.

109. Maud Anne Bracke and James Mark, eds., *Between Decolonisation and the Cold War: Transnational Activism and Its Limits in Europe, 1950s–90s*, special issue, *Journal of Contemporary History* 50, no. 3 (2015); Carole Fink, Philipp Gassert, and Detlef Junker, eds., *1968: The World Transformed* (Cambridge: Cambridge University Press, 1998).

110. Drayton, "Secondary Decolonisation," 117. See Fanon, *Wretched;* Kwame Nkrumah, *Neo-Colonialism: The Last Stage of Imperialism* (London: Nelson, 1965); Achille Mbembe, *On the Postcolony* (Berkeley: University of California Press, 2001).

111. Drayton, "Secondary Decolonisation," 117.

112. Lloyd Braithwaite, *Colonial West Indian Students in Britain* (1955; Kingston, Jamaica: University of the West Indies Press, 2001).

113. Eric Huntley interviewed by Anne Walmsley (April 28, 1986), CAM/6/31, GPI.

114. Interview with Horace Ové, in *Black and White in Colour: Black People in British Television since 1936*, ed. Jim Pines (London: BFI, 1992), 122.

115. Lloyd Hines, "Waiting for the Man!" *Nexus: The West Indian Students' Union Newsletter*, March 1968, WONG/1/5, BCA.

116. Locksley Comrie in "Conference Symposium 'The Artist in the Caribbean,'" September 1, 1968, CAM/4/2/7, GPI.

117. Hines, "Waiting for the Man!" On Comrie, see Locksley Comrie interviewed by Anne Walmsley, March 24, 1986, CAM/6/13, GPI; Walmsley, *Caribbean Artists Movement*.

118. Carmichael spoke at the West Indian Students' Centre on July 27, 1967. See "Warden's Report for the Month of July, 1967," "West Indian Students' Centre, Book Two," AS.

119. In reconstructing this picture of events at the West Indian Students' Centre, I have relied on archives of their papers collected at BCA, IRR, and AS, as well as conversations with Jessica and Eric Huntley, Ansel Wong, and Darcus Howe.

120. *Seminar on the Realities of Black Power, 16–18 August 1968* (London: West Indian Students' Centre, 1968), JLR/2/5/4, GPI. See also "West Indian Students' Centre: Warden's Report–August 1968" and "Report on Seminar Held at the West Indian Students' Centre on 16th–18th August 1968," AS.

121. Waters, "Student Politics," 25. See chapter 4.

122. Jessica Huntley and Eric Huntley, interviewed by Harry Goulbourne, May 20, 1992, 4463/F/07/01/001, LMA; Wild, "'Black Was the Colour of Our Fight,'" 144.

123. *Baldwin's Nigger*, dir. Ové (DVD).

124. Wild, "'Black Was the Colour of Our Fight,'" 98.

125. Ibid., 98–103; "Michael X Gives Warning of Bloodshed," *Daily Telegraph*, August 11, 1970.

126. Anne-Marie Angelo, "'Black Oppressed People All Over the World Are One': The British Black Panthers' Grassroots Internationalism, 1969–1973," *Journal of Civil and Human Rights*, forthcoming.

127. W. Chris Johnson, "Guerrilla Ganja Gun Girls: Policing Black Revolutionaries from Notting Hill to Laventille," *Gender & History* 26, no. 3 (2014): 664–65.

128. Althea Jones-Lecointe, interviewed by Diana Agunbiade-Kolawole and Jemella Binns, September 20, 2013, in Organised Youth, *British Black Panthers*, 134, 137.

129. Johnson and Sinclair interviewed by Rosie Wild, paraphrased in Wild, "'Black Was the Colour of Our Fight,'" 144. See also 98–99.

130. Johnson, "Guerrilla Ganja Gun Girls," 674.

131. See Raoul Pantin, *Black Power Day: The 1970 February Revolution* (Santa Cruz, CA: Hatuey Production, 1990); Selwyn D. Ryan and Taimoon Stewart, with Roy McCree, eds., *The Black Power Revolution, 1970: A Retrospective* (St. Augustine, Trinidad and Tobago: University of the West Indies Press, 1995).

132. David Millette, "Guerilla War in Trinidad: 1970–1974," in *Black Power Revolution*, ed. Ryan et al., 625–60.

133. Lennox Grant, "Did you get Beverley Jones' message, Sister?" *Tapia*, September 30, 1973.

134. Althea Jones-Lecointe, interviewed by Diana Agunbiade-Kolawole and Jemella Binns, September 20, 2013, in Organised Youth, *British Black Panthers*, 139.

135. Jones-Lecointe became most famous for her leadership in the 1971 Mangrove Nine trial. See chapter 3.

136. *Message to the Black People of Britain by Kwame Nkrumah* (Black Panther pamphlet, 1968), NEW/17/1, GPI; Egbuna, *Destroy This Temple*.

137. Bunce and Field, *Darcus Howe*, 72–91.

138. Open letter to Michael Manley, *Black Voice* 3, no. 3 (1972), NEW/14/8, GPI.

139. Millette, "Guerilla," 634, 642.

140. "Beverley Jones Murdered by Eric Williams' Police Force," *Freedom News: Black Community Bulletin*, September 22, 1973, NEW/17/20, GPI.

141. Margaret Andrews, *Doing Nothing is Not an Option: The Radical Lives of Eric and Jessica Huntley* (Southall, Middlesex, England: Krik Krak, 2014), 52.

142. Jessica Huntley and Eric Huntley, interviewed by Harry Goulbourne, May 20, 1992, 4463/F/07/01/001, London Metropolitan Archives (LMA).

143. Ibid.

144. Ibid.

145. Andrews, *Doing Nothing*, 71–75.

146. Ibid., 80–82.

147. See chapters 4 and 5.

148. Jessica and Eric Huntley interviewed by Philippa Ireland, January 9, 2007, in Philippa Ireland, "Material Factors Affecting the Publication of Black British Fiction" (PhD diss., Open University, 2010), 240.

149. Walter Rodney, *Walter Rodney Speaks: The Making of an African Intellectual* (Trenton, NJ: Africa World Press, 1990), 13.

150. See Rupert Charles Lewis, *Walter Rodney's Intellectual and Political Thought* (Detroit: Wayne State University Press, 1998), chap. 5.

151. Jessica and Eric Huntley interviewed by Ireland, January 9, 2007, in Ireland, "Material Factors."

152. See, e.g., Audvil King et al., *One Love* (London: Bogle-L'Ouverture, 1971), which brought together writers active in the little magazines—*Harambee, Bongo-Man, Blackman Speaks* and *Abeng*—that were flourishing in post–Rodney Riots Jamaica.

153. See Phyllis and Bernard Coard, *Getting to Know Ourselves* (London: Bogle-L'Ouverture, 1972). This history is taken up in chapter 4.

154. On this generation, see Lamming, *Pleasures of Exile*.

155. Walmsley, *Caribbean Artists Movement*, 43–46.

156. Lamming cited in Kate M. Houlden, "Sexuality in the Writing of Male Authors from the Anglophone Caribbean: Roger Mais, John Hearne, Jan Carew and Andrew Salkey" (PhD diss., Queen Mary University of London, 2010), 192. The extent of Salkey's work in this regard is evidenced in the enormous collection of correspondence held in his archive at the British Library.

157. See Andrew Salkey, *Havana Journal* (New York: Penguin, 1971); id., *Georgetown Journal: A Caribbean Writer's Journey from London via Port of Spain to Georgetown, Guyana, 1970* (London: New Beacon, 1972).

158. See Walmsley, *Caribbean Artists Movement*.

159. See Rob Waters, "Henry Swanzy, Sartre's Zombie? Black Power and the Transformation of the Caribbean Artists Movement," in *Cultures of Decolonisation: Transnational Productions and Practices*, ed. Ruth Craggs and Claire Wintle (Manchester: Manchester University Press, 2016), 67–85.

160. Brathwaite quoted in Anne Walmsley, "A Sense of Community: Kamau Brathwaite and the Caribbean Artists Movement," in *The Art of Kamau Brathwaite*, ed. Stewart Brown (Bridgend, Mid Glamorgan, Wales: Seren, 1995), 102.

161. Gary Burton, "Caribbean Artists Movement–West Indian Students' Centre Joint Symposium," August 1969, CAM/4/3/2, GPI.

162. "Thesis in Black," *Bumbo: Special Unity-Week Issue*, July 1970, JOU/7/10, GPI.

163. Andrew Salkey, "The Negritude Movement and Black Awareness" (1969), CAM/4/3/4, GPI.

164. Salkey, *Georgetown*, 124.

165. On the earlier history that Salkey hints at, see Winston James, "Migration, Racism and Identity Formation: The Caribbean Experience in Britain," in *Inside Babylon: The Caribbean Diaspora in Britain*, ed. Winston James and Clive Harris

(London: Verso, 1993): 231–87; Phillips and Phillips, *Windrush;* Henri Tajfel and John L. Dawson, eds, *Disappointed Guests: Essays by African, Asian, and West Indian Students* (London: Institute of Race Relations, 1965); Donald Hinds, *Journey to an Illusion: The West Indian in Britain* (London: Heinemann, 1966).

166. Gus John, interviewed by Anne Walmsley, February 15, 1988, CAM/6 /35, GPI.

167. Edwards, "Diaspora," 65–66.

168. Quoted in Craig, "Black Power," 73.

169. Andrew Salkey, *Come Home, Malcolm Heartland* (London: Hutchinson, 1976), 51, 73.

170. Sam Selvon, *Moses Ascending* (1975; Oxford: Heinemann, 1984); Sam Selvon, *The Lonely Londoners* (1956; London: Penguin, 2006).

CHAPTER 2. POLITICAL BLACKNESS:
BROTHERS AND SISTERS

1. Colin MacInnes, "Calypso Lament," *New Society*, April 6, 1972.

2. Alan Brien, "Soledad Brothers and Sisters," in *Speeches from the Soledad Brothers Rally, Central Hall, Westminster, 20/4/71*, ed. John Thorne (London: Friends of Soledad, 1971), 3.

3. A Black Woman, "The Black Woman," *Grassroots*, 2, no. 7 (1972), NEW/9/6, GPI.

4. Ibid.

5. MacInnes, "Calypso."

6. Brien, "Soledad Brothers and Sisters."

7. Anonymous interviewee quoted in Carter, *Shattering*, 81.

8. See Gail Lewis, "From Deepest Kilburn," in *Truth, Dare or Promise: Girls Growing Up in the Fifties*, ed. Liz Heron (London: Virago, 1985), 213–36.

9. See Michael Young and Peter Wilmott, *Family and Kinship in East London* (London: Routledge & Keegan Paul, 1957).

10. Lewis, "From Deepest Kilburn."

11. Ibid.

12. Ibid.

13. Gail Lewis, interviewed by Rachel Cohen, April 18, 2011, Sisterhood and After: The Women's Liberation Oral History Project (SA), British Library, London.

14. Natalie Thomlinson, *Race, Ethnicity and the Women's Movement in England, 1968–1993* (New York: Palgrave Macmillan, 2016).

15. Jessica Huntley and Eric Huntley, interviewed by Harry Goulbourne, May 20, 1992, 4463/F/07/01/001, LMA.

16. Lewis, "From Deepest Kilburn."

17. Pauline Black, *Black by Design: A 2-Tone Memoir* (London: Serpent's Tail, 2011), 81–82.

18. Kureishi, "London and Karachi," 273.

19. Lewis, interviewed by Cohen.

20. The *Black Power* book might also refer to Richard Wright's classic 1954 text, though this was far less popular than Carmichael and Hamilton's book among British Black Power groups.

21. Gail Lewis, interviewed by Marie Bernard, May 15, 2009, BWM22A, BCA.

22. Trew, *Black for a Cause*, 149.

23. Neil Kenlock, interviewed by Keanna Williams and Lyida Amoabeng, July 15, 2013, in Organised Youth, *British Black Panthers*, 67–68.

24. Linton Kwesi Johnson, interviewed by Anne Walmsley, June 18, 1986, CAM/6/36, GPI.

25. Farukh Dhondy, quoted in Bunce and Field, "Obi B. Egbuna," 407–8.

26. "Reading List in Black," *Black Dimension* 1, no. 3 (April 1969).

27. Pryce, *Endless Pressure*, 167.

28. "Libraries and Racism: A Poverty of Thinking," *Race Today*, October–November 1973, 301.

29. Ibid; Kureishi, "London and Karachi."

30. "Books: 'Herstorical' Conspiracy," *Fowaad!* 7 (November 1980), 13.

31. Cartoon by Sister Owaada, *Fowaad!* 7 (November 1980), 14.

32. Ambalavaner Sivanandan, interviewed by the author, July 25, 2012. Sivanandan and the IRR are discussed in greater detail later in this chapter, and in chapter 5.

33. "The IRR Library," *Race Today*, October–November 1973, 307. See also Ambalavaner Sivanandan, *Race and Resistance: The IRR Story* (London: Race Today Publications, 1974).

34. Kwesi Owusu, "The Struggle for a Radical Black Political Culture: An Interview with A. Sivanandan," in *Black British Culture and Society: A Text Reader*, ed. Kwesi Owusu (London: Routledge, 2000), 418.

35. Racial Adjustment Action Society, *The Black House: A Self Help Community Project in the Making* (London: Sir Joshua Reynolds Press, 1971).

36. On ACER, see chapter 4. On Garrison and the Black Cultural Archives, see Hannah J.M. Ishmael and Rob Waters, "Archive Review: The Black Cultural Archives," *Twentieth Century British History* 28, no. 3 (2017): 465–73.

37. See "Black Liberation: Stokely Carmichael & James Forman. No. 1 Pamphlet–Black Series 1968" (unpublished), GPI, uncatalogued, folder, Dream to Change the World. On New Beacon Books, see Brian Alleyne, *Radicals against Race: Black Activism and Cultural Politics* (Oxford: Berg, 2002); Ruth Bush, "New Beacon Books: The Pioneering Years" (2013), www.georgepadmoreinstitute.org/the-pioneering-years.

38. On Bogle-L'Ouverture, see Andrews, *Doing Nothing*.

39. Paul Warmington, *Black British Intellectuals and Education* (New York: Routledge, 2014), viii. I learned of the existence of many of the bookshops mentioned from www.leftontheshelfbooks.co.uk/images/doc/Radical-Bookshops-Listing.pdf.

40. See Sarah White, Roxy Harris, and Sharmilla Beezmohun, *A Meeting of the Continents: The International Book Fair of Radical Black and Third World Books—Revisited. History, Memories, Organisation and Programmes, 1982–1995* (London: New Beacon Books, 2005).

41. See Lucy Delap, "Feminist Bookshops, Reading Cultures and the Women's Liberation Movement in Great Britain, c. 1974–2000," *History Workshop Journal* 81 (2016): 171–96.

42. Colin A. Beckles, "'We Shall Not Be Terrorized Out of Existence': The Political Legacy of England's Black Bookshops," *Journal of Black Studies* 29, no. 1 (1998): 59.

43. Dada, quoted in ibid., 60.

44. "Support the Bookshop Joint Action," *Race Today*, January 1978, 3.

45. Several short-lived publications began in the late 1960s. Black Eagles's *Black Dimension* began in 1968 and was in production for around a year. The Black Radical Action Movement's *Black Ram* had a similarly brief run in 1969. South London groups produced stenciled newsletters *Uhuru* and *Ujamaa* from the late 1960s to the early 1970s, while Notting Hill's *Flambeau* ran for twelve months starting in 1971. Larger organizations achieved impressive longevity and reach in their periodicals. The Universal Coloured People's Association, initially publishing sporadic pamphlets and leaflets in 1967, began a regular publication, the *Black People's News Service*, in 1968, soon taken over by the BPM after the former organization split, and later renamed *Freedom News*. The publication continued into the mid-1970s, when the Panthers reorganized as the Black Workers Movement, but many former Panthers involved with the newsletter went on to play an important role in the radical monthly *Race Today*. The BUFP's *Black Voice* was founded in 1970, eventually ceasing publication in 1984. The BLF's *Grassroots* began in 1971 and continued into the late 1980s. These publications enjoyed nationwide circulation. By its third issue, *Grassroots* was distributed in Bristol, Birmingham, Wolverhampton, Bradford, Liverpool, Hull, Sheffield, and London, while the BUFP's Manchester branch began publishing its own newsletter in the 1970s. Outside London, Huddersfield's Black People's Liberation Party published *Black Chat* from 1971, while in Nottingham, the Black People's Freedom Movement published *BPFM Weekly* and *Uhuru*, and Coventry's Afro-Asian People's Liberation Movement published *Resistance*. Periodicals unaffiliated with black power organizations that covered black culture, art, and intellectual life also flourished. The Trinidadian community worker Courtney Tulloch and the British Asian writer Naseem Khan established *Hustler!* in 1968, a Notting Hill community-based newsletter combining crosswords, book reviews, and community advice with regular critiques of Notting Hill policing and the local rise of Powellism, and coverage of James Baldwin, Eldridge Cleaver, Michael Abdul Malik, and others. *Spirit*, a "black arts" journal, ran for a short period in 1969, published in north London alongside the *Backayard News Sheet*. From 1969 to 1971, the South Asian activist Ajoy Shankar Ghose, a founder-member of UCPA, regularly published a "black consciousness" journal, *TriContinental Outpost*, while former BUFP founder Alrick Xavier Cambridge published his *Black Liberator: A Theoretical*

Journal for Black Liberation between 1971 and 1978. *Black Liberator* and *Race Today* became national papers for black radical intellectual culture in 1970s Britain. Joining these two, in a more formal academic format, was *Race & Class*, published by the Institute of Race Relations from 1974, and still going today. In the later 1970s, black radical journals began to be produced by groups previously marginalized in the publications of an earlier generation. Asian Youth Movements in the Midlands and the north of England produced a raft of new publications: *Liberation* (Manchester), *Kala Tara* (Bradford), *Kala Mazdoor* (Sheffield), and *Kala Shoor* (Sheffield). Black women's groups produced *Speak Out* (BBWG), and *Fowaad!* (OWAAD).

46. Obi B. Egbuna, "Contradictions of Black Power," *Tricontinental Outpost* 22 (October–November 1972), 4.

47. Jenny Bourne, "When Black Was a Political Colour: A Guide to the Literature," *Race & Class* 58, no. 1 (2016): 122.

48. Vince Hines, *How Black People Overcame Fifty Years of Repression in Britain, 1945–1995*, vol. 1: *1945–1975* (London: Zulu Publications, 1998), 237.

49. "Reading List in Black," *Black Dimension* 1, no. 3 (April 1969); "TriContinental Outpost sold at," *TriContinental Outpost*, 13 (November 30, 1970), 8. Winston Trew remembers also buying the BPM's newsletters in Collets book shop. See Trew, *Black for a Cause*, 29.

50. Farukh Dhondy, "Speaking in Tongues," in *Voices of the Crossing: The Impact of Britain on Writers from Asia, the Caribbean and Africa*, ed. Ferdinand Dennis and Naseem Khan (London: Serpent's Tail, 2000), 170.

51. Trew, *Black for a Cause*, 190–91.

52. Leila Howe, interviewed by Catalina Velez and Patrick Ballesteros, July 24, 2013, in Organised Youth, *British Black Panthers*, 104.

53. Barbara Beese and Leila Hassan, "A Review of *Westindian World*," *Race Today*, September 1976, 187. Speakers' Corner had long been a location for anticolonial and anti-racist politics in Britain, and was visited by Roy Sawh as early as 1962. He continued to speak there regularly right up to his eventual return to Guyana in the early 1970s. The Universal Coloured People's Association also kept up a regular stall in Hyde Park, as did *Tricontinental Outpost*. See, e.g., "Speakers' Corner, London W.1," *Flamingo*, November 1962; Universal Coloured People's Association, *Black Power in Britain*, back cover; "Burn, Baby, Burn," *Illustrated London News*, May 18, 1968; "TriContinental Outpost sold at" (cited n. 49 above).

54. Dhondy, "Speaking in Tongues." The "discipline" of newspaper selling is satirized in Horace Ové's *Pressure*.

55. Roger Chartier, *Forms and Meanings: Texts, Performances and Audiences from Codex to Computer* (Philadelphia: University of Pennsylvania Press, 1995), 92.

56. On these texts as part of black material culture, see the final section of this chapter.

57. Unless otherwise attributed, all biographical details are from George Jackson, *Soledad Brother* (New York: Penguin, 1971).

58. Ibid., 40.

59. Jean Genet, "Preface," in Jackson, *Soledad Brother*, 21.

60. Jackson describes the prison conditions in his *Soledad Brother* and *Blood in My Eye* (New York: Penguin, 1975). See also the descriptions of contemporary conditions in New York's Attica prison in Heather Ann Thompson, *Blood in the Water: The Attica Prison Uprising and its Legacy* (New York: Pantheon Books, 2016). For a British iteration, see Obi Egbuna's prison memoir in his *Destroy This Temple*.

61. Historians of the British Black Power movement have often pointed to the dissimilarities. See Wild, "'Black Was the Colour of Our Fight'"; Angelo, "The Black Panthers in London"; Kelley and Tuck, *Other Special Relationship*. On black radicalism and responses to British policing and justice systems, see chapter 3.

62. Jackson, *Soledad Brother*, 240.

63. See ibid., 177, 240–41, 252–53, 290.

64. See Clive Webb, "Special Relationships: Mixed-Race Couples in Post-War Britain and the United States." *Women's History Review* 26, no. 1 (2016): 110–29; Hazel Carby, "Becoming Modern Racialized Subjects," *Cultural Studies* 23, no. 4 (2009): 650, 652; Paul Rich, *Race and Empire in British Politics* (Cambridge: Cambridge University Press, 1986), 120–44.

65. Lewis, interviewed by Cohen.

66. Ibid. Subsequent Lewis quotations are taken from this interview, unless cited otherwise. The obsession with masculinity identified by Lewis was echoed across the Black Power texts most favored by black radicals on both sides of the Atlantic. See Rolland Murray, *Our Living Manhood: Literature, Black Power and Masculine Ideology* (Philadelphia: University of Pennsylvania Press, 2007). More widely, Hazel Carby, *Race Men* (Cambridge, MA: Harvard University Press, 1998).

67. Lewis, interviewed by Cohen. See also Gail Lewis interviewed by Marie Bernard, May 15, 2009, BWM22A, BCA.

68. "Soledad Campaign Sister Here," *Observer*, April 18, 1971.

69. "Support Rally for Angela Davis," *West Indian Digest*, November–December 1971, 7; "Inez Williams Visits Britain," *Black Voice* 3, no. 4 (1972): 4; "Angela Davis (Angela Davis Defence Committee, etc.)," JLR/3/2/2, GPI.

70. See Jackson, *Soledad Brother*, 141–142.

71. Leila Hassan, "Soledad Sister: Conversations with Penny Jackson," *Race Today*, May 1971, 146.

72. "Soledad Sister," *Frendz*, June 4, 1971.

73. "Penny Jackson in London," *Grassroots* 1, no. 1, n.d. (1971), NEW/9/1, GPI. On the Metro case, see chapter 5.

74. Beverly Bryan, Stella Dadzie, and Suzanne Scafe, *The Heart of the Race: Black Women's Lives in Britain* (London: Virago, 1985), 143–44.

75. Thomlinson, *Race*, 65–67. See also Julia Sudbury, *"Other Kinds of Dreams": Black Women's Organisations and the Politics of Transformation* (London: Routledge, 1998).

76. See Brixton Black Women's Group, "Black Women Organizing," in *Many Voices, One Chant: Black Feminist Perspectives*, ed. Valerie Amos et al., special issue, *Feminist Review* 17 (1984): 84–89; Bryan et al, *Heart of the Race*.

77. See Bryan et al., *Heart of the Race;* Thomlinson, *Race,* 85–88; Sudbury, *"Other Kinds of Dreams."* 200–201; Tracey Fisher, *What's Left of Blackness: Feminisms, Transracial Solidarities, and the Politics of Belonging in Britain* (New York: Palgrave Macmillan, 2012). On policing and education campaigns, see chapters 4 and 5.

78. Thomlinson, *Race,* 72–73; Amrit Wilson, *Finding a Voice: Asian Women in Britain* (London: Virago, 1978); Southall Black Sisters, *Against the Grain: A Celebration of Survival and Struggle* (Southall, Middlesex, England: Southall Black Sisters, 1990).

79. See *Speak Out; Fowaad;* Southall Black Sisters, *Against the Grain;* Centre for Contemporary Cultural Studies, *The Empire Strikes Back: Race and Racism in 70s Britain* (London: Hutchinson, 1982); Amos et al., eds., *Many Voices.*

80. See Bryan et al., *Heart of the Race,* 145.

81. Gary Burton, "Black Women," letter to editor, *Race Today,* March 1974, 84–85. Burton was responding to Selma James, "Sex, Race and Working Class Power," *Race Today,* January 1974, 3–6.

82. Paulette McCulloch, letter to editor, *Race Today,* June 1975, 162.

83. Bryan et al., *Heart of the Race,* 2.

84. McCulloch, letter to editor.

85. See, e.g., the advert for a "Sisters Forum on the History of the Oppression of Black Women," *Freedom News,* March 4, 1972.

86. Editorial, *Speak Out,* 1 (1978): 2.

87. Cover image, *Speak Out,* 1 (1978).

88. Bryan et al., *Heart of the Race.*

89. Mia Morris, interviewed by Rachel Cohen, July 26–August 2, 2010, C1420/08, SA.

90. See Jacqueline Nassy Brown, "Black Liverpool, Black America, and the Gendering of Diasporic Space," *Cultural Anthropology* 13 (1998): 291–325. Also Kennetta Hammond Perry, "'U.S. Negroes, Your Fight Is Our Fight': Black Britons and the 1963 March on Washington," in Kelley and Tuck, *Other Special Relationship,* 18–19.

91. Thomlinson, *Race,* 76.

92. Avtar Brah, *Cartographies of Diaspora: Contesting Identities* (London: Routledge, 1996), 9.

93. Ibid., 13.

94. Ibid.

95. Avtar Brah, "The Early Days," in Southall Black Sisters, *Against the Grain,* 13.

96. Southall Black Sisters' Mandana Hendessi, speaking in 1982. In ibid., 10.

97. See, in particular, Jenny Bourne, ed., *The Colour of the Struggle, 1950s–1980s,* special issue, *Race & Class* 58, no. 1 (2016); Wild, "'Black Was the Colour of Our Fight.'"

98. Owusu, "Struggle," 9.

99. For a summary, see Valerie Allport, "Bibliography of Writings by A. Sivanandan," *Race & Class* 41, nos. 1–2 (1999): 217–24.

100. Ambalavaner Sivanandan "White Racism & Black," *Encounter* 31, no. 1 (1968): 96.

101. Ambalavaner Sivanandan, "The Liberation of the Black Intellectual," in *A Different Hunger? Writings on Black Resistance* (London: Pluto Press, 1983), 331, 333n.

102. Sivanandan, *Race and Resistance.*

103. Sivanandan, "RAT and the Degradation of Black Struggle," *Race & Class* 26, no. 4 (1985): 1–34.

104. Owusu, "Struggle," 12.

105. *National Conference on the Rights of Black People in Britain* (pamphlet, May 1971), JLR/3/2/13, GPI; Hines, *How Black People Overcame Fifty Years*, 71.

106. "We Are On the Move," *Black People's News Service*, May–June 1971, NEW/17/7, GPI.

107. Carmichael, with Thelwell, *Ready for Revolution*, 576.

108. See "Black Power in Britain," *Man Alive* (BBC2, February 27, 1968).

109. Derek Humphry and Gus John, *Because They're Black* (New York: Penguin, 1972), 134.

110. See, e.g., Tony Ballantyne, *Between Colonialism and Diaspora: Sikh Cultural Formations in an Imperial World* (New Delhi: Permanent Black, 2007), 134–46. This attraction is dramatized in Hanif Kureishi, *The Buddha of Suburbia* (London: Faber & Faber, 1990).

111. Wild, "'Black Was the Colour of Our Fight,'" 30.

112. See Roy Sawh, *From Where I Stand* (London: Hansib, 1987).

113. On Tony Soares, see Anne-Marie Angelo, "'We All Became Black': Tony Soares, African-American Internationalists, and Anti-Imperialism," in Kelley and Tuck, *Other Special Relationship*, 95–102.

114. See Southall Black Sisters, *Against the Grain.*

115. This is particularly evident in *Race Today* and *Race & Class*, both of which had prominent South Asian representation on the editorial boards throughout their lifetimes, but it is equally evident in many of the smaller publications of the era.

116. Jagmohan Joshi, quoted in Sivanandan, *Different Hunger?* 25.

117. See Wild, "'Black Was the Colour of Our Fight,'" 134–35, 214.

118. "Prime Minister's Conference," *Black Dimension* 1 (February 1969), JOU 35/1, GPI.

119. "We Are on the Move," *Black People's News Service*, May–June 1971, NEW/17/7, GPI.

120. The most prominent contestations of this narrative first emerged in the Subaltern Studies project of the 1980s. Representative essays can be found in Ranajit Guha and Gayatri Chakravorty Spivak, eds., *Selected Subaltern Studies* (Oxford: Oxford University Press, 1988).

121. A. X. Cambridge interviewed by Ted Bowden, "Questions on Black Power," *Black Liberator* 1, nos. 2–3 (1971): 67–73.

122. "An Examination of Racism Today and Its Historical Background," *Black Voice* 1, no. 1 (August–September 1970): 8, NEW/14/1, GPI.

123. See, e.g., "United We Stand! Divided We Fall!" *Black Voice* 2, no. 2 (1971): 3, NEW/14/5, GPI; "Black People's History," *Black People's News Service*, March 1970, NEW/17/2, GPI.

124. Anandi Ramamurthy, *Black Star: Britain's Asian Youth Movements* (London: Pluto Press, 2013), 10–29.

125. Quoted in ibid., 28.

126. Ibid., 70.

127. Ibid., 66.

128. Ibid., 66–67.

129. Ibid., 67–77. See also Diarmaid Kelliher, "Constructing a Culture of Solidarity: London and the British Coalfields in the Long 1970s," *Antipode* 49, no. 1 (2017): 106–24.

130. Bassi quoted in Ramamurthy, *Black Star*, 80. See also Yasmin Alibhai-Brown "To Be or Not to Be Black," *Race & Class* 41, nos. 1–2 (1999): 166.

131. Ramamurthy, *Black Star*, 83–84.

132. Michael Rothberg, *Multidirectional Memory: Remembering the Holocaust in the Age of Decolonization* (Stanford: Stanford University Press, 2009).

133. Chris Mullard, *Black Britain* (London: Allen & Unwin, 1973), 44.

134. "Paul Gilroy on Commemorations of the End of the Slave Trade," *Socialist Worker*, April 24, 2007, https://socialistworker.co.uk/art/11017.

135. *Speeches from the Soledad*, ed. Thorne.

136. David Udo, ibid., 25.

137. Penny Jackson, ibid. 13.

138. Alexander Kirby, "Power to the People," *Race Today*, May 1971, 145.

139. Joshi in *Speeches from the Soledad*, ed. Thorne, 30.

140. See, e.g., Brien, "Soledad Brothers and Sisters"; Kirby, "Power"; "Soledad Sister," *Frendz*, June 4, 1971; Courtney Tulloch, "Revolution and Rhetoric," *Race Today*, June 1971, 184.

141. This argument is forcefully made in Brown's *Dropping Anchor*.

142. Kirby, "Power." The black education movement is discussed in chapter 4.

143. Virdee, *Racism*.

144. See Stuart Hall et al., *Policing the Crisis*. The tensions between British Asians and British Caribbeans resulting from such moral panics was played for dark comedy in Selvon's *Moses Ascending*.

145. In this respect, see also Nydia A. Swaby, "'Disparate in Voice, Sympathetic in Direction': Gendered Political Blackness and the Politics of Solidarity," *Feminist Review* 108 (2014): 11–25.

146. Tariq Modood, "Political Blackness and British Asians," *Sociology*, 28, no. 4 (1994): 862. See also id., "'Black,' Racial Equality and Asian Identity," *New Community* 14, no. 3 (1988): 397–404.

147. See Carol Tulloch, *The Birth of Cool: Style Narratives of the African Diaspora* (London: Bloomsbury Academic, 2016); Ford, *Liberated*. The significance of black style as a site for the affirmation of black dignity and the integrity of the body has long been noted in African American history. See Marybeth Hamilton, "The Lure

of Black Style," *Journal of Contemporary History* 34, no. 4 (1999): 641–51; Shane White and Graham White, *Stylin': African American Expressive Culture from Its Beginnings to the Zoot Suit* (Ithaca, NY: Cornell University Press, 1998); Ward, *Just My Soul Responding*. On the black British dimensions of this longer history, see Stuart Hall, "Reconstruction Work: Images of Postwar Black Settlement," *Ten.8* 16 (1984): 2–9; Perry, *London*, 73. See also Steve Chibnall, "Whistle and Zoot: The Changing Meaning of a Suit of Clothes," *History Workshop Journal* 20, no. 1 (1985): 56–81; Sandra Courtman, "A Journey through the Imperial Gaze: Birmingham's Photographic Collections and Its Caribbean Nexus," in Faulkner and Ramamurthy, *Visual Culture*, 127–52.

148. Modood, "Political Blackness," 868.

149. See Paul Gilroy, "Introduction," in *There Ain't No Black in the Union Jack: The Cultural Politics of Race and Nation*, 2nd ed. (London: Routledge, 2002), xiv.

150. Modood, "Asian Identity," 400.

151. Cf. Stuart Hall, "New Ethnicities," in *Stuart Hall: Critical Dialogues in Cultural Studies*, ed. David Morley and Kuan-Hsing Chen (London: Routledge, 1996), 442–51.

152. See Sara Ahmed, *Willful Subjects* (Durham, NC: Duke University Press, 2014), 18, 209n27.

153. Brah, *Cartographies*, 9.

154. Frantz Fanon, *Black Skin, White Masks* (1952; London: Pluto Press, 2008), 84.

155. Sister Maxine, letter to editor, *Grassroots* 1, no. 4 (1971): 11.

156. Sivanandan, "Liberation."

157. William Mazzarella, "Affect: What Is It Good For?" in *Enchantments of Modernity: Empire, Nation Globalization*, ed. Saurabh Dube (London: Routledge, 2009), 293.

158. Michael Roper, "Slipping Out of View: Subjectivity and Emotion in Gender History," *History Workshop Journal* 59 (2005): 58.

159. Mazarella, "Affect," 292.

160. Frank Trentmann, "Materiality in the Future of History: Things, Practices, and Politics," *Journal of British Studies* 48 (2009): 288, 289.

161. Brian Massumi, "The Autonomy of Affect," *Cultural Critique* 31 (1995): 88.

162. Linton Kwesi Johnson, "Yout Rebels," in *Dread Beat and Blood* (London: Bogle-L'Ouverture, 1975), 21. See also, e.g., Colin Jones, *The Black House* (London: Prestel, 2006); Dennis Morris, *Growing Up Black* (London: Autograph ABP, 2012); Mike Sealey, ed., *Vanley Burke: A Retrospective* (London: Lawrence & Wishart, 1993); Armet Francis, Neil Kenlock, and Charlie Phillips, *Roots to Reckoning* (London: Seed, 2005); John Goto, *Lover's Rock* (London: Autograph ABP, 2014).

163. See Dick Hebdige, *Subculture: The Meaning of Style* (London: Methuen, 1979); id., *Cut 'n' Mix: Culture, Identity and Caribbean Music* (London: Comedia, 1987).

164. See Kobena Mercer, "Black Hair," in *Welcome to the Jungle: New Positions in Black Cultural Studies* (London: Routledge, 1994); Kamau Brathwaite, *History of*

the Voice: The Development of Nation Language in Anglophone Caribbean Literature (London: New Beacon, 1984).

165. Paul Gilroy, "Between the Blues and the Blues Dance: Some Soundscapes of the Black Atlantic," and Julian Henriques, "Sonic Domination and the Reggae Sound System," in *The Auditory Culture Reader*, ed. Michael Bull and Les Back (Oxford: Berg, 2003). See also Kieran Connell, "Dread Culture: Music and Identity in a British Inner City," in *Stories of Cosmopolitan Belonging: Emotion and Location*, ed. Hannah Jones and Emma Jackson (London: Routledge, 2014), 86–98.

166. Hebdige, *Subculture*, 43; Pryce, *Endless Pressure*, 167n.

167. Gilroy, "Between the Blues," 383.

168. Jan McKenley, interviewed by Rachael Cohen, April 18–19, 2011, SA.

169. Gail Lewis speaking at "BIMI in collaboration with BISR presents Horace Ové," Birkbeck Cinema, 43 Gordon Square, January 24, 2015; Lewis interviewed by Cohen.

170. Trew, *Black for a Cause*, 199. On Britain's reggae sound-systems, see Lloyd Bradley, *Bass Culture: When Reggae Was King* (London: Viking, 2000) and Lloyd Bradley, *Sounds Like London: 100 Years of Black Music in the Capital* (London: Serpent's Tail, 2013).

171. Michael La Rose, quoted in Brian Alleyne, "'Peoples' War': Cultural Activism in the Notting Hill Carnival," *Cambridge Journal of Anthropology* 20, nos. 1–2 (1998): 123. See also Michael La Rose in *Changing Britannia: Life Experience with Britain*, ed. Roxy Harris and Sarah White (London: New Beacon Books, 1999), 121–48. On the George Padmore Supplementary School, the Black Parents Movement, and the Black Youth Movement, see chapters 4 and 5.

172. Trew, *Black for a Cause*, 190–91.

173. "Black Images," advertisement, *Race Today*, September–October 1978, 144.

174. Editorial, *Hustler!* January 17, 1969.

175. The best examples are from film. See, e.g., the documentary films *Mangrove Nine*, directed by Franco Rosso (London: John La Rose Productions, 1973); *Step Forward Youth*, directed by Menelik Shabazz (London: Kuumba Black Arts, 1977); *Struggles for Black Community*, directed by Colin Prescod (London: Race & Class, 1984).

176. Trew, *Black for a Cause*, 149.

177. Akua Rugg, "Four Films with Blacks as Subjects," *Race Today Review*, December 1981–January 1982, 45.

178. Judith Lockhart, interviewed by Sheila Ruiz, March 2, 2009, BWM05A, BCA.

179. Emil Wilson, "Peter: Flat Mate and Revolutionary," in *Peter Moses: July 1945–December 1972* (pamphlet, n.d. [1973]), 4463/D/11/02/001, LMA.

180. Brien, "Soledad Brothers and Sisters," 3.

181. Ibid., 2.

182. Martin Francis, "Tears, Tantrums, and Bared Teeth: The Emotional Economy of Three Conservative Prime Ministers, 1951–1963," *Journal of British Studies* 41 (2002): 363–64.

183. Brien, "Soledad Brothers and Sisters," 2.

184. See *Speeches from the Soledad*, ed. Thorne.

185. Kirby, "Power."

186. Brien, "Soledad Brothers and Sisters," 2.

187. Roland Barthes, "The Grain of the Voice," in *Image, Music, Text* (New York: Noonday, 1977), 188. See also David Scott, *Stuart Hall's Voice: Intimations of an Ethics of Receptive Generosity* (Durham, NC: Duke University Press, 2017) 30–31.

188. Courtney Tulloch, "Revolution and Rhetoric."

189. Mazzarella, "Affect," 302.

CHAPTER 3. RADICAL BLACKNESS AND THE
POST-IMPERIAL STATE: THE MANGROVE NINE TRIAL

1. Shabazz, "The Trial of the Mangrove Nine: A Tribute to Justice Edward Clarke," in *'The Day I See Twelve Black Monkeys as Jurors Here . . . That's When I quit!,' Court Usher . . . Old Bailey DEC. '71* (pamphlet), NEW/38/2, GPI.

2. Sivanandan, *Different Hunger*, 33.

3. Hall et al., *Policing the Crisis*, 279.

4. See Jennifer Davies, "From 'Rookeries' to 'Communities': Race, Poverty and Policing in London, 1850–1985," *History Workshop Journal* 27 (1989): 66–85.

5. See Roy Porter, *London: A Social History* (London: Penguin, 2000), 258–60; Jennifer Davies, "Jennings Buildings and the Royal Borough: The Construction of the Underclass in Mid-Victorian England," in *Metropolis London: Histories and Representations since 1800*, ed. David Feldman and Gareth Stedman Jones (New York: Routledge, 1989), 11–39.

6. This lively but often tense mix is captured in some of the best of the early literature of West Indian migration. See especially Sam Selvon's *The Lonely Londoners* (1956) and George Lamming's *The Emigrants* (1954).

7. See Mike Phillips and Charlie Phillips, *Notting Hill in the Sixties* (London: Lawrence & Wishart, 1991); Phillips and Phillips, *Windrush*, 104–118; Malik, *Michael X;* Majbritt Morrison, *Jungle West 11* (London: Tandem, 1964).

8. See Colin MacInnes, *City of Spades* (London: MacGibbon & Kee, 1957); id., *Absolute Beginners* (London: MacGibbon & Kee, 1959); id., *England, Half English* (London: MacGibbon & Kee, 1961). MacInnes's writing enjoyed wide circulation and impact—Andrew Salkey even recalls meeting a drunken student in Havana reading a Spanish translation of *City of Spades* and fantasizing about the sexual abandon of London's underworld! See Salkey, *Havana*, 43–44.

9. See John Davis, "Rents and Race in 1960s London: New Light on Rachmanism," *Twentieth Century British History* 12, no. 1 (2001): 69–92. See also Pearl Jephcott, *A Troubled Area: Notes on Notting Hill* (London: Faber & Faber, 1964); Pilkington, *Beyond the Mother Country*.

10. See Pilkington, *Beyond the Mother Country;* Perry, *London*, chap. 3.

11. For first-hand accounts of Mosley's rallies in Notting Hill, see Box 46, Donald Chesworth Archive, Queen Mary University of London (PP2).

12. See Davis, "Containing Racism"; Jephcott, *Troubled Area.*

13. Critchlow in Pilkington, *Beyond the Mother Country*, 142.

14. Ibid., 142.

15. Ishmahil Blagrove Jr., ed., *Carnival: A Photographic and Testimonial History of the Notting Hill Carnival* (London: riceNpeas, 2014).

16. See Charlie Phillips, interviewed by Kelly Foster, August 14, 2013, ORAL/3/3, BCA.

17. Phillips and Phillips, *Windrush*, 278–79.

18. Mica Nava, *Visceral Cosmopolitanism: Gender Culture and the Normalisation of Difference* (Oxford: Berg, 2007).

19. "'Transparent Nonsense' in Evidence of Police Officers, says Counsel," *Kensington Post*, December 3, 1971.

20. *Mangrove Nine.* See also "Relationship between Police and Immigrants: Black Power Movement; Demonstration and March in Notting Hill (1970–1972)," HO 325/143, NA.

21. "Mangrove Nine Trial," *Grassroots* 1, no. 5 (1971): 1, 3.

22. "The Strange Case of P. C. Pulley," *Black Dwarf*, June 1, 1969.

23. Selma James, quoted in "'Riot and Affray': The Women in the Dock," *Kensington Post*, December 10, 1971. See also "Continuing: the Trial of the Mangrove Nine," *Kensington Post*, November 26, 1971; Black People's Information Service, *Justice for the Mangrove 9* (pamphlet, 1971), NEW/38/4, GPI.

24. Recording of Howe's speech in *Mangrove Nine.*

25. Ibid.

26. Quoted in "A Den of Iniquity," *Kensington Post*, October 22, 1971; "'Den of Iniquity' Busted," *Hustler!* January 17, 1969, NEW/3/8, GPI.

27. Quoted in "Constable's Comments 'rooted in prejudice,'" *Kensington Post*, October 22, 1971.

28. DI Stockwell to detective superintendent of Kensington BK1 Station, September 23, 1971, 26C, OG 12/70/350, MEPO 31/20, NA.

29. Quoted in Jill Palmer, "Notting Hill's Trouble Makers," *Evening Standard*, August 11, 1970.

30. Quoted in "Demo Sparked by Hustlers," *Kensington Post*, August 14, 1970.

31. "Police Critics Bitter," *Daily Telegraph*, August 11, 1970.

32. Derek Humphry, with Gus John, *Police Power and Black People* (London: Panther Books, 1972), 135.

33. Quoted in Louis Chase, "What Justice for the Mangrove Nine?" *Race Today*, February 1972, 38.

34. "Michael X Gives Warning of Bloodshed," *Daily Telegraph*, August 11, 1970.

35. "Inside Britain's Black Power HQ Red and Blue Drawing Pins Mark 'Areas of Possible Confrontation,'" *Daily Sketch*, August 11, 1970.

36. "Black Power File for Maudling," *Guardian*, 12 August 1970; "Black Power Intelligence Reports, 1967–1981," HO 376/154, and "Black Power Intelligence

Reports, 1968–1977," HO 376/155. Copies in possession of author, obtained under the Freedom of Information Act.

37. See "Relationship between Police and Immigrants: Black Power Movement; Demonstration and March in Notting Hill (1970–1972)," HO 325/143, NA.

38. "Justice for the Mangrove Nine."

39. Ibid.

40. Darcus Howe, quoted in Bunce and Field, *Darcus Howe*, 125.

41. "Why I'll Fight the Heavy Mob," *Kensington Post*, December 17, 1971; "The Abyss of No Return," *Kensington Post*, December 17, 1971. John La Rose, meeting supporters from the public gallery as they left the court following these speeches, records the electrifying effect of these closing addresses. "It was brilliant," said one. "That whole speech should be published" (John La Rose's diary, GPI, uncatalogued, folder, Dream to Change the World).

42. See, e.g., *Black People's News Service*, March 1970, NEW/17/2, GPI; *Black People's News Service*, May 1970, NEW/17/3, GPI. See also Mullard, *Black Britain*, 142; J. A. Hunte, *Nigger Hunting in England* (London: West Indian Standing Conference, 1966); Humphry, with John, *Police Power and Black People*.

43. "Demonstrators 'Used Violence on Police,'" *Guardian*, October 9, 1971.

44. "Portnall Road Clash Was 'Quite Spontaneous,'" *Kensington Post*, October 15, 1971.

45. "Why I'll Fight the Heavy Mob," *Kensington Post*, December 17, 1971.

46. Darcus Howe in *Mangrove Nine*.

47. "Mangrove Judge 'Tyrant,'" *Guardian*, December 14, 1971.

48. *Time Out*, September 10, 1971, quoted in Bunce and Field, *Darcus Howe*, 121.

49. *Freedom Meeting for Angela Davis & Mangrove 9* (flyer), October 14, 1971, AS.

50. *Friends of Soledad, Latest News* (pamphlet), November 10, 1971, JOU/32/3, GPI.

51. "Mangrove Judge 'Tyrant,'" *Guardian*, December 14, 1971.

52. "What We Stand For," *Black People's News Service*, July 1970, NA, MEPO 31/20.

53. "We are on the Move," *Black People's News Service*, May–June 1971, NEW/17/7, GPI.

54. *Mangrove Nine*.

55. *Black Voice*, quoted in Mullard, *Black Britain*, 142; Trew, *Black for a Cause*, 112–16. In 1976, when the police provoked a mass conflict between themselves and revelers at the Notting Hill Carnival, many black activists were also quick to point to the role of the presiding officer, Chief Superintendent Ron Patterson, in suppressing the Anguillan revolution. See Race Today Collective, *The Road Made to Walk on Carnival Day: The Battle for West Indian Carnival in Britain* (London: Race Today Collective, 1977). Exchanges of personnel, ideas, and tactics among British colonial police forces at the end of empire are noted in David Killingray and David M. Anderson, "An Orderly Retreat? Policing the End of Empire," in *Policing and Decolonisation: Politics, Nationalism and the Police, 1917–65*, ed. Killingray and Anderson (Manchester: Manchester University Press, 1992), 1–21. It would be

interesting to see what became of these colonial police officers, and their tactics, when (or if) they returned to the metropole.

56. A British Black Panther speaking in 1971, quoted in Watson, "Sociology of Black Nationalism," vi.

57. Darcus Howe, "Bringing it all Back Home," *Race Today*, March 1974, 67.

58. Humphry, with John, *Police Power and Black People*, 164.

59. *Mangrove Nine.*

60. "Fighting the Justice Machine," *Special Education Issue*, special issue, *Grassroots* (1972), NEW/9/7, GPI.

61. Ibid.

62. Jones Lecointe in *Mangrove Nine.*

63. John Heilpern, "Mangrove Nine Notebook: Old Bailey Showcase for Black Protest," *Guardian*, October 17, 1971. Alexander Kirby in a *Race Today* editorial similarly charged that "Britain's legal system shows every sign of advanced *rigor mortis.*" See "The Mangrove Nine," *Race Today*, January 1972, 1.

64. David Cannadine, *Ornamentalism: How the British Saw Their Empire* (London: Penguin, 2001), 172.

65. See Hall et al., *Policing the Crisis;* Gilroy, *Ain't No Black*, chap. 3.

66. E. P. Thompson, *Writing by Candlelight* (London: Merlin, 1980), viii.

67. "Attacks on Black Activists," *TriContinental Outpost*, January 1972.

68. Ibid. See also Schaffer, "Legislating."

69. "Crowd Besieges Police Station," *The Times*, July 28, 1970.

70. See Angelo, "Black Panthers."

71. "Tension Builders in Notting Hill," *Race Today*, December 1970, 457.

72. See A. X. Cambridge, "On the Metro Saga," *Black Liberator* 1, no. 4 (1972): 155–68.

73. Trew, *Black for a Cause.*

74. "Points of the Month," *Race Today*, May 1972, 150.

75. See Stuart Hall, *The Hard Road to Renewal: Thatcherism and the Crisis of the Left* (London: Verso, 1988); Hall et al., *Policing the Crisis*, chaps. 8 and 9. See also Whipple, "Ordinary People"; Marcus Collins, ed., *The Permissive Society and Its Enemies: Sixties British Culture* (London: Rivers Oram Press, 2007).

76. Editorial, *Black Liberator* 1, no. 1 (September–October 1971): 3.

77. In January 1971, an arson attack on a West Indian party at Sunderland Road, Forest Hill, left five in hospital, one critically ill, and six more treated for burns. Accusing the police of inaction in finding those responsible, the Black Unity and Freedom Party (BUFP) organized a march of 150 people to Lewisham's Ladywell police station, where A. X. Cambridge protested against police brutality against black people in the area. See "5 in Hospital after House-Party Blaze," *South London Press*, January 5, 1971; "Bombings: Call for Action," *South London Press*, January 22, 1971. See also *Fire Bombs Victims*, special issue, *Black Voice* 2, no. 1 (1971).

78. See Institute of Race Relations, *Police against Black People: Evidence Submitted to the Royal Commission on Criminal Procedure* (London: IRR, 1979), 14.

79. See Hall et al., *Policing the Crisis*, 284. For more on the Act, and its short life, see Fred Lindop, "The Dockers and the 1971 Industrial Relations Act, Part 1: Shop Stewards and Containerization," *Historical Studies in Industrial Relations*, 5 (1998): 33–72; Fred Lindop, "The Dockers and the 1971 Industrial Relations Act, Part 2: The Arrest and Release of the 'Pentonville Five,'" *Historical Studies in Industrial Relations*, 6 (1998): 65–100.

80. Hall et al., *Policing the Crisis*, 289.

81. Joe Jacobs, *Sorting Out the Postal Strike* (Bromley, Kent, England: Solidarity, 1971).

82. Tony Lane and Kenneth Roberts, *Strike at Pilkingtons* (London: Collins, 1971); "The Pilkingtons Strike," *International Socialism*, July–August 1970, 5–6.

83. See John Matthews, *Ford Strike: The Workers' Story* (London: Panther Books, 1972); Jon Murden, "Demands for Fair Wages and Pay Parity in the British Motor Industry in the 1960s and 1970s," *Historical Studies in Industrial Relations* 20 (2005): 18–25.

84. Gordon Carr, *The Angry Brigade: The Cause and the Case* (London: Gollancz, 1975); Jonathan Green, *Days in the Life: Voices from the English Underground, 1961–1971* (London: Pimlico, 1998), 356–62, 390.

85. See Martin Bright, "Look Back in Anger," *Observer Magazine*, February 3, 2002.

86. See John Sutherland, *Offensive Literature: Decensorship in Britain, 1960–1982* (London: Junction Books, 1982), 111–16.

87. Tony Palmer, *The Trials of Oz* (London: Blond & Briggs, 1971).

88. Frank Mort, "Scandalous Events: Metropolitan Culture and Moral Change," *Representations* 93 (2006): 109.

89. This is a key argument of Hall et al., *Policing the Crisis*.

90. Alan Brien, "Soledad Brothers and Sisters," in *Speeches from the Soledad*, ed. Thorne, 2.

91. Satnam Virdee, "Anti-Racism and the Socialist Left, 1968–79," in Smith and Worley, *Against the Grain*, 214.

92. See Satnam Virdee, *Racism, Class and the Racialized Outsider* (New York: Palgrave Macmillan, 2014), 113–19; Fred Lindhop, "Racism and the Working Class: Strikes in Support of Enoch Powell," *Labour History Review* 66, no. 1 (2001): 79–100; Liz Fekete, "Dockers against Racism: An Interview with Micky Fenn," *Race & Class* 58, no. 1 (2016): 55–60.

93. Miles and Phizacklea quoted in Virdee, *Racism*, 124.

94. See ibid., 123–44.

95. See Burkett, *Constructing Post-Imperial Britain*, chap. 9.

96. On the growth of the radical left in the 1960s and 1970s, see Smith and Worley, *Against the Grain*.

97. "Angela's Sister Appeals to Ford Men," *Morning Star*, October 14, 1971. See also "The Courage of Georgina Jackson," *Morning Star*, October 6, 1971; "Angela—Building a Shield against Fascism," *Morning Star*, October 13, 1971; "Urgent Plea to Save Angela's Life," *Morning Star*, October 13, 1971.

98. "Action of British People Especially Important—Angela," *Morning Star*, October 14, 1971.

99. "Angela Protest Tomorrow," *Morning Star*, September 25, 1971.

100. Cecil Gutzmore, untitled commentary, *Black Liberator* 1, no. 4 (1972): 172.

101. Gary Burton, "A Look at the Angela Davis Defence Committee and the British CP," *Black Liberator* 1, no. 4 (1972): 174.

102. Ibid., 175, 176.

103. "Black Defence Committee," *Red Mole*, January 1–5, 1971.

104. "Notting Hill: White Militants March in Solidarity with Black Struggle," *Red Mole*, November 16–30, 1970.

105. Ibid.

106. "Black Defence Committee."

107. Black Defence Committee, "Hands Off Black People: Smash the Immigration Bill!" poster for a public meeting at Conway Hall, June 10, 1971, BL.

108. "Black Defence Committee." On Joshua Francis, Darcus Howe, "From Bobby to Babylon: Blacks and the British Police. Part 3: Brixton before the Uprising," *Race Today*, February–March 1982, 61–69.

109. Steve Cohen, "Manchester: Solidarity with Black Militants Struggling against Oppression," *Red Mole*, August 1971.

110. Lucy Gray, "Repression in Britain: The Black People's Struggle," *Red Mole*, October 5, 1971.

111. Steve Cohen, "Solidarity with the Mangrove Nine," *Red Mole*, January 10, 1972.

112. On the underground press, see Nigel Fountain, *Underground: The London Alternative Press, 1966–74* (London: Routledge, 1988); Robert Dickson, *Imprinting the Sticks: The Alternative Press beyond London* (Brookfield, VT: Arena, 1997).

113. *Antiuniversity of London* 1 (1968), BL. On the connections between libertarian education and black radical politics, see chapter 4.

114. Malik, *Michael X;* John Williams, *Michael X: A Life in Black and White* (London: Century, 2008); Green, *Days in the Life*, 95.

115. See, e.g., Colin Campbell, "Beatniks, Moral Crusaders, Delinquent Teenagers and Hippies: Accounting for the Counterculture," and Willie Thompson and Marcus Collins, "The Revolutionary Left and the Permissive Society," in *Permissive Society*, ed. Collins, 97–111, 155–68; Arthur Marwick, *The Sixties: Cultural Revolution in Britain, France, Italy and the United States, c. 1958–c. 1974* (Oxford: Oxford University Press, 1998); Dominic Sandbrook, *White Heat: A History of Britain in the Swinging Sixties* (London: Little, Brown, 2006). Hints as to the influence of black cultures in the formation of the underground are found in the interviews in Jonathon Green's *Days in the Life* (10--11, 50, 97–98, 343–46), but his *All Dressed Up: The Sixties and the Counter-Culture* (London: Jonathan Cape, 1998) confines this issue to a separate chapter and marginal role.

116. Haynes in Green, *Days in the Life*, 126.

117. On slavery and the liberty of the body, see Gilroy, *Ain't No Black*, 226–27.

118. Caroline Coon and Rufus Harris, *The Release Report on Drug Offences and the Law* (London: Sphere Books, 1969), 14. See also Hall et al., *Policing the Crisis*, 239–40.

119. See Colin MacInnes, "RAAStus: WI in W.2.," *Oz*, February 1967; Courtney Tulloch, "The Reading Collective, 1967–68," *Race Today*, March 1972, 95–97; "Michael X and the Flower Children," *Oz*, November 1967.

120. On *International Times (IT)*, see Fountain, *Underground*, 30; on *Friends*, John Chesterman, interviewed by Margot Farnham, September 13–15, 1993, Hall-Carpenter Oral History Project, C456/123/01–09, BL; Green, *Days in the Life*, 362–64.

121. John Cunningham, "Short Order for the Law," *Guardian*, December 17, 1971.

122. Newton quoted in Bobby Seale, *Seize the Time: The Story of the Black Panther Party and Huey P. Newton* (London: Hutchinson, 1970), 404. See also Huey P. Newton, with J. Herman Blake, *Revolutionary Suicide* (London: Wildwood House, 1974), 164–66.

123. I am borrowing Raymond Williams's definition of keywords from his *Keywords: A Vocabulary of Culture and Society* (London: Croom Helm, 1976), 13.

124. Ibid., 13.

125. See, e.g., "Off the Pigs," *Friends*, May 15, 1970; "Pigs Rampage," *Friends*, May 29, 1970.

126. "Black Panthers: Statement by Black Panther Movement," *International Times*, August 15, 1970; "Hands off the Mangrove," *Friends*, September 13, 1970.

127. "Pigs Clutch Short and Curlies," *International Times*, October 22–November 5, 1970; "Pigs Double Cross Squatters," *International Times*, October 8–22, 1970; "Tory Pigs Pressure: Blacks & Poor Are First Target," *International Times*, November 5–19, 1970; "We Accuse Police at Metro Siege," *Frendz*, June 4, 1971.

128. "There's No Justice Like British Justice," *Frendz*, September 16, 1971.

129. "Who Were the Pigs of the Year?," *Frendz*, January 18, 1972.

130. *Ink*, January 7, 1972.

131. See Clive Emsley, "The English Bobby: An Indulgent Tradition," in *Myths of the English*, ed. Roy Porter (Cambridge: Polity Press, 1992), 114–35. See also Raphael Samuel's short history of the policeman as a national fiction "who invites attention, as a talisman of changing attitudes to authority," in his "Introduction: The Figures of National Myth," *Patriotism: The Making and Unmaking of British National Identity*, ed. Raphael Samuel, vol. 3, *National Fictions* (London: Routledge, 1989), xx–xxii.

132. "Obscenity: Who Really Cares?," *Friends*, March 25, 1970.

133. Neville in *Ink*, December 2, 1971.

134. "Evenin' All," *Oz*, September 1971.

135. Ian Birchall, "'Vicarious Pleasure?': The British Far Left and the Third World, 1956–79," in Smith and Worley, *Against the Grain*, 190.

136. *Black Liberator*, September–October 1971, 3.

CHAPTER 4. BLACK STUDIES

1. Farukh Dhondy, "Teaching Young Blacks," (1978) in Dhondy, Beese, and Hassan, *Black Explosion*, 9.

2. Christopher Knight, *The Making of Tory Education Policy in Post-War Britain, 1950–1986* (New York: Falmer Press, 1990), chap. 3; Brian Simon, *Education and the Social Order* (London: Lawrence & Wishart, 1999), 396–401; Whipple, "Ordinary People," chap. 5; Glen O'Hara, *Governing Post-War Britain: The Paradoxes of Progress* (New York: Palgrave Macmillan, 2012), 153–75; Rodney Lowe, *Education in the Post-War Years: A Social History* (London: Routledge, 1988); Centre for Contemporary Cultural Studies, *Unpopular Education: Schooling and Social Democracy in England since 1944* (London: Hutchinson, 1981).

3. See Centre for Contemporary Cultural Studies, *Unpopular Education*.

4. Carolyn Steedman, "State Sponsored Autobiography," in *Moments of Modernity: Reconstructing Britain, 1945–1964*, ed. Becky Conekin et al. (London: Rivers Oram Press, 1999), 41–54. More widely, Christopher Hilliard, *To Exercise Our Talents: The Democratization of Writing in Britain* (Cambridge, MA: Harvard University Press, 2006); Chris Waters, "Autobiography, Nostalgia, and the Changing Practices of Working-Class Selfhood," in *Singular Continuities: Tradition, Nostalgia, and Identity in Modern British Culture*, ed. George K. Behlmer and Fred M. Leventhal (Stanford: Stanford University Press, 2000), 178–95.

5. Marina Maxwell, "Violence in the Toilets," *Race Today*, September 1969, 137, 139.

6. Ibid., 136, 137.

7. Beryl Gilroy, *Black Teacher* (1979; London: Bogle-L'Ouverture, 1994), 147.

8. Select Committee on Race Relations and Immigration, Session 1975–76, *The West Indian Community: Minutes of Evidence. Thursday 20 May 1976* (London: Her Majesty's Stationery Office, 1976), 294.

9. "To School with Fear," *Spare Rib*, September 1977.

10. Carlton Duncan, in Phillips and Phillips, *Windrush*, 260.

11. Kureishi, "London and Karachi," 271; Gilroy, *Black Teacher*, 153.

12. Quoted in Bryan et al., *Heart of the Race*, 63.

13. Ibid., 63.

14. Carter, *Shattering Illusions*, 84.

15. Mullard, *Black Britain*, 14. Mullard was drawing here on Fanon's *Black Skin, White Masks*.

16. Brett Bebber, "'We Were Just Unwanted': Bussing, Migrant Dispersal, and South Asians in London," *Journal of Social History* 48, no. 3 (2015): 639, 657n20.

17. See E. J. B. Rose, *Colour and Citizenship: A Report on British Race Relations* (London: Institute of Race Relations, 1969), 267–73, 281–86; Bebber, "Bussing"; Warmington, *Black British Intellectuals*, 50.

18. See Winston Best in John La Rose Tribute Committee, *Foundations of a Movement* (London: John La Rose Tribute Committee, 1991), 12–19.

NOTES TO PAGES 125–130 · 255

19. Carter, *Shattering Illusions*, 88.

20. Warmington, *Black British Intellectuals*, 58.

21. Carter, *Shattering Illusions*, 92. The scale of the debate launched by Coard's book is evident in the volume of press cuttings assiduously collected by researchers at the Institute of Race Relations. See "Newspaper cuttings on Educationally Sub-Normal (ESN) Schools," folder, 01/04/04/01/05/08, IRR.

22. Bernard Coard, *How the West Indian Child Is Made Educationally Sub-Normal in the British School System: The Scandal of the Black Child in Schools in Britain* (London: New Beacon, 1971).

23. Bryan et al., *Heart of the Race*, 77–79; see also "Supplementary Education," folder, 01/04/04/01/04/01/21, IRR.

24. Beese and Hassan, "Who's Educating Whom?" (1975), in Dhondy, Beese, and Hassan, *Black Explosion*, 30.

25. See Heidi Safia Mizra and Diane Reay, "Spaces and Places of Black Educational Desire: Rethinking Black Supplementary Schools as a New Social Movement," *Sociology* 34, no. 3 (2000): 521.

26. Bryan et al., *Heart of the Race*, 59–61; Mary Chamberlain, *Narratives of Exile and Return* (New York: St. Martin's Press, 1997), 83.

27. John La Rose, "Introduction," in *Changing Britannia: Life Experience with Britain*, ed. Roxy Harris and Sarah White (London: New Beacon Books, 1999), vii. The school was attached to the Shepherd's Bush Social and Welfare Association, also founded by Wood. See Wilfred Wood in *Building Britannia: Life Experience with Britain*, ed. Roxy Harris and Sarah White (London: New Beacon Books, 2009), 129–61; C. Sealy, "Shepherd's Bush Social and Welfare Association," *Race Today*, November 1972, 355.

28. Quoted in Sally Tomlinson, "The Black Education Movement" in *Race and Gender: Equal Opportunities Policies in Education*, ed. Madeleine Arnot (Oxford: Pergamon, 1985), 70.

29. Supplementary schools are recorded in Bethnal Green, Brixton, Brockley, Camberwell, Clapham, Clapton, Dalston, Ealing, Finsbury Park, Fulham, Greenwich, Hammersmith, Harlesden, Holloway, Ladbroke Grove, Lewisham, Leyton, Luton, Peckham, Romford, Seven Sisters, Shepherd's Bush, Slough, Southall, Stoke Newington, Streatham, Tooting, Tulse Hill, Wandsworth, Westbourne Park, and West Green. Afro-Caribbean Education Resource Project, *Resource and Information Booklet* (London: ACER Project, 1980), 18–19, GARRISON/2/2/11, BCA; Afro-Caribbean Education Resource Project, *Resource and Information Guide*, 3rd ed. (London: ACER Centre, 1987), 33–35, GARRISON/2/2/13, BCA.

30. Tomlinson, "Black Education," 70; Beese and Hassan, "Who's Educating Whom?" 31; Kehinde Andrews, *Resisting Racism: Race, Inequality and the Black Supplementary School Movement* (London: Institute of Education Press, 2013), 13. For Liverpool, see Robert Moore, *Racism and Black Resistance in Britain* (London: Pluto Press, 1976), 97–98.

31. Jessica Huntley, in Phillips and Phillips, *Windrush*, 258–59.

32. Bryan et al., *Heart of the Race*, 59.

33. Race Today Women, "Caribbean Women and the Black Community," *Race Today*, May 1975, 112.

34. Ibid., 111–12.

35. Judith Lockhart, interviewed by Sheila Ruiz, March 2, 2009, BWM05, BCA.

36. Quoted in Bryan et al., *Heart of the Race*, 71.

37. "Firsthand Report: Birmingham," *Race Today*, May 1973, 145.

38. Ansel Wong in Waters, "Student Politics," 25.

39. Ibid; Carter, *Shattering Illusions*, 94; Valentino A. Jones, *We Are Our Own Educators! Josina Machel: From Supplementary to Black Complementary School* (London: Karia Press, 1986); Andrews, *Doing Nothing*, chap. 7; Sivanandan, *Different Hunger*, 30–31; "Supplementary Education," folder, 01/04/04/01/04/01/21, IRR; "The Malcolm X Montessori Programme," *Tricontinental Outpost*, February 1971, 2.

40. Phillips and Phillips, *Windrush*, 291.

41. "Firsthand Report: Birmingham," *Race Today*, May 1973, 145.

42. Carter, *Shattering Illusions*, 94.

43. Ibid.

44. Steedman, "State-Sponsored Autobiography"; Hilliard, *To Exercise Our Talents*, 280–281.

45. Steedman, "State-Sponsored Autobiography," 51.

46. Carolyn Steedman, *Landscape for a Good Woman: A Tale of Two Lives* (London: Virago, 1986), 122. Laura Tisdall emphasizes that for the planners of postwar social democracy, children's mental stability and sense of self were crucial. Not only was education deemed critical to the production of responsible social democratic citizens, but ideas about the child were the foil to this conception of what an adult social democratic citizen looked like. See "Education, Parenting and Concepts of Childhood in England, c. 1945 to c. 1979," *Contemporary British History* 31, no. 1 (2017): 24–46. See also Michal Shapira, *The War Inside: Psychoanalysis, Total War and the Making of the Democratic Self in Postwar* (Cambridge: Cambridge University Press, 2013); Mathew Thomson, *Lost Freedom: The Landscape of the Child and the British Post-war Settlement* (Oxford: Oxford University Press, 2013); Laura King, "Future Citizens: Cultural and Political Conceptions of Children in Britain, 1930s–1950s," *Twentieth Century British History* 27, no. 3 (2016): 389–411.

47. Paul Willis, *Learning to Labour: How Working Class Kids Get Working Class Jobs* (1977; Burlington, VT: Ashgate, 1993), 36.

48. Gilroy, *Black Teacher*, 139–40, 159, 183.

49. Coard, *How the West Indian Child Is Made Educationally Sub-Normal*, 27, 28.

50. Hilliard, *Talents*, 287. Mass-Observation was a social research project, launched in 1937, that studied everyday life in Britain, using volunteer observers.

51. See Richard Dyer, *Coronation Street* (London: BFI, 1981); Waters, "Auto-Biographical Writing"; Chris Waters, "Representations of Everyday Life: L. S. Lowry and the Landscape of Memory in Postwar Britain," *Representations* 65 (1999): 121–50.

52. See Darrell M. Newton, *Paving the Empire Road: BBC Television and Black Britons* (Manchester: Manchester University Press, 2011), 120–34; Schaffer, *Vision of a Nation*, 231–72. More widely, see *Black and White in Colour*, ed. Pines; Webster, *Imagining Home*.

53. For journalism see, in particular, Donald Hinds's "About People" series in the *West Indian Gazette*, and *Flamingo*'s long-running "Jason v. London" series. The 1950s and early 1960s also saw the publication of Samuel Selvon's *The Lonely Londoners* (1956), *Ways of Sunlight* (1957), and *The Housing Lark* (1965), George Lamming's *The Emigrants* (1954), and Andrew Salkey's *Escape to an Autumn Pavement* (1959), as well as Lloyd Reckord's film *Ten Bob in Winter* (1963).

54. Clair Wills, "Passage to England: Stories of Punjabi Immigrants," *Times Literary Supplement*, September 1, 2017. See also Clair Wills, *Lovers and Strangers: An Immigrants History of Post-War Britain* (London: Allen Lane, 2017).

55. Hilliard, *To Exercise Our Talents*, 6.

56. Ibid.; Waters, "Autobiography."

57. V. S. Naipaul, *A House for Mr Biswas* (London: Collins, 1963). The novel is a fictional account of Naipaul's father's path into writing. See also V. S. Naipaul, *Letters between a Father and a Son* (London: Picador, 2012).

58. Hilliard, *To Exercise Our Talents*, 235–45.

59. Glyne Griffith, "'This is London calling the West Indies': The BBC's Caribbean Voices,'" in *West Indian Intellectuals*, ed. Schwarz, 198. More widely, see Mary Chamberlain, *Empire and Nation-Building in the Caribbean: Barbados, 1937–66* (Manchester: Manchester University Press, 2010), chap. 6. See also Newcastle University's *Scripting Empire: West Indian and West African Literature at the BBC, 1939–1968*, https://research.ncl.ac.uk/bbcscriptingempire/abouttheproject.

60. See David Dabydeen, "West Indian Writers in Britain," in *Voices of the Crossing*, ed. Dennis and Khan, 70.

61. George Lamming, *The Pleasures of Exile* (1960; London: Pluto Press, 2005), 51. See also Chris Campbell, "Ariel over the Airwaves: George Lamming's Rituals of Revenant History," *Journal of Postcolonial Writing* 48, no. 5 (2012): 485–96.

62. Gail Low, *Publishing the Postcolonial: Anglophone West African and Caribbean Writing in the UK, 1948–1968* (London: Routledge, 2011).

63. See Waters, "Henry Swanzy, Sartre's Zombie?" in *Cultures of Decolonisation*, ed. Craggs and Wintle, 67–85; Walmsley, *Caribbean;* Brathwaite, *History of the Voice*. On Caribbean Black Power, see Quinn, *Black Power;* Obika Gray, *Radicalism and Social Change in Jamaica, 1960–1972* (Knoxville: University of Tennessee Press, 1991); Robert A. Hill, "From *New World* to *Abeng*: George Beckford and the Horn of Black Power in Jamaica, 1968–1970," *Small Axe* 24 (2007), 1–15; *Black Power Revolution of 1970*, ed. Ryan, Stewart, and McCree.

64. Brathwaite, *History of the Voice*, 13.

65. James Berry, "The Literature of the Black Experience," in *The Language of the Black Experience in Britain: Cultural Expression through Word and Sound in the Caribbean and Black Britain*, ed. David Sutcliffe and Ansel Wong (Oxford: Basil Blackwell, 1986), 88–89.

66. Ibid., 83.

67. Ken Worpole, *Local Publishing & Local Culture: An Account of the Work of the Centerprise Publishing Project, 1972–1977* (London: Centerprise Trust, 1977), 3–4, 13; Berry, "Literature of the Black Experience," 92. Centerprise's publications of black writing included Usherwood's *Poems* (London: Centerprise, 1972), *Talking Blues* (London: Centerprise, 1976), *Breaking the Silence: Writing by Asian Women* (London: Centerprise, 1984), and *Black Anthology Group, Not All Roses: Poetry & Prose* (London: Centerprise, 1987).

68. *Stepping Out: An Anthology of Writings, Including Plays and Poems, Published by the Commonplace Workshop, as a Conduit for Creative Expression for West Indian Youth in Great Britain* (London: Commonplace, 1976); Paul George, *Memories* (London: Commonplace, 1976); Bev Shaw, *Awakening* (London: Commonplace, 1978); Ranjit Sumal, *Back Home* (London: Commonplace, 1981).

69. Accabre Huntley, *At School Today* (London: Bogle-L'Ouverture, 1977); "At School Today," *Race Today*, November–December 1977, 166.

70. Michael McMillan, *The School Leaver* (London: Black Ink Collective, 1978); *Black Ink* (London: Black Ink Collective, 1978); Berry, "Literature of the Black Experience," 89.

71. See *Who Feels It Knows It* (Manchester: Gatehouse Project, 1980); *The Tip of My Tongue* (Manchester: Gatehouse Project, 1980); *Just Lately I Realise: Stories from West Indian Lives* (Manchester: Gatehouse Project, 1985).

72. See Asian Women Writers' Workshop, *Right of Way: Prose and Poetry by the Asian Women Writers' Workshop* (London: Women's Press, 1988), 2–3.

73. *Savacou*, nos. 9–10 (1974); *Bluefoot Traveller: An Anthology of West Indian Poets in Britain*, ed. James Berry (London: Limestone Publications, 1976). See also *News for Babylon: The Chatto Book of Westindian-British Poetry*, ed. James Berry (London: Chatto & Windus, 1984).

74. *Dread, Beat and Blood*, directed by Franco Rosso (Arts Council, 1979); "Reviewing '78," *Race Today*, January 1979, 3.

75. Farukh Dhondy, "Britain's Black Theatre," *Race Today Review*, December 1981–January 1982, 17–20.

76. See McMillan, *School Leaver*, 3–4. On Festac '77, see also Eddie Chambers, *Black Artists in British Art: A History since the 1950s to the Present* (London: I.B. Tauris, 2014), 42, 47, 58.

77. Berry, "Literature of the Black Experience," 89; Dhondy, "Black Theatre"; Rachael Gilmour, "Bluefoot Travellers: Black Literary Aesthetics," in *Flower/Power: British Literature in Transition*, vol. 2: *1960–1980*, ed. Kate McLoughlin (Cambridge: Cambridge University Press, forthcoming).

78. Quoted in Bryan et al., *Heart of the Race*, 207–8.

79. Quoted in ibid., 65. The affects of reading and writing are receiving increasing attention by historians of the emotions. See, e.g., Rachel Ablow, ed., *The Feeling of Reading: Affective Experience and Victorian Literature* (Ann Arbor: University of Michigan Press, 2010); Ute Frevert, Pascal Eitler, and Stephanie Olsen, *Learning*

How to Feel: Children's Literature and Emotional Socialization, 1870–1970 (Oxford: Oxford University Press, 2014).

80. Lauretta Ngcobo, "Introduction," in *Let It Be Told: Essays by Black Women in Britain*, ed. Ngcobo (London: Pluto Press, 1987), 1.

81. Mullard, *Black Britain*, 7.

82. See Gilmour, "Bluefoot Travellers"; Rachael Gilmour, "The University of Brixton: Postcolonial Linguistics on the Radio," in *Popular Postcolonialisms*, ed. Nadia Atia and Kate Houlden (London: Routledge, forthcoming).

83. Berry, "Literature of the Black Experience," 93.

84. Brathwaite, *History of the Voice*.

85. On black poetry in 1970s Britain, see Ian Dieffenthaller, *Snow on Sugarcane: The Evolution of West Indian Poetry in Britain* (Newcastle upon Tyne: Cambridge Scholars Publishing 2009).

86. Quoted in Bryan et al., *Heart of the Race*, 207.

87. Berry, "Literature of the Black Experience," 90.

88. On this rebellion and how it was thought about, see chapter 5.

89. Ansel Wong, "Creole as a Language of Power and Solidarity," in *Language of the Black Experience in Britain*, ed. Sutcliffe and Wong, 113.

90. Ngcobo, "Introduction," in *Let It Be Told*, 3–4.

91. Waters, "Autobiography," 186. Cf. Ben Jones, "The Uses of Nostalgia," *Cultural and Social History* 7, no. 3 (2010): 355–74.

92. Alleyne, *Radicals against Race*, 53–55.

93. Chris Searle, *Ferndale Fires: A Children's Story* (London: Centerprise, 1974).

94. *Books of the George Padmore School* (pamphlet, n.d.), BEM/3/1/5/2, GPI. "Report on the Work of the Albertina Sylvester and George Padmore Schools," 1974, BEM/3/1/3/1, GPI.

95. Roxy Harris, *Being Black: Selections from Soledad Brother & Soul on Ice. With Questions and Notes* (London: New Beacon Books, 1981), 4.

96. Steedman, "State-Sponsored Autobiography," 50–51.

97. Harris, *Being Black*, 4–5.

98. Ibid., 9, 12, 15, 27, 28. For the original lesson plans, see BEM/3/1/5, GPI.

99. Thomson, *Lost Freedom*, 194; Sam Wetherell, "Painting the Crisis: Community Arts and the Search for the 'Ordinary' in 1970s and '80s London," *History Workshop Journal* 76 (2013): 235–49.

100. See John Shotton, *No Master High or Low: Libertarian Education and Schooling in Britain 1890–1990* (Bristol: Libertarian Education, 1993).

101. See Thomson, *Lost Freedom*, 200; Shotton, *No Master;* Nigel Wright, *Free School: The White Lion Experience* (Bristol: Libertarian Education Press, 1989).

102. See Chris Searle, "Introduction," in *Classrooms of Resistance*, ed. Chris Searle (London: Writers and Readers Publishing Cooperative, 1975), 5–12; Chris Searle, *Stepney Words* (London: Reality Press, 1971).

103. Wetherell, "Painting the Crisis," 239.

104. See *Chris Searle: The Great Includer*, special issue, *Race & Class*, 51, no. 2 (2009).

105. Chris Searle, "Denigration," *Race Today*, July 1972, 232–33. See also Chris Searle, *The Forsaken Lover: White Words and Black People* (London: Routledge & Kegan Paul, 1972).

106. Chris Searle, letter to editor, *Race Today*, December 1975, 280–81.

107. Waters, "Student Politics." On the Radical Students Alliance, see Caroline M. Hoefferle, *British Student Activism in the Long Sixties* (New York: Routledge, 2013), 68–69.

108. Waters, "Student Politics." On Freire, see his *Pedagogy of the Oppressed* (1968; New York: Penguin, 1972). On the White Lion Free School, see Shotton, *No Master*, 226–38; Wright, *Free School*. On Neill, see Jonathan Croall, *Neill of Summerhill: The Permanent Rebel* (London: Routledge & Kegan Paul, 1983).

109. Susan Chin, "To My Black Teacher," in *Ahfiwe: Journal of the Ahfiwe School and Abeng* 1 (n.d.): 10. WONG/2/1, BCA.

110. "Foreword," in ibid.

111. Waters, "Student Politics."

112. Editorial, in *Ahfiwe: Journal of the Ahfiwe School and Abeng* 1 (n.d.).

113. Clive Robertson, "Black Youth Speaks," *Ahfiwe* 2 (n.d.): 10. WONG/2/2, BCA.

114. Poems quoted are from *Ahfiwe*, nos. 1 and 2.

115. Len Garrison, interviewed by Zhana, in Zhana, *Black Success Stories*, vol. 1: *Celebrating People of African Heritage* (London: Zhana Books, 2006), 77.

116. "Afro-Caribbean Education Resource Project" (n.d.), GARRISON/2/1/4, BCA.

117. "Self Image and Black Awareness: North Lewisham Project," in Afro-Caribbean Education Resource Centre, *Images and Reflections: Education and the AfroCaribbean Child* (London: ACER, n.d.), 12, GARRISSON/2/2/12, BCA.

118. *ACER Project Second Annual Report, 1979–1980* (London: ACER, 1980), 6, GARRISON/2/1/8, BCA.

119. *Black Youth Annual Penmanship Competition 1982 Winning Essays* (London: ACER, 1983), 2, GARRISON/2/2/12–13, BCA.

120. Ansel Wong, "Len Garrison–A Biography," in Len Garrison, *Beyond Babylon* (London: Black Star Publications, 1985), 5.

121. See *Peter Moses: July 1945–December 1972* (pamphlet, n.d. [1973]), 4463/D/11/02/001, LMA; Remembering Olive Collective, *Remember Olive Morris*.

122. "Afro-Caribbean Education Resource Centre: Phase II" (n.d. [1981]), 11, GARRISON/2/2/9, BCA.

123. ACER Project, "Racism & the Black Child," May 1982, 34, GARRISON/2/2/2, BCA.

124. *Black Youth Annual Penmanship Awards: 1983 Winning Essays* (London: ACER, 1984), p. ii, GARRISON/2/2/20, BCA.

125. Colin Shakes, "Let the Pen Speak for I," and Davy Hay, "A Black British Childhood," both in ibid., 77, 80.

126. Paul McGilchrist, "Introduction," in *Black Voices: An Anthology of ACER's Black Young Writers Competition*, ed. Paul McGilchrist (London: ACER, 1987), xi.

127. See Simon Gikandi, "On Culture and the State: The Writings of Ngũgĩ wa Thiong'o," *Third World Quarterly* 11, no. 1 (1989): 154–55.

128. Ngũgĩ wa Thiong'o, "A Call for Action," in McGilchrist, *Black Voices*, vii.

129. Martin Glynn, "Introduction," *ACER Black Young Writers (Penmanship) Award: 1985 Winning Entries* (London: ACER, 1986), n.p., GARRISON/2/2/21, BCA.

130. On black youth and "rebellion," see chapter 5.

131. Editorial, "Oral History and Black History," *Oral History* 8, no. 1 (1980): 4.

132. Ferdinand Dennis, "Journeys without Maps," in *Voices*, ed. Dennis and Khan, 43.

133. Berry, "Literature of the Black Experience," 85.

134. "Notes—Monday 16th November 1970," working file for Albertina Sylvester and George Padmore Schools. BEM/3/1/3/2/20, GPI.

135. "Polytechnic of Central London: Centre for Extramural Studies. Black Culture and Political Liberation," March 1974, BEM/3/1/5/1/11, GPI; "The Historical Experience of Black People," *Westindian World*, September 17–23, 1976.

136. "News for Teachers: The Black Experience," *Education and Community Relations* 11, no. 8 (1972): 5; "Tottenham College of Technology: Black Studies Course" (n.d.), DADZIE/4/7, BCA.

137. "Black Studies at the Holloway Institute" (n.d.), BEM/3/1/3/2/15, GPI.

138. See Achin Vaniak, "The Free University for Black Studies," *Race Today*, July 1972, 239.

139. Sawh, *From Where I Stand*, 44–47; Stephen Bulgin, "The Free University of Black Studies," *Race Today*, June 1970, 190.

140. "Black Studies on Radio London," *Teachers against Racism* 2 (June 1972): 15.

141. "The Question of Black Studies," *Teachers against Racism* 1 (February 1972): 2–4; "A Suggested Black Studies Syllabus," ibid. 2 (June 1972): 10–11; Nigel File and Chris Power, *Black Settlers in Britain, 1555–1958* (London: Heinemann Educational Books, 1981).

142. Jon Rex and Sally Tomlinson, *Colonial Immigrants in a British City* (London: Routledge & Kegan Paul), 186–87; "Firsthand Report: Birmingham," *Race Today*, May 1973, 144–45.

143. "Aims of T.A.R.," *Teachers against Racism* 2 (June 1972): 1.

144. See Chris Mullard, *Anti-Racist Education: The Three O's* (Watford, England: National Association for Multi-Racial Education, 1984), 7–8; Alastair Bonnett, *Radicalism, Anti-Racism and Representation* (London: Routledge, 1993), 109–12.

145. Quoted in Delap, "Feminist Bookshops," 181.

146. Moore, *Racism*, 99; "IRR Library," *Race Today*, October–November 1973, 307.

147. Mike Phillips, "The Acceptable Face of Racism," *Race Today*, October–November 1973, 306.

148. File and Power, *Black Settlers*, 91.

149. Susan Scafe, *Teaching Black Literature* (London: Virago, 1989), 1.

150. Ibid., 3.

151. Beese and Hassan, "Who's Educating Whom?" 31.

152. Scafe, *Teaching*, 15–16.

153. Barbara Beese, Leila Hassan, and Farukh Dhondy "The Black Explosion in British Schools," in Dhondy, Beese, and Hassan, *Black Explosion*, 50.

154. Hazel Carby, "Multicultural Fictions" (stencilled occasional paper), Centre for Contemporary Cultural Studies, University of Birmingham, 1979, i, http://epapers.bham.ac.uk/1813.

155. Dhondy, "Teaching," 18.

156. Bryan et al., *Heart of the Race*, 74.

157. Havel V. Carby, "Schooling in Babylon," in Centre for Contemporary Cultural Studies, *Empire Strikes Back*, 193.

158. Institute of Race Relations, "Anti-Racist Not Multicultural Education: IRR Statement to the Rampton Committee on Education," *Race & Class* 20, no. 1 (1980): 81–83.

159. Centre for Contemporary Cultural Studies, *Empire Strikes Back*, esp. chap. 2. See also Michael Keith, "How Did the Empire Strike Back? Lessons for Today from *The Empire Strikes Back: Race and Racism in 70s Britain*," *Ethnic and Racial Studies* 37, no. 10 (2014): 1815–1822.

160. Carby, "Schooling," 205.

161. "Black Studies Conference," *Race Today*, October–November 1973, 295.

162. An analogous approach from supplementary schools can be found in the literature of the Kwame Nkrumah Supplementary School. See *Kwame Nkrumah Supplementary School* (pamphlet, May 4, 1972), 01/04/04/01/04/01/21, IRR.

163. Sam Morris, *The Case and the Course: A Treatise on Black Studies* (London: Committee on Black Studies, 1973).

164. Sam Morris, "Black Studies in Britain," *New Community* 2, no. 3 (Summer 1973), 245–48.

165. A. Sivanandan, "Race, Class and the State" (1976), in *Different Hunger*, 114, 120.

166. Quoted in Carter, *Shattering Illusions*, 132–33.

167. On Sivanandan's position, see especially Sivanandan, *Communities of Resistance*. For an example of an analysis that follows this line of argument, see Wild, "'Black Was the Colour of Our Fight.'" In relation to education and anti-racism, a similar argument is also given in Bonnett, *Radicalism*.

168. Black Parents Movement and Black Students Movement, "Where We Stand" (n.d. [1976]), 2, B/02/01/001, LMA.

169. "CCR Will Keep Close Watch on School Report," *South London Press*, January 23, 1976.

170. "Document from the Black Youth Movement to be presented at the Annual Conference of the Black Parents Movement. October 1979," B/02/01/003, LMA; N.N. Pepukayi (secretary of Operation Headstart) to John La Rose, January 22, 1976, BEM/3/1/3/8, GPI. On Operation Headstart's funding, see "Operation Headstart: Background Information and Progress Report" (n.d.), BEM/3/1/3/8, GPI.

171. Ken Forge, letter to the editor, *Race Today*, March 1974, 83.

172. The best account remains Centre for Contemporary Cultural Studies, *Unpopular Education*.

CHAPTER 5. THINKING ABOUT RACE
IN A TIME OF REBELLION

1. See "Move as a Community," *Race Today*, June 1974, 167–73. For the 1963 boycott, see Madge Dresser, *Black and White on the Buses: The 1963 Colour Bar Dispute in Bristol* (Bristol: J. W. Arrowsmith, 1986).

2. Gus John, *In the Service of Black Youth* (Leicester: National Association of Youth Clubs Publications, 1981), 172.

3. Dhondy, "Teaching Young Blacks," *Race Today*, May–June 1978, 83.

4. See Martin Barker's important book *The New Racism: Conservatives and the Ideology of the Tribe* (London: Junction Books, 1981).

5. Alvin, a Jamaican man living in Birmingham, interviewed for Derek Bishton and Brian Homer, eds., *Talking Blues: The Black Community Speaks about Its Relationship with the Police* (Birmingham: AFFOR, 1978), 18.

6. Hunte, *Nigger Hunting*.

7. Rose, *Colour and Citizenship*, 349–66; Humphry, with John, *Police Power*, 11.

8. National Council for Civil Liberties, *Annual Report, 1971*, and National Opinion Poll research, 1971, both cited in Humphry, with John, *Police Power*, 1, 109.

9. See Great Britain, Parliament, House of Commons, Select Committee on Race Relations and Immigration, *Police/Immigrant Relations*, vols. 1–3 (London: Her Majesty's Stationery Office, 1972).

10. Institute of Race Relations, *Police against Black People*.

11. Gilroy, *Ain't No Black*, 74.

12. Hall et al., *Policing the Crisis*.

13. Detective Inspector Sergeant Ridgewell, quoted in ibid., 44.

14. Institute of Race Relations, *Police against Black People*, 41–42. See also Clare Demuth, *Sus: A Report on the Vagrancy Act 1824* (London: Runnymede Trust, 1978).

15. See *Breaking Point*, directed by Menelik Shabazz (London: ATV, 1978).

16. See Islington 18 Defence Committee, *Under Heavy Manners: Report of the Labour Movement Enquiry into Police Brutality and the Position of Black Youth in Islington Held on Saturday July 23rd 1977* (London: Islington 18 Defence Committee, 1977).

17. Institute of Race Relations, *Police against Black People*, 10.

18. Ibid., 5–6.

19. See A. X. Cambridge, "On the Metro Saga," *Black Liberator* 1, no. 4 (1972): 155–68.

20. "Trials of the Cricklewood 12 & the Stockwell 10," *Race Today*, November 1975, 244–246.

21. Institute of Race Relations, *Police against Black People*, 6–7.

22. "Caledonian Road," *Race Today*, September 1970, 334; Harry Goulbourne, *Caribbean Transnational Experience* (London: Pluto Press, 2002), 101–7.

23. "It's Blowin' Now," *Race Today*, August 1975, 173–74.

24. "'Remember, Remember, the Fifth of November': The Bonfire Night Case," *Race Today*, September 1976, 180–83; "Up Against the Police," *Race Today*, July–August 1976, 148.

25. Courtney Tulloch, "The Political Carnival," *Race Today*, May 1971, 159.

26. See Race Today Collective, *Road Made to Walk on Carnival Day*.

27. "250 Are Hurt as Notting Hill Carnival Erupts into Riot," *The Times*, August 31, 1976.

28. See Blagrove, *Carnival*, 80, 95.

29. See ibid., 226–27, 230–33, 243, 258–59. A first-hand account of the 1976 Carnival published in *Race Today* records a stall selling "revolutionary literature" among the sound systems camped under the Westway flyover. See "Last Week It Was Soweto, This Week It's Notting Hill," *Race Today*, September 1976, 177. The *Times* reporter David Leigh similarly noted "the black power posters and the radical newsheets [sic] on sale" at the Carnival. See David Leigh, "Confrontation Recalls 1958 Riots," *The Times*, August 31, 1976.

30. Cheddar, quoted in Blagrove, *Carnival*, 129.

31. "Last Week It Was Soweto," 176.

32. Gilroy, *Ain't No Black*, 93. For the youth club as a political space, see Gus John, *In the Service;* and, in fictional form, Michael McMillan, *Hard Time Pressure* (London: Young People's Theatre Scheme, [1980]).

33. Lionel Morrison, "Notting Hill—Heading for Confrontation," *Race Today*, November 1971, 385.

34. Keith Piper, *Step into the Arena: Notes on Black Masculinity & the Contest of Territory* (Rochdale, England: Rochdale Art Gallery, 1991), 3.

35. "Sir Robert Mark Will Not Allow 'No Go' Areas in London," *The Times*, September 1, 1976.

36. See Islington 18 Defence Committee, *Under Heavy Manners*.

37. *Great Is the Carnival and It Will Prevail* (London: Black Parents Movement and Black Students Movement, 1977), CVL/4/2/5, GPI.

38. See Pryce, *Endless Pressure*.

39. Quoted in "Pressure Mounting for Public Inquiry into Bristol Riot," *The Times*, April 5, 1980.

40. "Burn, Bristol, Burn," *Westindian World*, April 11–17, 1980.

41. "Mass Murder in Lewisham," *Westindian World*, January 23–29, 1981.

42. Joe Jarrett, "A Lot to Explain," letter to the editor, *Westindian World*, February 13–19, 1981.

43. See John La Rose, *The New Cross Massacre Story: Interviews with John La Rose* (London: Alliance of the Black Parents Movement, 1984).

44. Gus John, "The 1981 Moss Side Uprising" (1981), in *Taking a Stand: Gus John Speaks on Education, Race, Social Action and Civil Unrest, 1980–2005* (Manchester: Gus John Partnership, 2006), 527.

45. See *Blood Ah Go Run*, directed by Menelik Shabazz (London: Kuumba Black Arts, 1982).

46. Quoted in Leslie Scarman, *The Scarman Report: The Brixton Disorders 10–12 April 1981* (Harmondsworth, England: Penguin, 1982), 95.

47. Ibid., 38–72; John Benyon and John Solomos, "British Urban Unrest in the 1980s," in *The Roots of Urban Unrest*, ed. Benyon and Solomos (Oxford: Pergamon Press, 1987), 3.

48. Benyon and Solomos, "British Urban Unrest," 4.

49. Michael Nally, "Eyewitness in Moss Side," in *Scarman and After: Essays Reflecting on Lord Scarman's Report, the Riots, and Their Aftermath*, ed. John Benyon (Oxford: Pergamon Press, 1984), 55.

50. Benyon and Solomos, "British Urban Unrest," 4; *Black & Blue: Racism and the Police* (London: Communist Party, 1981), 1.

51. Quoted in Benyon and Solomos, "British Urban Unrest," 5.

52. Ibid., 6.

53. Ibid.

54. Ibid.

55. Martin Luther King Jr. aphorism used as the campaign slogan of the Liverpool 8 Defence Committee following the urban uprisings in Liverpool in July 1981. See Liverpool 8 Defence Committee flyer in *A Common History*, one of four films in the Colin Prescod video *Struggles for Black Community*.

56. For a more critical contemporary perspective, see Tony Gilbert, *Only One Died* (London: Beauchamp, 1975).

57. Brixton Defence Campaign, "Brixton Defence Campaign Says Boycott the Scarman Inquiry," *Race & Class* 23, nos. 2–3 (1981–82): 230.

58. Editorial, "After the Inquest Lord Scarman," *Westindian World*, May 22–28, 1981.

59. Scarman, *Scarman Report*, 215. An inquiry into the Bristol uprising requested earlier had similarly split black community activists between those willing to cooperate, and those denouncing the call. See Simon Peplow, "'A Tactical Manoeuvre to Apply Pressure': Race and the Role of Public Inquiries in the 1980 Bristol 'Riot,'" *Twentieth Century British History*, forthcoming.

60. "After the Inquest." For a longer perspective, see Stuart Hall, "Black Men, White Media," *Savacou*, nos. 9–10 (1974): 97–100.

61. Editorial, "The Police and the Young Blacks," *Race Today*, February–March 1982, 52–53.

62. Cecil Gutzmore, "Capital, 'Black Youth' and Crime," *Race & Class* 25, no. 2 (1983): 26.

63. See Centre for Contemporary Cultural Studies, *Empire Strikes Back;* John Solomos, *Black Youth, Racism and the State: The Politics of Ideology and Policy* (Cambridge: Cambridge University Press, 1988).

64. Geoff Eley, "The Trouble with 'Race': Migrancy, Cultural Difference, and the Remaking of Europe," in *After the Nazi Racial State: Difference and Democracy*

in Germany and Europe, ed. Rita Chin et al. (Ann Arbor: University of Michigan Press, 2009), 166.

65. See Dennis Dworkin, *Cultural Marxism in Postwar Britain: History, the New Left, and the Origins of Cultural Studies* (Durham, NC: Duke University Press, 1997).

66. Robert J. C. Young makes a convincing case for the debt of postcolonial theory more widely to anticolonialist Marxism in *Postcolonialism: A Historical Introduction* (Oxford: Blackwell, 2001).

67. See Cedric Robinson, *Black Marxism: The Making of the Black Radical Tradition* (1983; Chapel Hill: University of North Carolina Press, 2000).

68. See also Waters, "Thinking Black."

69. Report in the *Guardian*, quoted in Bunce and Field, *Darcus Howe*, 144.

70. Howe writing in 1974, quoted in ibid., 145.

71. On Brixton's political squats, see Matt Cook, "'Gay Times': Identity, Locality, Memory, and the Brixton Squats in 1970's London," *Twentieth Century British History* 24, no. 1 (2013): 84–109. *Race Today* was first based on Shakespeare Road, but moved to the adjacent Railton Road in 1982.

72. Bunce and Field, *Darcus Howe*, 153.

73. See Pryce, *Endless Pressure*.

74. Karl Marx, *Capital: A Critique of Political Economy. Vol.1, Book One: The Process of Capitalist Production* (1867; London: Lawrence & Wishart, 2003), 592.

75. Darcus Howe, "Editorial: The Police and the Black Wageless," *Race Today*, February 1975, 27.

76. John La Rose, "The Police and the Black Wageless," letter to the editor, *Race Today*, March 1975, 65.

77. Ian MacDonald, "The Creation of the British Police," *Race Today*, December 1973, 332.

78. La Rose, "Police and the Black Wageless," 65.

79. Howe, "Police and the Black Wageless," 27.

80. "Young Lions of Brixton," editorial, *Race Today*, May 1974, 131.

81. "Notting Hill and After," editorial, *Race Today*, October 1976, 194.

82. Goulbourne, *Caribbean*, 81.

83. Stella Dadzie, interviewed by Rachel Cohen, June 2–3, 2011, C1420/20, SA.

84. See A. X. Cambridge, "Black Workers and the State: A Debate inside the Workers' Movement," *Black Liberator* 2, no. 2 (1973–74): 183–186; A. X. Cambridge and Cecil Gutzmore, "The Industrial Action of the Black Masses and the Class Struggle in Britain," *Black Liberator* 2, no. 3 (1974–75): 195–206. A good extended analysis of the *Black Liberator* position on this is Hall et al., *Policing the Crisis*, 371–81.

85. Rudy Narayan, "Lessons of the Metro Trial," *Race Today*, July 1972, 241. See also Morrison, "Notting Hill—Heading for Confrontation."

86. "On the Metro Saga: Interview with Tony Mohipp and Ranny Duheal at the Black People's Information Centre," *Black Liberator* 1, no. 4 (1972): 164.

87. A.X. Cambridge, "Criminal Procedure and the Black Masses in the United Kingdom," *Black Liberator*, December 1978, 1–4.

88. Colin Prescod, "Black People against State Harassment (BASH) Campaign–A Report," *Black Liberator*, December 1978, 5–7.

89. Cecil Gutzmore, "Carnival, the State and the Black Masses in the United Kingdom," *Black Liberator*, December 1978, 10–27.

90. Ambalavaner Sivanandan, interviewed by author, July 25, 2012.

91. Stuart Hall, "Introduction," in Sivanandan, *Different Hunger*, x.

92. On the Spaghetti House Siege, see Jenny Bourne, "Spaghetti House Siege: Making the Rhetoric Real," *Race & Class* 53, no. 2 (2011): 1–13.

93. Ambalavaner Sivanandan, "Race, Class and the State: The Black Experience in Britain," *Race & Class* 17, no. 4 (Spring 1976): 101.

94. Ibid., 105.

95. Ibid., 117.

96. Ibid., 120.

97. Ibid., 121–22.

98. Ambalavaner Sivanandan, "Race: The Revolutionary Experience," *Race Today*, August 1969, 108–9.

99. Ambalavaner Sivanandan, "From Resistance to Rebellion: Asian and Afro-Caribbean Struggles in Britain," *Race & Class* 23, nos. 2–3 (1981–82): 111–52.

100. Ambalavaner Sivanandan, interviewed by Louis Kushnick and Paul Grant, "Catching History on the Wing: A. Sivanandan as Activist, Teacher, and Rebel," in *Against The Odds: Scholars Who Challenged Racism In The Twentieth Century*, ed. Benjamin P. Bowser and Louis Kushnick, with Paul Grant (Boston: University of Massachusetts Press, 2002), 237.

101. Paul Gilroy reviewing Martin Kettle and Lucy Hodge's *Uprising!* (1982), "Riotology," *Race Today Review* 14, no. 3 (1983): 185.

102. Hazel Carby, "The Racism behind the Rioting" (1982), in *Cultures in Babylon: Black Britain and African America* (London: Verso, 1999), 229.

103. Sivanandan, "Resistance to Rebellion," 146.

104. Ibid., 150, 151.

105. Hall et al., *Policing the Crisis*.

106. Hall, "Racism and Reaction," 29–30, 32.

107. See Kieran Connell, "*Policing the Crisis* 35 Years On," *Contemporary British History* 29, no. 2 (2015): 273–83.

108. See Hall, *Hard Road*.

109. Hall et al., *Policing the Crisis*, 331–32.

110. Ibid., 343–44.

111. Ibid., 347.

112. Stuart Hall, "Cultures of Resistance and 'Moral Panics,'" *Afras Review* 4 (1979): 11.

113. Hall et al., *Policing the Crisis*, 381–82.

114. Ibid., 394–97.

115. Centre for Contemporary Cultural Studies, *Empire Strikes Back*, 7–8. On Hall and blackness, see Claire Alexander, "Stuart Hall and 'Race,'" *Cultural Studies* 23, no. 4 (2009): 465–69; Stuart Hall and Les Back, "At Home and Not at Home: Stuart Hall in Conversation with Les Back," *Cultural Studies* 23, no. 4 (2009): 669; Rob Waters, "Strange Familiarity," *Identities* 25, no. 1 (2018).

116. Centre for Contemporary Cultural Studies, *Empire Strikes Back*, 9.

117. Keith, "How Did the Empire Strike Back?" 1816–17. Cf. Hall and Jefferson, *Resistance*.

118. Paul Gilroy, "You Can't Fool the Youths . . . Race and Class Formation in the 1980s," *Race & Class* 23 (1981–82), 208.

119. Ibid.

120. Gilroy, *Black Atlantic*.

121. Gilroy, "You Can't Fool the Youths," 209, 210.

122. Ibid., 210.

123. Ibid., 213, 217. Cf. Hebdige, *Subculture*.

124. Baldwin, quoted in Gilroy, *Ain't No Black*, 153.

125. Ibid., 159–60.

126. Ibid., 198.

127. Ambalavaner Sivanandan, "All That Melts into Air Is Solid: The Hokum of New Times" (1990), in id., *Communities of Resistance: Writings on Black Struggles for Socialism* (London: Verso, 1990), 19–59.

128. See Hall, "Introduction" in Sivanandan, *Different Hunger*; Centre for Contemporary Cultural Studies, *Empire Strikes Back*, 8. Reviewing Hall et al., *Policing the Crisis*, in *Race & Class*, Lee Bridges named it "probably one of the most important books to be written on race relations in Britain," though Bridges also complained that "the treatment of race is variable, irresolute," although "there are points [. . .] where the centrality of race [. . .] to the whole crisis, is recognised" (Bridges, "*Policing the Crisis*," 193, 194). See also Bridges's two reviews of *The Empire Strikes Back* in *Race & Class* 25, no. 1 (1983): 99–100, and no. 2 (1983): 94–95.

129. Hall, "Cultures of Resistance," 11.

130. Gilroy, in conversation with the author.

131. In particular, Linton Kwesi Johnson, Leila Hassan and John La Rose continued to hold both institutions in high regard.

132. Sivanandan, "Liberation of the Black Intellectual," 96.

133. Prescod, "Groundings."

134. Lee Bridges, "*The Empire Strikes Back*," *Race & Class* 25, no. 1 (1983): 100.

135. Hassan, quoted in Bunce and Field, *Darcus Howe*, 154.

136. Ibid., 154.

137. Ibid., 155–57. On Lindo, see "Free George Lindo," *Race Today*, May–June 1979, 54–56.

138. Bunce and Field, *Darcus Howe*, 167.

139. Ibid., 168.

140. Ibid., 188–202, 214.

141. Bogle-L'Ouverture's publisher's advertisement, in Johnson, *Dread, Beat and Blood*, inside cover.

142. Ngcobo, "Introduction," 8. See also Gilmour, "Bluefoot," and chapter 4 in this volume.

143. Dennis Bovell in conversation with Linton Kwesi Johnson, January 25, 1999, in Harris and White, *Building Britannia*, 1–46. Bovell's connection to Johnson reveals a closeness between music and politics at this time that could equally be traced through the career of the popular reggae performer Jah Shaka, who began life performing for the Fasimbas and at the West Indian Students Centre. See Trew, *Black for a Cause*, 199; Hines, *How Black People Overcame Fifty Years*, 206.

144. See *Dread, Beat an' Blood*, dir. Franco Rosso (London: Arts Council, 1979).

145. Ibid.; James Procter, *Dwelling Places: Postwar Black British Writing* (Manchester: Manchester University Press, 2003), 103–4.

146. A.X. Cambridge was a regular go-to for the *South London Press* in its coverage of racism and anti-racist politics.

147. See Cecil Gutzmore, "Carnival, the State and the Black Masses in the United Kingdom," in Winston James and Clive Harris, *Inside Babylon: The Caribbean Diaspora in Britain* (London: Verso, 1993), 229n1.

148. See Gutzmore's papers, GUTZMORE/1, BCA. See also Gail Lewis, interviewed by Rachel Cohen, April 15–18, 2011, SA, C1420/14, BL.

149. Ambalavaner Sivanandan, interviewed by the author, July 25, 2012.

150. Chris Mullard, *Race, Power and Resistance* (London: Routledge & Keegan Paul, 1985), 195.

151. Hall, "Introduction" in Sivanandan, *Different Hunger*, ix.

152. Colin Prescod, "Foreword," in Ambalavaner Sivanandan, *Catching History on the Wing: Race, Culture and Globalisation* (London: Pluto Press, 2008), vii.

153. Balvinder Bassi, quoted in Ramamurthy, *Black Star*, 10.

154. Hall, "Cultures of Resistance," 2; Kieran Connell and Matthew Hilton, "The Working Practices of Birmingham's Centre for Contemporary Cultural Studies," *Social History* 40, no. 3 (2015): 278.

155. Paul Gilroy, "Paul Gilroy Interview—2 June 2011," *Cultural Studies* 27, no. 5 (2013): 744. Gilroy is referring to the 1978 album *Handsworth Revolution* by Steel Pulse, a band with whom he also had existing ties.

156. Errol Lawrence, interviewed by Kieran Connell, May 29, 2013, www.birmingham.ac.uk/schools/historycultures/departments/history/research/projects/cccs/interviews.

157. Stuart Hall, "Cultural Studies and Its Theoretical Legacies," in Morley and Kuan-Hsing, *Stuart Hall*, 269.

158. Ibid., 267.

159. John Akomfrah in conversation with Alan Marcus, University of Aberdeen, March 11, 2008, https://vimeo.com/830033. See Morris, *Growing Up Black*.

160. Cedric Robinson, "An Inventory of Contemporary Black Politics," *Emergency* 2 (1984): 22.

1. Andrew Salkey to Jessica Huntley, following reports of racist attacks on bookshops, July 7, 1978, repr. in "No Colour Bar: Black British Art in Action, 1960–1990," Guildhall Art Gallery, July 10, 2015–January 24, 2016.

2. See Bookshop Joint Action, *We Won't Be Terrorised Out of Existence: Bookshop Joint Action Documentation, September 1977–April 1978* (pamphlet, 1978), 4462/J/01/002, LMA.

3. Colin A. Beckles, "'We Shall Not Be Terrorized Out of Existence': [. . .] England's Black Bookshops," 64.

4. Linton Kwesi Johnson, *Making History* (London: Island Records, 1983). LP.

5. On the drive to record the longer history of black settlement and black resistance in Britain, see Waters, "Thinking Black."

6. Mullard, *Black Britain*, 176.

7. *Blacks' Britannica*, directed by David Koff (Boston: WGBH, 1978); *Struggles for Black Community;* Darcus Howe, "From Bobby to Babylon," three parts in *Race Today*, May–June 1980, 8–14, November 1980, 31–41, and February–March 1982, 61–69. The Institute of Race Relations also produced an exhibition under the title "From Resistance to Rebellion" in the early 1980s, promoting it for hire to schools and community groups, and published a series of children's books on the history of immigration to Britain, and racism and black British politics.

8. Johnson, "Time Come," in id., *Dread, Beat and Blood*, 24–25.

9. Gilroy, *Ain't No Black*, 93.

10. James, *Black Power*, 12.

11. Akua Rugg, "Four Films with Black Subjects," *Race Today Review*, December 1981–January 1982, 48.

12. Menelik Shabazz, "Stories behind the Films," http://menelikshabazz.co.uk /stories-behind-the-films.

13. Mark Currie, *About Time: Narrative, Fiction and the Philosophy of Time* (Edinburgh: Edinburgh University Press, 2007), 11. See also Jacques Derrida, *Archive Fever: A Freudian Impression* (Chicago: University of Chicago Press, 1996).

14. Editorial, "The Political Pantry is Bare," *Race Today*, November/December 1979, 99.

15. David Scott, *Omens of Adversity: Tragedy, Time, Memory, Justice* (Durham: Duke University Press, 2014), 4.

16. Linton Kwesi Johnson, "Reggae Fi Radney (To the Memory of Walter Rodney)," *Race Today Review*, December 1981–January 1982, 12.

17. "Grenada," *Fowaad!* 7 (November 1980): 8. On the fallout of and soul-searching after Guyana and Grenada, see, e.g., "C.L.R. James on Walter Rodney," *Race Today*, November 1980, 28–30; Gus John's "A Revolution Betrayed," in *Emergency* 2 (1984): 37–42.

18. See Joshua Bloom and Waldo E. Martin Jr., *Black against Empire: The History and Politics of the Black Panther Party* (Berkeley: University of California Press, 2013); Quinn, *Black Power*.

19. Scott, *Omens*, 5.

20. Ibid., 2.

21. Kenan Malik, *From Fatwa to Jihad: The Rushdie Affair and Its Aftermath: How a Group of British Extremists Attacked a Novel and Ignited Radical Islam* (London: Melville House, 2014), quotation at xi. Ramamurthy, however, emphasizes that in the case of the Asian Youth Movements (AYMs) through which so many of these "black" Asians found this political identity "while the AYMs were secular, secularism was not an identity that they felt the need to profess. Their advocated identity was with an anti-imperialist blackness which was secular through its inclusive nature" (Ramamurthy, *Black Star*, 5).

22. See Ramamurthy, *Black Star*, chap. 8. On local struggles in the 1980s against this turn from radical blackness to radical Islam, see Southall Black Sisters, *Against the Grain*.

23. Ambalavaner Sivanandan, "RAT and the Degradation of Black Struggle," *Race & Class* 26, no. 4 (1985): 2.

24. Ibid., 6.

25. This was particularly the case in the Black Education Movement, explored in chapter 4, and in the campaign against "sus" policing.

26. Sivanandan, "RAT," 10.

27. Ibid., 6.

28. Darcus Howe, "As I See It: Black Sections for the Black Middle Class. I Say Yes," *Race Today*, August–September 1985, 10.

29. Sydney Jeffers, "Black Sections in the Labour Party: The End of Ethnicity and 'Godfather' Politics?" in *Black and Ethnic Leaderships: The Cultural Dimensions of Political Action*, ed. Pnina Werbner and Muhammad Anwar (London: Routledge, 1991), 45.

30. Farukh Dhondy, "Speaking in Whose Name?" *New Statesman*, April 24, 1987.

31. Labour Party Black Sections, *Seven Steps to Forming Black Sections* (1985), cited in Jeffers, "Black Sections," 45.

32. Tariq Modood, "'Black', Racial Equality and Asian Identity," *New Community* 14, no. 3 (1988): 398.

33. Ibid., 399. In *The Voice* at this time, too, Ferdinand Dennis would argue for a rejection of the term "black" to describe communities of African descent in Britain, preferring the term "Afro-British." See Ferdinand Dennis, "History—Fact or Fiction?" *The Voice*, March 25, 1987.

34. Yasmin Ali, "Echoes of Empire," in *Enterprise and Heritage: Crosscurrents of National Culture*, ed. John Corner and Sylvia Harvey (London: Routledge, 1991), 207.

35. Hall, "New Ethnicities," 444.

36. Coco Fusco, *Young British and Black: The Work of Sankofa and Black Audio Film Collective* (Buffalo, NY: Hallwalls / Contemporary Arts Centre, 1988); Mercer, *Welcome to the Jungle; Black Experiences*, special issue, *Ten.8*, no. 22, ed. David A. Bailey (1986); Centre for Contemporary Cultural Studies, *Empire Strikes Back;*

Many Voices, One Chant: Black Feminist Perspectives, special issue, *Feminist Review*, no. 17, ed. Valerie Amos et al. (Autumn 1984); Chambers, *Black Artists;* Blk Art Group Research Project 2012, www.blkartgroup.info.

37. Hall, "New Ethnicities," 445.

38. Ferdinand Dennis, *Behind the Frontlines: Journey into Afro-Britain* (London: Gollancz, 1988). The marginalizations and the passions contained in celebrations of black "frontline" politics of street confrontation were analyzed in two classic films of the late 1980s—*Handsworth Songs* and *Territories*.

39. James, *Black Power*, 11.

40. *From Black Power to Pan-Africanism: Kwame Ture Speaks* (flyer, 1984), DADZIE/4/22/2.

41. Linton Kwesi Johnson, "Youths of Hope" (1973), in id., *Voices of the Living and the Dead* (London: Race Today, 1983), 29.

42. Linton Kwesi Johnson, "Voices of the Living and the Dead" (1973), in id., *Voices*, 7.

43. Amitav Ghosh, *In an Antique Land* (London: Granta, 1994), 201.

44. See Bill Schwarz, "Actually Existing Postcolonialism," *Radical Philosophy* 104 (2000), 16.

SELECTED BIBLIOGRAPHY

ARCHIVES CONSULTED

Andrew Salkey collection, British Library, London (AS)
BBC Written Archives Centre, Reading (WAC)
Black Cultural Archives, London (BCA)
British Film Institute, London (BFI)
Donald Chesworth Archive, Queen Mary University of London (PP2)
George Padmore Institute, London (GPI)
Institute of Race Relations, London (IRR)
London Metropolitan Archives (LMA)
National Archives, Kew (NA)
Sisterhood and After, British Library, London (SA)

NEWSPAPERS AND PERIODICALS

Backayard News Sheet
Black Dimension
Black Dwarf
Black Liberator
Black People's News Service
Black Voice
Brixton Advertiser
Bumbo
Daily Express
Daily Mail
Daily Mirror
Daily Sketch
Daily Telegraph

Education and Community Relations
Encounter
Evening Standard
Flamingo
Fowaad!
Freedom News
Friends/Frendz
Grassroots
Guardian
Hustler!
Illustrated London News
International Socialism
International Times
Kensington Post
Magnet
Morning Star
New Community
New Society
New Statesman
Observer
Oral History
Oz
Race & Class
Race Today
Race Today Review
Red Mole
Savacou: A Journal of the Caribbean Artists Movement
Soledad Brothers Newsletter
South London Press
Spare Rib
Speak Out
The Spectator
Spirit
Sunday Telegraph
Sunday Times Magazine
Tapia
Teachers against Racism
The Times (London)
TriContinental Outpost
Trinidad Guardian
Voice
West Indian Gazette
West Indian Students Union Newsletter
Westindian World

Abernethy, Graeme. "'Not Just an American Problem': Malcolm X in Britain." *Atlantic Studies* 7, no. 3 (2010): 285–307.

Ablow, Rachel, ed. *The Feeling of Reading: Affective Experience and Victorian Literature.* Ann Arbor: University of Michigan Press, 2010.

Adi, Hakim. *West Africans in Britain 1900–1960: Nationalism, Pan-Africanism and Communism.* London: Lawrence & Wishart, 1998.

Ahmed, Sara. "Affective Economies." *Social Text* 22, no. 2 (2004): 117–39.

———. *Willful Subjects.* Durham, NC: Duke University Press, 2014.

Alexander, Claire. "Stuart Hall and 'Race.'" *Cultural Studies* 23, no. 4 (2009): 457–82.

Ali, Yasmin. "Echoes of Empire." In *Enterprise and Heritage: Crosscurrents of National Culture*, ed. John Corner and Sylvia Harvey, 194–211. London: Routledge, 1991.

Alibhai-Brown, Yasmin. "To Be or Not to Be Black." *Race & Class* 41, no. 1–2 (1999): 163–70.

Alleyne, Brian. "'Peoples' War': Cultural Activism in the Notting Hill Carnival." *Cambridge Journal of Anthropology* 20, no. 1–2 (1998): 111–35.

———. *Radicals against Race: Black Activism and Cultural Politics.* Oxford: Berg, 2002.

Ambar, Saladin M. *Malcolm X at the Oxford Union: Racial Politics in a Global Era.* Oxford: Oxford University Press, 2014.

Amos, Valerie, Gail Lewis, Amina Mama, and Pratibha Parmar, eds. *Many Voices, One Chant: Black Feminist Perspectives.* Special issue, *Feminist Review*, no. 17 (Autumn 1984).

Andrews, Kehinde. *Resisting Racism: Race, Inequality and the Black Supplementary School Movement.* London: Institute of Education Press, 2013.

Andrews, Margaret. *Doing Nothing Is Not an Option: The Radical Lives of Eric and Jessica Huntley.* Southall, Middlesex, England: Krik Krak, 2014.

Angelo, Anne-Marie. "'Black Oppressed People All Over the World Are One': The British Black Panthers' Grassroots Internationalism, 1969–1973." *Journal of Civil and Human Rights*, forthcoming.

———. "The Black Panthers in London, 1967–1972: A Diasporic Struggle Navigates the Black Atlantic." *Radical History Review* 103 (2009): 17–35.

———. *Global Freedom Struggle: The Black Panthers of Israel, the United Kingdom, and the United States.* Chapel Hill: University of North Carolina Press, forthcoming.

Austin, David. *Fear of a Black Nation: Race, Sex, and Security and Sixties Montreal.* Toronto: Between the Lines, 2013.

Bailey, David A., ed. *Black Experiences.* Special issue, *Ten.8*, no. 22 (1986).

Bailkin, Jordanna. *The Afterlife of Empire.* Berkeley: University of California Press, 2012.

Baker, Houston A., Jr., Manthia Diawara, and Ruth H. Lindeborg, eds. *Black British Cultural Studies: A Reader.* Chicago: University of Chicago Press, 1996.

Baldwin's Nigger. Directed by Horace Ové. DVD. 1969; London: British Film Institute, 2005.

Ballantyne, Tony. *Between Colonialism and Diaspora: Sikh Cultural Formations in an Imperial World*. New Delhi: Permanent Black, 2007.

Barker, Martin. *The New Racism: Conservatives and the Ideology of the Tribe*. London: Junction Books, 1981.

Barthes, Roland. *Image, Music, Text*. New York: Noonday, 1977.

Bebber, Brett. "'We Were Just Unwanted': Bussing, Migrant Dispersal, and South Asians in London." *Journal of Social History* 48, no. 3 (2015): 635–61.

Beckles, Colin A. "'We Shall Not Be Terrorized Out of Existence': The Political Legacy of England's Black Bookshops." *Journal of Black Studies* 29, no. 1 (1998): 51–72.

Benyon, John, ed. *Scarman and After: Essays Reflecting on Lord Scarman's Report, the Riots, and Their Aftermath*. Oxford: Pergamon Press, 1984.

Benyon, John, and John Solomos, eds. *The Roots of Urban Unrest*. Oxford: Pergamon Press, 1987.

Berry, James. *Fractured Circles*. London: New Beacon, 1979.

Bishton, Derek, and Brian Homer, eds. *Talking Blues: The Black Community Speaks about Its Relationship with the Police*. Birmingham: All Faiths for One Race (AFFOR), 1978.

Black, Lawrence. *Redefining British Politics: Culture, Consumerism and Participation, 1954–70*. New York: Palgrave Macmillan, 2010.

Black, Lawrence, and Hugh Pemberton. *An Affluent Society? Britain's Post-War "Golden Age" Revisited*. Burlington, VT: Ashgate, 2004.

Black, Pauline. *Black by Design: A 2-Tone Memoir*. London: Serpent's Tail, 2011.

Black & Blue: Racism and the Police. London: Communist Party of Great Britain, 1981.

Blackett, R. J. M. *Building an Antislavery Wall: Black Americans in the Atlantic Abolition Movement, 1830–1860*. Baton Rouge: Louisiana State University Press, 1983.

Blacks' Britannica. Television documentary directed by David Koff. Produced by David Koff and Musindo Mwinyipembe. Boston: WGBH, 1978.

Blagrove, Ishmahil, Jr., ed. *Carnival: A Photographic and Testimonial History of the Notting Hill Carnival*. London: riceNpeas, 2014.

Bleich, Erik. *Race Politics in Britain and France: Ideas and Policymaking since the 1960s*. Cambridge: Cambridge University Press 2003.

Blood Ah Go Run. Directed by Menelik Shabazz. London: Kuumba Black Arts, 1982.

Bookshop Joint Action, *We Won't Be Terrorised Out of Existence: Bookshop Joint Action Documentation, September 1977–April 1978* (pamphlet, 1978), 4462/J/01/002, LMA.

Bloom, Joshua, and Waldo E. Martin, Jr. *Black against Empire: The History and Politics of the Black Panther Party*. Berkeley: University of California Press, 2013.

Bocking-Welch, Anna. "Ghost Hunting: Amateur Film and Travel at the End of Empire." In *The British Abroad since the Eighteenth Century*, ed. Martin Farr and

Xavier Guégan, vol. 2: *Experiencing Imperialism*, 214–31. New York: Palgrave Macmillan, 2013.

Bonham-Carter, Mark. "The Liberal Hour and Race Relations Law." *Journal of Ethnic and Migration Studies* 14, no. 1–2 (1987): 1–8.

Bonnett, Alastair. *Radicalism, Anti-Racism and Representation*. London: Routledge, 1993.

Bourne, Jenny, ed. *The Colour of the Struggle, 1950s–1980s*. Special issue, *Race & Class* 58, no. 1 (2016).

Bracke, Maud Anne, and James Mark, ed. *Between Decolonisation and the Cold War: Transnational Activism and Its Limits in Europe, 1950s–90s*. Special issue, *Journal of Contemporary History* 50, no. 3 (2015).

Bradley, Lloyd. *Bass Culture: When Reggae Was King*. London: Viking, 2000.

———. *Sounds Like London: 100 Years of Black Music in the Capital*. London: Serpent's Tail, 2013.

Brah, Avtar. *Cartographies of Diaspora: Contesting Identities*. London: Routledge, 1996.

Brathwaite, Kamau. *History of the Voice: The Development of Nation Language in Anglophone Caribbean Literature*. London: New Beacon, 1984.

———. "Timehri." *Savacou*, no. 2 (1970): 35–44.

Brathwaite, Lloyd. *Colonial West Indian Students in Britain*. Kingston, Jamaica: University of the West Indies Press, 2001.

Breaking Point. Directed by Menelik Shabazz. London: ATV, 1978.

Brien, Alan. "Soledad Brothers and Sisters." In *Speeches from the Soledad Brothers Rally, Central Hall, Westminster, 20/4/71*, ed. John Thorne. London: Friends of Soledad, 1971.

Brother Outsider: The Life of Bayard Rustin. Directed by Nancy D. Kates and Bennett Singer. Boston: PBS, 2003.

Brown, Jacqueline Nassy. "Black Liverpool, Black America, and the Gendering of Diasporic Space." *Cultural Anthropology* 13 (1998): 291–325.

———. *Dropping Anchor, Setting Sail: Geographies of Race in Black Liverpool*. Princeton, NJ: Princeton University Press, 2005.

Brown, Stewart, ed. *The Art of Kamau Brathwaite*. Bridgend, Mid Glamorgan, Wales: Seren, 1995.

Bryan, Beverly, Stella Dadzie, and Suzanne Scafe. *The Heart of the Race: Black Women's Lives in Britain*. London: Virago, 1985.

Buettner, Elizabeth. *Empire Families: Britons and Late Imperial India*. Oxford: Oxford University Press, 2004.

———. "'We Don't Grow Coffee and Bananas in Clapham Junction You Know!': Imperial Britons Back Home." In *Settlers and Expatriates: Britons over the Seas*, ed. Robert Bickers, 302–28. Oxford: Oxford University Press, 2010.

———. "'Would You Let Your Daughter Marry a Negro?': Race and Sex in 1950s Britain." In *Gender, Labour, War and Empire: Essays on Modern Britain*, ed. Philippa Levine and Susan R. Grayzel, 219–237. New York: Palgrave Macmillan, 2009.

Bull, Michael, and Les Back. *The Auditory Culture Reader*. Oxford: Berg, 2003.

Bunce, Robin, and Paul Field. *Darcus Howe: A Political Biography*. London: Bloomsbury, 2014.

———. "Obi B. Egbuna, C. L. R. James and the Birth of the Black Power Movement in Britain." *Twentieth Century British History* 22 (2011): 391–414.

Burkett, Jodi. *Constructing Post-Imperial Britain: Britishness, "Race," and the Radical Left in the 1960s*. New York: Palgrave Macmillan, 2013.

Burning an Illusion. Directed by Menelik Shabazz. London: British Film Institute, 1981.

Bush, Ruth. "New Beacon Books: The Pioneering Years." 2013. www.georgepadmore institute.org/the-pioneering-years.

Campbell, Chris. "Ariel over the Airwaves: George Lamming's Rituals of Revenant History." *Journal of Postcolonial Writing* 48, no. 5 (2012): 485–96.

Cannadine, David. *Ornamentalism: How the British Saw Their Empire*. London: Penguin, 2001.

Carby, Hazel V. "Becoming Modern Racialized Subjects." *Cultural Studies* 23, no. 4 (2009): 624–57.

———. *Cultures in Babylon: Black Britain and African America*. London: Verso, 1999.

———. "Multicultural Fictions." Stencilled Occasional Paper, Centre for Contemporary Cultural Studies, University of Birmingham, 1979, http://epapers.bham .ac.uk/1813.

———. *Race Men*. Cambridge, MA: Harvard University Press, 1998.

Carew, Jan. *Ghosts in Our Blood: With Malcolm X in Africa, England, and the Caribbean*. Chicago: Lawrence Hill, 1994.

Carmichael, Stokely. *Stokely Speaks: Black Power Back to Pan-Africanism*. New York: Random House, 1971.

Carmichael, Stokely, and Charles V. Hamilton. *Black Power: The Politics of Liberation*. London: Jonathan Cape, 1968.

Carmichael, Stokely, with Ekwueme Michael Thelwell. *Ready for Revolution: The Life and Struggles of Stokely Carmichael (Kwame Ture)*. New York: Scribner, 2003.

Carr, Gordon. *The Angry Brigade: The Cause and the Case*. London: Victor Gollancz, 1975.

Carson, Clayborne. *The Autobiography of Martin Luther King*. London: Abacus, 2000.

Carter, Trevor. *Shattering Illusions: West Indians in British Politics*. London: Lawrence & Wishart, 1986.

Centre for Contemporary Cultural Studies. *The Empire Strikes Back: Race and Racism in 70s Britain*. London: Hutchinson, 1982.

———. *Unpopular Education: Schooling and Social Democracy in England since 1944*. London: Hutchinson, 1981.

Chamberlain, Mary. *Empire and Nation-Building in the Caribbean: Barbados, 1937–66*. Manchester: Manchester University Press, 2010.

———. *Narratives of Exile and Return*. New York: St. Martin's Press, 1997.

Chambers, Eddie. *Black Artists in British Art: A History Since the 1950s to the Present.* London: I. B. Tauris, 2014.

Chartier, Roger. *Forms and Meanings: Texts, Performances and Audiences from Codex to Computer.* Philadelphia: University of Pennsylvania Press, 1995.

Chibnall, Steve. "Whistle and Zoot: The Changing Meaning of a Suit of Clothes." *History Workshop Journal* 20, no. 1 (1985): 56–81.

Clemons, Michael L., and Charles E. Jones, "Global Solidarity: The Black Panther Party in the International Arena." In *Liberation, Imagination, and the Black Panther Party: A New Look at the Black Panthers and Their Legacy*, ed. Kathleen Cleaver and George Katsiaficas, 20–39. New York: Routledge, 2001.

Coard, Bernard. *How the West Indian Child Is Made Educationally Sub-Normal in the British School System: The Scandal of the Black Child in Schools in Britain.* London: New Beacon, 1971.

Coard, Phyllis, and Bernard Coard. *Getting to Know Ourselves.* London: Bogle-L'Ouverture Publications, 1972.

Collins, Marcus, ed. *The Permissive Society and Its Enemies: Sixties British Culture.* London: Rivers Oram Press, 2007.

Connell, Kieran. "Dread Culture: Music and Identity in a British Inner City." In *Stories of Cosmopolitan Belonging: Emotion and Location*, ed. Hannah Jones and Emma Jackson, 86–98. London: Routledge, 2014.

———. "*Policing the Crisis* 35 Years On." *Contemporary British History*, 29, no. 2 (2015): 273–83.

Connell, Kieran, and Matthew Hilton, "The Working Practices of Birmingham's Centre for Contemporary Cultural Studies." *Social History* 40, no. 3 (2015): 287–311.

Cook, Matt. "'Gay Times': Identity, Locality, Memory, and the Brixton Squats in 1970's London." *Twentieth Century British History* 24, no. 1 (2013): 84–109.

Coon, Caroline, and Rufus Harris. *The Release Report on Drug Offences and the Law.* London: Sphere Books, 1969.

Cooper, David, ed. *The Dialectics of Liberation.* London: Penguin, 1968.

Craggs, Ruth, and Claire Wintle, eds., *Cultures of Decolonisation: Transnational Productions and Practices.* Manchester: Manchester University Press, 2016.

Craig, Susan. "Black Power Groups in London, 1967–1969." Master's thesis, University of Edinburgh, 1970.

Croall, Jonathan. *Neill of Summerhill: The Permanent Rebel.* London: Routledge & Kegan Paul, 1983.

Currie, Mark. *About Time: Narrative, Fiction and the Philosophy of Time.* Edinburgh: Edinburgh University Press, 2007.

Darian-Smith, Kate, Patricia Grimshaw and Stuart Macintyre, eds. *Britishness Abroad: Transnational Movements and Imperial Cultures.* Melbourne: Melbourne University Press, 2007.

Darwin, John. *The Empire Project: The Rise and Fall of the British World System.* Cambridge: Cambridge University Press, 2009.

Davies, Jennifer. "From 'Rookeries' to 'Communities': Race, Poverty and Policing in London, 1850–1985." *History Workshop Journal*, 27 (1989): 66–85.

———. "Jennings Buildings and the Royal Borough: The Construction of the Underclass in Mid-Victorian England." In *Metropolis London: Histories and Representations since 1800*, ed. David Feldman and Gareth Stedman Jones, 11–39. London: Routledge, 1989.

Davies, Tom Adam. *Mainstreaming Black Power.* Oakland: University of California Press, 2017.

Davis, Angela. *An Autobiography.* London: Hutchinson, 1975.

Davis, John. "Rents and Race in 1960s London: New Light on Rachmanism." *Twentieth Century British History* 12, no. 1 (2001): 69–92.

Dean, Dennis. "The Race Relations Policy of the First Wilson Government." *Twentieth Century British History* 11, no. 3 (2000): 259–83.

Delap, Lucy. "Feminist Bookshops, Reading Cultures and the Women's Liberation Movement in Great Britain, c. 1974–2000." *History Workshop Journal* 81 (2016): 171–96.

Demuth, Clare. *Sus: A Report on the Vagrancy Act 1824.* London: Runnymede Trust, 1978.

Dennis, Ferdinand. *Behind the Frontlines: Journey into Afro-Britain.* London: Gollancz, 1988.

Dennis, Ferdinand, and Naseem Khan, eds. *Voices of the Crossing: The Impact of Britain on Writers from Asia, the Caribbean and Africa.* London: Serpent's Tail, 2000.

Derrida, Jacques. *Archive Fever: A Freudian Impression.* Chicago: University of Chicago Press, 1996.

Dhondy, Farukh, Barbara Beese, and Leila Hassan, *The Black Explosion in British Schools.* London: Race Today, 1982.

Dialectics of Liberation. LP. Liberation Records, 1968.

Dickson, Robert. *Imprinting the Sticks: The Alternative Press beyond London.* Brookfield, VT: Arena, 1997.

Dieffenthaller, Ian. *Snow on Sugarcane: The Evolution of West Indian Poetry in Britain.* Newcastle-upon-Tyne: Cambridge Scholars Publishing 2009.

Dowd Hall, Jacquelyn. "The Long Civil Rights Movement and the Political Uses of the Past." *Journal of American History* 91 (2005): 1233–63.

Dread, Beat an' Blood. Directed by Franco Rosso. London: Arts Council, 1979.

Dresser, Madge. *Black and White on the Buses: The 1963 Colour Bar Dispute in Bristol.* Bristol: J. W. Arrowsmith, 1986.

Dworkin, Dennis. *Cultural Marxism in Postwar Britain: History, the New Left, and the Origins of Cultural Studies.* Durham, NC: Duke University Press, 1997.

Dyer, Richard. *Coronation Street.* London: BFI, 1981.

Edwards, Brent Hayes. *The Practice of Diaspora: Literature, Translation, and the Rise of Black Internationalism.* Cambridge, MA: Harvard University Press, 2003.

———. "The Uses of Diaspora." *Social Text* 19, no. 1 (2001): 45–74.

Egbuna, Obi. *Destroy This Temple: The Voice of Black Power in Britain.* London: MacGibbon & Kee, 1971.

Eley, Geoff. "The Trouble with 'Race': Migrancy, Cultural Difference, and the Remaking of Europe." In *After the Nazi Racial State: Difference and*

Democracy in Germany and Europe, ed. Rita Chin, Heide Fehrenbach, Geoff Eley, and Atina Grossman, 137–81. Ann Arbor: University of Michigan Press, 2009.

Emsley, Clive. "The English Bobby: An Indulgent Tradition." In *Myths of the English*, ed. Roy Porter, 114–35. Cambridge: Polity Press, 1992.

Fanon, Frantz. *Black Skin, White Masks*. 1952. London: Pluto Press, 2008.

———. *The Wretched of the Earth*. New York: Penguin, 1967.

Faulkner, Simon, and Anandi Ramamurthy, eds. *Visual Culture and Decolonisation in Britain*. Burlington, VT: Ashgate, 2006.

Fekete, Liz. "Dockers against Racism: An Interview with Micky Fenn." *Race & Class* 58, no. 1 (2016): 55–60.

File, Nigel, and Chris Power. *Black Settlers in Britain, 1555–1958*. London: Heinemann Educational Books, 1981.

Fink, Carole, Philipp Gassert, and Detlef Junker, eds. *1968: The World Transformed*. Cambridge: Cambridge University Press, 1998.

Fisher, Tracey. *What's Left of Blackness: Feminisms, Transracial Solidarities, and the Politics of Belonging in Britain*. New York: Palgrave Macmillan, 2012.

Ford, Tanisha C. *Liberated Threads: Black Women, Style, and the Global Politics of Soul*. Chapel Hill: University of North Carolina Press, 2015.

Fountain, Nigel. *Underground: The London Alternative Press, 1966–74*. London: Routledge, 1988.

Francis, Armet, Neil Kenlock, and Charlie Phillips. *Roots to Reckoning*. London: Seed, 2005.

Francis, Martin. "Tears, Tantrums, and Bared Teeth: The Emotional Economy of Three Conservative Prime Ministers, 1951–1963." *Journal of British Studies* 41 (2002): 354–87.

Freire, Paulo. *Pedagogy of the Oppressed*. 1968. New York: Penguin, 1972.

Frevert, Ute, Pascal Eitler, Stephanie Olsen, Uffa Jensen, Margrit Pernau, Daniel Brückenhaus, Magdalena Beljan, Benno Gammerl, Anja Laukötter, Bettina Hitzer, Jan Plamper, Juliane Brauer, and Joachim C. Häberlen. *Learning How to Feel: Children's Literature and Emotional Socialization, 1870–1970*. Oxford: Oxford University Press, 2014.

Fryer, Peter. *Staying Power: The History of Black People in Britain*. London: Pluto Press, 1984.

Fusco, Coco. *Young British and Black: The Work of Sankofa and Black Audio Film Collective*. Buffalo, NY: Hallwalls/Contemporary Arts Centre, 1988.

Gaines, Kevin K. *American Africans in Ghana: Black Expatriates and the Civil Rights Era*. Chapel Hill: University of North Carolina Press, 2006.

Garrison, Len. *Beyond Babylon*. London: Black Star Publications, 1985.

Ghosh, Amitav. *In an Antique Land*. London: Granta, 1994.

Gilbert, Tony. *Only One Died*. London: Beauchamp, 1975.

Gilmour, Rachael. "Bluefoot Travellers: Black Literary Aesthetics." In *Flower/Power: British Literature in Transition*, vol. 2: *1960–1980*, ed. Kate McLoughlin. Cambridge: Cambridge University Press, forthcoming.

————. "The University of Brixton: Postcolonial Linguistics on the Radio." In *Popular Postcolonialisms*, ed. Nadia Atia and Kate Houlden. London: Routledge, 2017.

Gilroy, Beryl. *Black Teacher*. 1979. London: Bogle-L'Ouverture Publications, 1994.

Gilroy, Paul. *The Black Atlantic: Modernity and Double Consciousness*. London: Verso, 1993.

————. "Commemorations of the End of the Slave Trade." *Socialist Worker*, April 24, 2007, https://socialistworker.co.uk/art/11017/.

————. "Paul Gilroy Interview–2 June 2011." *Cultural Studies* 27, no. 5 (2013): 744–56.

————. *There Ain't No Black in the Union Jack: The Cultural Politics of Race and Nation*. London: Hutchinson, 1987. 2nd ed. London: Routledge, 2002.

————. "You Can't Fool the Youths . . . Race and Class Formation in the 1980s." *Race & Class* 23 (1981–82): 207–22.

Gikandi, Simon. "The Embarrassment of Victorianism: Colonial Subjects and the Lure of Englishness." In *Victorian Afterlife: Postmodern Culture Rewrites the Nineteenth Century*, ed. John Kucich and Dianne F. Sardoff, 157–85. Minneapolis: University of Minnesota Press, 2000.

————. "On Culture and the State: The Writings of Ngũgĩ wa Thiong'o." *Third World Quarterly*, 11, no. 1 (1989): 148–156.

————. "Pan-Africanism and Cosmopolitanism: The Case of Jomo Kenyatta." *English Studies in Africa* 43 (2000): 3–28.

Glaude, Eddie S., Jr., ed. *Is It Nation Time? Contemporary Essays on Black Power and Black Nationalism*. Chicago: University of Chicago Press, 2002.

Goto, John. *Lover's Rock*. London: Autograph ABP, 2014.

Goulbourne, Harry. *Caribbean Transnational Experience*. London: Pluto Press, 2002.

Gray, Obika. *Radicalism and Social Change in Jamaica, 1960–1972*. Knoxville: University of Tennessee Press, 1991.

Great Britain. Parliament. House of Commons. Select Committee on Race Relations and Immigration. *Police/Immigrant Relations*. 3 vols. London: Her Majesty's Stationery Office, 1972.

————. *The West Indian Community: Minutes of Evidence. Thursday 20 May 1976*. London: Her Majesty's Stationery Office, 1976.

Green, Jonathon. *All Dressed Up: The Sixties and the Counter-Culture*. London: Jonathan Cape, 1998.

————. *Days in the Life: Voices from the English Underground, 1961–1971*. London: Pimlico, 1998.

Guha, Ranajit, and Gayatri Chakravorty Spivak, eds. *Selected Subaltern Studies*. Oxford: Oxford University Press, 1988.

Guild, Joshua. *In the Shadows of the Metropolis: Cultural Politics and Black Communities in Postwar New York and London*. Oxford: Oxford University Press, forthcoming.

Guillory, Monique, and Richard C. Green. *Soul: Black Power, Politics, and Pleasure*. New York: New York University Press, 1998.

Hall, Stuart. "Black Men, White Media." *Savacou*, nos. 9–10 (1974): 97–100.

———. "Cultures of Resistance and 'Moral Panics.'" *Afras Review* 4 (1979): 2–18.

———. *The Hard Road to Renewal: Thatcherism and the Crisis of the Left*. London: Verso, 1988.

———. *Familiar Stranger: A Life between Two Islands*. London: Allen Lane, 2017.

———. "New Ethnicities." In *Stuart Hall: Critical Dialogues in Cultural Studies*, ed. David Morley and Kuan-Hsing Chen, 442–51. London: Routledge, 1996.

———. "Reconstruction Work: Images of Postwar Black Settlement." *Ten.8* 16 (1984): 2–9.

———. "Racism and Reaction." In *Five Views on Multi-Racial Britain*, ed. Commission for Racial Equality, 23–35. London: Commission for Racial Equality, 1978.

Hall, Stuart, and Les Back. "At Home and Not at Home: Stuart Hall in Conversation with Les Back." *Cultural Studies* 23, no. 4 (2009): 658–87.

Hall, Stuart, Chas Critcher, Tony Jefferson, John Clarke, and Brian Roberts. *Policing the Crisis: Mugging, the State, and Law and Order*. London: Macmillan, 1978.

Hall, Stuart, and Tony Jefferson, eds. *Resistance through Rituals: Youth Sub-cultures in Post-war Britain*. London: Hutchinson, 1976.

Hamilton, Marybeth. "The Lure of Black Style." *Journal of Contemporary History* 34, no. 4 (1999): 641–51.

Harris, Roxy. *Being Black: Selections from Soledad Brother & Soul on Ice. With Questions and Notes*. London: New Beacon Books, 1981.

Harris, Roxy, and Sarah White, eds. *Building Britannia: Life Experience With Britain*. London: New Beacon Books, 2009.

———, eds. *Changing Britannia: Life Experience with Britain*. London: New Beacon Books, 1999.

Hebdige, Dick. *Cut 'n' Mix: Culture, Identity and Caribbean Music*. London: Comedia, 1987.

———. "Reggae, Rudeboys and Rastas." In Stuart Hall and Tony Jefferson, eds., *Resistance through Rituals: Youth Sub-cultures in Post-war Britain*. London: Hutchinson, 1976.

———. *Subculture: The Meaning of Style*. London: Methuen, 1979.

Heineman, Benjamin W., Jr. *The Politics of the Powerless: A Study of the Campaign against Racial Discrimination*. London: Institute of Race Relations, 1972.

Hill, Robert A. "From *New World* to *Abeng*: George Beckford and the Horn of Black Power in Jamaica, 1968–1970." *Small Axe* 24 (2007): 1–15.

Hilliard, Christopher. *To Exercise Our Talents: The Democratization of Writing in Britain*. Cambridge, MA: Harvard University Press, 2006.

Hinds, Donald. *Journey to an Illusion: The West Indian in Britain*. London: Heinemann, 1966.

Hines, Vince. *How Black People Overcame Fifty Years of Repression in Britain, 1945–1995*, vol. 1: *1945–1975*. London: Zulu Publications, 1998.

Hiro, Dilip. *Black British, White British*. London: Eyre & Spottiswoode, 1971.

Hoefferle, Caroline M. *British Student Activism in the Long Sixties*. New York: Routledge, 2013.

Houlden, Kate M. "Sexuality in the Writing of Male Authors from the Anglophone Caribbean: Roger Mais, John Hearne, Jan Carew and Andrew Salkey." PhD diss., Queen Mary University of London, 2010.

Humphry, Derek, and Gus John. *Because They're Black*. New York: Penguin, 1972.

———. *Police Power and Black People*. London: Panther Books, 1972.

Hunte, J. A. *Nigger Hunting in England*. London: West Indian Standing Conference, 1966.

Hunter, Emma. *Political Thought and the Public Sphere in Tanzania: Freedom, Democracy, and Citizenship in the Era of Decolonization*. Cambridge: Cambridge University Press, 2015.

Institute of Race Relations. *Police against Black People: Evidence Submitted to the Royal Commission on Criminal Procedure*. London: IRR, 1979.

Ireland, Philippa. "Material Factors Affecting the Publication of Black British Fiction." PhD diss., Open University, 2010.

Ishmael, Hannah J.M., and Rob Waters. "Archive Review: The Black Cultural Archives." *Twentieth Century British History* 28, no. 3 (2017): 465–73.

Islington 18 Defence Committee. *Under Heavy Manners: Report of the Labour Movement Enquiry into Police Brutality and the Position of Black Youth in Islington Held on Saturday July 23rd 1977*. London: Islington 18 Defence Committee, 1977.

Jackson, Ben, and Robert Saunders, eds. *Making Thatcher's Britain*. Cambridge: Cambridge University Press, 2012.

Jackson, George. *Blood in My Eye*. New York: Penguin, 1975.

———. *Soledad Brother*. New York: Penguin, 1971.

Jacobs, Joe. *Sorting Out the Postal Strike*. Bromley, Kent, England: Solidarity, 1971.

James, C. L. R. *Black Power: Its Past, Today, and the Way Ahead*. London: Frank John, 1968.

James, Winston. *Holding Aloft the Banner of Ethiopia: Caribbean Radicalism in Early Twentieth Century America*. London: Verso, 1998.

James, Winston, and Clive Harris, eds. *Inside Babylon: The Caribbean Diaspora in Britain*. London: Verso, 1993.

Jeffers, Sydney. "Black Sections in the Labour Party: The End of Ethnicity and 'Godfather' Politics?" In *Black and Ethnic Leaderships: The Cultural Dimensions of Political Action*, ed. Pnina Werbner and Muhammad Anwar, 43–57. London: Routledge, 1991.

Jephcott, Pearl. *A Troubled Area: Notes on Notting Hill*. London: Faber & Faber, 1964.

John, Gus. *In the Service of Black Youth*. Leicester: National Association of Youth Clubs Publications, 1981.

———. *Taking a Stand: Gus John Speaks on Education, Race, Social Action and Civil Unrest, 1980–2005*. Manchester: Gus John Partnership, 2006.

John La Rose Tribute Committee. *Foundations of a Movement*. London: John La Rose Tribute Committee, 1991.

Johnson, Linton Kwesi. *Dread, Beat and Blood*. London: Bogle-L'Ouverture Publications, 1975.

———. *Inglan Is a Bitch*. London: Race Today, 1981.

———. *Making History*. LP. Island Records, 1983.

———. *Voices of the Living and the Dead*. London: Race Today, 1983.

Johnson, W. Chris. "Guerrilla Ganja Gun Girls: Policing Black Revolutionaries from Notting Hill to Laventille." *Gender & History* 26, no. 3 (2014): 661–787.

Jones, Ben. "The Uses of Nostalgia." *Cultural and Social History* 7, no. 3 (2010): 355–74.

Jones, Colin. *The Black House*. London: Prestel, 2006.

Jones, Valentino A. *We Are Our Own Educators! Josina Machel: From Supplementary to Black Complementary School*. London: Karia Press, 1986.

Joseph, Peniel E., ed. *The Black Power Movement: Rethinking the Civil Rights–Black Power Era*. London: Routledge, 2006.

———. *Stokely: A Life*. New York: Basic Civitas, 2016.

———. *Waiting 'Til the Midnight Hour: A Narrative History of Black Power in America*. New York: Holt, 2006.

Keith, Michael. "How Did the Empire Strike Back? Lessons for Today from *The Empire Strikes Back: Race and Racism in 70s Britain*." *Ethnic and Racial Studies* 37, no. 10 (2014): 1815–22.

Kelley, Robin D. G., and Stephen Tuck, eds. *The Other Special Relationship: Race, Rights and Riots in Britain and the United States*. New York: Palgrave Macmillan, 2015.

Kelliher, Diarmaid. "Constructing a Culture of Solidarity: London and the British Coalfields in the Long 1970s." *Antipode* 49, no. 1 (2017): 106–24.

Killingray, David, and David M. Anderson. "An Orderly Retreat? Policing the End of Empire." In *Policing and Decolonisation: Politics, Nationalism and the Police, 1917–65*, ed. David Killingray and David M. Anderson, 1–21. Manchester: Manchester University Press, 1992.

King, Audvil, Althea Helps, Pam Wint, and Frank Hasfal, with Andrew Salkey. *One Love*. London: Bogle-L'Ouverture, 1971.

Knight, Christopher. *The Making of Tory Education Policy in Post-War Britain, 1950–1986*. New York: Falmer Press, 1990.

Kureishi, Hanif. *The Buddha of Suburbia*. London: Faber & Faber, 1990.

———. "London and Karachi." In *Patriotism: The Making and Unmaking of British National Identity*, ed. Raphael Samuel, vol. 2: *Minorities and Outsiders*, 270–87. London: Routledge, 1989.

Lamming, George. *The Pleasures of Exile*. 1960. London: Pluto Press, 2005.

Lane, Tony, and Kenneth Roberts. *Strike at Pilkingtons*. London: Collins, 1971.

La Rose, John. *The New Cross Massacre Story: Interviews with John La Rose*. London: Alliance of the Black Parents Movement, 1984.

Layton-Henry, Zig. *The Politics of Immigration: Immigration, 'Race' and 'Race' Relations in Post-war Britain*. Oxford: Blackwell, 1992.

Lent, Adam. *British Social Movements since 1945: Sex, Colour, Peace and Power*. New York: Palgrave, 2001.

Levine, Philippa, and Susan R. Grayzal, eds. *Gender, Labour, War and Empire: Essays on Modern Britain*. New York: Palgrave Macmillan, 2009.

Lewis, Gail. "From Deepest Kilburn." In *Truth, Dare or Promise: Girls Growing Up in the Fifties*, ed. Liz Heron, 213–36. London: Virago, 1985.

———. *Walter Rodney's Intellectual and Political Thought*. Detroit: Wayne State University Press, 1998.

Lindop, Fred. "The Dockers and the 1971 Industrial Relations Act, Part 1: Shop Stewards and Containerization." *Historical Studies in Industrial Relations* 5 (1998): 33–72.

———. "The Dockers and the 1971 Industrial Relations Act, Part 2: The Arrest and Release of the 'Pentonville Five.'" *Historical Studies in Industrial Relations* 6 (1998): 65–100.

———. "Racism and the Working Class: Strikes in Support of Enoch Powell." *Labour History Review* 66, no. 1 (2001): 79–100.

Low, Gail. *Publishing the Postcolonial: Anglophone West African and Caribbean Writing in the UK, 1948–1968*. London: Routledge, 2011.

MacInnes, Colin. *Absolute Beginners*. London: MacGibbon & Kee, 1959.

———. *City of Spades*. London: MacGibbon & Kee, 1957.

———. *England, Half English*. London: MacGibbon & Kee, 1961.

Magaziner, Daniel R. *The Law and the Prophets: Black Consciousness in South Africa, 1968–1977*. Athens: Ohio University Press, 2010.

Makalani, Minkah. *In the Cause of Freedom: Radical Black Internationalism from Harlem to London, 1917–1939*. Chapel Hill: University of North Carolina Press, 2011.

Malchow, H. L. *Special Relations: The Americanization of Britain?* Stanford, CA: Stanford University Press, 2011.

Malcolm X. *Malcolm X: February 1965. The Final Speeches*, ed. Steve Clark. New York: Pathfinder, 1992.

Malik, Kenan. *From Fatwa to Jihad: The Rushdie Affair and Its Aftermath: How a Group of British Extremists Attacked a Novel and Ignited Radical Islam*. London: Melville House, 2014.

Malik, Michael Abdul. *From Michael de Freitas to Michael X*. London: André Deutsch, 1968.

Mangrove Nine. Directed by Franco Rosso. DVD. London: John La Rose Productions, 1973.

Marwick, Arthur. *The Sixties: Cultural Revolution in Britain, France, Italy and the United States, c. 1958–c. 1974*. Oxford: Oxford University Press, 1998.

Marx, Karl. *Capital: A Critique of Political Economy. Vol.1, Book One: The Process of Capitalist Production*. 1867. London: Lawrence & Wishart, 2003.

Massumi, Brian. "The Autonomy of Affect." *Cultural Critique* 31 (1995): 83–109.

Matera, Marc. *Black London: The Imperial Metropolis and Decolonization in the Twentieth Century*. Oakland: University of California Press, 2015.

Matthews, John. *Ford Strike: The Workers' Story*. London: Panther, 1972.

Mazzarella, William. "Affect: What Is It Good For?" In *Enchantments of Modernity: Empire, Nation Globalization*, ed. Saurabh Dube, 291–309. London: Routledge, 2009.

Mbembe, Achille. *On the Postcolony*. Berkeley: University of California Press, 2001.

McLeod, John. "A Night at 'the Cosmopolitan': Axes of Transnational Encounter in the 1930s and 1940s." *Interventions* 4, no. 1 (2002): 53–67.

McGilchrist, Paul, ed. *Black Voices: An Anthology of ACER's Black Young Writers Competition*. London: ACER, 1987.

McMillan, Michael. *The Front Room: Migrant Aesthetics in the Home*. London: Black Dog Publishing, 2010.

———. *Hard Time Pressure*. London: Young People's Theatre Scheme, 1980.

———. *The School Leaver*. London: Black Ink Collective, 1978.

Mercer, Kobena. *Welcome to the Jungle: New Positions in Black Cultural Studies*. London: Routledge, 1994.

Mizra, Heidi Safia, and Diane Reay. "Spaces and Places of Black Educational Desire: Rethinking Black Supplementary Schools as a New Social Movement." *Sociology* 34, no. 3 (2000): 521–44.

Modood, Tariq. "'Black', Racial Equality and Asian Identity." *New Community* 14, no. 3 (1988): 397–404.

———. "Political Blackness and British Asians." *Sociology*, 28, no. 4 (1994): 859–76.

Morris, Dennis. *Growing Up Black*. London: Autograph ABP, 2012.

Morris, Sam. *The Case and the Course: A Treatise on Black Studies*. London: Committee on Black Studies, 1973.

Morrison, Majbritt. *Jungle West 11*. London: Tandem, 1964.

Mort, Frank. "Scandalous Events: Metropolitan Culture and Moral Change." *Representations* 93 (2006): 106–37.

Mullard, Chris. *Anti-Racist Education: The Three O's*. Watford, England: National Association for Multi-Racial Education, 1984.

———. *Black Britain*. London: Allen & Unwin, 1973.

———. *Race, Power and Resistance*. London: Routledge & Kegan Paul, 1985.

Murden, Jon. "Demands for Fair Wages and Pay Parity in the British Motor Industry in the 1960s and 1970s." *Historical Studies in Industrial Relations* 20 (Autumn 2005): 1–27.

Murray, Rolland. *Our Living Manhood: Literature, Black Power and Masculine Ideology*. Philadelphia: University of Pennsylvania Press, 2007.

Murugkar, Lata. *Dalit Panther Movement in Maharashtra: A Sociological Appraisal*. Bombay: Popular Prakashan, 1991.

Naipaul, V. S. *A House for Mr Biswas*. London: Collins, 1963.

———. *Letters between a Father and a Son*. London: Picador, 2012.

Nava, Mica. *Visceral Cosmopolitanism: Gender Culture and the Normalisation of Difference*. Oxford: Berg, 2007.

Newton, Darrell M. *Paving the Empire Road: BBC Television and Black Britons*. Manchester: Manchester University Press, 2011.

Newton, Huey P., with J. Herman Blake. *Revolutionary Suicide*. London: Wildwood House, 1974.

Ngcobo, Lauretta, ed. *Let It Be Told: Essays by Black Women in Britain*. London: Pluto Press, 1987.

Nkrumah, Kwame. *Neo-Colonialism: The Last Stage of Imperialism*. London: Nelson, 1965.

Ogbar, Jeffrey O. G. *Black Power: Radical Politics and African American Identity*. Baltimore: John Hopkins University Press, 2004.

O'Hara, Glen. *Governing Post-War Britain: The Paradoxes of Progress*. New York: Palgrave Macmillan, 2012.

Olden, Mark. *Murder in Notting Hill*. Winchester, England: Zero Books, 2011.

Ongiri, Amy Abugo. *Spectacular Blackness: The Cultural Politics of the Black Power Movement and the Search for a Black Aesthetic*. Charlottesville: University of Virginia Press, 2010.

Organised Youth. *The British Black Panthers and Black Power Movement: An Oral History and Photography Project*, ed. Lizzy King. London: Photofusion Education Trust, 2013.

Owusu, Kwesi. "The Struggle for a Radical Black Political Culture: An Interview with A. Sivanandan." In *Black British Culture and Society: A Text Reader*, ed. Kwesi Owusu, 416–24. London: Routledge, 2000.

Palmer, Tony. *The Trials of Oz*. London: Blond & Briggs, 1971.

Pantin, Raoul. *Black Power Day: The 1970 February Revolution*. Santa Cruz, Trinidad and Tobago, West Indies: Hatuey Productions, 1990.

Paul, Kathleen. *Whitewashing Britain: Race and Citizenship in the Postwar Era*. Ithaca, NY: Cornell University Press, 1997.

Pennybacker, Susan. *From Scottsboro to Munich: Race and Political Culture in 1930s Britain*. Princeton, NJ: Princeton University Press, 2009.

Peplow, Simon. "'A Tactical Manoeuvre to Apply Pressure': Race and the Role of Public Inquiries in the 1980 Bristol 'Riot.'" *Twentieth Century British History*, forthcoming.

Perry, Kennetta Hammond. *London Is the Place for Me: Black Britons, Citizenship, and the Politics of Race*. Oxford: Oxford University Press, 2015.

Phillips, Mike. *London Crossings: A Biography of Black Britain*. London: Continuum, 2001.

Phillips, Mike, and Charlie Phillips. *Notting Hill in the Sixties*. London: Lawrence & Wishart, 1991.

Phillips, Mike, and Trevor Phillips. *Windrush: The Irresistible Rise of Multi-Racial Britain*. London: HarperCollins, 1998.

Pilkington, Edward. *Beyond the Mother Country: West Indians and the Notting Hill White Riots*. London: I. B. Tauris, 1988.

Pines, Jim, ed. *Black and White in Colour: Black People in British Television since 1936*. London: BFI, 1992.

Piper, Keith. "Passing the Cricket Test." 2015. www.keithpiper.info/crickettest.html.

———. *Step into the Arena: Notes on Black Masculinity & the Contest of Territory*. Rochdale, England: Rochdale Art Gallery, 1991.

Porter, Roy. *London: A Social History*. London: Penguin, 2000.

Pressure. Directed by Horace Ové. DVD. 1975; London: British Film Institute, 2005.

Procter, James. *Dwelling Places: Postwar Black British Writing*. Manchester: Manchester University Press, 2003.

Pryce, Ken. *Endless Pressure: A Study of West Indian Life-Styles in Bristol*. New York: Penguin, 1979.

Putnam, Lara. *Radical Moves: Caribbean Migrants and the Politics of Race in the Jazz Age*. Chapel Hill: University of North Carolina Press, 2013.

Quinn, Kate, ed. *Black Power in the Caribbean*. Gainesville: University Press of Florida, 2014.

Race Today Collective. *The Road Made to Walk on Carnival Day: The Battle for West Indian Carnival in Britain*. London: Race Today Collective, 1977.

Racial Adjustment Action Society. *The Black House: A Self Help Community Project in the Making*. London: Sir Joshua Reynolds Press, 1971.

Ramamurthy, Anandi. *Black Star: Britain's Asian Youth Movements*. London: Pluto Press, 2013.

Ramchand, Kenneth. "The Colour Problem at the University: A West Indian's Changing Attitudes." In *Disappointed Guests: Essays by African, Asian, and West Indian Students*, ed. Henri Tajfel, and John L. Dawson, 27–37. London: Institute of Race Relations, 1965.

Ramdin, Ron. *The Making of the Black Working Class in Britain*. Burlington, VT: Ashgate, 1986.

Rex, Jon, and Sally Tomlinson. *Colonial Immigrants in a British City*. London: Routledge & Kegan Paul, 1979.

Rhodes, Jane. *Framing the Black Panthers: The Spectacular Rise of a Black Power Icon*. New York: New Press, 2007.

Rice, Alan J., and Martin Crawford. *Liberating Sojourn: Frederick Douglass & Transatlantic Reform*. Athens: University of Georgia Press, 1999.

Rich, Paul. *Race and Empire in British Politics*. Cambridge: Cambridge University Press, 1986.

Robinson, Cedric. *Black Marxism: The Making of the Black Radical Tradition*. 1983. Chapel Hill: University of North Carolina Press, 2000.

Rodney, Walter. *The Groundings with My Brothers*. London: Bogle-L'Ouverture Publications, 1969.

———. *Walter Rodney Speaks: The Making of an African Intellectual*. Trenton, NJ: Africa World Press, 1990.

Roper, Michael. "Slipping Out of View: Subjectivity and Emotion in Gender History." *History Workshop Journal* 59 (2005): 57–72.

Rose, E. J. B. *Colour and Citizenship: A Report on British Race Relations*. London: Institute of Race Relations, 1969.

Rothberg, Michael. *Multidirectional Memory: Remembering the Holocaust in the Age of Decolonization*. Stanford, CA: Stanford University Press, 2009.

Rush, Anne Spry. *Bonds of Empire: West Indians and Britishness from Victoria to Decolonization*. Oxford: Oxford University Press, 2011.

Rushdie, Salman. *Imaginary Homelands: Essays and Criticism, 1981–1991.* London: Granta, 1991.

———. *The Satanic Verses.* London: Penguin, 1988.

Ryan, Selwyn D., and Taimoon Stewart, with Roy McCree, eds., *The Black Power Revolution of 1970: A Retrospective.* St. Augustine, Trinidad and Tobago: University of the West Indies Press, 1995.

Salkey, Andrew. *Come Home, Malcolm Heartland.* London: Hutchinson, 1976.

———. *Georgetown Journal: A Caribbean Writer's Journey from London via Port of Spain to Georgetown, Guyana, 1970.* London: New Beacon, 1972.

———. *Havana Journal.* New York: Penguin, 1971.

Samuel, Raphael, ed. *Patriotism: The Making and Unmaking of British National Identity.* Vol. 2: *Minorities and Outsiders.* Vol. 3: *National Fictions.* London: Routledge, 1989.

Sandbrook, Dominic. *White Heat: A History of Britain in the Swinging Sixties.* London: Little, Brown, 2006.

Sawh, Roy. *From Where I Stand.* London: Hansib, 1987.

Scafe, Susan. *Teaching Black Literature.* London: Virago, 1989.

Scarman, Leslie, Baron. *The Brixton Disorders 10–12 April 1981.* Harmondsworth, England: Penguin, 1982.

Schaffer, Gavin. "Legislating against Hatred: Meaning and Motive in Section Six of the Race Relations Act of 1965." *Twentieth Century British History* 25, no. 2 (2014): 251–75.

———. *The Vision of a Nation: Making Multiculturalism on British Television, 1960–1980.* New York: Palgrave Macmillan, 2014.

Schofield, Camilla. *Enoch Powell and the Making of Postcolonial Britain.* Cambridge: Cambridge University Press, 2013.

Schwarz, Bill. "Actually Existing Postcolonialism." *Radical Philosophy* 104 (2000): 16–24.

———. "Black Metropolis, White England." In *Modern Times: Reflections on a Century of English Modernity*, ed. Mica Nava and Alan O'Shea, 176–207. London: Routledge, 1996.

———. "Claudia Jones and the West Indian Gazette: Reflections on the Emergence of Post-Colonial Britain." *Twentieth Century British History* 14 (2003): 264–85.

———. *Memories of Empire*, vol. 1: *The White Man's World.* Oxford: Oxford University Press, 2011.

———. "'The Only White Man in There': The Re-Racialisation of England, 1956–1968." *Race & Class* 38 (1996): 65–78.

———, ed. *West Indian Intellectuals in Britain.* Manchester: Manchester University Press, 2003.

Scott, David. *Conscripts of Modernity: The Tragedy of Colonial Enlightenment.* Durham, NC: Duke University Press, 2004.

———. *Omens of Adversity: Tragedy, Time, Memory, Justice.* Durham, NC: Duke University Press, 2014.

———. "On the Very Idea of a Black Radical Tradition." *Small Axe* 17 (2013): 1–6.

———. *Stuart Hall's Voice: Intimations of an Ethics of Receptive Generosity*. Durham, NC: Duke University Press, 2017.

Seale, Bobby. *Seize the Time: The Story of the Black Panther Party and Huey P. Newton*. London: Hutchinson, 1970.

Sealey, Mike, ed. *Vanley Burke: A Retrospective*. London: Lawrence & Wishart, 1993.

Searle, Chris, ed. *Classrooms of Resistance*. London: Writers and Readers Publishing Cooperative, 1975.

———. *Ferndale Fires: A Children's Story*. London: Centerprise, 1974.

———. *The Forsaken Lover: White Words and Black People*. London: Routledge & Kegan Paul, 1972.

———. *Stepney Words*. London: Reality Press, 1971.

Self, Robert O. *American Babylon: Race and the Struggle for Postwar Oakland*. Princeton, NJ: Princeton University Press, 2003.

———. "The Black Panther Party and the Long Civil Rights Era." In *In Search of the Black Panther Party: New Perspectives on a Revolutionary Movement*, ed. Jama Lazerow and Yohuru Williams, 15–55. Durham, NC: Duke University Press, 2006.

Selvon, Sam. *The Lonely Londoners*. 1956. London: Penguin, 2006.

———. *Moses Ascending*. 1975. Oxford: Heinemann, 1984.

Sewell, Mike. "British Responses to Martin Luther King Jr and the Civil Rights Movement, 1954–68." In *The Making of Martin Luther King and the Civil Rights Movement*, ed. Brian Ward and Tony Badger, 194–212. New York: Macmillan, 1996.

Shapira, Michal. *The War Inside: Psychoanalysis, Total War and the Making of the Democratic Self in Postwar*. Cambridge: Cambridge University Press, 2013.

Sherwood, Marika. *Malcolm X: Visits Abroad, April 1964–February 1965*. Oare, Kent, England: Savannah Press, 2010.

Sherwood, Marika, with Donald Hinds, Colin Prescod, and the 1996 Claudia Jones Symposium. *Claudia Jones: A Life in Exile*. London: Lawrence & Wishart, 1999.

Shilliam, Robbie. *The Black Pacific: Anticolonial Struggles and Oceanic Connections*. London: Bloomsbury Academic Press, 2015.

Shotton, John. *No Master High or Low: Libertarian Education and Schooling in Britain 1890–1990*. Bristol: Libertarian Education, 1993.

Shukra, Kalbir. *The Changing Pattern of Black Politics in Britain*. London: Pluto Press, 1998.

Simon, Brian. *Education and the Social Order*. London: Lawrence & Wishart, 1999.

Singh, Nikhil Pal. "The Black Panthers and the 'Undeveloped Country' of the Left." In *The Black Panther Party (Reconsidered)*, ed. Charles E. Jones, 57–105. Baltimore: Black Classics, 1998.

Sivanandan, Ambalavaner. *Catching History on the Wing: Race, Culture and Globalisation*. London: Pluto Press, 2008.

———. *Communities of Resistance: Writings on Black Struggles for Socialism*. London: Verso, 1990.

———. *A Different Hunger? Writings on Black Resistance*. London: Pluto Press, 1983.

———. "From Resistance to Rebellion: Asian and Afro-Caribbean Struggles in Britain." *Race & Class* 23, nos. 2–3 (1981–82): 111–52.

———. *From Resistance to Rebellion: Asian and Afro-Caribbean Struggles in Britain*. Race & Class pamphlet no. 10. London: Institute of Race Relations, 1986.

———. *Race and Resistance: The IRR Story*. London: Race Today Publications, 1974.

———. "Race, Class and the State: The Black Experience in Britain." *Race & Class* 17, no. 4 (Spring 1976): 347–68.

———. "Race: The Revolutionary Experience." *Race Today*, August 1969, 108–9

———. "RAT and the Degradation of Black Struggle." *Race & Class*, 26, no. 4 (Spring 1985): 1–34.

———. "White Racism & Black." *Encounter* 31, no. 1 (1968): 95–96.

Sivanandan, Ambalavaner, interviewed by Louis Kushnick and Paul Grant. "Catching History on the Wing: A. Sivanandan as Activist, Teacher, and Rebel." In *Against the Odds: Scholars Who Challenged Racism in the Twentieth Century*, ed. Benjamin P. Bowser and Louis Kushnick, with Paul Grant, 227–42. Boston: University of Massachusetts Press, 2002.

Slate, Nico, ed. *Black Power Beyond Borders: The Global Dimensions of the Black Power Movement*. New York: Palgrave Macmillan, 2012.

Smith, Anne Marie. *New Right Discourse on Race and Sexuality: Britain, 1968–1990*. Cambridge: Cambridge University Press, 1994.

Smith, Evan, and Matthew Worley, eds. *Against the Grain: The British Far Left from 1956*. Manchester: Manchester University Press, 2014.

Solomos, John. *Black Youth, Racism and the State: The Politics of Ideology and Policy*. Cambridge: Cambridge University Press, 1988.

Southall Black Sisters. *Against the Grain: A Celebration of Survival and Struggle*. Southall, Middlesex, England: Southall Black Sisters, 1990.

Steedman, Carolyn. *Landscape for a Good Woman: A Tale of Two Lives*. London: Virago, 1986.

———. "State-Sponsored Autobiography." In *Moments of Modernity: Reconstructing Britain, 1945–1964*, ed. Becky Conekin, Frank Mort, and Chris Waters, 41–54. London: Rivers Oram Press, 1999.

Step Forward Youth. Directed by Menelik Shabazz. London: Kuumba Black Arts, 1977.

Stokely Carmichael at the Dialectics of Liberation, London 1967. DVD. Directed by Peter Davies. 1967; Vancouver: Villon Films, 2012.

Street, Joe. "Malcolm X, Smethwick, and the Influence of the African American Freedom Struggle on British Race Relations in the 1960s." *Journal of Black Studies* 38 (2008): 932–50.

Struggles for Black Community. Directed by Colin Prescod. DVD. 1984; London: Race & Class, 2008.

Sudbury, Julia. *"Other Kinds of Dreams": Black Women's Organisations and the Politics of Transformation*. London: Routledge, 1998.

Sutcliffe David, and Ansel Wong, eds. *The Language of the Black Experience in Britain: Cultural Expression through Word and Sound in the Caribbean and Black Britain*. Oxford: Basil Blackwell, 1986.

Sutherland, John. *Offensive Literature: Decensorship in Britain, 1960–1982*. London: Junction Books, 1982.

Swaby, Nydia A. "'Disparate in Voice, Sympathetic in Direction': Gendered Political Blackness and the Politics of Solidarity." *Feminist Review* 108 (2014): 11–25.

Swan, Quito. *Black Power in Bermuda: the Struggle for Decolonization*. New York: Palgrave Macmillan, 2009.

Tabili, Laura. *We Ask for British Justice: Workers and Racial Difference in Late Imperial Britain*. Ithaca, NY: Cornell University Press, 1994.

Thomlinson, Natalie. *Race, Ethnicity and the Women's Movement in England, 1968–1993*. New York: Palgrave Macmillan, 2016.

Thompson, Andrew, ed. *Britain's Experience of Empire in the Twentieth Century*. Oxford: Oxford University Press, 2012.

Thompson, E. P. *Writing by Candlelight*. London: Merlin, 1980.

Thompson, Heather Ann. *Blood in the Water: The Attica Prison Uprising and Its Legacy*. New York: Pantheon Books, 2016.

Thomson, Matthew. *Lost Freedom: The Landscape of the Child and the British Post-War Settlement*. Oxford: Oxford University Press, 2013.

Thorne, John, ed. *Speeches from the Soledad Brothers Rally, Central Hall, Westminster, 20/4/71*. London: Friends of Soledad, 1971.

Times News Team. *The Black Man in Search of Power: A Survey of Black Revolution across the World*. London: Nelson, 1968.

Tisdall, Laura. "Education, Parenting and Concepts of Childhood in England, c. 1945 to c. 1979." *Contemporary British History* 31, no. 1 (2017): 24–46.

Tomlinson, Sally. "The Black Education Movement." In *Race and Gender: Equal Opportunities Policies in Education*, ed. Madeleine Arnot, 65–80. Oxford: Pergamon, 1985.

Trentmann, Frank. "Materiality in the Future of History: Things, Practices, and Politics." *Journal of British Studies* 48 (2009): 283–307.

Trew, Winston N. *Black for a Cause, Not Just Because: The Case of the 'Oval 4' and the Story of Black Power in 1970s Britain*. Derby, England: Derwent Press, 2010.

Trometter, Alyssa L. "'The Fire in the Belly': Aboriginal Black Power and the Rise of the Australian Black Panther Party, 1967–1972." PhD diss., University of Melbourne, 2013.

Tuck, Stephen. *The Night Malcolm X Spoke at the Oxford Union: A Transatlantic Story of Antiracist Protest*. Berkeley: University of California Press, 2014.

Tulloch, Carol. *The Birth of Cool: Style Narratives of the African Diaspora*. London: Bloomsbury Academic, 2016.

Universal Coloured People's Association. *Black Power in Britain: A Special Statement*. London: Universal Coloured People's Association, 1967.

Van Deburg, William. *New Day in Babylon: The Black Power Movement and American Culture, 1965–1975*. Chicago: University of Chicago Press, 1992.

Virdee, Satnam. *Racism, Class and the Racialized Outsider*. New York: Palgrave Macmillan, 2014.

Walmsley, Anne. *The Caribbean Artists Movement, 1966–1972: A Literary and Cultural History*. London: New Beacon Books, 1992.

Ward, Brian. *Just My Soul Responding: Rhythm and Blues, Black Consciousness, and Race Relations*. Berkeley: University of California Press, 1998.

———. "A King in Newcastle: Martin Luther King, Jr. and British Race Relations." *Georgia Historical Quarterly* 79, no. 3 (1995): 599–632.

Ward, Stuart, ed. *British Culture and the End of Empire*. Manchester: Manchester University Press, 2001.

Warmington, Paul. *Black British Intellectuals and Education*. New York: Routledge, 2014.

Warner, Michael. "Publics and Counterpublics." *Public Culture* 14, no. 1 (2002): 49–89.

Waters, Chris. "Autobiography, Nostalgia, and the Changing Practices of Working-Class Selfhood." In *Singular Continuities: Tradition, Nostalgia, and Identity in Modern British Culture*, ed. George K. Behlmer and Fred M. Leventhal, 178–195. Stanford, CA: Stanford University Press, 2000.

———. "Representations of Everyday Life: L. S. Lowry and the Landscape of Memory in Postwar Britain." *Representations* 65 (1999): 121–50.

Waters, Rob. "Black Power on the Telly: America, Television, and Race in 1960s and 1970s Britain." *Journal of British Studies* 54, no. 4 (2015): 1–24.

———. "Henry Swanzy, Sartre's Zombie? Black Power and the Transformation of the Caribbean Artists Movement." In *Cultures of Decolonisation: Transnational Productions and Practices*, ed. Ruth Craggs and Claire Wintle, 67–85. Manchester: Manchester University Press, 2016.

———. "Strange Familiarity," *Identities* 25, no. 1 (2018): 61–66.

———. "Student Politics, Teaching Politics, Black Politics: An Interview with Ansel Wong." *Race & Class* 58, no. 1 (2016): 17–33.

———. "Thinking Black: Peter Fryer's *Staying Power* and the Politics of Writing Black British History in the 1980s." *History Workshop Journal* 82 (2016): 104–20.

Watson, G. Llewellyn. "The Sociology of Black Nationalism: Identity, Protest and the Concept of 'Black Power' Among West Indian Immigrants in Britain." PhD diss., University of York, 1972.

Webb, Clive. "Britain, the American South, and the Wide Civil Rights Movement." In *The U.S. South and Europe: Transatlantic Relations in the Nineteenth and Twentieth Centuries. New Directions in Southern History*, ed. Cornelis A. van Minnen and Manfred Berg, 243–63. Lexington: University Press of Kentucky, 2013.

———. "Special Relationships: Mixed-Race Couples in Post-War Britain and the United States." *Women's History Review* 26, no. 1 (2016): 110–29.

Webster, Wendy. *Englishness and Empire, 1939–1965*. Oxford: Oxford University Press, 2005.

———. *Imagining Home: Gender, "Race" and National Identity, 1945–64*. London: UCL Press, 1998.

West, Michael O., William G. Martin, and Fanon Che Wilkins, eds. *From Toussaint to Tupac: The Black International since the Age of Revolution*. Chapel Hill: University of North Carolina Press, 2009.

Wetherell, Sam. "Painting the Crisis: Community Arts and the Search for the 'Ordinary' in 1970s and '80s London." *History Workshop Journal* 76 (2013): 235–49.

White, Sarah, Roxy Harris, and Sharmilla Beezmohun. *A Meeting of the Continents: The International Book Fair of Radical Black and Third World Books–Revisited. History, Memories, Organisation and Programmes, 1982–1995*. London: New Beacon Books, 2005.

White, Shane, and Graham White. *Stylin': African American Expressive Culture from its Beginnings to the Zoot Suit*. Ithaca, NY: Cornell University Press, 1998.

Whipple, Amy C. "'Ordinary People': The Cultural Origins of Popular Thatcherism in Britain, 1964–79." Ph.D diss., Northwestern University, 2004.

Wild, Rosalind Eleanor. "'Black Was the Colour of Our Fight': Black Power in Britain, 1955–1976." Ph.D diss., University of Sheffield, 2008.

Wilder, Gary. *Freedom Time: Negritude, Decolonization, and the Future of the World*. Durham, NC: Duke University Press, 2015.

Williams, John. *Michael X: A Life in Black and White*. London: Century, 2008.

Williams, Raymond. *Keywords: A Vocabulary of Culture and Society*. London: Croom Helm, 1976.

Willis, Paul. *Learning to Labour: How Working Class Kids Get Working Class Jobs*. 1977. Burlington, VT: Ashgate, 1993.

Wills, Clair. *Lovers and Strangers: An Immigrants History of Post-War Britain*. London: Allen Lane, 2017.

Woodard, Komozi. *A Nation within a Nation: Amiri Baraka (LeRoi Jones) and Black Power Politics*. Chapel Hill: University of North Carolina Press, 1999.

Worpole, Ken. *Local Publishing & Local Culture: An Account of the Work of the Centerprise Publishing Project, 1972–1977*. London: Centerprise Trust, 1977.

Wright, Nigel. *Free School: The White Lion Experience*. Bristol: Libertarian Education Press, 1989.

Young, Michael, and Peter Wilmott. *Family and Kinship in East London*. London: Routledge & Kegan Paul, 1957.

Young, Robert J. C. *Postcolonialism: A Historical Introduction*. Oxford: Blackwell, 2001.

Zhana. *Black Success Stories*, vol. 1: *Celebrating People of African Heritage*. London: Zhana Books, 2006.

INDEX

busing, 129–30
Butler, Rab, 19

Cambridge, Alrick Xavier (Ricky), 76,
    184–87
Campaign Against Racial Discrimination
    (CARD), 21, 23, 27–29, 71
Carby, Hazel, 159–61
Carew, Jan, 23–25
Caribbean Artists Movement (CAM),
    45–46, 138–40
Caribbean Education and Community
    Workers' Association (CECWA), 130
Caribbean Voices, 137–38
Carmichael, Stokely: British government's
    response to, 33–34; legacy of, 218–19;
    media response to, 26; opposition to, 7,
    27; politics of, 30–33; popularity among
    African and Caribbean people in Brit-
    ain, 15–17, 26–27, 29–30; popularity
    among South Asians in Britain, 72; style
    of, 30–32
Carter, Trevor, 130, 134, 162
Centerprise, 139
Centre for Contemporary Cultural Studies
    (CCCS), 160, 168, 180, 192–98, 199,
    204–5
Cleaver, Eldridge, 32, 55, 56, 89, 145
Coard, Bernard, 130, 135–36, 213
Cochrane, Kelso, 18, 210–11
Commission for Racial Equality (CRE),
    162, 217
Communist Party of Great Britain, 18, 43,
    116–18
Community Relations Commission
    (CRC), 161–62, 179, 189, 215
Comrie, Locksley, 37, 38
Conservative Party, 18–20, 126
counterculture, 113–14, 118–22
Critchlow, Frank, 95–97, 120

Dadzie, Stella, 9, 68, 184–85
Davis, Angela, 28, 55, 58, 63–68, 88*fig,* 104,
    115–17
decolonization: in Britain, 8–13, 107–9,
    123–24, 199; cultural, 44–45, 136–39;
    economic realignments of, 189; failures
    of, 214; in Guyana, 42–43; in Jamaica,

44; secondary, 36; telos of, 213; in
    Trinidad and Tobago, 40–42; violence
    of, 25
de Freitas, Michael: anti-police activism of,
    119–20, 170; with Malcolm X, 232n59;
    with RAAS, 24, 28; with Stokely Car-
    michael, 31–34; trial of, 110. *See also*
    Black House
Dhondy, Farukh, 125–26, 159–60, 166, 201,
    216
Dialectics of Liberation Congress, 30–32,
    118

education: educationally subnormal (ESN)
    schools, 80, 130–31, 133; policy, 125–27;
    state schools, 128–29, 154–63; supple-
    mentary schools, 39, 131–34, 143–51, 162,
    188. *See also* busing
Egbuna, Obi B.: arrest and imprisonment
    of, 41, 110; with Kwame Nkrumah, 42;
    with Stokely Carmichael, 31, 33, 34;
    with Universal Coloured People's
    Association, 28

Fanon, Frantz, 25, 83, 87, 196
Fasimbas: education work of, 58, 86; music
    of, 85, 270n143; Oval Four, 106, 111;
    women in, 67
feminism. *See* black women's movement
Flamingo, 19, 137
free schools, 146
Free University for Black Studies, 156

Gandhi, Mohandas Karamchand
    (Mahatma), 76
Garrison, Len, 60, 151, 157, 163, 210
George Padmore Supplementary School,
    143–46, 162, 163
Gilroy, Beryl, 128, 135
Gilroy, Paul: at Centre for Contemporary
    Cultural Studies, 195–99, 205; on
    history, 79, 221; on memory, 172, 221; on
    music, 84–85; on political blackness, 82;
    There Ain't No Black in the Union Jack,
    3, 9, 82
Glean, Marion, 21–23
Gordon, Rhodan, 101, 103, 184
Gordon Walker, Patrick, 20